Copyright 2016 © Roho Publishing. All rights reserved. Printed in the United States.

ISBN: 978-0-9894338-6-0

Cover and Design: Jenna Stanbrough

On the Cover:

The legendary tradition of Emporia State University Track and Field is represented in the three pictures on the cover. Archie San Romani, who placed 4th in the Olympic 1500 meters in 1936, represents the past. Josh Honeycutt, national champion triple jumper, represents the men's present. Honeycutt has represented the U.S.A. in international competition and has been ranked among the top eight triple jumpers in the U.S. for three consecutive years, 2013-2015. Heather Leverington represents the women's program. She was a five-time national champion in the shot put and set the NCAA DII National Outdoor meet record in her career.

Roho Publishing

4040 Graphic Arts Rd

Emporia, KS 66801

www.rohopublishing.com

Steve Hawkins originally wrote *A History of the Track/Field and Cross Country Teams at Emporia State University, 1900-1984* as his master's thesis. Over the last thirty years, ESU teams have continued to add to the legendary tradition. Mark Stanbrough added the years from 1984-2015 and edited the original Hawkins thesis to fit into a book format. Pictures have been added to help tell the historical story.

About Roho Publishing

When Kip Keino defeated Jim Ryun in the 1968 Olympic Games at 1500 meters he credited the win to "Roho." Roho is the Swahili word for spirit demonstrated through extraordinary strength and courage. The type of courage and strength that can be summoned up from deep within that will allow you to meet your goals and overcome the challenges in life. Roho Publishing focuses on the spirit of sport and is designed to inspire, encourage, motivate and teach valuable life lessons.

Dedication

I would like to thank my daughter, Jenna Stanbrough, for being my right hand person. She has been an integral part in editing, designing and creating the final product of this book.

A special thanks goes to my family. My mom and dad supported me in my desire to be an athlete. My wife, Wendy, has encouraged me throughout my career. My three daughters, whom I was fortunate enough to coach all three in cross country and track, are lifetime cross country and track and field fans.

I would like to thank all the coaches and fellow teammates I have had over the years who made a difference in my life. I would also like to thank the athletes whom I have had the privilege to coach over the years. Each of these individuals has taught me much about the qualities to be successful in life – good character, integrity, a strong work ethic, dedication and perseverance.

Mark Stanbrough

I would like to thank Dr. Patricia McSwegin, Dr. Bill Tidwell, Dr. Richard Keller and Dr. Fred Markowitz for their help and guidance with this project.

A special thanks goes to Coach Tidwell, who inspired the project and for whom it is written.

Thanks also to Mom, Dad and John for their assistance with the project.

Steve Hawkins

Acknowledgements

Special thanks go to Kylie Lewis from ESU Archives for her help in retrieving much needed information and the ESU Archives for allowing us to use the information in the book. Thanks to ESU Media and Marketing for the courtesy use of photos and information. The ESU Athletic Department, particularly Don Weast, Steve Blocker, and Eric Wellman provided valuable help in finding results.

Preface

I came to Emporia State in the fall of 1974 full of excitement to be a college student-athlete. I loaded up my 1969 Chevrolet Impala and drove the 100 miles from the small town of Mound City, Kansas to the big city of Emporia. As a graduate in the first class of Jayhawk-Linn High School in 1973, my high school had only offered football, basketball and track, and I enjoyed playing all three. When I came to ESU, I had never ran cross country, in fact, I had never seen a cross country race and had no idea how far you had to run. After meeting with Coach Philip Delavan in the summer of 1974, he recommended I run cross country. His famous words of, "It will make you a better 800 runner" eventually became prophetic. However, when I arrived at ESU, I had no idea what I was about to get into. Within a couple of weeks I went from my 25 miles a week training to 100 miles a week. It's a miracle my body survived! My first year was a challenge to say the least, but as the body and mind adapted, I did improve every year as a cross country runner.

My main event in track and field was the 800 meters and Coach Delavan was right. In a supporting ESU environment, I improved to compete at the national level. As I reflect back on my experiences as an athlete, I don't remember every race; however, my strongest memories are of the people that I was able to associate with on a daily basis- my teammates. It was during my running days at ESU that I began to learn of the legendary ESU cross country/track and field history. Bill Tidwell was the athletic director and I knew he held the school 800 record. I heard people talk about world-class shot putter Al Feuerbach and I was fortunate to be a teammate with Kathy Devine, the collegiate record holder in the shot put. However, my knowledge of ESU track and cross country history was very limited.

In 1984, a mere 10 years after a naïve student-athlete began attending ESU, I became the head cross country and track and field coach at ESU. It was during those eight years as the head coach that I began to deeply appreciate the magnificent history of the legendary ESU program.

After coaching at ESU, I remained teaching at ESU, in various roles of professor, department chair and director of coaching education. I have remained in close contact with ESU coaches and athletes and the sports of track and field and cross country as a high school coach and official. My appreciation of and respect for the ESU legends has continued to grow. When I share the stories with current athletes, most have little knowledge of the athletes that came before them. I believe it is important to tell the stories. The stories of legendary ESU athletes are motivating, energizing and create a tremendous sense of pride. I am a Hornet and I am proud to have ran, coached and have been associated with ESU for over forty years. This book is dedicated to the many athletes and coaches who have established the proud, legendary tradition of cross country and track and field and at Emporia State University.

-Coach Mark Stanbrough, B.S.E. 1977, M.S. 1979

Preface

In the spring of 1984, I sat with my coach, advisor and mentor, Dr. Bill Tidwell, to discuss ideas for my master's thesis. He casually proposed the idea of writing about the history of track & field at ESU. Although my major was Physical Education, I was intrigued. The ESU Athletics Hall of Fame was in its infancy, and I'd seen several impressive track & field alumni inducted, including Coach Tidwell, so I took on the challenge. As I reached into the history of the program, I was drawn in more than I ever imagined that I could be. Hour upon hour was spent viewing microfiche in William Allen White Library, and the more that I discovered, the more that I wanted to know. I could not believe how incredible the history of the program was. Luck was on my side as well; one day a baseball coach approached me and asked did I want the track junk they had found in Welch Stadium. I assumed it was old equipment, but I said yes all the same. There was indeed old equipment, but there was also a binder that contained track & field results dating from the 1920s up through the 1960s. It turned out Coach Welch had been a meticulous record keeper. These records allowed me to confirm results gleaned from stories in the Gazette, yearbooks and other sources, as well as to establish top 10 performer lists for all events. Letters sent to alumni brought a response rate far greater than I ever expected, and provided amazing and amusing stories to include in the document. I still recall the sense of relief and disappointment that I felt when I sent the paper to the binder. I was relieved that the project was complete, as I had worked harder on that project than perhaps any other before or since. However, it was tinged with disappointment, as I didn't believe that I had completely encapsulated the history of the program, and I knew that the history was not going to stop with 1984. I'm very pleased that Mark continued to record the history of the ESU track and cross country programs, and is bringing this book to life. I'm also very proud to be a part of the ESU track and cross country heritage.

-Steve Hawkins, B.S.E. 1983, M.S. 1985

Table of Contents

The History of Emporia State Track and Field: A Legendary Tradition

Foreword	1
Introduction	5
Men's 1900s	5-9
Men's 1910s	9-13
Men's 1920s	13-28
Men's 1930s	28-43
Men's 1940s	43-48
Men's 1950s	48-62
Men's 1960s	62-83
Men's 1970s	83-91
Men's 1980s	92-99
Men's 1990s	99-108
Men's 2000s	109-116
Men's 2010s	116-123
Women's 1970s	124-130
Women's 1980s	130-139
Women's 1990s	139-150
Women's 2000s	150-158
Women's 2010s	158-164
Hornet History	165-190
Men's All-Time Participants	190
Women's All-Time Participants	207
Resources	212
Photo Credits	213
About the Authors	214

Foreword

I started coaching at Iowa State University and I always had a great respect for Fran Welch and the Emporia State program. After Iowa State, I went to the University of Central Missouri as the head track and field coach. Fran Welch called one day and asked if I would be interested in the track job at Emporia and I said, "you bet." He asked me not to tell anyone that I had the job. Fran hand-picked me as the coach.

Emporia State was one of the greatest jobs in the world. I loved being in Emporia and clearly loved coaching there and working with All-American and world record holders. After Emporia State I went to the University of Texas and retired but came out of retirement to coach at Round Rock High School. I told the Round Rock High athletes stories of the great athletes at Emporia State like Al Feuerbach and it helped them to work harder as they were inspired by the stories.

Emporia State was a very important part of my coaching career. Emporia State will always be a special place that is near and dear to my heart where Mary Jane and I spent some of the best years of our lives.

-Coach Phil Delavan

The reader of this book will be presented with the comprehensive history of the track and field/cross country program at Kansas State Normal School, Kansas State Teachers College and currently Emporia State University. The rich heritage of track and field at ESU was made possible by several outstanding state, national and internationally known coaches. These coaches have been successful working with modest facilities and budget.

As Fran Welch once said, "give me a talented athlete and he/she will make me a good coach." One may wonder why so many talented athletes choose to attend ESU. I believe for two reasons; first the personalities, knowledge, and skills of the coaches and second; ESU has always had the philosophy of promoting the academic program as well as the athletic program. My experience and observation has been that student-athlete programs motivate students to do the very best they can in the classroom and in athletics. Strong student-athlete programs provide the student with knowledge, skills and awareness to be successful in life.

ESU will continue to attract talented new students by providing high quality student athletics "for the common good."

-Coach Bill Tidwell

When I came to ESU in August of 1992, the university was in a transition period. We were moving into NCAA DII and full membership in MIAA. It was not hard for me to adjust, as I had been in the NCAA at the University of Nebraska the previous 7 years. But I got the feeling in talking to the coaches that they were really used to NAIA and their history had been that for so long that they and the programs were going to have to adjust. I also had run at the MIAA level at Northeast Missouri State University (Truman). I knew it was a great DII Conference to belong to.

In the fall of 1992, I took on the challenge of heading up the Cross Country and Track and Field program with a facility that was on its last days. That first year was the worst year I have ever had to train athletes, and in fact ran many workouts on a cinder track down at the junior high athletic fields by Peter Pan Park. I also moved the cross country course from around the campus fields to Jones Park in Emporia, where we began to paint a line around it every two weeks for workouts and our one home meet. This park was a vital part of my hill training for sprinters, jumpers, and middle distance/distance runners.

We had a small team of less than 40 athletes both men and women, and very few new freshmen and two graduate assistant coaches in Will Waubaunsee and Don Farmer. Jonathon Oshel walked into my office that year and became an All-American Javelin thrower. Between the facilities, budget, and adjustments with athletes, I almost felt I had made a mistake taking up Dr. Quayle's decision to hire me. At Nebraska, our phone budget was larger than the operations budget at ESU for CC/T&F. I remember my wife Kathy and I having many talks that first semester and especially with her help saying to me "you wanted to be the head of your own program" and telling me she knew I could do this. We went about making the best of the situation and we said, "let's commit to making Emporia State our program." With that, we took ownership in every part of the program for 19 years.

Recruiting was just going to work and reaching out to Kansas High schools – getting in the car and going out to schools and homes. Dr. Quayle gave me a university car with lots of miles on it and I proceeded to put many more on it and in fact ran it off the road in a flood coming back to Emporia at about one o'clock in the morning one night. Two men recruits in that first class, Troy Derley and Jason Stuke, bought into my idea of the new track coming and wanted to be a part of building a solid DII program. I knew in visiting in their homes and with their parents they were the kind of young men and leaders that I needed. At the time, I could not have understood the effect of them coming on the small amounts of scholarship aid I offered to what we began to accomplish in the years to come. They were certainly the cornerstone of getting the respect our program gained the first day they stepped on campus. I am indebted to them seeing my vision of ESU Track and Field as my first recruiting class. Three other men came in the second year of recruiting that added to that impact - Jermaine Mitchell, a very talented distance runner, Tim Vietti, and Brandon Masters - with their talent for so many events helped us win a conference title in just the 3rd year of being in the NCAA/MIAA. The team grew to 90 plus men and women. The women's efforts were slightly slower but with another cornerstone recruiting class of Deandra Doubrava, Gillian Curtiss, and Heather Leverington, it was just a matter of time before the women gained the respect of the league with a championship and this group was the leader of the 1999 team that won the first NCAA trophy for ESU since joining DII. Deandra became, in my opinion, the greatest athlete in ESU athletic history. Heather became an All-American class thrower that just dominated the MIAA and NCAA DII. Jason Stuke laid out the work ethic under Coach Will for the throwers and Heather and the others followed, making our throws squad a point machine. Gillian was this little books scholarship athlete that I could never have seen doing what she did, going to 2nd in the nation twice in the 400 hurdles. There are so many athletes over the 19 years to mention, but without these student athletes laying a foundation and the respect they brought to the program, many of the others who came later would not have been possible. I am forever indebted to them for helping me build ESU to one of the most respected DII programs in the nation.

Essentially, one of the greatest transitions for Emporia State Track and Field was the building of a first class track inside Welch Stadium from 1993-1994. It was wonderful to see the bulldozers come in and take the old track out. At one time that track had been state of the art but over time the rubberized asphalt track had hardened and cracked and I really did not like to put athletes out on it. We also could not have any home meets, which meant the athletes traveled all the time with no indoor or outdoor facilities for meets. The track and field project headed up by Clair Hutchinson and Frank Karnes and under the pride of head contractor Fred Kipp (an ESU Alum and former major league pitcher) totally changed ESU Track and Field for decades to come. Watching the transformation of Welch Stadium was very interesting with the lights being moved behind the stands and nothing but dirt, then rock base, then asphalt to provide the surface for the new track. So many people had contributed funds and now we were seeing a state of the art facility in an old Kansas limestone rock stadium built in the WPA days come to life. I made a decision one day to ask AD Dr. Bill Quayle if it would be okay if we bid for the national outdoor championships. The track was not finished but I wanted to take on the challenge of showcasing our facility. I was pretty young then and naïve to think the NCAA Committee would listen to me and I think Bill Quayle just did not want to say no. I went to the 1994 National Indoor Championships in Fargo, North Dakota with a proposal to the DII committee to ask if we could be put in the rotation to host the meet in 1995. We had not run one meet on our new facility yet. I guess the committee was in the mood to come to the Midwest and give a new NCAA DII school an opportunity and in the weeks after my presentation, they gave ESU a year to get ready and host their first NCAA Championship. Teams came to run at ESU in 1994 and 1995 to get a look at the facility and kept coming back. We later hosted the 1999 and 2006 NCAA Championships. Many in the athletic department helped in putting on these championships and Emporia certainly benefited economically from regular season home meets and the national meets. Other facilities that benefited our program was a weight room for our team and great throwing facilities in the fields surrounding the PE Building. We also transformed Gym A into the best workout facility we could for training in the space we had. AD Kent Weiser helped to provide a track surface over the whole gym, which allowed us to wear spikes and made it forever for track and field. We had to make do indoors in training but outdoors the track in Welch Stadium witnessed top collegiate, American and even World Class Olympic athletes competing in Emporia.

Over the years of ESU athletic history many people have played a key role in this university being respected in track and field. During the years from 1992-2011 many assistant coaches helped to train athletes each day of every school year to be the best they could be. It is not possible for one coach to train all the specialties of our sport. I counted on graduate assistants and part-time volunteers to coach events and I really gave them ownership in their coaching. I really think they felt in the short time that they were at ESU that they had an effect and they benefited their own coaching careers. For most of the time I was at ESU the Physical Education department hired graduate assistant coaches with tuition and fee waivers and stipends. They were mostly just out of college and eager to work, recruit and coach. Throughout my years at ESU, just about every two years we would replace these coaches as they would obtain their master degree and go on to fulltime jobs. It was a constant cycle, but personally I really find it rewarding to see a coaching tree in the track and field profession of those that came through ESU. I am indebted to all of these individuals too numerous to name here. They helped student athletes achieve and our university to be one of the most respected in the NCAA, and I think they learned a lot about administering a track and field program.

Kathy and I having many good memories of the student athletes, coaches, and administrators in the 19 years of coaching cross country and track and field program at Emporia State University.

-Coach David Harris

Foreword

Hard work, dedication and over-achievement are the words that come to mind when I think of Emporia State Track and Field/Cross Country. Prior to my interview to become assistant coach in summer of 2009, I could not have found Emporia, Kansas on a blank map. However, I had heard so many positive things about the program, I felt as though I'd been there before and I knew I was privileged to be hired.

I believe that God brought me to Emporia State and there could be no other place I would rather coach. The challenges, the tradition, and the over-achievement truly make this a special place. This program is one of the last greatest programs that has not been corrupted by the superficial belief that material objects are required in order to be successful. Facilities are not the only thing that builds champions. There is no replacement for hard work and commitment in reaching one's fullest potential as an athlete. I can recall days which our team ran hills in 9-degree weather and our coaching staff had to shovel snow off the track in order for our athletes to get a workout in just prior to the indoor national championships. All of these things make our program stronger. We may not always win every big title, but often times, opposing coaches are wondering what we do so consistently well at ESU. The answer is work hard.

My mission is to maintain what I feel is one of the proudest track and field traditions in the nation. Every day I come into campus, I know I am truly blessed to be a part of such an amazing legacy built by ordinary folks who demonstrated extraordinary commitment to their sport. It is more than a mere coincidence that I have come to Emporia State. I love this program dearly and I hope to continue to produce citizens who have learned some of their greatest lessons through the best program in the country!

GO HORNETS!

-Coach Steve Blocker

Men's Track and Field
Introduction

The sport of track and field began with the ancient Greek civilizations. The Greeks' love of athletics, the European word for track and field, originated very early in their history and reached its pinnacle in the ninth century B.C. Footraces, favorites of the Greeks, were run regularly in Elis on the plain of Olympia. Eventually, discus and javelin events were added and, as more cities participated, the event became quite popular, being held every four years. Thus began the Olympic Games, for which formal record keeping started in 776 B.C. The Romans took over the games in 336 B.C., adding boxing, wrestling and the pentathlon, and the Olympics continued until A.D. 393 when the Roman Emperor Theodosius I abolished the games as a pagan spectacle. At the time of their demise, the Olympic Games were famous in all parts of the world and were attended by athletes from many countries.

Modern track and field began in England with the formation of athletic clubs. The first clubs were formed at Oxford and Cambridge in the early 1850s, and in 1857, the first intercollegiate contest was held between the two schools. Athletic clubs served as the foundation for the establishment of track in the United States as well. Modeled after its English counterparts, the New York Athletic Club was organized in 1868. Enrollment soared to 300 members in only a few months, prompting the first contest held on November 8th, 1868. The New York Club was in many ways the pioneer of track and field in this country. Besides sponsoring the first contest in the U.S., the NYAC built the first cinder track in the United States and brought the first spiked shoes into the country. The New York Club acted as the pattern and the stimulus for similar organizations in various parts of the country. By 1886, major athletic clubs were located in every section of the United States, and two years later, the first national meet of the Amateur Athletic Union of the United States was held. There were 120 athletes from all parts of the country entered in this event. The meet was a complete success and, by the 1890s, club athletics had grown to be very successful.

Track did not develop as quickly in the colleges. The sport was taken up in the eastern colleges in the early 1870s, and the first intercollegiate contest was held between the Ivy League schools in 1874. There were five events in that first meet: the mile run, the 100-yard dash, the three-mile run, the 120-yard hurdles, and the seven-mile walk. Curiously enough, spectators at these early meets took more interest in events such as the seven-mile walk than in the other events. The midwest was about 20 years behind the east in beginning intercollegiate track contests, due in part to the conservative views of the administration and faculty of the midwest colleges. It was not until well into the 1880s and 1890s that interest spread throughout the country. Growth in intercollegiate track developed just in time to replace the athletic clubs, which were declining due to professionalism among the competitors and bickering among the different clubs. Track survived in the United States because it had a firm hold in the nation's colleges.

The modern Olympic Games were first held in Athens, Greece. Track and field was dominated by the United States, who won nine of the 12 events. The success of the U.S. team helped ignite the success of U.S. Track and Field.

1900-1909

Track at the Kansas State Normal School did not have an auspicious beginning. In the late 1890s and early 1900s the only track event was the all-school field day. The field day was a competition among the four societies (social organizations) at the Normal, and included all the events contested in a regular track meet. Normal School students anticipated the meet with a great deal of interest, and downtown merchants offered prizes for the winners. In the next decade, the field day was replaced by the interclass meet, with the intent of drumming up interest to compete on the established track team. It provided a means for the coach to locate talent that was not out for the track team. However, by the 1920s, these events had lost all importance in the development of KSN track.

In 1896, KSN helped form "The Interstate League of Normal Schools," of which Kansas, Missouri, Iowa, Wisconsin, and Illinois were members. Each year in May, these schools would gather on one of the campuses for a debate and oration contest, a baseball game, and a track meet. Student publications from this period suggest that KSN was strongly represented in the debate and oration contests during the early years of the Interstate League. However, no record of participation in the baseball game or track meet can be found.

The students and faculty at KSN were not satisfied with this lack of interest in field athletics. In April of 1900, a new constitution for the Athletic Association was developed outlining a new plan for KSN athletics. The association, made up of representatives from the faculty, the students, and the alumni, represented seven sections (teams), one of which was track. Each team was managed by the students with close faculty supervision. It was hoped that interest in field athletics would be increased greatly under the new plan.

These efforts led to KSN's first participation in the track meet at the seventh annual interstate contest in 1902. This contest, held in Emporia, had a positive impact on the growth of track on the KSN campus. Major influences were both the performances of the KSN athletes and the fine showing of the Iowa and Illinois teams. Considering the infancy of the program, KSN's athletes made a respectable showing, gathering a 1st in the hammer, and 2nds in the hammer, broad jump, 220-yard dash and 440-yard dash. The following excerpt from the Student Index shows the impact this success had on the KSN campus:

> The ease with which Drake and Davies, the only boys on our team who had made any special practice for the interstate meet, took 1st and 2nd places (in the hammer) shows what our school could do if all were to work as they should. (Student Index, Vol. 1, No. 17)

The greatest impact on the KSN program, however, came from the outstanding performances of the Iowa and Illinois teams. The success of these two schools, winning 10 of the 11 events and taking a majority of the 2nds and 3rds between them, acted as a decided stimulus to track and field at KSN.

Earl M. Carney: Coach
Earl M. Carney took charge of the development of all athletics at the Kansas State Normal School in 1899, and directed activities in the early years. During his last year, KSN participated in its first interschool contest. Carney left KSN in 1904 to enroll in the KU Medical School.

During September 1902, 16-18 KSN men, inspired by the training practices and performance results of the Iowa and Illinois men, started training to prepare for the 1903 interstate meet. This work paid off as the Emporia Normal scored 17 points to place 4th in the meet. John Davies, the 2nd place winner in the hammer the year before, was the individual star for KSN, winning the shot put and the hammer and placing 2nd in the discus. Davies set a school record of 112-7 in the hammer. This mark still stood when the javelin replaced the hammer as an event in 1912 and lasted until the 1960s when competition in the hammer was renewed.

Three men led the development of the KSN

track program during its initial decade. Earl M. Carney took charge of the development of all athletics at the Normal in 1899. During his last year, KSN participated in its first interschool contest other than the interstate meet, a rain shortened dual loss to Kansas University.

Carney left KSN in 1904 to enroll in the KU Medical School. His replacement, Paul B. Samson, also had charge of all the sports teams at the Normal. Samson coached the track teams at KSN for four seasons, during which time the program became solidly established.

In 1904 the Kansas Conference, a league composed of all colleges in the state, was formed. The first conference track meet was held in 1906, and the Normal finished 3rd behind the Kansas Agricultural College (Kansas State's predecessor) and the College of Emporia. KSN improved to 2nd in the state meet in 1907 and placed 3rd the following year. By the time Samson left in 1908, the track teams at the Normal were among the strongest in the state.

The third man who helped in the development of the track program was Dr. Norman Triplett. He was an ardent supporter of track on the Normal campus. Triplett even temporarily took over the reins of the track squad for the 1909 season, when Samson's resignation after the 1908 football season left KSN without a track coach. But his main role was as faculty advisor, a responsibility Triplett held for 30 years until his retirement in 1931.

> **Paul Samson: Coach**
> Paul B. Samson was in charge of all the sports teams at the Kansas Normal School. Samson coached the track teams at KSN for four seasons, during which time the program became solidly established. Samson immediately initiated dual meets with Baker and the College of Emporia, both of which would develop into strong rivalries. Samson also was the football coach and had a football coaching record of 16-16.
>
>

Many outstanding performers represented KSN during these early years. One of the first was Leonard Hargiss, who was a star hurdler and sprinter on the 1902-1905 teams. He was followed to KSN in the fall of 1905 by his younger brother, Homer W. "Bill" Hargiss, who became the outstanding performer of the decade and one of the all-time greats in Emporia State University athletic history.

The performers of this period were characterized by great versatility. Many participated in four or five events at each meet; Bill Hargiss was no exception. He ran the sprints and hurdles, broad jumped, threw the hammer, and usually anchored KSN's mile relay. His specialty, however, was the hurdles. During his junior season, Hargiss ran under the state record in the high hurdles in a dual meet with Fairmount College of Wichita and also won the 220-yard low hurdles at the state meet. There was little doubt that Bill Hargiss would own both state marks in the hurdles after his senior year and his performance in the opening meet of the 1909 season was spectacular. In that meet, a dual against Fairmount, Hargiss won the broad jump, the hammer, the high hurdles, and anchored KSN's mile relay to victory. Hargiss' tremendous ability is shown in this account of the mile relay from the KSN Bulletin:

> The relay race was the most exciting event. Fairmount kept the lead for the first three laps. When Hargiss started he had twenty-five yards to gain (sic) a good man against him. On the first half lap he did not gain much, but when he came to the 220 yard line he started to sprint. He gained on his man at every step and crossed the line a few inches ahead of him (KSN Bulletin, Vol. 8, No. 32)

Unfortunately Hargiss' great promise went unfulfilled. His season came to an end shortly after the Fairmount meet when he came down with the mumps. The shortness of his senior track season does not diminish the greatness of his athletic accomplishments at KSN, nor would it be the end of Bill Hargiss's association with KSN track.

Other standouts during the decade include H.D. Davis, who was the first state champion for KSN, winning the two-mile in 1906. Sidney Miller was the two-mile state champion in 1907, and he came back to win the mile at the 1908 state meet. Aubrey Davidson was another champion in the 1908 state meet, winning the half-mile. W. Roy Campbell, the state champion pole vaulter in 1908, 1909 and 1910, was also outstanding for KSN, even though he was almost the cause of cancellation of the 1907 track dual. On May 2nd, 1907, the day of the Baker dual, the Athletic Board declared Campbell ineligible because of low grades. The rest of the Normal team thought the decision unfair and refused to run. The meet was called off and Baker went home. However, peace returned to the Normal team when Campbell was reinstated, and KSN went on to defeat C. of E. in a dual meet and finish 2nd in the state meet behind Fairmount College.

> **Harry Cole: Three Decade Career**
> A unique feature of this period was the participation of high school students from the Normal Training School on KSN's athletic teams. In 1908, a high school student named Harry Cole began the longest and one of the most successful associations with Normal athletics of any athlete in ESUs history. Cole was a weight man, and his specialty was the discus. He finished 2nd in that event in the 1908 state meet, and before his career with KSN ended in 1923, it would extend over parts of three decades and include three state championships. Cole participated on the KSN track team for five years as a high school student and for two years as a college student.
>
>

In 1907, the Kansas Conference set a limit of four years on the athletic eligibility in college competition. This ruling had little effect on the Normal program, though, as it was then common for college students to leave school after one or two years of study. Students were able to do this because KSN offered a two-year course of study as well as a four-year course of study, allowing students to get teaching jobs after only two years of college education. Also, many students would leave school at any time during the year for a job, then return a few years later to finish their degree. Why this rule did not affect Harry Cole and other such cases is not known, perhaps his high school standing was the reason. Whatever the reasoning was, Cole participated on the KSN track team for five years as a high school student and for two years as a college student.

A development that greatly strengthened the KSN track program was the addition of a permanent cinder track, completed in time for the 1909 season. The new track provided KSN with one of the best facilities in the state. It also allowed KSN to host the state meet almost every year during the next decade. Besides the new facility, two other occurrences highlighted the 1909 season. KSN dropped athletic relations with C. of E. due to incidents of poor sportsmanship that had marred many of the athletic contests between the two schools during the preceding years, including two track meets. Bad feelings had emerged after the 1906 and 1907 dual meets over what both schools considered unfair starts in the dashes. The second occurrence was a dual loss to Washburn College and their head coach Garfield Weede. Ten years later, Weede moved to Pittsburg Normal as the head coach of all sports and began a long career with that school that included a fierce rivalry on the track with the Emporia Normal School.

Although the success of the initial decade of competition in track at KSN could not be demonstrated in wins and losses, the experience had been gained and the commitment made to field a strong track program in the coming years. From 1904, when dual competition started at KSN, until 1909, Normal thinclads split 10 duals, winning five and losing five. The results from four other duals on the schedule are not available. KSN tracksters made strong showings in the first four years of the Kansas conference meet, both as individuals and as a team. Only once in the four years did KSN finish lower than 3rd, finishing 5th in 1909 when Bill Hargiss was out.

1910

1910 Team Picture

Fred Honhart came to HSN as the head track and field coach for 1910. KSN's developing track program reached a high point in 1910 when the Normal won the state championship. The Normal tracksters defeated the two-time defending champ Kansas State Aggies by three points to take the team title. Outstanding for KSN was Roy Campbell, who won the pole vault for the third straight year, won the high hurdles in state record time, and finished 2nd in the low hurdles and 3rd in the broad jump. Harry Cole set a new state record in winning the discus, as well as grabbing a 2nd and 3rd in the shot put and hammer respectively. Marcus Gambill was the only other individual winner for KSN, taking 1st in the mile run. The Aggies won seven individual titles to four for KSN, but the Normal thinclads placed in every event to win the meet. The victory set off quite a celebration on the Normal campus, with a parade, a bonfire, and speeches by KSN's president and the outstanding athletes.

In addition to winning the state championship, the 1910 team went undefeated in dual competition. In their three dual meets, the Normal athletes easily defeated Washburn, Baker and Fairmount. The traditional dual with C. of E. was not held that year, because the Normal Athletic Association had decided not to resume athletic relations with C. of E. and risk stirring up the bad feelings that had been prominent a few years earlier.

Fred Honhart: Coach

Fred Honhart was the track and field coach at Emporia State (then Kansas State Normal School) from 1910-1912. He was also the football coach at the university compiling a 13-8-2 record. After leaving ESU, Honhart graduated from the Louisville Medical College at Louisville, Kentucky with a medical degree and practiced medicine in the Detroit, Michigan area for the remainder of his life.

1911

KSN's representative on the cinder paths in 1911 was again strong, despite the loss of Roy Campbell and Marcus Gambill. The loss of Campbell's skills was completely offset by the addition of Leonard Hurst. Competing in the same events Campbell had starred in for the previous four years, Hurst performed in spectacular fashion. In a dual victory over Southwestern College, Hurst scored 20 points, winning the pole vault, both hurdles, and the broad jump. His mark of 20-6 in the broad jump in this meet set a new school record. At the state meet, Hurst won the high hurdles and the pole vault, setting a state record of 11-0 in the vault. However, Kansas State regained the state title defeating KSN by 5 ½ points. Besides Hurst and Harry Cole, the latter who defended his title in the discus and placed 2nd in the hammer and 3rd in the shot put, only four other Normal tracksters were able to place. Cole's winning toss of 121-7 in the discus broke his own state record by almost seven feet.

1912

Fred Honhart came to KSN in the fall of 1909 and coached until 1912. Unfortunately, Honhart's last year at KSN was dampened by a dual loss to Baker and a 4th place finish in the state meet. Cole was the only individual state champion that returned from the championship and near championship seasons of 1910 and 1911, and he won his third consecutive crown in the discus while extending his state record by almost seven and one-half feet to 129-3. His 2nd place finish in the shot put was the next highest finish for KSN as no other Normalite could place above 3rd in an event. The bright spot of the season was an easy dual victory over C. of E., celebrating resumption of athletic relations between the two schools.

1913-1914

George Crispen succeeded Honhart in 1913, but his two years at the Normal were frustrating ones. The Kansas Conference ruling in 1912 barring high school students from college athletics kept Harry Cole from participating, and weakened the team in several other places. KSN suffered another loss when Welford Diggs, captain of the 1913 team, quit school before the season started. Diggs, the school record holder in the 100 and 220-yard dashes, had placed in both events at the 1912 state meet. These developments left KSN without well-rounded teams, and the Normal tracksters were winless in five duals in 1913 and 1914, losing to Baker, C. of E. twice, Haskell and Kansas State. KSN slipped to 5th in the state meet in 1913, and withdrew from the Kansas Conference before the 1914 state meet. KSN's withdrawal from the conference was precipitated by problems with player's eligibility. The breakup of the conference soon after KSN's withdrawal led to cancellation of the 1914 state meet. In the summer of that year, an attempt was made to form a new conference composed of Kansas and Missouri colleges. However, the new conference never materialized, and the Kansas Conference was reformed that fall. KSN was voted back into the conference in December of 1914, and resumed participation in the state track meet in 1915.

1913 Track Squad

George Crispen: Coach
George Crispen was the fourth track and field coach in ESU history, coaching two years in 1913 and 1914. Crispin came to KSN in 1912 originally as a physical education instructor but was given coaching duties when previous coach Fred Honhart resigned to pursue a medical degree.

Despite being unable to gain team victories, Crispen's teams were not without outstanding performers. James Nichols set a school record of 52.5 seconds in the 440 in 1914, equaling the state record; however, this did not count as a state record because it was not recorded in the state meet. John Bollin set a school record of 2:04.6 in the half-mile in winning the event against Kansas State in 1914. Gambill, the 1910 state mile run champion, was back in school in 1914, but because of the breakup of the conference, he did not get a chance to repeat.

1915

In 1915, the familiar face of H.W. Bill Hargiss appeared to guide the athletic fortunes of KSN. Hargiss left the head football job at Kansas University to return to his alma mater as coach for all sports. He had been at KU for only one year, but confusion among athletic policy makers at the State University prompted Hargiss to accept KSN President Thomas Butcher's offer. Prior to coaching at KU, Hargiss had been at the Normal's crosstown rival, C. of E., for three years as head football and track coach.

Hargiss brought renewed enthusiasm to the Normal team and immediate success was realized from this enthusiasm. KSN regained the state championship in Hargiss' first year, winning easily with 51 ½ points. Bollin continued his success from 1914, winning the half-mile at the state meet in a school and state record time of 2:02.6. Three newcomers also helped KSN win the championship. Cloudsley Lockman and Charles Weber, both sophomores new to the program, won their respective events. Lockman took 1st in the high hurdles tying the state record, while Weber won the two-mile in the outstanding time of 10:19.8, setting a state and school record. This time would stand as a state record until 1924 and as a school record until 1927 despite the tremendous development in track throughout the state following World War I. The third newcomer was freshman distance runner Bruce T. Portwood. Portwood won the mile for the first of three times, although these titles would not be consecutive because of the outbreak of the World War. KSN also won the state mile relay as the team of Harry Van Campen, Bollin, Harris, and Carpenter set a school record of 3:35.0.

1916

The 1916 season opened as one of great promise and Normal fans were not disappointed. The season began with a new twist for the KSN thinclads when they participated in an indoor dual meet with Kansas University. This was the first indoor meet ever entered by the Normal and, although KU won easily, this participation signified another step toward the development of a consistently strong track program at KSN. Two weeks after the KU meet, KSN athletes entered the Kansas City Athletic Club Invitation Indoor meet, competing against athletes from all over the United States. According to newspaper accounts of the event, the Normalites made good showings in the events they entered despite not placing. A unique feature of this meet was the method of contesting the relay races. The track at the Convesantion Hall in Kansas City was only four lanes wide and was banked. Therefore, to prevent excessive fouling during the races, the fields were kept small. Two or three schools would be matched against each other in a race, the pairing usually based on the size of the schools. The first year KSN was paired against William Jewell College. In later years, this format paired KSN against Pittsburg Normal (now Pittsburg State) and the two conference rivals rarely failed to produce a close and exciting race.

Bill Hargiss: Coach
Bill Hargiss came to Emporia State University in 1905 and participated in football, basketball, baseball, and track. He returned to Emporia as the head track and field and football coach. Hargiss coached four seasons from 1915-1918. He compiled a 62-23-11 record as the head football coach. His track teams won seven state titles. Hargiss is a member of the NAIA Hall of Fame.

The 1916 outdoor season opened with a convincing victory over the Haskell Indians, who were well known for their strong teams and outstanding individuals. This victory was a sign of how strong the Normal team had become. Guy Cross, a freshman, emerged as the new KSN star, winning the 440-yard dash and the broad jump with school record efforts in both, as well as beating the state record in the 440 by almost one second. Cross also ran on the winning mile relay and placed 2nd in the 100-yard dash. Another freshman, Lloyd Sharpe, set a school record in the shot put. With this outstanding new talent, plus veterans Portwood, Weber and Lee Stites, KSN overwhelmed the competition in taking a second straight state title. Portwood and Weber repeated as state champions in the mile and two-mile respectively. Stites won the javelin with the state record toss of 170-0, placed 2nd in the low hurdles, and ran on the winning mile relay team with King, Carpenter and Cross. Rounding out the individual champions for KSN were Hamill in the 880-yard run and Cross in the 440 and broad jump, the latter with a state record jump of 22-1 ¼.

1917

KSN won a third straight state title in 1917, winning eight events and scoring in all but the high jump. However, the accomplishment was diminished by the impending war. Many schools had dropped spring athletics from the schedule in mid-April, therefore, only eight schools entered the meet held on the Normal campus, half as many as had participated in 1916. Some of the top performers in the state were in training camp for the war or had gone back to the farm to work, further reducing the quality of the meet. KSN was not hit as hard by these losses in 1917 as many schools were, losing only Lee Stites, and retained enough individual talent and depth to win. Cloudsley Lockman won his second title in the high hurdles, equaling his own state record set in the 1915 state meet. Harry Van Campen finished on top in the 440-yard dash, and Sharpe won the shot put. Arthur Garrison upset teammate Cross in the broad jump, and Claude Galbraith won the javelin. Galbraith had broken the state javelin record at the 1916 meet, but the record lasted only a few minutes as teammate Stites broke the mark on his next throw to win the event. The most outstanding accomplishments of the meet, however, belonged to Cross, as this account from the Emporia Gazette relates:

1917 Gymnasium

> Cross, of the Normal, was the leading point winner. His performance yesterday was phenomenal. He won two 1sts, a 2nd and a tie for 3rd, and he had to get up out of bed to come to the meet. He has been sick for two weeks with appendicitis. His weakened condition showed up in the broad jump and he tied for 3rd. Last year he set a new record in this event. However, it was the brilliant race of Cross which won the mile relay for the Normal. He came from behind in the last lap in a great burst of speed. (Emporia Gazette, 1917, p. 7)

Cross's two 1sts were in the 100 and 220-yard dashes, with the 2nd in the high hurdles.

The state meet was the only outdoor meet held in 1917, as the war caused cancellation of four scheduled dual meets. Normal trackmen did participate in the indoor season, losing duals to KU and Kansas State. The top KSN athletes again participated in the KC Athletic Club indoor meet, where Harry Van Patten's tie for 1st in the pole vault with Atwood of KU at 11-3 set a school record. No other places were earned by KSN athletes, and the Normal relay team was defeated by KU in their section of the race.

1918-1919

The effect of the war could not be avoided forever, leading to disappointing seasons for KSN in 1918 and 1919. KSN slipped to 6th and 4th in the 1918 and 1919 state meets, respectively, as most of the stars from the previous three years had graduated or were in military service. Sharpe was the only individual champion remaining on the 1918 team, and his 2nd place in the shot put was the highest finish by a KSN athlete at the state meet that year. Portwood returned from military service for the 1919 season and finished his career by winning the mile run at state for the third time. Jim "Tubby" Vaughn also ended his career with a victory in the 1919 state meet, winning the shot put. Vaughn had performed during the previous two seasons in the shadow of Sharpe, KSN's star shot putter, usually placing 2nd behind him. With Sharpe gone in 1919, Vaughn was able to cop the victory.

1917 Track Squad

H.D. McChesney: Coach
H.D. McChesney was the head track and field coach at Kansas State Normal School in 1919. After one year, McChesney moved into the athletic director position.

KSN's meet record was not the only disappointment of 1918 and 1919. Coach Bill Hargiss resigned after the 1918 season to accept a position with the Oregon State Agricultural College in Corvallis. Hargiss's coaching record was a testimony to his ability to inspire young men to their highest potential, and his presence was sorely missed. But he would return in 1921 to lead another resurgence in Normal track fortunes. H.D. McChesney took over the head track position for the 1919 season and performed admirably considering the circumstances.

1920

For the Kansas State Normal track program, the third decade of century did not begin with great distinction. H.D. McChesney had moved up to athletic director, and the 1920 team inherited by George W. McClaren returned only three lettermen. The lack of experience showed as KSN dropped duals to Ottawa, Friends, C. of E., and Washburn. The Normal finished 8th in the state meet, the worst finish by a KSN team since the meet began in 1906. Lloyd McGahan was a bright spot for McLaren during the season, breaking the school record in the high jump twice, the second time at the state meet when he won the event with a leap of 5-10.

KSN's yearbook, the Sunflower, contained an account of the 1920 season that would prove prophetic for the rest of the decade:

> This year will mean much to K.S.N. in the way of track. Experience was gained and the foundation laid for a team next year that undoubtedly will bring back lost prestige. All the men will be back and new stars will enter to make a team that will make history for K.S.N., in track athletics. (Sunflower, 1920, p. 168)

KSN track athletes would indeed make history during this decade.

George McClaren: Coach

George McClaren coached the track and field team at Kansas State Normal School in 1920. McClaren was an All-American football player at the University of Pittsburg coached by the legendary Pop Warner. McClaren also was the head football coach during 1919 season and went 1-5-2. He later was the head football coach at the University of Arkansas and was inducted into the College Football Hall of Fame.

1921

The first major event of this history was the return of Coach Bill Hargiss from Oregon in 1921. Hargiss had led KSN to three consecutive state track championships during his previous tenure as head coach. His return brought a resurgence of enthusiasm to the track program at Normal, resulting in KSN's most successful season since 1916. Normal thinclads resumed participation in the KCAC indoor meet, and defeated Baker, Pittsburg, Friends and C. of E. in dual competition. KSN's only loss in a dual meet was to Washburn, and the season ended with a 4th place finish in the state meet. McGahan repeated as the champion in the high jump.

A familiar face on the 1921 Normal team was Harry Cole, who had been on the 1908-1912 teams as a high school boy. After being declared ineligible in 1913 because of his high school standing, Cole began a long and eventful odyssey. He enrolled at the Oregon Agricultural College in 1914 and stayed for two years. In 1916, while competing for Oregon Agriculture College, Cole broke the world record for the indoor discus with a throw of 140-9. When World War I broke out, Cole enlisted in the army, and he was on the ship Tuscania when it was torpedoed off the Irish coast. While in France, Cole entered an international track meet, which was in Paris during the spring of 1918. However, Cole broke his ankle training prior to the meet and was unable to compete. After being discharged from the service, Cole entered the Normal in 1920 as a junior.

During the 1921 season, Cole was among the best discus throwers in nation. When he threw 134-11 in the Washburn dual, Cole qualified to attend the Pennsylvania State Relay Carnival in Philadelphia. The Penn Relays were the largest meet in the world at time, and it was a great honor for one of KSN's athletes to attend. When the athletic department could not afford to send Cole, money to pay the expenses for the trip was raised by the student body to support the Normal athlete. Unfortunately, Cole did not place in the top three at Penn, and although an account of his performance is not available, there is evidence to suggest that Cole did not perform up to his usual standards. The discus was won by Weiss of the University of Illinois with a throw of 138-8, while 3rd place was taken with a mark of 126-3. Cole had thrown consistently around 135 feet during the season and had marks around 139 feet in practice, either of which would have easily earned Cole a place in the Penn meet, and potentially the victory.

However, Cole did not need to travel to Philadelphia to find competition. Harland Wiley of Friends College in Wichita had broken Cole's eight year old state discus record in 1920, and in 1921, Wiley was also one of the best throwers in the nation. Wiley defended his state championship that year in defeating Cole by one-half inch, setting a new state record of 135-4 ½.

1922

When the 1922 track season opened, Cole was not in school. However, a large number of promising freshmen had been added to the squad, the best of whom was Earl McKown. McKown won the state high school pole vault in 1921, setting a record of 11-9. In addition to the new talent, KSN added a new 16-lap to the mile indoor track which was one of the best in the state. This greatly facilitated Yellowjacket training in the early season. KSN's athletes had picked up the new nickname, the Yellowjackets, because of the color of the football team's uniforms, and the moniker began to be used quite exclusively when discussing Normal athletics.

Indoor Track: 1922
KSN's 16 lap to the mile indoor track was one of the best in the state.

KSN opened the 1922 indoor season with the annual KCAC meet. McKown won the pole vault for the only Emporia place. KSN ended the indoor season with a convincing dual victory over C. of E. on the Normal track. This was KSN's first-ever indoor dual against a Kansas Conference school, and it ended heavily in the Normal's favor.

The 1922 outdoor season was KSN's most successful up to this point. The Yellowjackets trounced Baker, Pittsburg and C. of E. in dual competition, won a triangular meet against Southwestern and C. of E., and won the state championship easily with 48 points. A dual loss to Kansas State was the only smudge on the season record. Normal trackmen broke 10 school records during the season, many of them more than once. KSN won seven events at the state meet, setting four new records and tying two. McKown won the pole vault with a record jump of 12-4, 1 ¼ inches less than his school record set earlier in the year. Team captain Cleyon Stewart won the 440-yard dash with a state and school record time of 51.2 seconds. Maurice Myer made up for the disappointment from 1921, setting a state and school record of 1:59.6 in winning the 880-yard run. After having an outstanding season in 1921, Myer missed the state meet when his entry was not properly certified. Merritt Sherer and Robert Dunning won the low and high hurdles respectively, both tying the state record and setting school records. Elijah Williams won KSN's sixth individual title, taking the 100-yard dash in 10.0 seconds, a new school record. A freshman from Emporia High School, "Lige," as he was nicknamed, was highly regarded as a high school sprinter, and had been recruited by some of the largest schools in the country. Lige chose to attend KSN so he could stay close to his family. The Yellowjackets' final victory was in the mile relay, the team of Myer, Sherer, George Holtfrerich and Stewart setting another state and school record.

Two Yellowjackets bettered state records during the season, but could not repeat their performance at the state meet. Lloyd McGahan bettered his own state and school record with a leap of 5-10 ½, and Holtfrerich threw the javelin 172-3 ½ to better the state record set by KSN's Lee Stites in 1916. Both marks counted as school records, but not state records as they were not recorded in the state meet. The final school record was set by Williams in the 220-yard dash. Unfortunately, the great success of the year was marked by tragedy. Claude Galbraith was forced to give up track early in the season due to an illness which resulted in his death in April. Galbraith was a member of the 1916-17, and 1919-22 teams, winning the javelin at the state meet in 1917. His contributions were greatly missed during the 1922 season.

The KSN program had progressed to the point where some of the athletes were of a caliber to compete in championship meets beyond the state meet. During the summer of 1922, six KSN trackmen entered the Annual Mid-West AAU track meet in St. Joseph, Missouri, and earned 3rd place for the Normal behind KU and the University of Iowa. McKown won the pole vault with a jump of 12 feet, Myer placed 2nd in the 880-yard run behind Morrow of Iowa, and McGahan finished 2nd in the high jump. Sherer earned the final points for the Normal, taking 3rd in the high hurdles.

1923

In March of 1923, Kansas State Normal's name was changed to Kansas State Teachers College of Emporia. This had more significance for the program than would be expected, as the name change designated a shift from two-year normal courses to a full four-year teacher training program. It would no longer be common for students to leave school after one or two years to teach.

The 1923 season opened as usual with the annual KCAC indoor meet. Earl McKown, KSTC's sophomore pole vaulter, turned in a phenomenal performance, clearing 12-10 to break the world record for the indoor vault by one inch. The following account from the KSTC Bulletin describes McKown's record setting vault:

> Having won the event (at 12-6), McKown asked that the bar be raised. The bar was then placed at 13 feet on the standards, but by actual measurement was 12 feet 10 inches high. The Normal athlete failed to clear the bar on the first attempt. After a more careful measurement of distance for the second trial, he cleared the bar with inches to spare. (KSTC Bulletin, Vol. 22, No. 36, P. 1)

McKown completed the indoor season with a 2nd place finish at the Illinois Relays in Urbana.

The Yellowjacket thinclads had another banner year during the 1923 outdoor season. After an initial loss to Oklahoma A. & M., KSTC swamped Baker, Friends and C. of E. in duals. They defeated Pittsburg in a dual without McKown and Lige Williams who were competing at the Drake Relays. Normal tracksters competed in the First Annual Kansas University Relays, taking 4th place as a team. At KU, McKown claimed 1st in the pole vault at 12-9, and the KSTC two-mile relay team of Merle Tate, Francis Talbott, Ralph Summers and Maurice Myer took 1st with a time of 8:31.6. Lige Williams won KSTC's other place, taking 3rd in the 100-yard dash. Williams only lost by inches despite being set back a yard from the starting line for jumping the

False Start Rule
A standard practice for a false start at this time resulted not in an athlete getting thrown out of the race, but of being set back one yard. If that runner false started again, they were set back another yard. Note the runners digging holes as their starting blocks.

gun. Williams remembers this race in the following account:

> "I ran a dead heat against Roland Locke of Nebraska, 9.6 seconds. I had been set back one yard for a false start although I was not guilty. Bill Hargiss raised Cain. We both almost were put out of the race." (E. Williams, personal communication, June 1984)

Harry Cole, who was competing again after sitting out during 1922, was ruled ineligible after taking 2nd in the discus. NCAA rules did not allow men with three years of track competition or freshmen to compete in open or university class events, and Cole was disqualified because he was in his fourth year of college competition as a college athlete. Robert Dunning was ruled ineligible before he ran the high hurdles, costing the Hornets a possible place in the event. Dunning was ruled out because he had attended Kansas University in the fall of 1922, and the Missouri Valley required a year's residence at a school for eligibility.

> **Drake Relays**
> The inaugural Drake Relays were held in 1910. The first meet drew just 100 spectators and 82 athletes, all from Des Moines-area colleges and high schools. The second year; however, drew 250 athletes and a crowd of some 500 spectators. In 1914, the Relays saw its first world record set. By 1922, the Relays had been expanded into a two-day event that drew 10,000 fans and became the first major track and field event broadcast on the radio. It is regarded as one of the top track and field events in the United States.
>
> **DRAKE RELAYS**
> *america's athletic classic*

The following week, while the remainder of the KSTC team took on Pitt in a dual, Williams and McKown participated in the Drake Relays. KSTC's first venture to Des Moines, Iowa, was successful as Williams took 3rd in the 100-yard dash and McKown placed 4th in the pole vault. Hargiss thought Williams had won the 100 and filed a protest. The first three men, Williams, Irvin, and Locke of Nebraska, were all timed in 9.8 seconds, which tied the Drake record. After a 20-minute delay, the judges picked Red Irvin of Kansas State the winner. Three of the sprinters Williams defeated in this race made the U.S. Olympic team in 1924.

KSTC defended its state championship in 1923, more than doubling the score on runner-up College of Emporia. The performances of Lige Williams were magnificent, as he won the 100 and 220-yard dashes in 9.7 seconds and 21.8 seconds respectively. Both were school and state records, and his 9.7 in the 100 equaled the American Intercollegiate record and was within one-tenth of a second of the world intercollegiate record. Merritt Sherer repeated in the 220- yard low hurdles with the record time of 15.4 seconds, and Bob Dunning won his second consecutive title in the high hurdles. Dunning equaled his state record time of 15.6 seconds, but it was not allowed because he knocked down two hurdles. McKown repeated in the pole vault with a jump of 12-0, four inches below his state record and 13 inches below his school record set earlier in the season. McKown's school record of 13-1 tied the American Intercollegiate record, but his feat was not officially recognized as it was set in dual competition. Cole again lost to Wiley of Friends in the discus, both beating the old state record.

Williams' heroics were not finished with the state meet. The week after, when KSTC was defeating C. of E. in their traditional dual, Lige tied the world record for the 220-yard dash around a curve, blazing to time of 21.8 seconds. Unfortunately, this was not recognized as a world record because no "official" AAU timer was present. Williams, Dunning and McKown qualified for the NCAA meet in Chicago held June 15 and 16, becoming the first KSTC athletes to compete in national championship competition. Cole had qualified also, but again the four-year rule kept him from competing. In the national meet, McKown tied for 1st in the pole vault with Brooker of Michigan at 13 feet, adding six inches to the old NCAA record. The KSTC vaulter cleared 13 feet on his first attempt, while Brooker did not get over until his third attempt. Both missed three attempts at 13-4, so they were awarded a tie for 1st. According to rules in force in 1923, the height cleared determined the winner, not the number of attempts.

Williams and Dunning were both met with hard luck in the NCAA meet. Williams qualified for the finals of the 100-yard dash, but had to withdraw because of a leg injury sustained in the semi-final race. Dunning was barely nosed out of the finals in the high hurdles; then while leading his semi-final heat in the low hurdles, he tripped and fell over the third hurdle. Dunning describes the latter race in this account from the KSTC Bulletin:

> "I got off to a wonderful start in the low hurdle race," he said, but I was too eager, and running faster than I even (sic) run before. I was on the third path and passing around the man ahead, when zip zowie - my leg caught the third hurdle. The force of the impact sent me almost straight into the air, while at the same time my legs doubled in, and I landed in a heap. The race was about over by the time I was able to get up." (The Bulletin, Vol. 22, No. 54, p. 5)

Lige Williams: Collegiate Record and World Record Time

Lige Williams ran 9.7 in the 100-yard dash and equaled the American Intercollegiate record at the 1923 State meet. The next week in a KSTC- College of Emporia dual, Lige Williams tied the world record for the 220-yard dash around a curve running 21.8 seconds. Unfortunately, this was not recognized as there was no "official" AAU timer present.

Competing in the Midwest AAU later that summer, McKown took 1st in the pole vault, and Dunning placed 2nd in the high hurdles and 3rd in the low hurdles. Cole was eligible to enter this meet because the only requirement was amateur status. However, he was working in the harvest fields and was unable to get back to Emporia. Thus, Cole's successful career with KSN ended, his best performance in the discus being 144-5 set in the 1923 Pitt dual. This mark stood as a school record until 1948.

Hurdle Rules

In the early days of the sport, hurdles were much more of a barrier. The stationary, heavy hurdle was more likely to knock over the runner. When lighter hurdles were introduced, athletes were disqualified if they knocked over more than three hurdles, a rule that prevailed until the L-shaped hurdle was introduced in 1935.

Due to the great success being experienced by the KSN program, trackmen began working out early during the fall of 1923. About 25 of the new men were enrolled in a track class, taught by Bob Dunning that met three days a week.

Another interesting development in training occurred in early January of 1924. A new mat stuffed with hay was purchased to be used by the indoor jumpers and vaulters. Until this time jumpers had not had such luxury. Outdoors, the vaulters and jumpers continued to land in sand pits. Considering this and the fact that the poles used in vaulting were bamboo poles, the heights that McKown was making in the event were truly outstanding.

1924

In 1924, McKown began his third year of competition by repeating his victory in the pole vault at the annual KCAC indoor. He did not match his world record effort of the year before, but his winning height of 12-6 was still exceptionally good. Dunning and Roy Pringle were entered in the high hurdles, but failed to arrive at the arena in time for the preliminaries. The starting time for the event had been moved forward and Hargiss had not been informed. This mistake cost the Yellowjackets' only other entries in the meet a chance to earn a place.

Competing in the Illinois Relays, McKown tied for 2nd in the vault with a leap of 12-9 ¼. Lige Williams, competing in the 75-yard dash, did not qualify for the finals. There was a question about whether Williams did qualify, as McKown insisted Lige took an easy 2nd in his heat; however, only two of the six judges supported McKown's claim.

The 1924 outdoor season opened as one of great promise. McKown, Williams, Dunning and Maurice Myer returned as state record holders, and former state record holder Guy Cross was back in school and on the team. Cross had set the state record in the broad jump in 1916, but left school the next year to teach. His state record had stood until 1923, and Cross was back to try to reclaim it. New men on the team included some outstanding sprinters. Lois Williams, freshman from Chanute, had set state high school records in the 100 and 220-yard dashes the previous spring, and another freshman, Frank Harris, had a best mark of 10.0 seconds in the 100-yard dash. These men helped make KSTC's sprint teams very strong.

The sprint teams showed their strength in the second year of KSTC's participation at the Kansas and Drake Relays. At KU, an 880-yard relay team of Ibra Brown, Fred Lighter, Lois Williams and Lige Williams finished 2nd to Occidental College of Los Angeles. This loss to Occidental was not a mark against the Yellowjackets, as three of the men who ran on the Californians winning relay also placed in the finals of the 100-yard dash at KU. The next week at the Drake Relays, the KSTC team, with Harris substituted for Brown, won the event in the time of 1:32.4.

> **Earl McKown: World Record**
> Earl McKown set his first world record in 1923, vaulting 12-10 indoors. The greatest performance of the 1925 Kansas Relays was turned in by McKown. Mac, as he was nicknamed, shattered all his previous records with a vault of 13-2 ⅞, to establish a new world intercollegiate record, a new Kanas Relays record, and a school record that would stand for over 20 years. McKown, pushed hard by his competition, often had to set records in order to win the event outright.

KSTC's sprint teams were not the only winners at the big relay meets. At KU, McKown defended his title in the pole vault, raising his meet record to 13-½ while just missing at 13-3. The two-mile relay team of Wilbur Myer, Clem Tuggle, John Swaze, and Roy Coats finished 2nd to Occidental. The Yellowjackets' two fastest half-milers, Maurice Myer and Bill Upson, ran on the medley relay team instead of the two-mile team. However, the medley team was unable to place. Lige Williams' disqualification in the 100-yard dash cost the Yellowjackets perhaps another gold watch. Lige was ruled out on the protest of the Marquette University coach after easily winning his qualifying heat. Williams had attended Marquette in the fall of 1923 and did not meet the residence requirement. Dunning, who had missed the 1923 KU meet on the same ruling, qualified for the finals of the high hurdles but did not place in the top three.

1924 Drake Relays Teams

880 Relay Team
Harris, Lighter, Williams (Lois), Williams (Lige), Hargiss

Two-Mile Relay Team
Upson, Myer (Maurice), Hargiss, Myer (Wilbur), Coats

McKown won his first Drake Relays title the next week, setting a new relays record of 13-0. This was an exceptional performance because the runways were soggy from heavy rains. The two-mile relay, with Maurice Myer and Upson in place of Tuggle and Swaze, finished 4th.

The Pittsburg Normal track team had been steadily improving since Garfield "Doc" Weede took over the program in 1919, and Weede won his first state championship with Pittsburg in 1924 when Pitt defeated KSTC by 8 ½ points. In that meet, KSTC was handicapped by the conference rule limiting entries to 15 per team, resulting in six potential point winners being left at home. The meet was the best ever held in the Kansas Conference, as eight records were broken and one was tied. Yellowjacket athletes had held five of the records that fell. The only KSTC trackman to break a record was McKown, who upped his own record to 12-6 in winning his third consecutive vault title. George Holtfrerich, the school record holder in the javelin, threw 170-6 in the prelims of the event to break KSTC's Lee Stites' state record set in 1915. However, Holtfrerich's record only lasted until the finals, when Skelton of Pittsburg threw 172-7 to win the event. Joe Weber tied the state record in taking 1st in the low hurdles. Weber first came into the limelight by winning both hurdle events in the 1924 Pitt dual, defeating teammate Dunning in both. He continued this success in the state meet with his victory in the low hurdles and a close 2nd in the highs. Weber was relegated to 2nd in the highs by Dunning, who won the event for the third straight year, although Dunning did not come close to his state record in the event. Also repeating was Lige Williams, who tied for 1st in the 100-yard dash with Hooper of Pittsburg to win his third consecutive title in the event, and won the 220-yard dash for the second straight time. However, neither of Williams' winning times was close to his meet records.

In 1924, the Mid-Western section of the AAU was renamed the Missouri Valley Association, and the meet that year was designated an Olympic Trials qualifying event. McKown and Williams represented KSTC with a great deal of success at the meet held in Lincoln, Nebraska. McKown won his specialty with a vault of 12-8 5/16, while Lige took 2nd in the 100 and 200-meter dashes. For his performance,

McKown was chosen by the Olympic committee to represent the Western United States in the Olympic Trials. Williams ran a close 2nd to Irwin of Kansas State in both dashes, with Irwin's time in the 100-meter equaling the winning time posted by Charles Paddock of the U.S. at the 1920 Olympic Games. Williams, Irwin and Locke of Nebraska were recognized as the top three sprinters in the country, and the three had already qualified for the trials. Unfortunately, Williams injured his leg 10 days before the trials and was unable to compete. Irwin also missed the trials with an injury, and Locke was unable to compete, keeping the United States top sprinters out of the Olympics. As he left for Boston and the Olympic trials, McKown was considered a sure bet to make the U.S. Olympic team. He still jointly held the American Intercollegiate record at 13-1, although his world indoor record had been broken. At the trials, McKown was one of 10 men to qualify for the finals, but hard luck hit the day of the finals. McKown woke that day feeling ill, and was thought to have tonsillitis. He competed despite the illness, but failed to earn a place on the Olympic team. The four qualifiers cleared 13-0, a height McKown had consistently cleared during his outstanding years at KSTC. If not for the illness, McKown would probably have represented the United States and KSTC in the Paris Olympics. When he returned home, it was found that his illness was the mumps.

1925

When the 1925 season rolled around, John Kuck, a freshman from Wilson, Kansas, was gaining all the laurels despite the presence of KSTC's two senior world class performers, McKown and Lige Williams. Kuck had gained national fame by breaking the world interscholastic record for the 12-pound shot put with a toss of 56-8 ¾ at the 1924 Kansas state high school meet. Kuck had chosen to attend KSTC despite offers from some of the largest schools in the country, and he made his presence felt in the first meet of the season, winning the shot in the annual KCAC indoor. He was the only KSTC entry to place, as McKown and Williams did not attend the meet.

Kuck continued his success during the outdoor season. In a romp over C. of E., while most of the stars who were to compete in the Kansas Relays the next day sat in the bleachers, Kuck set a new American Intercollegiate record in the 16-pound shot, throwing 48-11. He also exceeded the state record in the javelin. However, his intercollegiate record lasted only until the next day when Herbert Schwarze of Wisconsin broke the record with a toss of 49-10 ¾ while competing at the KU Relays.

The greatest performance of the 1925 Kansas Relays was turned in by Earl McKown. Mac, as he was nicknamed, shattered all his previous records with a vault of 13-2 ⅞, to establish a new world intercollegiate record, a new relays record, and a school record that would stand for over 20 years. McKown, pushed hard by his competition, had to set the record in order to win the event outright. The Yellowjacket two-mile relay team of Aaron Fink, Bill Upson, Clem Tuggle, and Wilbur Myer placed 4th in the college division at KU.

McKown was the only Yellowjacket to place at Drake the next week, winning his second vault title with a jump of 12-9. Kuck could not participate in either of the big relay meets because of his freshman standing. Lige Williams, KSTC's world class sprinter, was bothered by severe rheumatism in his hips throughout the entire year, and never reached the level of performance that had come to be expected of him.

Incidents of racial discrimination were, unfortunately, common in the early days of sport in the United States, and KSTC was not immune to the effects. During the 1925 season, KSTC met the University of Missouri in a dual in Columbia. However, black athletes were not allowed to compete in the state of Missouri, which kept Lois and Lige Williams, the Yellowjackets' top sprinters, from competing. KSTC men performed admirably, winning five events, but without their star sprinters, the Yellowjacket team was noticeably weakened and Missouri won handily. This would not be the last time racial discrimination would affect the KSTC track team, although in later years under the direction of Fran Welch, the KSTC team would not participate in a meet where all their athletes were not welcome.

Alfred Quasebarth
Quasebarth was the school record holder in the high jump using the western roll technique.

KSTC regained the state title in 1925, defeating Pitt by 18 points. The meet was once again of very high quality, with nine new records being set, six by Yellowjacket thinclads. McKown again won the pole vault, increasing his record height to 13-2. Lois Williams ran the greatest race of his life, winning the 220-yard dash in the school and state record time of 21.4 seconds. Lois also won the 100-yard dash in 9.9 seconds, defeating teammate Lige in both events. Kuck and Joe Weber were double winners for the Yellowjackets as well. Kuck won the shot put and javelin, setting records with marks that would have set records in nearly any conference in the country. Weber won both hurdle races, setting a record of 24.8 seconds in the low hurdles. Alfred Quasebarth was the final Yellowjacket record setter, tying for 1st in the high jump with a leap of 6-0. This was one and three-fourths inch below his school record set earlier in the year.

At the NCAA meet, in his final college appearance, McKown tied for 1st in the pole vault for the second time. He tied with four other men, all who cleared a height of 12-4. McKown ended his collegiate career holding the world intercollegiate record, the NCAA record, the Kansas Relays record, the Drake Relays record, the Missouri Valley AAU record, and the KCAC indoor meet record. He was KSTC's first Olympic trials competitor, beginning a tradition of KSTC representation in the U.S. Olympic Trials and the Olympic Games. McKown's accomplishments helped make Kansas State Teachers College track famous throughout the nation.

Earl McKown: National Champion
Earl McKown was a world-class pole vaulter while a member of the Emporia State University track & field team from 1922-25. He won the national championships in 1923 and 1925. In 1922, he established the world indoor record with a vault of 12-10. Two years later, his winning vault of 13-2 7/8 at the Drake Relays set a world collegiate record for an outdoor meet. During most of his career, he held the pole vault record in nearly every meet he had competed in, including the NCAA, Kansas Relays, the Drake Relays, and the Kansas Conference.

Although he had completed his collegiate competition, McKown was able to represent KSTC one last time at the National AAU meet in San Francisco. Because eligibility for AAU competition was not limited by class status, freshman John Kuck was eligible to compete in this meet as well. The AAU meet was divided into two sections based on the junior and senior college rating of the contestants. Since he was a freshman and had never competed in a national meet, Kuck was able to enter the shot, discus and javelin in the junior division. However, a contestant was allowed to compete in a division higher than his rating, so Coach Hargiss entered Kuck in the same three events in the senior division also. Kuck performed quite admirably, establishing a new junior national AAU shot put record of 48-2 4/5, breaking a record that had stood since 1905. In the senior division, Kuck placed 2nd in the javelin and 3rd in the shot. The two men who beat him in the shot, Bud Houser and Glenn Hartranft of the United States, had finished 1st and 2nd at the 1924 Olympics, with Kuck nosing out the man who had placed 3rd at Paris. McKown ended up 3rd in the senior division pole vault. Mac was one of six men who tied for 1st at 13-0 when all six failed to clear 13-6. To determine a winner, the bar was gradually lowered until two men cleared at 12-11 ½, gaining a tie for 1st. McKown cleared the bar at 12-10 ½ for 3rd. This is similar to the procedure used today to break ties in championship meets, with one major difference being that after the two men both cleared at 12-11 ½, the bar would have been raised up again to determine an outright winner.

1926

KSTC supporters had come to expect world record performances from the Yellowjacket thinclads. They were not disappointed in 1926 despite the graduation of McKown and Lige Williams, for John Kuck remained, and he was coming into his own as the greatest all-around weight man in the world. At the KCAC meet in his first outing, Kuck set a new world indoor record of 49-¼ for the 16-pound shot. One month later, at the Illinois Indoor Relays, Kuck smashed his own record with a tremendous toss of 50-6 ¾.

Kuck's new record didn't stand for long. Again it was Herbert Schwarze who bested Kuck's mark while defeating Kuck at the National AAU indoor only one week after the Illinois meet. Kuck retained the world intercollegiate indoor record, however, because Schwarze competed unattached.

Kuck was not the only outstanding performer for the Yellowjackets in 1926. Joe Weber and Lois Williams, both double winners in the 1925 state meet, returned to the Yellowjacket team, as well as Kuck's brother, Frank, an outstanding weight man in his own right. Robert Greenwade would also become one of KSTC's all-time greats before his career was completed. These men, plus many others, gave KSTC another strong representative on the cinder paths for the 1926 season. John Kuck continued his superlative performances during the outdoor season. He won the shot put and javelin at the Kansas and Drake Relays, setting meet records in both events at Drake. At Kansas, the AAU organized a special shot put event so that Kuck could meet Schwarze, who was no longer a

> **Call Your Shot: World Record**
>
> The following account from the KSTC Bulletin describes the record setting throw at the Illinois State Relays.
>
> The time came for him (Kuck) to perform in the finals. Forty feet from the ring from which he was to throw the shot was a white mark. A similar line marked every foot from forty to fifty. Kuck walked to the fifty-foot mark. Taking off his white sweat jersey, Kuck placed it a little beyond the fifty-foot mark. He walked back to the circle. The crowd, sensing that something unusual was taking place, fought for advantageous positions from which to watch the event.
>
> Kuck picked up the 16-pound iron ball. Easily and with perfect form, he tossed it. The shot landed squarely in the middle of his sweat jersey, which made it appear that he know to the inch how far he could throw it. The crowd went wild. The record was no fluke. Kuck's two other heaves were well beyond the fifty-foot chalk line.
>
> (KSTC Bulletin, Vol. 25, No. 44, p.1)

collegian, in a battle for the world record. Schwarze won the event, but no record was set. At the Drake Relays, Kuck took 2nd place in the discus to go along with his two 1sts.

Two other Yellowjackets placed at the Kansas Relays. Weber took 3rd in the high hurdles and Frank Kuck, John's brother and an excellent thrower placed 4th in the shot put. The mile relay team of Frank Harris, Aaron Fink, Robert Greenwade and Lois Williams placed 2nd at the Drake Relays.

No track meet in the history of the state had ever aroused as much attention as the 1926 state meet at Pittsburg. Although the Yellowjackets were favored to win, Pitt had whipped them in a dual the week before the state meet. Both KSTC and Pitt were loaded with national caliber athletes, and the meet promised to be one of the best in the midwest. Track fans were not disappointed as KSTC scored 58 points to defend their state title in a very high quality meet. The most sensational performance was turned in by John Kuck, who tossed the javelin 214-2 ⅛ for a new world intercollegiate record, only two feet off the world record. Kuck also set a new state record in the shot put, tossing the iron ball 50-5 ¼, less than seven inches off the world record in that event. Kuck ended his day by winning the discus with a fine throw of 133-6. His performance firmly established Coach Hargiss's claim that he was the best all-around weight man in the world. Lois Williams defended his titles, winning the 100 and 220-yard dashes while setting a new record of 21.3 seconds in the 220-preliminary heat. Weber also set a new record in the prelims, running the high hurdles in 15.5 seconds. He came back in the finals to win both hurdle races for the second consecutive year. Robert Greenwade rounded out the Yellowjacket champions, winning the 440-yard dash in 49.4 seconds. Kuck continued his record-breaking spree into the summer. At the NCAA meet in June, Kuck established a new national intercollegiate record of 50-¾ in the shot put, and placed 3rd in the javelin with a toss of 187-11. He was hindered in the javelin by a very muddy field, and was able to take only two steps and throw rather than use his normal approach.

Competing in Yankee Stadium

Two KSTC athletes competed in Yankee stadium in 1926. John Kuck broke the world record for the 8 pound shot and the 12 pound shot. He then defeated the Olympic champion in the 16 pound shot. To top off the performance he won the javelin, defeating the world record holder. Robert Greenwade won the 440-yard dash in the same meet, but it was not known until the athletes returned to Emporia because of the publicity given to Kuck.

In July, Kuck and Greenwade entered two major events in the East. The first was the National AAU meet held in Philadelphia. Kuck won the javelin with a throw of 199-7, a new National AAU senior division record, and finished 2nd to Schwarze in the shot. Greenwade competed in both the junior and senior divisions, but failed to place in either. The second meet was a benefit meet for the Cathedral of St. John the Divine in New York City. The meet was held in Yankee Stadium and attracted many of the best track athletes in the world. Kuck's performance was magnificent, as he won four events and broke world records. Kuck broke the world record for the eight-pound shot with a throw of 68-7 ⅝, and the world record for the 12-pound shot with a toss of 57-9 ¾. Both marks had stood for nearly 20 years. Kuck also won the 16-pound shot, defeating Bud Houser, the 1924 Olympic champion, and Schwarze. Kuck's fourth win was in the javelin throw, where he defeated Jonni Myyra, the world record holder. Kuck's performance was so outstanding that though Greenwade had won the 440-yard dash in the same meet, it was not known until the athletes returned to Emporia because of the publicity given to Kuck.

Because of their outstanding performances in New York City, Kuck and Greenwade were invited on a month-long tour through Finland, Holland, Norway and Sweden. They left in early August and returned the middle of September. Kuck's and Greenwade's performances while on the tour brought great praise to the Kansas State Teachers College. They competed in eight meets and won a place in all of them. Kuck won most of the events he entered, his outstanding performance being a javelin throw of 215-2, the best mark posted in the world that year and within inches of the world record. In the shot, Kuck broke the European record with a toss of 49-0. Greenwade was just as successful, tying the world amateur record of 48.7 seconds in the 400-meter dash. He also broke the European record in the 100-meter by running 10.7 seconds, and he tied the European 200-meter record of 22.2 seconds.

> **John Kuck: Olympic Champion**
> Although he had left school before the 1928 Olympic Games held in Amsterdam, John Kuck became the only ESU track and field athlete to win an Olympic gold medal. In 1928, he broke the world record in the shot put three times, the third time at the Amsterdam Olympics where he won with an Olympic record setting throw of 52-0 13/16. Kuck has since been inducted into the Drake Relays of Fame, the Emporia State Athletic Hall of Honor and the Kansas Sports Hall of Fame.
>
>

The Scandinavian tour was the last time John Kuck participated under KSTC's colors. John and Frank Kuck withdrew from school in early February of 1927. The loss of the Kuck brothers severely damaged Yellowjacket hopes for a third consecutive state title. John went to compete for the Los Angeles Athletic Club. In 1928, he broke the world record in the shot put three times, the third time at the Amsterdam Olympics where he won with an Olympic record setting throw of 52-0 13/16. Kuck has since been inducted into the Drake Relays of Fame, the Emporia State Athletic Hall of Honor and the Kansas Sports Hall of Fame.

Although team strength was greatly reduced by the loss of the Kucks, KSTC had several outstanding runners remaining. Lois Williams, Greenwade, Aaron Fink, John Concannon, Menzo Hainline, and Earl Howard were on hand to provide a strong sprint team. Chester Davenport, in his third year, became one of the best milers in the state to provide another strong point for the team.

In the KCAC meet, the Yellowjacket mile relay entry of Fink, Greenwade, Hainline and Howard posted the best college time of the meet in defeating Pittsburg, the first mile relay victory ever for KSTC in the meet. Davenport finished 3rd in a classy field of milers, making the Yellowjackets venture to Kansas City a very successful one. The next stop on the indoor circuit was the Illinois Relays, where the Yellowjackets placed 2nd in both the medley and mile relays. KSTC's medley team had the fastest time in the heats, but a mix-up by the judges gave 1st to Michigan. Although available records do not list who ran on these relays, it can be surmised from the KSTC entries that Fink, Williams, Greenwade and Davenport were on the medley team and Fink, Williams, Greenwade, and Hainline were on the mile team.

1927

The opening of the 1927 outdoor season found Normal thinclads participating for the first time in the Texas Relays, the first stop on the Midwest Relay circuit. Success in the meet came early, as the medley relay team of Greenwade, Howard, Concannon, and Davenport won the college class event, setting a Texas Relays record of 3:37. The mile relay team, with Fink in place of Davenport, finished 4th. The same mile relay team entered the Rice Relays the following day and won in the meet record time of 3:23.5.

The next stop on the relay circuit was the Kansas Relays. Again the medley team won, after a brilliant anchor leg dual between KSTC's Davenport and Osif of Haskell College. The KSTC medley, a version of the distance medley with Greenwade running 440 yards, Concannon 220 yards, Fink 880 yards, and Davenport a mile, posted a winning time of 7:45.3. The Yellowjacket mile relay team finished 4th. Unfortunately, the KSTC medley team was upset at Drake in their quest for the Triple Crown. Haskell got revenge for the KU loss, outrunning KSTC in record time. Again, the outcome of the race hinged on the anchor leg, and although Davenport ran the fastest mile of his career, it was not enough to beat Osif, who was the National AAU six-mile champ. The mile relay team scored a near miss as well, finishing one-tenth of a second behind Oklahoma Baptist for 2nd place.

Despite having these outstanding relay teams, Hargiss did not have the depth necessary to field a strong team, and KSTC slipped to a tie for 3rd with C. of E. in the state meet. Lois Williams was the only individual winner for the Yellowjackets, taking the 220-yard dash. Williams was upset in the 100-yard dash, taking a controversial 2nd. The first three men in the 100 (one of whom was Williams) were in a photo finish at the tape, and it was only after a long and heated discussion that the judges gave 1st place to Puckett of McPherson.

This was the last KSTC participation in the Kansas Conference. In November of 1927, seven schools withdrew from the conference and formed the Central Intercollegiate Athletic Conference. The seven schools in the new conference were KSTC, Southwestern, College of Emporia, Fort Hays, Pittsburg, Wichita, and Washburn.

Bill Hargiss Era
During his 12 years as KSTC's track coach, the Yellowjacket teams won seven state championships. Hargiss coached five men who held world records at some time in their career, as well as numerous men who developed into state champions under his tutelage. His coaching record rates him as one of the all-time greats in Emporia State athletic history. He was inducted into the ESU Athletic Hall of Honor as one of the charter inductees.

Chester Davenport was the only Yellowjacket who went on to compete in a championship meet after the 1927 season. Davenport entered the mile at the National AAU meet in Lincoln, Nebraska. Though he did not place, his participation was great experience, because this was the largest amateur meet in the country.

Early in December of 1927, Bill Hargiss accepted the head football job at Kansas University. He stayed on as KSTC's head track coach through the 1928 season, although he missed part of the season while directing spring football at KU. Hargiss served as head football coach at Kansas for five years. After stepping down as football mentor, he handled other athletic duties until 1933, when he took over as KU's head track coach. Hargiss stayed on as Kansas' track coach for 10 years. After World War II, he served as athletic commissioner for KU until his retirement in 1961.

1928

KSTC athletes competed in the 1928 KCAC and Illinois Indoor Relays without a great deal of success. The only place won in either meet was a 3rd by the medley team of Oscar Kutchinski, John Concannon, Dave Massey and Chet Davenport at Illinois. Fran Welch was in charge of the thinclads while Hargiss was officiating in the NAAU Basketball tournament and holding spring football at KU. His last season at KSTC was not one of great success. The Yellowjackets lost duals to Wichita, C. of E., and Pittsburg, and finished 2nd to Wichita in a quadrangular. The Yellowjackets ended the season with a 4th place finish in the first CIC meet. However, several individuals experienced success on the relay circuit. At the Oklahoma University Relays, Earl Bevan took 1st in the javelin, setting a meet record. Ray Beals won another 1st for KSTC in the high jump. These two men also placed well at the Kansas and Drake Relays. Beals tied for 2nd in the high jump at KU and placed 5th in the event at Drake. Bevan took 3rd at KU and 4th at Drake in his specialty. The medley relay team of Massey, Kutchinski, Harold Hunter, and Davenport also placed 3rd at Kansas.

> **Francis Welch: Coach**
> Francis G. "Fran" Welch was chosen to succeed Hargiss as head football and track coach. Welch came to KSTC in 1914 as an undergraduate and earned letters in football, basketball and baseball. After a stint in the service during the World War, Welch attended Kansas State as a graduate student. In 1922, after coaching at Roosevelt High School for two years, Welch became a full-time coach and teacher at the College. Welch assisted Bill Hargiss in football and track from 1922 to 1928.
>
>

Pittsburg easily won the first CIC track title, the first string of 10 consecutive victories in the conference meet. For the Yellowjackets, Bevan won the javelin and Beals won the broad jump. As this was the initial year for the meet, all winning performances stood as conference records.

1929

Francis G. "Fran" Welch was chosen to succeed Hargiss as head football and track coach. In 1922, after coaching at Roosevelt High School for two years, Welch became a fulltime coach and teacher at KSTC. Welch assisted Hargiss in football and track from 1922 to 1928, and the athletes had confidence in his ability to lead them. However, this confidence was not shared by some members of the administration, and Welch's hiring was supposed to last for only a year or two until a big name coach could be found. As history shows, Welch lasted quite a bit longer than was originally intended.

Bevan continued his success during the 1929 season. Only a 2nd place finish at the Kansas Relays kept him from winning the Triple Crown in the javelin. Bevan won at Texas with a meet record throw of 206-4, and came back the next day to win his specialty in the Southern Methodist Relays, setting another meet record. His SMU throw of 208-6 stood as the top mark made in the United States during the 1929 season. After his 2nd place finish at KU, Bevan won at Drake with a toss of 186-6. KSTC relay teams gained prominence during the season as well. The mile relay team of Kutchinski, Massey, Forrest Morgan and Raymond Paines won at the KCAC indoor and placed 5th at the Illinois Indoor relays. At KU, the two-mile relay team of Arvil Dixon, Frank Pecinovsky, Raines and Massey finished 2nd to Pitt. Taking 3rd at Drake was the sprint medley team of Massey, Kutchinski, Claude Freeman, and Morgan.

The Yellowjacket thinclads ended the season and the decade with a 3rd place finish in the CIC meet. The finals on Saturday were held in a downpour with water ankle deep on the track. Because of the weather, only one record was broken. Bevan broke his own record in the javelin prelims with a throw of 187-7. The only other Yellowjacket to place 1st was George Brady, who won the discus, upsetting favored Green of Pittsburg.

Beginning in this era, with KSTC participating in the big relay meets, many of the dual meets were scheduled to coincide with the Texas, Kansas and Drake Relays. This was so the majority of the team, who were not able to qualify to attend the relay carnivals, would be able to compete. KSTC was able to win most of these dual meets without the services of the "stars," underlining the depth and quality of the athletes in the Yellowjacket program.

1930

What would become an exciting and spectacular era for the track program at KSTC had a slow beginning. Coach Welch's teams in the early 1930s maintained the tradition of strong relay teams, but lacked the depth needed to win team championships. Strong performances in the middle distances, a characteristic of the early 1930s teams, was to become a trademark of the Yellowjackets during the Welch era.

> The 1930 CIC meet had the distinction of being the first major meet in Kansas to be held under floodlights.

The middle distance performers showed up well during the 1930 season despite the loss of Forrest Morgan, who did not return to school. The mile relay team of Carl Fields, Verne Hiskey, Jimmy Knight, and Oscar Kutchinski placed 4th at the Illinois Indoor Relays, the Texas Relays, and the Southern Methodist Relays. The medley team composed of the same men, with the exception of Dave Massey for Fields, placed 4th at both the Texas and SMU Relays. These same relay teams took a 2nd and a 4th at Drake in the medley and mile, respectively.

Dale Burnett was a star on the 1926-1929 Yellowjacket football teams, as well as a very good hurdler for the Normal track team. He was twice an all-conference and all-state performer on the gridiron, and went on to play professional football for 11 years with the New York Giants.

The KSTC thinclads finished 3rd in the CIC meet behind Pittsburg and Wichita. Bert Morrill was the Yellowjackets' only winner, taking the javelin with a toss of 172-6 ¼. Knight suffered his only loss of the season in the 440-yard dash losing to Palmer Snodgrass of Pittsburg. The first three finishers in each event at the CIC earned the right to compete in the Kansas-Missouri Interstate meet at Warrensburg, where Knight won the 440-yard dash, gaining revenge by defeating Snodgrass. Knight was the only Hornet to place in the meet.

> **Robert Greenwade: Starting Blocks**
> A new development in track and field was initiated in 1930 by a former Yellowjacket. Robert Greenwade, in his training at San Antonio, was using starting blocks, the first to appear in the Midwest section of the country. The implements had recently been approved by the National AAU and the NCAA. Up until this time, the athletes had dug holes in the track for their feet as a means of improving their start. Greenwade had been very successful since his days at KSTC, setting a world record in the 300-yard dash and running close to the world record in the 440-yard dash.
>
>

1931

Coach Welch took a leave of absence in the spring of 1931 to work on his master's degree, leaving the program in the hands of Paul Kutnink. Kutnink had served as Welch's assistant coach for two years. He had competed for the 1920-1923 KSTC track teams and was well liked and respected by the Yellowjacket athletes. Kutnink performed very capably in Welch's absence.

The Yellowjacket team was strengthened when Forrest "Frosty" Morgan returned to school in 1931. Morgan, along with veterans Massey, Knight, and freshman Bernard Grant, formed a particularly strong mile relay team. This team opened the season with a victory at the KCAC meet, defeating Pittsburg and Baker by 30 yards. They continued their success by winning at the Texas Relays and finishing a close 2nd to Abilene Christian at the Rice Relays the next day. Both teams bettered the old Rice Relays record. The winning relay combination unfortunately ended when Massey pulled a muscle during the C. of E. dual. Kutnink did not have a capable replacement, and the team could only manage a 5th place finish at the KU Relays.

The Yellowjackets repeated their CIC performance of 1930, finishing 3rd behind Pittsburg and Wichita in the 1931 conference. Pitt was a dominant force, taking nine 1sts while scoring in every event. The outstanding effort for the Yellowjackets was turned in by Knight. In the 440-yard dash, he was 2nd to Widney of Wichita in a race so close that two of the judges called it a tie. Both men were timed in 49.7 seconds for a new CIC record. Knight, on the anchor, failed by only a few yards to catch up. However, Pitt was disqualified for fouling and KSTC gained the victory.

Because of a shortage of middle distance men, Welch moved Norman Rhoads up to the 880-yard run during the outdoor season. Rhoads met with outstanding success at this new distance, completing the regular season unbeaten in the half-mile and breaking the school record twice. His best time of 1:56.3, recorded at the Pitt dual, bettered the CIC mark for the event by .2 of a second. Rhoads defeated Elton Brown of Pitt, the conference record holder, in the meet. At the CIC meet, Rhoads again defeated Brown to win the 880 with a time just off the meet record.

Rhoads was also a part of KSTC's success on the relay circuit. At the Drake Relays, the mile relay team of Rhoads, A. J. Holder, Grant, and Knight ran a 3:21.8 qualifying time in the prelims, the fastest time ever posted by a KSTC team in the event. Due to the strength of the field, however, Welch pulled them out of the finals and entered the same foursome in the sprint medley relay, in which they placed 3rd. The two-mile relay team of Knight, Rhoads, Morgan, and Grant took another 3rd for the Yellowjackets. This same quartet had placed 2nd in the two-mile relay and 4th in the mile relay at KU the week prior to Drake.

1932

KSTC improved to 2nd place at the 1932 CIC meet, but Pittsburg was still dominant, winning by over 20 points. The Yellowjackets were much improved over recent years, scoring in 11 events to gain the best finish for KSTC since the conference began. Besides Rhoads' victory, KSTC earned one other 1st when Morrill regained the conference javelin title after his disappointing 3rd place finish in 1931. Holder tied the conference mark of 10.0 seconds in the 100-yard dash during his preliminary heat but was defeated by Swisher of Pitt in the finals.

After several years' absence, KSTC returned to compete in the Missouri Valley AAU meet, where five Yellowjackets earned 3rd place for KSTC. Rhoads won the 880-yard run, setting a meet and school record of 1:55.7. Orsie Poff, a sophomore two-miler, won that event with the school record time of 1:55.4.

When a Record is Not a Record
Orsie Poff had broken the 880-yard school record numerous times. However, he had finished 2nd or 3rd on these occasions, and only 1st place times could be counted as school records. This policy was due to the unreliable timing of second and third places. First was the only place timed by meet officials, so 2nd and 3rd place times were recorded only by the team's coach. Thus, there was the possibility that a non-winning performance might not be timed when there was a record broken. For the sake of uniformity, the plan of accepting only 1st place times for records was adopted.

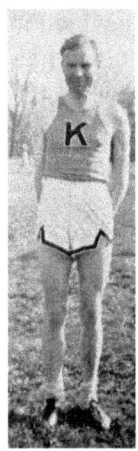

Lee Haring, who had missed most of the 1932 season with the mumps, came on strong at the end of the year to reveal his potential. He won the high hurdles at the Missouri Valley meet and placed 2nd in the lows. Haring had never run over a hurdle before he came to KSTC in 1930. In a freshman physical education class he took that fall semester, Haring started working on the hurdles with Warren Cook, a KSTC hurdler who was in charge of the class. When Haring returned to school in 1932 after his one-year layoff, he went back to running hurdles, and his efforts in the MVAAU meet helped salvage the season cut short by his ordeal with the mumps.

Rhoads was the only Yellowjacket to compete in the national intercollegiate meet that summer. The meet was an Olympic Trials qualifying event, with the top three in each event earning a berth in the U.S. Olympic Trials. Rhoads ran the two fastest races of his career, posting times of 1:54.8 in the prelims and 1:54.4 in the finals. Despite these performances, he could manage only a 7th place finish, even though he came in only seven yards behind the winner, and did not qualify for the trials. Shortly after this meet, the Los Angeles Athletic Club rated Rhoads as the fifth best half-miler in the United States.

1933

The Hornets fielded another large track team in the spring of 1933. Despite the effects of the depression on college enrollment and extra activities by students, 55 men reported for practice in early January. Several outstanding new men joined with the returning stars to form the strongest Hornet track team since 1926. Except for the annual clash with Pittsburg, the thinclads won every dual meet entered, including a 69-62 victory over Kansas State.

The KSTC relay teams experienced great success in the indoor and outdoor relay meets. At the Butler Indoor Relays in Indianapolis, the quartet of Paul Bridges, Jimmy Knight, Forrest Morgan and Norman Rhoads won the mile and two-mile relays. However, the team was disqualified from the two-mile event when a judge ruled that Rhoads had fouled on the

1932 Hornet
For several years, the KSTC athletic teams had been referred to as Hornets, a shortened version of Yellowjackets that most found easier to use. In the fall of 1932, the name of Hornets was officially adopted by KSTC.

anchor carry. Brown of Pittsburg had attempted to pass Rhoads on the inside during the final lap and was tripped.

The same quartet won the two-mile relay at the Kansas Relays, setting a college division record of 7:50.5. Three other Hornet teams placed at KU: the half-mile team of Duward Crooms, Claude Fisher, Alva Gould, and Lee Haring finished 2nd; the distance medley foursome of Morris Clark, Fisher, Tyree Mack, and Morgan finished 3rd; and the mile team of Paul Bridges, Bernard Grant, Knight, and Rhoads was also 3rd. The mile relay time of 3:19.7 was under the KU record for the event. Haring ran 2nd in the high hurdles to Bill Schiefly of Minnesota, the Big 10 champion in the event.

At the Drake Relays the following week, the two-mile team, composed of the same men who ran at KU, ran a dead heat with Pitt to tie for 1st. The time of 7:52.6 was a new college division Drake record. The mile quartet of Grant, Crooms, Holder and Mack placed 2nd to Oklahoma Baptist. The Hornet team "officially" set a school record of 3:22.2 in winning their preliminary heat. The old mark had stood since 1927, and although it had been broken numerous times during the six years it had stood, no team finished 1st when beating the mark. According to the policy in effect, the times could not be counted as a record. The Hornets also gained a 3rd place in the sprint medley, with the team of Crooms, Holder, Knight and Mack. Haring rounded out the KSTC scoring again placing 2nd to Schiefly in the high hurdles.

Pittsburg continued their domination of the CIC, taking a sixth consecutive title in 1933. The Hornets had hoped to challenge for the title, and although this did not occur, KSTC closed the gap between themselves and Pitt. Haring won both hurdle races, setting conference and school records of 15.0 seconds in the highs and 23.7 seconds in the lows. Morrill added another victory, winning the javelin for the third time in four years with a toss of 175-10. The outstanding performance of the meet was turned in by Rhoads, who won the 880-yard run, setting a new conference and school record of 1:52.8. Rhoads' time was only 1.2 seconds off the world record and was believed to be the best time ran in the U.S. during the 1933 season. Rhoads also came back to run an outstanding quarter on the mile relay. This team ran the superb time of 3:16.7, yet lost to Pittsburg by one-tenth of a second. In a very close decision, Holder lost to Swisher of Pitt in the 100-yard dash for the second straight year.

Meeting Jesse Owens

I got to take the trip to Chicago (World Fair year of 1933) that summer. Educationally I learned a lot. We rode the rails both ways and bunked in Hotel Sherman. That's where Norman Rhoads ordered dinner sent up to the room. $4.00 for three people. Fran climbed the wall and hit the roof. I met and talked with Jesse Owens there on the infield of Soldiers and Sailors Field. He was a high school senior headed for Ohio State and destined to make Woody Hayes a great coach. I remember his blue eyes. I also remember he ran a 9.6 one hundred yard dash and jumped 24 feet. This isn't bad for a high school kid...even today...I didn't place at Chicago. I did see some things at the Fair that I would never have seen...except for track.

(Lee Haring, personal communication, June 1984)

The Hornets competed in the MVAAU the weekend after the CIC and placed 3rd for the second consecutive year. Welch was saving Rhoads for the NCAA meet and did not enter him in his specialty, a decision that caused disappointment among track fans because Rhoads' entry in the 880 would have meant a dual with Glenn Cunningham, KU's star miler. Instead, Rhoads entered the 400-meter, and was barely nosed out of 1st in the time of

49.0 seconds. Haring won both hurdle events, a feat he had accomplished seven times during the season. Bridges and Poff ended the Hornet scoring, finishing 2nd in the 1500 and 5000-meter runs, respectively.

Haring and Rhoads went on that summer to compete in the NCAA meet in Chicago, but neither Hornet was able to place in their event.

Haring and Rhoads earned a place on the National Collegiate Honor Roll for their performances during the season, as did the Hornet two-mile relay.

1934

Three members of the record setting two-mile relay team were missing in 1934. Knight and Morgan had completed their eligibility, while Rhoads had not recovered from a broken foot suffered while playing baseball in the summer of 1933. However, the Hornets maintained a strong team, due mainly to the efforts of the sprinters.

For the first time in several years, KSTC did not open the season at the Butler Indoor Relays. Instead, Welch took three men to the Tulsa Invitational Indoor. Haring won both the 40-yard low and the 40-yard high hurdles, defeating Sam Allen of Oklahoma Baptist, one of the top hurdlers in the country. Bridges gained the Hornets other points, taking 2nd in the 880-yard run.

Once again, KSTC defeated Kansas State by a score of 74 ⅓-56 ⅔ to open the outdoor season. Hornet thinclads next turned their attention to the KU Relays, where they took 2nd to Pittsburg in the college division. Crooms was outstanding, winning the open 100-yard dash in 9.8 seconds and anchoring the 880-relay team of Jim Fraley, Eustace Shannon and Holder to 1st with the time of 1:28. The two-mile relay team of Bridges, Mack, Paul Mahoney, and Carl Van Weldon finished 2nd to Pitt, and the mile team of Fraley, Elwood Miller, Mack, and Bridges finished 3rd. Haring again took 2nd in the high hurdles, this year to Allen of OBU.

> **Racial Discrimination**
>
> Racial discrimination reached into Kansas during this period, as blacks were not allowed to compete on the athletic teams at KU, the state university. However, KSTC had for a number of years allowed black athletes to participate, and the school, coaches and athletes strongly supported all members of the team.
>
> On a trip to Lawrence, the team stopped for dinner at the Eldridge Hotel. We were told that the colored boys could not eat with us. The rest of us (team and coaches) told them that we all ate or none of us would-we all ate together.
>
> (O.L. Poff, personal communication)

The Hornets' success continued the next weekend at the Drake Relays. The mile relay team of Holder, Mack, Bridges, and Crooms captured 1st, defeating Pitt and OBU. These same men finished 2nd in the sprint medley, and the two-mile team of Van Weldon, Mahoney, Mack and Bridges placed 3rd. Crooms finished 3rd in the open 100-yard dash to Ralph Metcalfe of Marquette, the world record holder, and to Hall of Kansas. Eustace Shannon placed 3rd in the open long jump to complete the Hornets scoring.

At the Kansas Relays, Kansas State's 480-yard shuttle hurdle team had set a world record of 1:01.7. At Drake, a special team consisting of Herring from Texas A&M, Fisher from LSU, Allen from OBU, and

Haring from KSTC ran the event in 59.8 seconds to beat the time set by K-State, and run the event in less than one minute for the first time in history. This was accomplished despite running the event in the middle of the football field. The mark was submitted as a world record, but for reasons unknown, it was never accepted.

The Hornets again finished 2nd to Pittsburg in the CIC as the Gorillas had too much depth for KSTC. Haring and Crooms were the individual stars for KSTC. Haring repeated in both hurdle races, his times of 14.6 seconds in the prelims and 14.7 seconds in the finals of the highs bettering the conference record. However, neither time was allowed as a record because they were wind-aided. Crooms won the 100 and finished 2nd in the 220 and the broad jump. His times of 9.6 seconds and 21.1 seconds in the dashes, posted during the prelims, were also better than the existing conference marks, but again the wind velocity was over the allowable limit. The mile relay team of Bridges, Haring, Holder and Mack took KSTC's final victory.

The Hornets' last meet of the season was the Missouri Valley AAU. KSTC thinclads earned a 3rd place tie with Oklahoma University, behind Pittsburg and KU. Haring continued his outstanding performances by winning the high and low hurdles, while Bridges finished 3rd in the 880-yard run behind KU's Glenn Cunningham and Pittsburg's Brown. Crooms won his qualifying heat of the 100, but had to withdraw from the final because of a pulled muscle.

> **Archie San Romani:**
> **Dream to Make the Olympic Team**
> In the summer of 1933, Fran Welch received a letter that, according to the author, read something like this:
>
> Dear Mr. Welch:
> I would like to enter your school. I will do my very best in my studies. I want to be on your track team. I want to make the Olympic Team in 1936. My time is 4 minutes and 29 and 9 tenths seconds.
>
> The author of the letter was Archie San Romani. San Romani had attended Bethany College in 1932-33 and wanted to transfer to KSTC because of the outstanding music and athletic programs.
>
> I sent that letter to Mr. Welch. I can imagine how he felt and what he thought of a man with that time trying to make the Olympic team of 1936. He wrote back to me and said, "If you come here and work hard, I will see you have a roof over your head and something in your belly." That is just the way he put it. He gave me the break.
>
> -Archie San Romani (*The Pan American Track & Field Journal, Clinic Notes, 1960*

Later that summer, Haring and Crooms earned a great honor for themselves and KSTC. Both were selected to attend the NCAA meet in Los Angeles with their expenses paid by the NCAA, an honor that only the eight best in each event throughout the country received. For KSTC to have two athletes of this caliber spoke very highly of the Hornet program. The NCAA committee approved Bridges also, but he had to arrange his own expenses.

Against the national competition, the Hornet stars showed that they were worthy of this honor. Both Haring and Crooms qualified for the finals in their respective events, and both ran well in the finals. The judges did not place Haring in the high hurdles final, but the picture showed that he was actually 6th. Unfortunately, what the Hornets gained, they also lost. Crooms was picked by the judges as placing 6th in the 100-yard dash, but the picture moved

> **Photo Timing**
> In the 1934 NCAA meet in Los Angeles, the judges used a new photographic timing device to confirm placings picked by the timers, and this system caused a revision of many of the places in the finals, including the placing of both Lee Haring in the hurdles and Duane Crooms in the 100 yard dash.
>
>

him back to 7th place. Bridges also ran well, posting the fastest 880 of his career, but he did not qualify for the final. The three men who defeated Bridges in his heat finished 1st, 3rd, and 4th in the 880 final.

1935

Archie San Romani attended KSTC during the 1933-34 school year, but was ineligible to compete because of the transfer rule. He was eligible when the 1935 season opened, and the addition of San Romani gave the Hornets a very bright outlook. Five school record holders were on the team: Crooms in the 100 and 220, Haring in both hurdles, Rhoads, recovered from his foot injury, in the 880, Bridges in the mile, and Perry Kirkpatrick in the broad jump.

KSTC resumed participation in the KCAC indoor meet in 1935 after a six-year absence. Haring won the 50-yard high hurdles and finished 2nd in the 50-yard lows, while freshman Ken DeMott took 4th in the highs. San Romani ran the mile, finishing 3rd. The Hornets returned to the Butler Indoor Relays to conclude the indoor season and took 1st in the college division, 3rd overall behind Michigan and Ohio State. The two-mile relay team of Tyree Mack, Wendall Frame, Rhoads, and Bridges set a meet record of 8:02 in winning the event. The mile relay team also won, setting a meet record of 3:27.2. Eustace Shannon, Rhoads, Bridges, and Crooms ran on this team. The distance medley team of Clinton Bamtz, Frame, Holder, and San Romani finished 2nd when San Romani moved them up from 6th place on the anchor carry. Forty minutes, later San Romani came back to take 3rd in the open mile. Haring was ill with the measles and did not compete, costing the Hornets valuable points in the hurdles.

KSTC opened the outdoor season with impressive victories over Wichita and Kansas State, the third straight over the Aggies who had recently won the Big 6 Indoor Championship. The Hornets next journeyed to the Kansas Relays, where they met with remarkable success. Crooms repeated his 1934 victory in the 100-yard dash, defeating a strong field, including Jim Owens of the University of Iowa. Owens ran anchor on the teams that held world records in the 440 and 880 relays. San Romani won the open 1500-meter in 3:57.2, then anchored the Hornets' distance medley to victory in the college division. Holder, Mack, and Bridges joined San Romani on this team. The Hornets' fourth victory was in the 880 relay, the team of Shannon, Austin, Holder and Crooms winning with the time of 1:29. Welch entered a team in the university class 480-yard shuttle hurdles, and the Hornet hurdlers won the event. Unfortunately, they were not eligible to receive an award because Ken DeMott and Dick Dodd were freshmen and ineligible to compete in university class events. Jerome Carroll and Lee Haring were the other members of the team. Haring was unable to compete in the open high hurdles, an event he had placed 2nd in the previous two years, because he had used up his three years of NCAA eligibility. The two-mile relay team of Mack, Frame, Bridges and Rhoads was beaten by inches at the tape when the Pittsburg anchorman made up 15 yards on Rhoads, costing the Hornets a sixth Relays victory. Shannon, Rhoads, Austin and Frame ran on the mile team that placed 4th, while Shannon earned the last points for the Hornets with a 2nd in the broad jump. Shannon was in 1st and seemed assured of winning, when Pitts of Kansas leaped past him by one-fourth of an inch on his last jump.

> **Finishing Behind Jesse Owens' Record Performances**
> Duward Crooms competed against the legendary Jesse Owens in the 100-yard dash at the Drake Relays. Crooms finished a very respectable 5th in the 100 while Owens tied the world record at 9.5 seconds. Eustace Shannon competed against Owens in the broad jump, leaping 24-6 ¼ to set a new school record; however, he could only finish 4th behind the American record of Owens in 26-1 ¾.

Seven Hornets attended the Drake Relays the following week and performed well, although they did not match their success at KU. The mile relay team of Mack, Holder, Rhoads, and Crooms won the event and set a school record of 3:20.0, while the two-mile team of Mack, Rhoads, Bridges, and San Romani was defeated by Pitt by a scant yard for the second time in a week. The Hornets finished 2nd to Pitt in the sprint medley as well, with the team of Mack, Holder, Crooms and Bridges. Shannon turned in a spectacular performance in the broad jump, leaping 24-6 ¼ to break his school record by seven inches. However, this jump was good for only 4th in a very strong field, including Jesse Owens of Ohio State, who set a new American record of 26-1 ¾. Crooms also competed against Owens in the 100-yard dash and finished 5th while Owens tied the world record of 9.5 seconds.

The biggest victory of the season came two weeks later in the annual Pittsburg dual. KSTC defeated Pitt 69 1/3 to 61 2/3, Pitt's first dual loss in 11 years, and broke a string of 30 consecutive dual victories by the Gorillas. The Hornets outscored Pitt by 23 points on the track, and took 1st in the final three events to win the meet.

The success against the Gorillas was short lived, however, as the Weedesmen came back to nip the Hornets by 2 ½ points to win the CIC title. Winners for the Hornets included San Romani in the mile and two-mile, Haring in both hurdles, Leo Colton in the shot put, and Crooms in the 100 and 220-yard dashes. Crooms also took 2nd in the long jump. KSTC scored heavily in all the running events, but weakness in the field cost the Hornets the title.

For a while, the names of Yellowjacket and Hornet were used interchangeably. The evolution of the school mascot went from a stereotypical hornet to "Corky" the Hornet, who first appeared in 1934 by student Paul Edwards.

One of the most interesting and amusing incidents in the history of the program occurred on this trip. This account from the KSTC Bulletin describes the incident:

On the recent trip to Pittsburg for the conference meet, Lee Haring, Norman Rhoads, Harold Cook, and Eustace Shannon were incarcerated in the city calaboose Friday evening and spent two hours cooling their heels while city officials looked up the past records, present occupations, and future prospects of this quartet of desperadoes.

The difficulty started when Coach Fran Welch's proteges, after qualifying a good number for the meet Saturday, decided to take a little airing before retiring Friday evening. Without going into the details, suffice it to say that Haring, Rhoads, Cook, and Shannon created quite a disturbance, according to the chief of police, on one of Pittsburg's main thoroughfares. The chief, with one of his trusty retainers, drove up in the municipal and asked the four Hornets to accompany them to the lock-up.

Haring, feeling especially courageous, argued the point.

"Let me see your badge," said the Hornet timber topper.

"Climb in the wagon," growled the upholder of law and order, flashing a shiny gold badge. The offenders crawled. They rode to the station, where they were promptly escorted to the one and only cell and locked in.

While the chief of police communicated with the mayor, Dr. Garfield Weede, track coach at Pittsburg, and other people of importance, the Hornets organized a quartet and worked up a special version of If I Had the Wings of an Angel, and I'm in the Jail House Now, with special effects by Cook and Shannon. The rest of the time was spent reading the literary contributions left on the walls of the cell by former occupants.

The news of the arrest finally reached the ears of Kenneth DeMott, another hurdler, who proceeded to carry the information to Coach Fran Welch.

"How are the beds", the Hornet mentor calmly asked the troubled freshman.
"All right, I guess," he replied.
"Then we'll let them stay," said Welch. "They'll get a good nights rest."
"But Fran," protested Woody Teichgraeber, discus thrower, "The ventilation is terrible. It's stuffy down there."

After due consideration, it was finally decided that if the four lads would promise to behave themselves for the remainder of the trip, they would be allowed to leave the jail. Haring, still showing a disposition to remonstrate with the chief of police, was advised by the mayor that everything he said would be held against him, and he was finally led away, still muttering protests.

"The jail was terrible," said Harold Cook, in speaking of the incident. "I'm going to start a society for the improvement of municipal lock-ups. Haring is vice-president, Rhoads secretary, and Shannon is sargeant-at-arms."

There will be no treasurer, for obvious reasons. *(KSTC Bulletin, Vol. 34, No. 62, p. 1)*

The "disturbance" which led to the arrest of the four Hornets was a game of penny pitching, not a major crime by today's standards.

Archie San Romani: National Champion

Archie San Romani won the National Collegiate mile in 1935 and the 1500-meter run in 1936. He anchored the Hornet's distance medley relay team to a new world record in 1936.

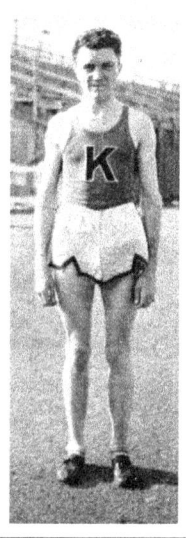

At the Missouri Valley AAU meet the weekend after conference, Haring and San Romani were winners for the Hornets. Haring won both hurdle events, setting a meet record of 14.8 seconds in the 110-meter highs. Sam Romani won the 1500-meter in the record time of 4:00.7. Rhoads finished 2nd in the 400-meter, while 3rds were earned by Bridges in the 800-meter, Shannon in the triple jump, Cecil Dryer in the shot put, and the mile relay team of Mack, Shannon, Bridges, and Rhoads. All these men qualified for the National AAU meet with their performances.

The next meet on the schedule however, was the NCAA meet in Berkeley, California, where San Romani, Shannon, Crooms, Rhoads and Haring competed for the Hornets. San Romani turned in a superb performance in winning the mile with the time of 4:19.1, upsetting the favorites with a thrilling sprint finish to win by a chest. No other Hornet was able to place.

On the basis of Sam Romani's effort, KSTC trackmen were invited to stay in California and run in the Far West AAU meet the following week. Haring won the high hurdles and took 3rd in the low hurdles, defeating many of the men who had beaten him at the NCAAs. San Romani finished 2nd in the mile behind Norman Bright of the Olympic Club.

San Romani and Haring were the only Hornets Welch entered in the National AAU meet in Lincoln, Nebraska. The competition in this meet was the best in the country, as any man with amateur status was eligible to enter. Sam Romani finished 3rd in the 1500-meter behind two of the best milers in the world, Glenn Cunningham, the world record holder, and Gene Wenzke. Haring did not qualify for the finals, and thus ended his career as one of KSTC's great track and field performers. Haring was listed on the 1935 National Honor Roll for the third consecutive year.

1936

In 1936, Archie San Romani, by then recognized as one of the top milers in the United States, was invited to compete in both the Millrose Games held at Madison Square Garden and the Boston Athletic Association Games. These were two of the four big eastern indoor meets to which only the top athletes in the country were invited. San Romani placed 4th behind Wenzke, Cunningham, and Joe Mangan at both meets.

Welch Stadium

In the fall of 1935, construction began on a new stadium north of Lake Wooster. The project was a part of the government's work program and meant jobs for the men of the city and for students. The stadium was completed in 1937, and the track was first used during the 1938 season. This facility is known today as Welch Stadium.

KSTC added a new event to the 1936 indoor schedule by attending the Ozark AAU Indoor Relays in St. Louis, Missouri. Ken DeMott proved an adequate replacement for Haring by winning the 55-yard high hurdles in both the collegiate and open divisions, while Dick Dodd placed 3rd in both divisions of the same event. San Romani finished 2nd to Mel Truitt of Indiana in an unusually slow mile. Cecil Dryer placed 2nd in the shot put to Don Elser of Notre Dame. Also placing 2nd were the Hornet mile and two-mile relay teams with foursomes of Al Locke, Loren Austin, Rhoads, and Crooms on the mile relay, and John Zimmerman, San Romani, Rhoads, and Bridges on the two-mile team.

At the annual Butler Relays, KSTC again won the college division and placed 3rd overall, behind the same two teams as in 1935. The team of Crooms, Bridges, Frame, and San Romani set a Relays record of 10:32 in winning the college distance medley, while the mile team of Crooms, Austin, Bridges, and Locke won, tying the meet record set by KSTC in 1935. Dryer and DeMott gained 2nds in the shot and high hurdles respectively. The two-mile team of Mack, Frame, Rhoads and Locke finished 3rd behind Pittsburg and Butler University. Fourths were earned by DeMott in the low hurdles and Crooms in the 60-yard dash.

The Hornet thinclads resumed participation in the Texas Relays when the outdoor season opened. However, only five KSTC men competed because of the discrimination rule against blacks competing in Texas. The 1936 season was one of only three years during the decade that KSTC participated at Texas, and this was due at least partially to the ban on black athletes. The five who did compete were very successful, as the distance medley team of Austin, Rhoads, Bridges, and San Romani won the university class event in the record time of 10:22.5, and Cecil Dryer placed 2nd in the open shot put.

When Crooms failed to qualify for the finals of the 100-yard dash at the Kansas Relays, an event he had won the two previous years, Welch decided to shoot the works in the distance medley relay. He scratched San Romani from the 1500-meter and Bridges and Rhoads from the two-mile relay. The latter relay team, with Eugene Foster, Zimmerman, Mack, and Frame running, finished 2nd to Pittsburg. Welch entered the team of Crooms, Rhoads, Bridges, and San Romani in the university class distance medley, and their performance was spectacular. In winning the event, they established a new Kansas Relays, American, and world record with the time of 10:12.7.

World Record Distance Medley Relay
The team of Duane Crooms, Norman Rhoads, Paul Bridges and Archie San Romani set a new world record in winning the Kansas Relays distance medley relay in 1936. The team ran 10:12.7 to win the university division. In a display of outstanding depth and quality of Hornet distance running, a second team of Locke, Mack, Zimmerman and Frame won the college division.

Crooms *Rhoads* *Bridges* *San Romani*

The depth and quality of the Hornet distance runners was shown when Welch entered another foursome in the college distance medley, and the team of Locke, Mack, Zimmerman and Frame also won with the time of 10:40.3. KSTC gained two other 2nd places, from Dryer in the shot and the shuttle hurdle team of

Jim Fraley, Werne Sumner, Dodd, and DeMott. The half-mile relay team of Harold Haywood, Austin, Locke, and Crooms took 3rd.

At the Drake Relays, the Hornet medley quartet was denied a shot at a triple crown. The three-year eligibility rule was enforced at Drake, keeping Crooms, Rhoads, and Bridges out of the university class. Welch entered Frame, Rhoads, Bridges, and San Romani in the two-mile relay, and this foursome won the event in a Drake record time of 7:52.0. KSTC also placed 3rd in the sprint medley relay and the mile relay. Available records do not list the runners on these teams, but Welch had previously announced that Austin, Crooms, Locke, and San Romani would run the sprint medley and Austin, Crooms, Locke, and Mack would run the mile.

KSTC defeated the Pittsburg Gorillas for the second straight year in the annual dual, winning by 17 points, and the Hornets were favored to finally take the CIC title away from Pitt. The Weedesmen pulled off the upset, though, winning 64-63 ½ for their ninth straight conference title. KSTC had a ½-point lead with the low hurdles and mile relay remaining when hard luck hit. Werne Sumner, the favorite to win the low hurdles, was leading when he tripped over the next to last hurdle and did not place. Pitt gained a 2nd place in the event and a lead the Hornet victory in the mile relay could not make up. Sam Romani and Crooms were the workhorses for KSTC. San Romani won the mile and two-mile and placed 2nd in the 880, while Crooms took 2nd in the 100, 220, broad jump, and ran on the Hornets' winning mile relay along with Locke, Rhoads and Bridges. Bridges took 1st in the 880 with the time of 1:59.5, and Harold Cook won the pole vault, jumping 11-10. Cecil Dryer earned the Hornets final victory, winning the shot put with the conference record throw of 48-5 ½.

Two weeks later, San Romani broke his own Missouri Valley record in the 1500-meter, winning the event at the MVAAU meet in 4:00.0. Bridges was also a winner, taking the 800-meter, while Dryer placed 2nd in the shot put. DeMott and Frame closed out the Hornet scoring, taking 3rds in the high hurdles and 5000-meter respectively.

San Romani was the only KSTC athlete to continue competition into the summer, and he did so quite successfully. He first entered the NCAA meet in Chicago to defend his mile title, and won the 1500-meter while setting a new NCAA record of 3:53.0. By winning the NCAA, he earned the right to compete in the final Olympic trials. However, Welch decided to enter San Romani in the Olympic sectional meet at Milwaukee and the National AAU at Princeton, New Jersey, and San Romani finished a close 2nd to Glenn Cunningham in the 1500-meter in both meets.

San Romani went to the U.S. Olympic Trials in New York still considered by most experts to be an outside shot for the Olympic team. To get on, he would have to break up the big three on the American mile scene: Glenn Cunningham, the world record holder in the mile, Gene Wenzke, the former world record holder in the indoor mile, and Bill Bonthron, the world record holder in the 1500-meter. San Romani not only broke them up, he almost won the event. Both he and Cunningham were timed at 3:49.9, but the former KU star was given the victory. San Romani became the first athlete to officially represent KSTC at the Olympic Games.

San Romani left for Berlin on July 15th of 1936, accompanied by Coach Welch. The students of KSTC and the townspeople of Emporia had worked together to raise $500 so Welch could accompany San Romani during the most important races of his life. San Romani went determined to win the race, but ended up 4th behind Jack Lovelock of New Zealand, Glenn Cunningham, and Luigi Beccali of Italy, the 1932 Olympic 1500-meter champion. Lovelock set a new Olympic and world record of 3:47.8, while San Romani's time of 3:50.0 was under the old Olympic record by 1.2 seconds. After the Games, San Romani stayed in Europe and participated in the AAU sponsored tour of the Scandinavian countries, a tour required of the U.S. Olympians by the AAU.

Two months after the Olympic Games, San Romani met Lovelock and Cunningham in a special mile race promoted by Princeton University. Run at halftime of the Princeton-Williams football game, the race was set up to give Lovelock one final shot at Cunningham's world record of 4:06.7 in the mile, as Lovelock would retire after the race. San Romani upset the favorites, though, winning in 4:09. In defeating Lovelock by eight yards, San Romani ran the fastest last quarter ever run at the end of a mile. This was the first in a series of major victories that would establish San Romani as the number one miler in the World for 1937.

San Romani's next victory came at the Sugar Bowl Game in "The Mile of the Century." Run at halftime of the Sugar Bowl Game in New Orleans, he defeated Cunningham by inches in the time of 4:14, which bettered the Southern record set by Cunningham in 1936. Sam Romani next moved indoors where, due to a lack of training facilities, his success was not as great. He finished a distant 4th to Cunningham's meet record in the Boston Knights of Columbus Games, then finished 3rd to Cunningham and Wenzke in the Millrose Games' Wanamaker Mile. San Romani had planned to enter the Baxter Mile at the New York Athletic Club Games, but bad weather forced cancellation of the trip.

Archie San Romani: Olympian

Archie San Romani became the first athlete to officially represent KSTC at the Olympic Games by qualifying for the U.S. Olympic team in the 1500 meters. At the Olympic Trials, San Romani and Glenn Cunningham were both timed in 3:49.9 with Cunningham given the victory.

At the 1936 Olympic Games in Berlin, Germany, San Romani finished 4th behind Jack Lovelock of New Zealand, Glenn Cunningham, and Luigi Beccali of Italy, the 1932 Olympic 1500-meter champion. Lovelock set a new Olympic and world record of 3:47.8, while San Romani's time of 3:50.0 was under the old Olympic record by 1.2 seconds.

The next stop on the indoor circuit for San Romani was the National AAU meet in New York, where he scored a thrilling victory in the 1500-meter, bursting past Luigi Beccali (the bronze medalist at 1500 meters in the 1936 Olympic Games) in the last five yards to win in 3:51.2. Cunningham had withdrawn from the race. San Romani and Cunningham met again a few weeks later at the Chicago Indoor Relays, and San Romani defeated the world record holder. Ken DeMott joined San Romani at Chicago, but did not place due to a pulled muscle that kept him out for most of the season.

1937

San Romani joined the Hornet squad after the Chicago meet to participate in the regular season schedule. Graduation losses had been heavy, with Rhoads, Bridges, Crooms, Mack, Locke, Austin and Dryer gone from the 1936 team. Nevertheless, the 1937 squad remained one of the best small college teams in the Midwest on the strength of several outstanding performers. Though strong in the big relay meets, the Hornets did not have the depth necessary to challenge Pittsburg for conference honors.

To open the season, KSTC athletes attended the 1st Annual Mid-West Intercollegiate Indoor meet in Naperville, Illinois. The Hornets finished 3rd behind North Central College and Pittsburg. Sam Romani won the mile, setting a field house record of 4:27. Sumner set another fieldhouse record in winning the 60-yard high hurdles. Frame earned the Hornets' final victory, winning the two-mile and also finishing 2nd to San Romani in the mile. Archie Shepard finished right behind his teammate to take 2nd in the high hurdles. This meet underscored the Hornets' strength in the distances and hurdles.

San Romani made one more venture into the indoor invitational meets during 1937, competing in the New York Knights of Columbus Games. He finished just two-tenths of a second behind Glenn Cunningham in the mile run at 4:08.9. Cunningham's time of 4:08.7 was just off his world indoor record for the mile of 4:08.4. These two men were developing quite a rivalry, and they met again at the Butler Indoor Relays. San Romani won this round, defeating Cunningham by two yards with the time of 4:21. The Hornet distance medley also came up with the victory, taking the college class event with the team of James McAlpine, Zimmerman, Bill Skinner, and Frame running a time of 10:53.4.

A new twist had been added to the KSTC-Pittsburg rivalry in 1936. The Hornets and Gorillas met in a dual relay meet, where all running events were contested as relays. Welch and Weede staged the event to give hometown fans a chance to see the outstanding relay teams that had dominated the college relay circuit since 1933. In the 27 relay races entered by either team since that year, only twice had one or the other failed to win, and even then they took 2nd and 3rd. Of the 25 remaining contests, the two squads finished 1st and 2nd in 20 of them.

In the first year of the event, KSTC and Pitt had split the events. KSTC won the distance relays and weight events, while Pitt won the sprint relays and jumps. In 1937, the field events were contested as relays as well, and KSTC again won the weights while Pitt took the jumps. However, the Hornets were able to win only two of the seven running relays, the two-mile and distance medley. The Gorillas used their great depth to an advantage in winning the meet.

After the dual relay, the Hornets moved on to the Kansas Relays, where the thinclads turned in some outstanding individual performances. San Romani ran the feature mile race, outkicking hometown favorite Cunningham to win in 4:14.1. Sumner, who was fast becoming one of the best hurdlers in the nation, won the high hurdles in 15.0 seconds. Lawrence Hague broke John Kuck's 11-year-old meet record in the javelin with a toss of 208-10 ½. Unfortunately, he finished 2nd to Terry of Hardin-Simmons College, Abilene, Texas, who set an intercollegiate record of 229-2 ½. The Hornet distance medley team won in the college division for the third consecutive year, taking permanent possession of the Jenny Wren Challenge Trophy. McAlpine, Zimmerman, Frame, and San Romani ran on that team. The two-mile team of Romine, Zimmerman, Skinner, and Frame finished 2nd to Pittsburg.

At the Drake Relays, Sam Romani was again entered in a feature race. This was a 1 ½ mile race against the famous Rideout twins of North Texas State College. San Romani won by over 200 yards with the time of 6:46.9, only four seconds off Paavo Nurmi's 12-year-old world record for the distance. Frame finished 3rd in the open two-mile, and Hague placed 4th in the javelin. Summer was disappointed, as he tripped over a hurdle in the highs and did not place. The only Hornet relay team to place was the two-mile, the foursome of Skinner, Romine, Zimmerman, and Frame taking 3rd behind Pitt and Butler.

KSTC placed 2nd behind Pitt at the CIC meet for the sixth consecutive year. The Hornet stars shown bright, as four men accounted for six 1sts and five new CIC records. But again, KSTC did not have the depth to challenge for the team championship. San Romani won the mile and two-mile, setting records of 4:13.5 and 9:23.8, respectively. Sumner was also a double winner, setting a CIC record of 14.8 seconds in the high hurdles and winning the lows. Hague took the javelin with the record throw of 196-3 ½. Anthony

Lohkamp was the Hornets' final winner, the giant sophomore heaving the shot 48-6 ⅞ to break Dryer's 1936 record.

San Romani's performances in his next two appearances firmly established him as the top miler in the world for the year. At the Missouri Valley AAU, he won the 1500-meter with the time of 3:50.3, a new meet record and the best time in the nation during 1937. Two weeks later, in the Princeton mile, San Romani won with the time of 4:07.2, the second fastest mile ever run in the world, and just one-half second off Cunningham's world mark.

San Romani was unable to defend his title in the NCAA meet because of the three-year eligibility rule, so his last performance as a Hornet was in the National AAU meet. San Romani was leading the pack in the 1500-meter with 200 meters to go when Cunningham stepped on his heel and San Romani fell. He got back up and managed to finish 4th in the race. San Romani ended his career as one of Emporia State University's all-time greats.

> **Archie San Romani: Post ESU Career**
> Archie San Romani was one of the charter inductees into the Emporia State University Athletic Hall of Honor. San Romani is also in the NAIA, Drake Relays, and Kansas Sports Halls of fame. He continued his successful running after graduation from KSTC. In August of 1937, San Romani again went to the Scandinavian countries, and while touring there, set a new world record of 5:16.7 in the 2000-meter run. In 1938, he set a new American indoor record of 8:27.4 for the 3000-meter run, just one second shy of Paavo Nurmi's world record. San Romani continued running up through 1940 in hopes of making the U.S. Olympic team again. However, World War II caused cancellation of the Games that year and crushed those hopes.

Two Hornets did enter the 1937 NCAA meet at Berkeley, California. Sumner, with record setting performances in the low and high hurdles at the Missouri Valley meet, had earned the ranking as one of the top six hurdlers in the nation, and went to the meet with expenses paid by the NCAA. Lohkamp was entered in the shot put for KSTC. Sumner lived up to the ranking, placing 3rd in the low hurdles and 4th in the highs. He was placed on the National Collegiate Honor Roll for his performances. Lohkamp was unable to place in his event.

1938

The absence of San Romani in 1938 robbed that season of much of the color enjoyed during previous seasons. However, the year was not without highlights. Ken DeMott returned from his 1937 injury to give the Hornets an extremely strong shuttle hurdle team. The team of Winston Smith, Archie Shephard, DeMott, and Sumner finished 2nd to the University of Michigan in the 320-yard shuttle hurdles at the Illinois Indoor Relays. The same foursome came back to win the 480-yard event at Drake, setting a Drake Relays record of 60.1, a mark only .3 of a second off the world record held by USC.

The Hornets maintained strong middle distance and distance teams despite the loss of most of the stars of the previous five years. At the Kansas Relays, the two-mile team of Wilcox, Skinner, Liby, and Frame placed 2nd to Pittsburg, while Liby, Skinner, Zimmerman, and Frame formed the distance medley team that placed 3rd. The same two-mile foursome, with Romine in place of Wilcox, was beaten at Drake, again by Pitt. Pitt won by inches in setting a Relays record of 7:47.6.

The highlight of the season was the upset of Pittsburg in the CIC meet. The Hornets had defeated Pitt in the dual relay meet, winning one more event than the Gorillas, then had been defeated in the regular format dual by one point. At the CIC meet, Pitt won eight events compared to six wins for the Hornets. Emporia scored in every event, however, and consistency with 2nds and 3rds gave KSTC a six-point victory over the Gorillas. Sumner repeated in the hurdles, tying his own record in the highs and setting a new record of 23.6 seconds in the lows. Lohkamp and Hague were repeat champions as well, taking the shot and javelin respectively. Lohkamp broke his own meet record with the toss of 50-¾. Frame, in his senior year, won the mile and two-mile for the first time. Frame had finished 2nd in both races to San Romani in the three previous years, and was KSTC's other star miler during those years, rarely losing to anyone besides his well-celebrated teammate.

The Hornets final participation of 1938 was at the Missouri Valley meet in Kansas City. Summer and Lohkamp led KSTC to a 2nd place finish by winning their respective events. Sumner took both hurdle races, while Lohkamp upset Elmer Hackney of K-State, the Big 6 shot put champion in that event. Frame finished 2nd in both the 1500 and 5000-meter races. Bob Liby took 2nd in the 800-meter, and Al Locke, who returned after an absence in 1937, finished 3rd in the 400-meter.

1939

With the CIC title to defend, the Hornet trackmen began working out early for the 1939 season. KSTC upheld the tradition of strong middle distance teams, winning the two-mile relay at the Kansas Relays with the team of Romine, Wilcox, Chet Peterson and Liby. KSTC gained points in three other events at Kansas. The distance medley and mile teams placed 3rd, and Lohkamp placed 2nd to Hackney of K-State in the shot put. At Drake, with Wayne Goldsmith in place of Romine, the Hornet two-mile relay was barely nosed out by George Pepperdine College, California. Pepperdine's time of 7:43.4 was a Relays record, while the Hornets' time of 7:43.6 set a new school record.

In 1939, Pittsburg State was once again the class of the conference. The Gorillas defeated KSTC in the dual relay meet, then swamped the Emporia thinclads by 50 points in the dual. Pitt regained the CIC title with a 13 point victory over the Hornets. KSTC won only four events, but 2nds and 3rds kept them close. Winners for Emporia were Lohkamp in the shot and discus, Wilcox in the two-mile, and Liby in the 880. In winning the 880, Liby scored a big upset over Bedillon of Pitt, the defending champ.

The 1939 Missouri Valley AAU meet was held in KSTC's new stadium, giving local fans a chance to see the top performers in the Midwest in action. The Hornets finished 3rd behind Kansas and Pittsburg, who tied for 1st. Three Emporia athletes earned 1sts, Lohkamp in the discus, Bob Liby in the 800-meter, and Wayne Goldsmith in the 400-meter hurdles. Goldsmith's time of 53.9 seconds in the 400 hurdles was a meet and school record. Lohkamp also placed 2nd in the shot to Hackney, who was the top shot putter in the world during the season, and Liby placed 2nd behind Goldsmith in the 400 hurdles. Chet Peterson ended the Hornet scoring, taking 3rd in the 1500-meter. Lohkamp went on to participate in the National AAU meet in Lincoln, Nebraska, and placed 3rd in the junior division shot put with the toss of 48-11 ½. Also participating at this meet was a former KSTC athlete named Francis Swaim. Swaim had never had any exceptional performances while competing for the Hornets, but his performance at the Missouri Valley meet earlier in the summer was truly outstanding, as he won the broad jump with a leap of 24-11. If he had been able to repeat this mark at the national meet, he would have won the junior division easily. He did not, though, and was unable to place.

1940

In the fall of 1939, a freshman from Harrison High School in New York named Freddie Wassallo enrolled at KSTC. Wassallo was on the 1940 track team, but it was not his accomplishments on the cinders that warrant his mention. He ran for the Hornets for only one season before transferring. What does warrant mention is that he came to KSTC because of the school's track reputation, and on the recommendation of his high school coach, Jim Fraley. Fraley had starred on the Hornet football and track teams from 1931-1935. Wassallo was the first of what would become hundreds of New York athletes who attended

Emporia State on the recommendation of Fraley. Included in these would be some of E-State's all-time greats in track and field.

Hornet thinclads opened competition in the new decade at the Missouri Valley AAU indoor meet in Kansas City. Charles Zarker, a freshman, earned 2nd place in the open mile, while two relays placed 2nd in the university/college class. The sprint medley team of Ted Downs, Bernard Taylor, Dick Givens, and Bob Liby finished 2nd behind KU and the two-mile team of Wassallo, Jim Wilcox, Chet Peterson, and Liby was defeated by Pittsburg. This was the only indoor meet entered by the Hornets, as a trip to Butler University was cancelled due to weather.

The middle distance performers continued to be the strength of the team when the 1940 outdoor season opened. After a trip to Texas in which no places were earned, the team entered the Kansas Relays. Charles Hayen, Wassallo, Liby and Peterson formed the two-mile relay team that placed 2nd behind Abilene Christian, Abilene beating the Relays record set by KSTC in 1933. The Hornets also placed 3rd in the distance medley event with the team of Givens, Peterson, Wilcox and Zarker. Peterson, running the 880-yard leg on the distance medley, tripped 50 yards from the handoff and lost 30 yards on the field. Wilcox was timed in 3:05 for his 1320-yard leg to get E-State back in the race. The mile team of Sam Butterfield, Elmer Cross, Hayen, and Liby took 2nd to Oklahoma Baptist to round out the Hornet scoring at KU.

> **East Coast Connection: Jim Fraley**
> Jim Fraley had starred on the Hornet football and track teams from 1931-1935. Fraley went back to coach at Sewanahaka High School in New York and had a highly successful coaching career. Two of his best-known athletes were Al Oerter, a four-time Olympic Gold medalist in the discus, and John Camien, a world class miler at ESU. In 1940, the first of Fraley-coached athletes came to ESU. Freddie Wassallo was the first of what would become hundreds of New York athletes who attended Emporia State on the recommendation of Fraley. Included in these would be some of E-State's all-time greats in track and field.
>
>

The next week, Welch split his middle distance performers and sent them to two different meets. The reason for this is not known, but it might have been because the distance medley relay, an event in which KSTC had a strong representative, was not offered for colleges at Drake. In any event, Welch sent his long medley team to the Boulder Colorado Relays, where the team of Cross, Dick Sheridan, Wilcox, and Zarker placed 2nd behind the University of Colorado.

The remainder of the team went to Drake, where five men earned places in three relays. Liby, Goldsmith, Givens, and Peterson took 2nd in the sprint medley, then Hayen replaced Givens and the quartet placed 2nd in the two-mile relay. The final relay to place was the mile, the team of Hayen, Peterson, Givens, and Liby earning 3rd place.

Pittsburg easily won the CIC title in 1940, winning 11 events. The excitement in the meet was provided by the race for 2nd between KSTC and Wichita. Wichita edged the Hornets to win the mile relay, and, apparently, 2nd in the meet. However, the Shockers were disqualified from the event for one of their runners leaving his lane too early. This gave Emporia their only victory of the meet and 2nd place as a team. Butterfield, Cross, Givens, and Peterson made up the winning mile relay team.

1941

Wichita withdrew from the Central Conference after the 1940 season, and although they were no longer a conference team, E-State retained them on the schedule until 1960. Washburn, one of the original members of the CIC in 1927, rejoined the conference in 1942 after having been a member of the Missouri Valley Conference for eight years.

World War II began to have an effect on the program in 1941, as a number of KSTC's top performers were either in the service or working when the season opened. Bob Liby, Charles Zarker, and Charles Hayen had entered the service, and Dick Givens was working in an airplane factory. These losses, combined with the graduation of Jim Wilcox and Dick Sheridan, the transfer of Freddie Wassallo, and the ineligibility of Elmer Cross, robbed the team of most of the middle distance performers of the previous year. However, three men, Wayne Goldsmith, Sam Butterfield, and Chet Peterson, returned, and they combined with sophomore Randy Woelk to once again give KSTC strong relay teams. Woelk had broken Glenn Cunningham's Kansas Relays high school mile record as a senior in 1939, but had a non-eventful first year at E-State. Woelk started his sophomore year at KSTC with a 2nd place finish in the mile at the Missouri Valley indoor meet, then teamed with Goldsmith, Butterfield and Peterson to place 4th in the distance medley at Texas, 2nd in the event at Kansas, and 1st in the event at Colorado. Woelk also garnered 4th place in the 3000-meter run at Texas, while Goldsmith placed 4th in the open high hurdles at the same meet.

At the Kansas Relays, KSTC won one other 2nd and two 4ths. The two-mile team of Roland Myers, Peterson, Butterfield, and Woelk placed 2nd, while Goldsmith again took 4th in the high hurdles. The Hornet speedsters also got into the act, taking 4th in the 880 relay with the team of Jim Smith, Jim South, Bernard Taylor, and Goldsmith. This same sprint team placed 3rd in the 880 relay and 4th in the 440 relay at the Colorado Relays. The Hornets participated at Boulder instead of going to Drake because more of the team could compete, and the E-State thinclads earned 3rd place as a team behind Kansas State and the host team.

Pittsburg State won their 13th CIC title in 14 years in 1941, while KSTC took 2nd for the eighth time in the same number of years. Once again though, the Hornets were closing the gap. The Gorillas had defeated E-State by only seven points in the annual dual, the Hornets taking most of the seconds and 3rds in the meet to offset Pitt's 10 victories. At the conference meet, Pittsburg won nine events to five victories for the Hornets, but KSTC placed in all but two events to stay close. Winners for Emporia were Goldsmith in the high hurdles, Peterson in the 880, Ralph Wedd in the shot put, Elmer Carpenter in the discus, and Keith Caywood in the broad jump.

1942

In dual competition, the Hornets lost twice to Pittsburg, in the relay meet and the regular dual, and defeated Wichita and Hays easily. At KU, E-State won a 3rd in the 880-relay and a 2nd in the two-mile relay. The teams were Clinton Squier, Gail DeMott, Bernard Taylor, and Goldsmith in the 880, and Elton Davis, Don Mettler, Prentice Gary, and Woelk in the two-mile relay. Goldsmith was unable to compete in the open

> The United States' direct involvement in the World War during 1942 cut deeply into the track program. The draft and general defense work took a large number of men from the college. Five trackmen, including CIC champions Peterson, Carpenter and Wedd were lost to the service and military employment. General tire restrictions severely limited travel, and prevented KSTC's attendance at the Texas Relays, Colorado Relays and Drake Relays. It was no longer possible to charter cars or buses for trips, so the team had to travel by train, which limited the number of athletes who could make the trip. KSTC's only participation in 1942 was in dual meets, the Kansas Relays and the CIC meet.

hurdles because of the three-year eligibility rule.

The high note came at the last event of the season. For only the second time since the Central Conference was organized in 1928, the Hornets toppled Pittsburg State off the top of the conference. Wayne Goldsmith was the workhorse for KSTC, winning the high and low hurdles and placing 2nd in the 100 and 220-yard dashes. Randy Woelk was also a double winner for the Hornets, taking the 880 and mile. Bernard Taylor took 1st in the 100-yard dash, and Bernard Ruddick won the high jump, setting a school record of 6-2 ¼. The final winner for Emporia was Elmer Carson in the broad jump.

1943-44

The effects of the success of the 1942 season were put on hold for several years, though, as there would be no more track competition at KSTC until after the war.

> **Emporia Track Program Cancelled**
> In January of 1943, Fran Welch, a captain in the Special Services branch of the army, left for Lexington, Washington. One month later, the cancellation of the track program was announced. Declining male enrollment, the cut in athletic funds, and transportation problems had made it impossible to support the program.

1945

In May of 1945, the victory bell at KSTC was ringing for the first time in three years. There was peace in Europe and the process of returning to normal began. In September of that year, the Central Conference was reorganized. Active participation as an established athletic conference did not begin until September 1, 1946, and any sports participation between the spring of 1943 and September 1, 1946 were "forgotten" as far as the CIC was concerned.

Fran Welch returned from the service in December 1945 to assume duties as head of the physical education department and director of athletics. The major problem facing Welch in the rebuilding of the athletic program was finances. He outlined a budget requiring $14,000 to field a complete athletic program. To raise that kind of money required a great deal of help, and the KSTC Student Council and K-Club provided that support. These groups drew up a petition to raise the athletic fee from $1.50 per semester per student to $5.00 per semester per student. This increase would be in effect for two years according to the petition. Eighty percent of the student body at KSTC signed this petition, and it was then sent to the Board of Regents where it was approved. Athletics at Emporia State were on sound financial footing!

1946

The rebuilding process of the track program took until the middle of May 1946 to reach completion. In the meantime, Welch decided to field a track team. Several pre-war performers had returned to school, and they provided a nucleus around which to build the team. Among these were Randy Woelk, Chet Peterson, Elmer Cross, Prentice Gary, Bernard Ruddick, and Elmer Carpenter.

The Hornets' first participation was at the Kansas Relays. Just as in the pre-war days, KSTC's strength was in the middle distances. The two-mile relay team of John Lane, Tom Carr, Peterson, and Gary won with the time of 8:36.8. With Harold Smith replacing Carr, the foursome won the mile relay in the time of

3:31.7. Also placing for the Hornets at KU was the distance medley team in 2nd, and Carpenter taking 4th in the discus.

The Drake Relays were the second meet of the season for KSTC. The same two-mile foursome that won at KU placed 5th in the event at Drake, held during a steady downpour. The mile and distance medley teams, as well as the individual entries, failed to place. The final meet of the season was a two point dual loss to Wichita.

Although the times and results of this short season were not outstanding, a base had been laid upon which to rebuild the great tradition of the Hornet thinclads. Under the guiding hand of Fran Welch, KSTCs track program would again gain the stature enjoyed by the pre-war teams.

1947

The Hornets won the initial ESU Relays meet, defeating Wichita by two and one-half points. KSTC scored in every event, and won the two-mile, shot put, and discus relays.

The remainder of the season was not so successful, as the Emporia thinclads lost duals to KU, Pittsburg, Ottawa, and Washburn. The season ended with a 3rd place finish in the CIC meet. Fort Hays won their first ever track title, with Washburn edging the Hornets by one point for 2nd place. For KSTC, Dwight Waddell won the mile, Bob Grimm took the discus, and Roland Yergler won the broad jump. The Hornets also gained a tie for 1st in the high jump from Bob Stokes.

> **ESU Relays Begin**
> The 1947 track season was highlighted by the hosting of the first annual Emporia State Relays. This was one of the outstanding and unique meets in the Midwest, with all the running events and field events contested as relays. This was accomplished in the field events by adding together the best height or distance of the four participants from each school. The team with the highest total won the event.

1948

In 1948, the Hornets reversed the results of the dual meets with Pitt, Ottawa and Washburn, winning each by large margins. KSTC also whipped Wichita in a dual contest. The team strength was the middle and long distances and the weight events, and these strengths were underscored at the Emporia Relays. Waddell came from behind on the anchor leg in both the two-mile and distance medley relays to get the victory for KSTC. The Hornets also won the shot put, discus, and broad jump relays. These victories were not enough to overcome Hays, though, as the Tigers won the team title. At the Kansas Relays, the middle distance relays performed well with both the two-mile and distance medley teams placing 3rd. Bob Blair, Maynard Mitchell, Harold Butterfield, and Waddell competed on the two-mile team, and Ralph Summers, Blair, Mitchell and Waddell were on the medley team. The Hornets were unsuccessful at the other stops on the major relay circuit.

E-State and Fort Hays tied for the 1948 CIC crown with 57 points each. Hays offset the Hornets' strength in the distances and field by dominating the sprints, and gained the tie by defeating KSTC in the mile relay. Hornet freshman Roger Ruth began his outstanding record of performances in the conference meet, winning the broad jump and pole vault, and taking 3rd in the high jump. Dwight Waddell repeated in the mile, and took 2nd in the 880-yard run. Grimm was another repeat winner for the Hornets, taking the discus. Earlier in the season, Grimm had set a new school record in the event, breaking Harry Cole's 1924 record by four inches. Bill Wygle won the shot put for the Hornets' final victory, and placed 3rd in the discus.

After several years' absence, Emporia State resumed participation in the Missouri Valley AAU meet that summer. Ruth turned in an outstanding performance, winning the pole vault with a jump of 13-0. Wygle and Grimm finished 2nd, and 3rd, respectively, in the discus, and Maynard Mitchell's 3rd in the 1500-meter was the Hornets' final place. Waddell was unable to compete due to a pulled muscle.

1949

The Hornets had a banner year in 1949 to end the decade on a successful note. Team strength was still in the middle distances and weights, and the middle distance performers showed up well at the Oklahoma A & M Relays, the Kansas Relays and the Drake Relays. At Oklahoma, the distance medley team of Jim Widrig, Burl Purkeypile, Maynard Mitchell and Dwight Waddell finished 4th. Waddell ran a superb anchor, coming from far behind and just nipping the University of Oklahoma man at the wire. Waddell came back to anchor the two-mile team of Harold Butterfield, Jim Hobson, and Widrig to 3rd.

At the Kansas Relays, the distance medley team turned in another strong performance. With Butterfield in place of Purkeypile, the quartet won the college division event, posting the sixth fastest time ever for the event at KU. Hobson replaced Butterfield in the two-mile team, and this foursome placed 2nd. In the race, Waddell was beaten by inches by the Abilene Christian College anchorman, both schools timed in 7:57. The same team of Hobson, Mitchell, Widrig, and Waddell combined to take 3rd in the two-mile relay at Drake. The distance medley was not offered for the college class, so that outstanding team was unable to run.

With balanced scoring and depth in nearly every event, KSTC gained sole possession of the CIC track crown in 1949 for only the third time since the beginning of the meet. E-State scored at least two places in 10 events, and swept the mile run. Ruth and Waddell were outstanding for the Hornets. Ruth won the broad jump, tied for 1st in the pole vault, and took 2nd in the high jump. Waddell doubled with a victory in the 880-yard run and a repeat win in the mile. Jack Larkin upset teammate Bill Wygle to win the discus with the second best throw ever by a Hornet. The only mark better than Larkins was set by Wygle, who earlier in the season, had broken Grimm's year old school record with a toss of 147-11. However, Wygle did repeat in winning the shot put. Ralph Summers was the final Hornet champion, winning the 100-yard dash as well as finishing 2nd in the 220-yard dash.

The season and decade came to an end at the Missouri Valley AAU, where three Hornets gained places. Ruth copped 2nd in the broad jump and pole vault, while Waddell finished 3rd in the mile. Summers ended KSTC's scoring, placing 4th in the low hurdles.

1950

Many of the outstanding performers who helped lead KSTC to CIC titles in 1948 and 1949 returned to open the sixth decade of this century, four of whom were defending CIC champions (Dwight Waddell, Ralph Summers, Jack Larkin, and Roger Ruth). Also returning were Bob Klotz, Jim Widrig, and Maynard Mayberry, high place winners in the 1949 CIC. Another conference champion returned, but his title was almost a decade old. Ralph Wedd had won the CIC shot put title in 1941, but the army interrupted his career in 1942. Wedd finally returned to KSTC in 1950, but never reached the form that had won him the shot title nine years earlier.

With all the returning talent, the Hornets set their sights on winning a third consecutive conference crown. The KSTC thinclads opened their quest at the Oklahoma A & M Relays. Larkin and Ruth starred for the Hornets, Larkin winning the discus and Ruth placing 3rd in the broad jump, pole vault and high jump.

The sprint medley team of Waddell, Gerald Shadwick, Don Hufford, and Widrig also placed 3rd. The success of the meet was marked, however, when Summers suffered a season-ending injury.

The Hornets moved next to the Midwest Relay circuit. Six men attended the Texas Relays, but none were able to place. However, tracksters met with more success at the Kansas and Drake Relays. The distance medley team of Bill Dudley, Jim Hobson, Widrig, and Waddell won the college event at KU with the time of 10:41.7, and placed 3rd in the event at Drake, the first year the distance medley had been offered for colleges at the meet. KSTC also won a 2nd place in the two-mile relay, with the team of Bill Dixon, Hobson, Widrig, and Waddell.

The Hornets' quest was realized at the conference meet as the thinclads took top honors, defeating 2nd place Hays by 29 points. Senior Waddell closed out a brilliant career by winning the 440-yard dash and the 880-yard run, and also anchoring the mile relay team. His 440 time of 49.3 seconds was a new record. Waddell established a new standard for the conference meet by winning the 440, 880, and mile during his four-year career. Ruth won the broad jump and pole vault, setting a school record of 13-5 in the vault, erasing his own school mark set earlier in the year. Ruth had set the old mark in the Pitt dual, breaking Earl McKown's 25-year-old record. Larkin repeated in the discus, breaking the school record with the toss of 148-4. However, the record was not accepted when it was found the throw had been made with a discus that was too light. Widrig and Fred Willson rounded out the Hornet champions, winning the mile and low hurdles, respectively.

Emporia ended the year with a 4th place finish in the Missouri Valley meet. Kansas won the meet, followed by K-State, Wichita and Emporia. Ruth was the only winner for the Hornets, taking the pole vault with the jump of 12-6. Widrig and Larkin earned 3rds in the mile and discus, respectively.

1951

In the spring of 1950, a youngster from Kiowa High School named Billy Tidwell won the Kansas State High School mile, upsetting rival Wes Santee of Ashland. Tidwell's time of 4:27.1 broke Glenn Cunningham's 20-year-old high school record. Tidwell and Santee had quite a rivalry during their high school days, and this continued through 1956, both starring for their respective schools and armed service branches. Santee went on to compete for the Kansas Jayhawks, while Tidwell was instrumental in leading the KSTC program back to the national prominence it had enjoyed in the 1920s and 1930s.

Although he did not originally come to KSTC, Tidwell was on hand when the 1951 season opened. Tidwell attended KU in the fall of 1950, and for five days of the second semester, before transferring to Emporia. This kept him from competing in open events at NCAA approved meets during 1951, but did not affect his eligibility with the CIC.

Another outstanding newcomer for the Hornets was Henry "Hank" Thompson. Thompson was a sprinter and hurdler who, along with Tidwell, would help lead the Hornets back to national prominence. He joined an already strong sprint team and helped KSTC experience success in the sprint events on the relay circuit.

The Hornets opened the 1951 season at the Preview Relays sponsored by Oklahoma A & M. Ruth turned in an outstanding performance, setting a school record of 13-7 ½ in winning the pole vault, and also finishing 2nd in the broad jump while bettering the old meet record with a 23-9 leap. Tidwell gained a second victory for KSTC, winning the 3000-meter run in 8:57. Other place winners were Don Holst, 3rd in the discus, and Hugh Lewick, 4th in the javelin. The 880-relay team of Gene Reed, Ralph Summers, Bob Klotz, and Thompson took 5th. Ruth competed at the Texas Relays one week later, taking 4th in the broad jump and tying for 4th in the pole vault. These were the only places won by KSTC. Tidwell was ineligible to compete in open events and black athletes were still not allowed to compete at Texas, keeping Hank Thompson off any Hornet relay teams that might have been entered. When Ruth was declared ineligible for open events at Kansas and Drake because he was a four-year athlete, the Hornets' hopes lay with the relays, and the teams came through at KU, winning four places. The two mile team of Bob Stauffer, Bill Dixon, Thompson, and Tidwell placed 2nd. Taking 3rd was the 880 team of Klotz, Ruth, Gerald Shadwick, and Summers, and with Thompson in place of Ruth, the foursome placed 4th in the mile relay. The final place won was a 5th in the distance medley by the team of Fred Willson, Bill Hutchinson, Dixon, and Tidwell.

Because of the ruling against Ruth, Welch entered the Hornets in the Colorado Relays instead of at Drake. Ruth again starred for KSTC, winning the broad jump and pole vault, while Lewick placed 4th in the discus. The final place was a 3rd in the distance medley, with Hutchinson, Stauffer, Woodward, and Tidwell running on the team.

KSTC took their fourth straight conference title in 1951, winning easily over 2nd place Hays. Ruth's final CIC performance was outstanding, as he set two conference scoring records while winning the broad jump and pole vault, taking 2nd in the 100-yard dash, and tying for 4th in the high jump. This set an individual single meet record of 13 ¼ points, breaking the record held jointly by KSTC's Archie San Romani in 1936 and Ralph Summers in 1949. Ruth also broke the career individual record held by Manning of Wichita, the former ending his career with 47 ½ points scored. Klotz and Tidwell were also double winners. Klotz won the 100 and 220-yard dashes and Tidwell won the mile and two-mile. Summers rounded out the Hornet victories, winning the 220-yard low hurdles.

> **Emporia hosts first NAIA meet**
> On June 2, 1951, Emporia State was host to an experimental track and field meet. The meet, sponsored by the National Association of Intercollegiate Basketball (NAIB), was designed to give all schools operating under the four-year athletic plan the opportunity to enter freshmen and fourth year athletes into competition in a large meet. NCAA sponsored meets did not allow four-year men to enter, a rule which severely handicapped schools such as KSTC. Two hundred and eleven schools in 22 Midwestern states were invited to the mid-west regional meet. Due in part to the success of KSTC's regional meet, the NAIB decided in 1952 to expand into the National Association of Intercollegiate Athletics to fill the need for an extensive postseason events program for the nation's smaller colleges.
>
>

Two weeks later, Emporia State athletes garnered three victories at the MVAAU meet. Two were earned by Ruth, as he won the pole vault with a jump of 13-5 and added a new event to his list of specialties by winning the triple jump. The Hornets defeated K-State and Kansas to win the 440 relay with the team of Shadwick, Summers, Willson and Klotz. Klotz also finished 2nd to Thane Baker of K-State in the 100 and 220-yard dashes. Summers and Willson took 2nd and 3rd, respectively, in the low hurdles.

In 1951, Emporia hosted a meet sponsored by the National Association of Intercollegiate Basketball. KSTC was very successful in this initial NAIA experimental track meet. The Hornets won the meet, winning the team title by three points over Abilene Christian, Texas. Ruth and Klotz picked up individual victories for the Hornets, Ruth in the pole vault and broad jump, and Klotz in the 100-yard dash. Klotz also finished 4th. Second place winners for the Hornets were Summers in the low hurdles, Lewick in the javelin, and Tidwell in the mile.

Bob Klotz went on to compete in the National AAU meet in Berkeley, California. He ran in the 100 and 220-yard dashes in both the junior and senior divisions, but did not place in either. Roger Ruth was scheduled to compete, but suffered a back injury in practice and missed the meet.

1952

Coach Welch was faced with the task of rebuilding his track team in 1952. The team had suffered heavy losses to graduation and the military draft. Ruth and Summers were among the most conspicuous lost to graduation, while sophomores Tidwell and Thompson went to the military. The Hornets, unable to overcome these losses, slipped in team strength and lost duals to Wichita, Ottawa and Pittsburg. The loss to Pitt was the first in seven seasons. At the CIC, Emporia fell to a tie for 3rd with Pitt as Hays easily won the event. Despite the loss in team depth, KSTC still had outstanding individuals. The greatest strengths were in the sprints and with Hugh Lewick in the javelin. Don Edwards, Edward McArdle, Fred Willson, and Klotz formed a strong sprint relay team that won the 440 and 880 relays at the Emporia Relays, placed 4th in both events at Drake, and 4th in the 880 event at KU. Lewick placed 2nd in the javelin at the Oklahoma A & M Relays and 5th at the Drake Relays. Willson was the only other individual place winner for the Hornets in the big relay meets, taking 3rd in the 220-yard intermediate hurdles at Oklahoma.

Klotz picked up the Hornets' only two victories at the CIC. He won the 100-yard dash, tying the CIC record of 9.7 seconds, and the 220-yard dash in 21.3 seconds. KSTC picked up most of their points in the two short dashes. Lewick was upset in the javelin and finished 2nd. Klotz and Lewick were the top performers for Emporia State in the MVAAU and the NAIA national meets. At the Missouri Valley, Klotz took 2nd in the 100 and 220-yard dashes to Thane Baker of K-State, one of the nation's top sprinters. Lewick placed 3rd in the javelin. A week later, they led KSTC to a 9th place finish among 58 colleges in the NAIA championships; Klotz taking 2nd in the 100 and 5th in the 220 and Lewick, with the best toss of his career, finishing 3rd in the javelin.

1953

KSTC's team strength was improved in 1953 as the Hornets defeated Wichita and Ottawa in duals. However, the Hornets lost the annual Pitt dual and again finished 3rd in the CIC behind Pitt and Hays. With Klotz graduated, Hornet relay teams fell off from the previous year, and the only place won on the relay circuit was a 4th in the mile relay at Kansas with the team of Robert Bonar, Don Edwards, Fred Willson and Bob Harsh.

The Hornets had four individual winners at the 1953 conference meet. Ed Hosking won the high jump and discus with marks of 6-2 and 126-3, respectively, and also placed 3rd in the broad jump. Harsh won the 440-yard dash and Willson took the high hurdles. The final winner for KSTC was Wayne "Tiny" Goodell, a giant 285-pound freshman who won the shot with a 45-4 ½ toss.

The conference meet in 1953 was an unusual affair, as the CIC and Kansas Conference held their championships at KSTC's stadium on the same day. The purpose was that the top three finishers in each event from each conference were to meet the next day in the NAIA District 10 meet to decide the qualifiers for the NAIA Nationals. However, the district meet was cancelled due to very heavy rain the morning of the meet, and Coach Welch, Coach Francis of Fort Hays, and Coach Peters of Ottawa selected the district's representatives to the national meet. Hosking and Goodell were the only Hornets selected by the committee to compete at the NAIA meet, and Goodell earned All-American honors by taking 3rd in the shot put. Hosking ended in a six-way tie for 4th in the high jump.

1954

Coach Fran Welch predicted a lean season for 1954, and this proved to be an accurate prediction despite the return of Henry Thompson from the service. Only five lettermen returned from 1953, and Goodell was lost to academic eligibility. The Hornets lost three of four dual meets, and slipped to 4th in the CIC. However, Hank Thompson was a bright spot for Welch during the season. In three of the four dual meets KSTC competed in, Thompson won the 100, 220 and 440-yard dashes, and anchored the winning mile relay. At the Oklahoma A & M Relays, he took 2nd in the university college class 100-yard dash, and ran on the 440 and sprint medley relay teams that placed 3rd and 2nd, respectively. At the Kansas Relays, Thompson ran strong legs on the 3rd place mile relay along with Don Blow, Clair Hutchinson, and Dick Bliss, and the 2nd place sprint medley team with Don LeVieux, R. L. Coberly and Bliss. Thompson, Hutchinson, Coberly and Bliss formed a sprint medley team that placed 5th at Drake.

Hank Thompson: National Champion
After coming to ESU as a freshman in 1951, Thompson had his career interrupted by two years of military service. He continued to compete while in the Army and won the 100 and 200 at the 1952 European Army Championships. He returned to ESU and won the 1954 national championship in the 440-yard dash and ended his career as a three-time All-American.

Thompson finished the season in spectacular fashion, winning the 220 and 440-yard dashes in the CIC meet, setting a school record of 49.0 seconds in the quarter. At the MVAAU meet, Thompson took 2nd in the 440 to Bill Jones of KU and broke his two week-old school record with the time of 48.4 seconds. Hank ended the season at the NAIA Championships in Abilene, Texas, winning the 440 in 49.1 seconds to become KSTC's first national champion since Archie San Romani in 1936. Dick Utter was the only other Hornet to win an event in the CIC, finishing in a six-way tie for 1st in the pole vault.

1955

Bill Tidwell returned from the army in the fall of 1954 to greatly strengthen the Hornet thinclads. While in the army, Tidwell had competed for the Sixth Army track team with outstanding results. In the spring of 1954, Tidwell won the 880-yard run at the All-Armed Services meet, outrunning Wes Santee of the Marine Corps. Later that spring Tidwell, finished 2nd in the event to Mal Whitfield, the 1952 Olympic 800-meter champion, at the National AAU meet.

Following in the footsteps of Archie San Romani, Tidwell became KSTC's second miler to compete in the Sugar Bowl meet and the big eastern indoor meets. In New Orleans, Tidwell finished 2nd, 10 yards behind Wes Santee. Two weeks later at the Knights of Columbus Games in Boston, Tidwell competed in the first indoor meet of his career, finishing 3rd in the mile with the time of 4:12.7 behind Gunnar Neilson of Denmark and Fred Dwyer. Tidwell returned to Boston several weeks later to compete in the Boston Athletic Association meet, and finished 4th in the mile while improving his time to 4:11.5. Wes Santee won the event, setting a new world indoor record of 4:03.8. One week later at the Millrose Games, Tidwell again finished 4th in the event, improving his time again to 4:10.6. Neilson won this round from Santee, breaking Santee's week old world mark by .2 of a second.

The Hornets had planned to attend the Texas Relays to open the outdoor season, but cancelled the trip after Coach Welch was informed by officials in Austin that the colored members of the squad would not be allowed to compete. KSTC instead attended the Arkansas Relays and met with a great deal of success, finishing 3rd in the meet behind Kansas and Pittsburg. Tidwell and Utter earned victories for E-State in the mile and pole vault respectively, and Tidwell also anchored the mile relay team of Don Blow, Robert Hawk, and Henry Thompson to 2nd place behind KU. Thompson finished 4th in the 100-yard dash and Blow took 3rd in the long jump to round out the Hornet scoring.

The Hornets moved on to the Kansas Relays, and on the strength of two outstanding anchor runs by Tidwell, placed 2nd to North Texas State in both the mile and sprint medley relays. Thompson led off the medley with a strong quarter, and after Blow and Bill Davis ran the 220 legs, Tidwell blazed a 1:50.2 880-yard anchor to make up 15 yards, but came up just short. In the mile relay, Tidwell was clocked in 47.1 seconds for his carry to haul the team of Blow, Ed Rowley, and Thompson to 2nd.

At the Drake Relays one week later, the KSTC sprint medley team turned in a memorable performance. The Hornet team won the event in 3:21.9, one of the 10 fastest times ever recorded in the event, and just off the world record of 3:20.2 held by KU. Tidwell's sterling effort on the anchor made the difference for the Hornets, as he blazed a 1:48.4 to make up 20 yards on North Texas. This was the second fastest 880 ever run, although it was not recorded as such because it was accomplished with a running start. Thompson, Hutchinson, and Davis rounded out the record-setting team. The Hornets also took 3rd in the mile relay behind North Texas and Pittsburg, with Thompson and Tidwell turning in strong carries for the same foursome that ran at Kansas.

Despite these outstanding performers, KSTC did not have the depth to challenge for the conference team title and remained 3rd in the CIC behind Pitt and Hays. Tidwell and Thompson were the workhorses for E-State, keeping the Hornets within eight points of team champ Pitt with their efforts. Tidwell won the 440 in 49.3, the 880 in 1:56.7, the mile in 4:31.6, and anchored the winning mile relay team, completing this amazing performance with only five minutes rest between the mile and the 440. Thompson won the 220-yard low hurdles, finished 2nd in the 220 and 440, and ran on the winning relay. Richard Scott won his second CIC long jump title, but only his first for KSTC. Scott won his first title a few years earlier while competing for Fort Hays.

Richard Utter: National Champion
Richard Utter became a national champion in 1955 at the NAIA National Championships. Utter set an NAIA and school record of 13-10 ¼ in winning the pole vault. Utter also placed 2nd in the 1956 national meet.

One week after the conference meet, Tidwell was invited to compete in the Coliseum Relays in Los Angeles, California, and he finished 2nd to Wes Santee while posting the fastest collegiate mile of the season of 4:07.4. Tidwell rejoined the Hornet squad to compete in the MVAAU meet, and he won the mile and 880, his time of 1:52.8 in the latter setting a new meet record and tying Norman Rhoads' school mark. Thompson finished 2nd in the low hurdles to Charlie Tidwell of KU, who during 1958-1960 set world bests in the 200-meter and 220-yard low hurdles, tied the world record in the 100-yard dash, and set the world mark in the 100-meter dash. Dick

Utter and Reece Bohannon earned 3rds in the pole vault and high jump, respectively, to complete the Hornet scoring.

Several Hornet thinclads turned in outstanding performances to earn 2nd place for KSTC behind Abilene Christian, Texas, in the NAIA Nationals. Utter turned in the top Hornet effort, setting an NAIA and school record of 13-10 ¼ in winning the pole vault, while teammate Bohannon tied for 3rd in the event at 12-0. Tidwell was a double winner, taking 1st in the 880-yard run in 1:53.7 and the mile in 4:14.2. The victory in the mile began a decade long domination of the NAIA mile event by KSTC runners. Thompson slipped to 4th in the 440 after winning the event in 1954, but earned All-America honors by taking 3rd in the 220-yard low hurdles.

Tidwell Runs Faster than World Record
Bill Tidwell turned in a spectacular performance at the National AAU meet running faster than the officially recognized world record by .5 of a second in running 1:48.1. However, Tidwell finished 3rd behind Arnie Sowell of the University of Pittsburg, who won the event in 1:47.6, and Tom Courtney of Fordham University, 2nd in 1:48.0. Lon Spurrier of the U.S. Army, who finished 5th in the race, had posted a time of 1:47.5 earlier in the year, but the mark was still pending recognition as an official world record.

Tidwell and Utter went on to compete in the NCAA and National AAU championship meets later that summer. Tidwell finished 4th in the mile at the NCAAs, running 4:08.6, but his season's collegiate best in the event was broken by Jim Bailey and Bill Dellinger of Oregon who placed 1st and 2nd. Tidwell stepped down to the 880 at the National AAU meet, and he turned in a spectacular performance when he broke the officially recognized world record by .5 of a second in running 1:48.1. However, Tidwell finished 3rd behind Arnie Sowell of the University of Pittsburg, who won the event in 1:47.6, and Tom Courtney of Fordham University, 2nd in 1:48.0. Utter was unable to place in either meet.

In October of 1955, Tidwell competed in the Olympic Carnival in Madison Square Garden, held to raise funds for the 1956 U.S. Olympic team, and finished 3rd in the mile behind Wes Santee and Fred Dwyer. This meet marked Santee's last competition as an amateur, as he was suspended by the AAU a short time after the event for accepting excessive expense money.

1956

In January of 1956, Tidwell was invited back to the Sugar Bowl Classic and again finished 2nd, losing by .2 of a second in the 1500-meter race to Jim Bailey of Oregon. Tidwell's next competition was at the Washington Evening Star Indoor Games, where he was nipped at the wire in the mile by George King, the AAU two-mile champ. Since Welch had decided not to enter him in as many indoor meets in 1956, Tidwell's final competition on the indoor circuit was at the Boston Athletic Association Games. He ran the fastest mile of his career in setting a school record of 4:06.3, yet finished 5th in a very strong field.

KSTC opened the outdoor season at the Oklahoma A & M Relays and Welch entered two relay teams in the university class with noteworthy results. The two-mile relay scored a near miss when Tidwell blistered a 1:51 anchor to make up 30 yards on Oklahoma's Johnny Dahl, but came up five yards short. E-State gained the victory in the distance medley with Tidwell anchoring the team of Clair Hutchinson, Artie Dunn, and Lawrence Jones. Dick Utter began an outstanding season in the pole vault finishing in a three-way tie for 2nd place.

The Texas Relays, which were allowing participation by black athletes for the first time, was the Hornets next stop on the relay circuit. Tidwell was again superb, scorching a 1:47.4 anchor on the sprint medley to bring the Hornets from 30 yards back and gain the victory. Tidwell's split was one-tenth of a second better than the world record for the 880, but was not considered as a record because it was accomplished with a running start. Hutchinson, Blow, and George Gibbs ran on this team with Tidwell. Rounding out the Hornet place winners were Utter in a three-way tie for 1st in the pole vault at 14-0, and freshman Warner Wirta placing 5th in the 5000-meter run.

The sprint medley team met with hard luck at the Kansas Relays when Hutchinson pulled a muscle on the 440 leg and was forced to drop out. The Hornets made up for this disappointment by winning the distance medley with the team of Autrey Calloway, Dunn, Jones, and Tidwell, who again made up a large deficit on the anchor carry. Other point winners for KSTC were the mile relay team of Calloway, Dunn, Bill Dickey and Tidwell which placed 3rd, and Utter with a 2nd place finish in the pole vault with a jump of 14-0.

Pittsburg State won a fourth consecutive CIC title in 1956, while KSTC remained 3rd behind the Gorillas and Fort Hays. The Hornets' lack of depth to challenge for the title showed, as they were shut out of the scoring in eight events. Tidwell was the star for E-State, setting conference marks of 1:52.2 and 4:12.3 in winning the 880 and mile respectively, and anchoring the winning mile relay team of Calloway, Hutchinson and Davis. Utter and Wirta garnered the Hornets final victories, winning the pole vault and two-mile, respectively. Utter's winning height was well below his school record of 14-4 set earlier in the season at the Emporia Relays, a vault which was also the best ever made by a Kansas collegian.

Bill Tidwell: National Champion
Bill Tidwell won four NAIA championships, winning the 880 and the mile in the 1955 meet and the 800 and 1500 in 1956. During his career, he held the NAIA national record for the 880 yard and mile runs and still holds the 800-meter record at ESU, a record that has stood for over 60 years. Tidwell just missed making the Olympic team, finishing 5th in the 800 meters. The top three finishers made the Olympic team and went on to all place in the top six in the Olympic final. Tidwell has since been inducted into the NAIA Track and Field Hall of Fame, the Drake Relays Hall of Fame, the Kansas Sports Hall of Fame and was a charter inductee into the Emporia State Athletic Hall of Honor.

After victories in the mile and pole vault by Tidwell and Utter, respectively at the annual MVAAU meet, the Hornets traveled to San Diego, California, for the NAIA Nationals. Tidwell, with his sights set on qualifying for the Olympic Trials, repeated in the 800-meter and 1500-meter and established NAIA records of 1:49.1 and 3:51.3 respectively. Utter finished in a tie for 2nd in the vault, losing to Bob Gutowski of Occidental College, who placed 2nd in the Olympic Games pole vault later that summer. Wirta earned the final points for the Hornets, taking 4th in the 5000-meter run. KSTC finished 4th as a team in the NAIA meet.

Tidwell's Olympic hopes received a blow a few days before the NCAA meet when he incurred a calf injury during a workout. This injury forced him to scratch from the NCAAs and left only the NAAU meet in which to qualify for the U.S. trials. Because of the injury, Tidwell ran only the 800-meter at the AAUs, but he met the qualifying standard by running 1:48.5 to finish 5th in a very strong field. Unfortunately, E-State's star runner was unable to overcome the injury, and finished 6th in the Olympic Trials 800-meter against one of the strongest fields ever to qualify at the distance. Tom Courtney won the event, setting an American record of 1:46.4, followed by Arnie Sowell and Lon Spurrier. The three American qualifiers placed 1st-4th-6th respectively in the Olympic 800-meter final. Another indication of the strength of the Olympic Trials field was that Mal Whitfield, the 1948 and 1952 Olympic 800-meter champ, finished 5th and failed to qualify. Because the injury had prevented Tidwell from qualifying for the trials in the 1500-meter, Welch appealed at the last minute for a chance for Tidwell to run in the 1500-meter race, but the appeal was denied by the U.S. Olympic Committee.

However, there was some consolation for Tidwell and others who did not qualify for the Olympic Games. Tidwell and 11 other men were selected by the AAU to compete in an AAU sponsored European tour. Tidwell toured Finland and Denmark, winning nine of the 13 races he competed in, including a victory in the 1500-meter over Josef Barthel, the 1952 Olympic champion at that distance. Tidwell's time of 3:45.2 in the race set a school record and bettered the top mark made in the U.S. Olympic trials 1500. Tidwell also set a school record of 48.3 seconds in the 400-meter. Two of Tidwell's four losses were to Roger Moens of Belgium in the 800-meter, the latter the world record holder at that distance.

1957

In January of 1957, Tidwell whipped Fred Dwyer between halves of the Sugar Bowl game to win that event for the first time in three tries, setting a new meet record of 3:51.5 for the 1500-meter. However, according to available sources, this was the only participation for Tidwell outside that of the Hornet squad, as no record of participation in the eastern indoor circuit can be found.

The 1957 Hornet track team was not strong enough to challenge for the conference title, but KSTC fielded extremely potent sprint medley and mile relay teams on the relay circuit, both with Tidwell on the anchor. These teams first flexed their muscles at the Oklahoma A & M Relays, with the sprint medley team of Dick Bliss, Duane McIntire, Harold Thompson, and Tidwell winning the college/university event in meet record time while defeating Oklahoma University and Kansas State. With Autrey Calloway running in place of Thompson, the foursome won the college mile relay as Tidwell made up 15 yards on Bob Wooten, the Pittsburg anchor. Utter placed 2nd in the pole vault and Blow finished 3rd in the long jump to round out the Hornet scoring.

At the Texas Relays, Welch entered sprint medley teams in both the university and the college class events. The team of Bliss, Thompson, Gibbs, and Tidwell finished 3rd in the university event behind and KU and the team of McIntire, Carstell Pitts, Bob Heaney, and Tidwell won the college class event with the time of 3:23.6. Tidwell blazed two superb anchor half-miles of 1:47.2 and 1:48.6 within the space of 50 minutes on those two relays. Utter earned the Hornets' final place, finishing 2nd in the pole vault with the jump of 14-0.

The "Kiowa Flyer," as Tidwell was being referred to in the newspapers, continued his superlative performances at the Kansas Relays, unreeling a half-mile anchor carry of 1:49.5 in the sprint medley and a cleanup quarter of 46.5 in the mile relay to hoist E-State to baton titles. Both Hornet relay teams set new KU Relays records; the mile team of Heaney, Bliss, McIntire, and Tidwell running 3:15.1, and the medley team of McIntire, Gibbs, Heaney, and Tidwell posting a mark of 3:22.6. The medley time was better than the winning time and the meet record in the university section of the sprint medley. For his performance,

Tidwell was voted the "Outstanding Performer" of the 1957 Kansas Relays, becoming the only small college athlete ever to win that honor. One other KSTC relay team earned a place, the 880 team of Pitts, Thompson, Gibbs, and McIntire taking 4th.

The Hornet sprint medley team claimed the Triple Crown the next week, winning the event at the Drake Relays in 3:22.6 with the foursome of Bliss, Pitts, Heaney and Tidwell. KSTC's winning time was five seconds better than the time KU posted to win the university event at Drake, and was two seconds better than the Villanova quartet which won the event at the Penn Relays the same weekend. The mile relay team of Calloway, McIntire, Bliss and Tidwell set their second meet record in a week in winning the college event with the time of 3:15.1. Tidwell continued his superlative efforts on the anchor carries, posting splits of 1:47.6 and 46.9 on the two relays. Utter placed 3rd in the pole vault to earn KSTC's final points.

Fort Hays ended Pittsburg State's reign as CIC champion in 1957, but E-State remained 3rd behind both rivals. Tidwell

> **Historic Day in Texas**
> Bill Tidwell turned in two outstanding half-mile times in the sprint medley relay in less than an hour at the Texas Relays. Running in the University class he unwound a 1:47.2 880 carry on the anchor leg, but was over 60 yards behind when he got the baton, and could only get the Hornets into 3rd. Fifty minutes later he was back to run in the College division sprint medley and ran a 1:48.6 anchor, which won the race for Emporia. Legendary coach Fran Welch commented, "I've never heard of a runner turning in two such outstanding times for one race is such a short amount of time."
>
> How good were the efforts? The world record time for 880 yards was 1:46.4 at that time. Tidwell had ran less than a second off world record pace in his first effort and slightly slower than two seconds off world record pace in his second race.
>
> But Tidwell wasn't done for the day. He came back to finish fifth in the open mile race and for good measure split 48.4 on his anchor leg of the mile relay team.
>
>
>
> *Don Blow, Clair Hutchinson, Bill Tidwell, George Gibbs*

repeated in the mile and half-mile, breaking his own conference record in the 880 with the time of 1:51.3, and also anchored the mile relay team of Heaney, Bliss, and McIntire to victory with the blazing split of 46.7 seconds. Besides running on the mile relay, freshman Duane McIntire won the shot put, finished 2nd in the 220 and 440-yard dashes, and took 4th in the discus. McIntire had been one of the top athletes in the state during his senior year at Gardner High School, winning the 100 and 220-yard dashes, the shot put, and anchoring Gardner's winning 880 relay team at the 1956 state high school meet. McIntire set state high school records in the 100 and 220. McIntire attended KU in the fall of 1956 to play football, but transferred to Emporia because of the size of the school. With his great diversity, McIntire was to become Emporia State's greatest all-around track and field performer. Blow and Utter also picked up conference victories for KSTC, in the long jump and pole vault respectively, with Utter tying for 1st in the vault.

Don Blow was KSTC's only entry in the NAIA meet that summer, and no reason can be found for Tidwell and Utter not being entered. Blow earned a 5th place in the long jump in the national championships. The remainder of the summer meets annually attended by KSTC athletes were not attended, and again, no reason for this is available. Tidwell's outstanding career thus came to an end, his performances having led Emporia State back into the national limelight, and his dazzling anchor carries on KSTC's relay teams having entertained track fans throughout the Midwest. Tidwell has since been inducted into the NAIA Track and Field Hall of Fame, the Drake Relays Hall of Fame, the Kansas Sports Hall of Fame and was a charter inductee into the Emporia State Athletic Hall of Honor.

Another outstanding Kansas track figure ended his career in 1957. Garfield "Doc" Weede, Pittsburg State's head track coach since 1919, retired at the end of the track season. In his 39 years as track coach, Pitt teams had won 19 league championships, 17 of which were CIC titles. Emporia State and Pitt State had dominated the CIC for most of its existence until Fort Hays, with Alex Francis taking over as head coach in 1946, entered the picture following World War II. Weede had produced many national caliber performers in track and field, and his contributions to the sport were outstanding.

1958

The 1958 Hornet track team was the strongest since 1951. Top returnees Duane McIntire, Bob Oden and Gonzalo Javier combined with outstanding newcomers Paul Whiteley, a junior transfer, and freshmen Rex Ressler, Landis Franklin, Noel Certain, Bill Favrow, Dennis Matheson and Monroe Fordham to provide a great deal of depth to the Hornet squad. These men were to form the nucleus of the group that was to key the Hornets return to the top of the CIC in the final years of the decade.

Whiteley had a great deal of success in the three indoor meets entered by the Hornet thinclads, winning the mile and two-mile in both the Omaha dual and Omaha triangular meets while setting meet records of 4:17.2 and 9:32.0 in the latter. At the KSU Indoor, Whiteley anchored the Hornet distance medley team of Franklin, Matheson, and Wirta to 2nd place behind Colorado University, running a 4:14.6 mile split.

Hornet relay teams continued this success into the outdoor relay circuit. At Texas, KSTC relay teams picked up two 3rds and two 4ths, with the two-mile team of Autrey Calloway, Matheson, Dick Bliss and Whiteley and the 880 team of Bob Heaney, Harold Thompson, Ressler, and McIntire taking the 3rd place. The sprint medley team of Franklin, Ressler, McIntire, and Whiteley, and the 440 team of James Hayes, Heaney, Thompson, and Ressler, earned the 4ths.

At the Kansas Relays, the outstanding performance for KSTC was turned in by the distance medley team of Franklin, Calloway, Javier, and Whiteley, which finished 2nd in setting a school record of 10:09.7. The mark this foursome erased had been a world record when set at KU in 1936. The sprint medley team of Franklin, McIntire, Ressler and Whiteley also finished 2nd, and the final place was earned by the Hornet 880 team of Hayes, Franklin, McIntire, and Ressler which placed 3rd.

KSTC experienced both success and disappointment at the Drake Relays, the success coming from the middle distance teams and the disappointment being provided by the sprint teams. The sprint medley foursome that competed at KU again finished 2nd in the event, and the mile team of Jim Hammond, McIntire, Bliss, and Franklin placed 3rd. Unfortunately, the strong distance medley team was unable to compete, as the event was once again not offered in the college division at Drake. The sprint teams, both of which qualified for the finals, met with hard luck when Bill Fleming pulled a muscle on his carry in the 440 relay and the team did not finish, and the 880 team dropped the baton and came in last.

Emporia State improved their placing in the CIC in 1958, finishing 2md behind Pitt State by only 10 points. Ressler turned in the outstanding performance of the meet, winning the 100 and 220-yard dashes in upsetting Bob Wooten of Pitt, who had won both events for three straight years. Ressler's time of 20.8 seconds in the 220 was a new CIC record. Other winners for KSTC were Franklin in the quarter, Whiteley in the 880, Javier in the mile, and Oden, who tied for 1st in the pole vault. KSTC's strengths were in the distance events and the shot put, with Hornet thinclads finishing 1-2-5 in the mile, 2-3-4-5 in the two-mile, and 2-3-4 in the shot.

Rex Ressler: National Champion
Rex Ressler was the 220-yard national champion as a freshman in 1958. He also placed 2nd in the 100-yard dash. His school record time of 20.92 for 200 meters stood for 53 years.

Ressler continued his superb performances into the summer, defeating Charlie Tidwell, Kansas University's world record holder, in winning the MVAAU 100 and 220-yard dashes in 9.8 seconds and 21.0 seconds respectively. Whiteley and Wirta earned victories for E-State in the mile and two-mile, respectively, while Oden finished in a tie for 3rd in the pole vault.

At the NAIA meet in San Diego, Ressler won the 220-yard dash in 21.5 seconds and placed 2nd in the 100-yard dash in 9.6 seconds. Ressler's time in the 100 tied Duward Crooms' 1936 school record in the event. Whiteley finished 2nd in the mile in 4:12.2 to help lead KSTC to a 3rd place team finish. Other place winners for the Hornets were Franklin, 5th in the 440, and Oden, tied for 5th in the vault. After the NAIA, Ressler stayed in California for two more weeks to compete in the National AAU meet and the NCAA meet. He did not place in the AAU meet, and was forced out of the NCAA semifinals with a pulled muscle after qualifying for the semis in both the 100 and 220-yard dashes.

1959

The Central Conference added an indoor championship to the track schedule in 1959, and the Fort Hays Tigers walked off with the team title in the first annual event. Two bad breaks cost KSTC a shot at the title: Ressler pulled a muscle in the semifinals of the 60-yard dash, an event in which he was a heavy favorite, and Gonzalo Javier, the favorite in the 880-yard run, cut in too soon while passing teammate Frank Hicks in the final of the event and fell, giving the victory to a Fort Hays runner. Whiteley was a double winner for the Hornets, taking the mile and two-mile, while Noel Certain won the broad jump, and Bob Oden took top honors in the pole vault, setting a fieldhouse record of 13-10 ¼.

KSTC's success at the Texas Relays in opening the outdoor season was tempered by the costly loss of Ressler, who reaggravated the injury from the CIC indoor and did not run again until the conference outdoor meet. Bob Oden earned the highest place for the Hornets, tying for 2nd in the pole vault at 14-0, while the two-mile relay team of Hicks, Dennis Matheson, Javier, and Whiteley took 3rd. Other places earned by KSTC thinclads were a 4th by Monroe Fordham in the high jump, and a 5th and a 6th by the 880 and 440 relay teams, respectively.

Bob Oden: National Champion

Bob Oden was a two-time NAIA National Champion in the pole vault, winning back-to-back national championships in 1959 and 1960. He won the conference championship three times and set conference and school records.

The distance relays continued the success at the second stop on the relay circuit, the long medley team of McIntire, Matheson, Javier, and Whiteley finishing 2nd in 10:24.1. With Hicks replacing McIntire, the foursome placed 3rd in the two-mile event with the time of 7:56.8. Other Hornet place winners at KU were Fordham with a 2nd place tie in the high jump, and Oden, who cleared 13-6 for a tie for 4th in the vault. The distance medley quartet that ran at KU placed 4th in the event at Drake, improving their time to 10:22.5. Welch entered a sprint medley team at Drake rather than the two-mile team, and the foursome of McIntire, Dick Corwin, Eddie Washington and Whiteley took 2nd in 3:25.4. Oden garnered the Hornets' final place at the Drake Relays, finishing in a four-way tie for 5th in the vault at 14-0.

E-State won the CIC crown in 1959 for the first time in eight years, scoring 91 ½ points to outdistance 2nd place Fort Hays. Ressler returned from his injury to become the meets only double winner, repeating in the 100 and 220-yard dashes. Oden, who had tied for 1st in the 1958 CIC, won the title outright in 1959 and set a new CIC record of 14-2 ½. Whiteley led a KSTC sweep in the mile, finishing in front of teammates Javier and Wirta, then came back to win the 880. Unfortunately, Whiteley was disqualified in the 880 for cutting too soon on the first curve. Other winners for the Hornets were Wirta in the two-mile, Washington in the 440 in 48.6 seconds, and the mile relay team of Don Smith, Certain, McIntire, and Washington. Despite not winning an individual event, McIntire was the meet's high scorer, placing 2nd in the 440-dash, 5th in the 220-dash, 2nd in the discus and 3rd in the shot put, as well as running anchor on the winning relay.

Ressler's season came to an end, as well as the Hornets' chances to challenge for the NAIA team title, when he reinjured the pulled muscle while practicing for the MVAAU meet. At the Missouri Valley meet, Whiteley began a string of exceptional performances, winning the mile and two-mile while running the fastest times of his career, 4:08.1 and 9:11.2, respectively. The two-mile time broke his own school record by six seconds. Oden also captured 1st for the Hornets, tying in the pole vault at 14-2, while Fordham tied for 2nd in the high jump and Certain placed 3rd in the triple jump.

The next meet for KSTC was the NCAA regional meet, in which the Hornets finished 2nd behind Central Missouri State. Individual winners in the region meet qualified for the NCAA National meet in Lincoln, Nebraska. Earning this distinction for KSTC were: Whiteley, a double winner in the mile at 4:15.0 and the three-mile at 14:18.3 while lapping the entire field in the latter; McIntire, also a double winner in the 100 and 220-yard dashes; Javier in the 880-yard run; and Oden in the pole vault. Other places earned by Hornet thinclads included a 2nd in the high jump by Fordham, a 3rd in the mile, and 4th in the three-mile by Javier, and a 3rd in the discus by McIntire.

Five Hornet thinclads attended the 1959 NAIA meet in Sioux Falls, South Dakota, and all five placed to earn 4th place team honors for KSTC. Whiteley was again outstanding, winning the mile in 4:11.2 and setting a new NAIA record of 9:06.0 while taking the two-mile. Oden was also an individual champion for KSTC, winning the pole vault with the jump of 13-7. McIntire finished 5th in the 100 and 220-yard dashes, while Javier and Fordham earned 6ths in the mile and high jump, respectively, to round out the Hornet scoring.

Whiteley's next performance was his most spectacular, as he won the NCAA three-mile title with the time of 13:59.1 in a thrilling finish over Miles Eisenman of Oklahoma State. Oden cleared 14-0 in the pole vault to garner 6th place and score one point for KSTC. Whiteley and Oden ended the 1959 track season one week after the NCAAs, competing in the National AAU meet in Boulder. Whiteley finished a disappointing 8th in the 5000-meter, but this was due to the effects of the high altitude, as Whiteley describes in this account from the KSTC Bulletin:

Paul Whiteley: National Champion

Paul Whiteley won the 1959 NAIA championships in the mile and two-mile runs, setting a meet and school record in the latter. He also won the NCAA championship in the three-mile run. Whitely was also outstanding in cross country, leading ESU to national titles in 1958 and 1959, finishing 3rd and 2nd individually.

"Unless you're used to the altitude, it can hurt you," he (Whiteley) said. "Although I usually have a strong finish, this time I just about walked in. Gee, was I ever sick after that." (KSTC Bulletin, Vol. 59, No. 17, p. 4)

Paul Whiteley's career as a Hornet ended after this race because he graduated in January of 1960. He stayed in Emporia through the spring, training for the 1960 Olympic trials, racing with outstanding success in many of the same meets as the E-State tracksters. Whiteley qualified for the U.S. Olympic Trials by placing 3rd in the 1960 National AAU 5000-meter with a time of 14:37.0. Unfortunately, Whiteley failed to win a place on the U.S. Olympic team, placing 4th in 14:28.4. Whitely defeated Billy Mills, who later went on to win the 1964 Olympic Games 10,000 meters.

Fran Welch: Olympic Coach

Coach Fran Welch was chosen as one of the coaches for the 1960 United States Women's Olympic Track and Field Team. Welch was recognized by his peers as one of the top track coaches in the United States, as demonstrated by his selection as an Olympic coach. In 1958, Welch had charge of a group of AAU stars that toured Europe, and he was also named field coach for the 1959 Pan American Games team. Welch had been president of the Missouri Valley Association of the AAU and was a member of the National AAU Track and Field Committee, as well as being one of the original inductees into the NAIA Track and Field Hall of Fame in 1954.

1960

The 1960 track season was one of the most successful in Hornet track history and began the most successful decade in the history of the program. The success in 1960 was accomplished despite the loss of Paul Whiteley and Warner Wirta to graduation and Rex Ressler to eligibility. Seventeen lettermen returned to provide the Hornets with outstanding talent and depth in nearly every event. This was shown in the total domination of the CIC Indoor meet, in which E-State won nine of 11 events to win by 36 points over the defending champion Fort Hays Tigers. Individual winners for KSTC included Gonzalo Javier in the mile and 880 in record time for the latter race, Eddie Washington in the 60 and 440-yard dashes, Noel Certain and Bob Oden with meet records in the long jump and pole vault respectively, David Ohlde in the two-mile, and Duane McIntire in the 60-yard low hurdles. The final victory for KSTC was provided by the mile relay team of Don Smith, Landis Franklin, McIntire, and Washington in meet record time.

> **Success at the Drake Relays**
> In 1959, the Emporia State track program was rewarded as one of the top five winners in the first 50 years of the Drake Relays. Hornet thinclads had picked up 15 victories at Drake since 1923, their initial year of competition in the meet. This was quite an accomplishment for KSTC as the Drake Relays were the most competitive event on the Midwest relay circuit.
>
>
> DRAKE RELAYS
> america's athletic classic

The Hornet thinclads continued their winning ways at the Kansas State Indoor Relays, claiming the college division title by winning three of four college relays and garnering two individual places in the university/open division. Washington gave a strong performance, winning the 300-yard dash in 31.5 seconds and running a leg on the victorious mile relay team with Franklin, Clarke, and McIntire. The other winning relays were the distance medley and two-mile foursome of Clarke, Hicks, Matheson, and Javier, while McIntire earned the Hornets' final points with a 4th place finish in the 75-yard high hurdles.

Noel Certain made ESU history by setting a new school record in the broad jump by leaping an outstanding 24-10 in the 1960 indoor season.

The Hornets continued to roll during the outdoor season, winning six events at the Oklahoma State Relays while setting two records and tying another. Lynn Davis and Monroe Fordham won their individual events, the high hurdles and the high jump respectively, with Fordham setting a school record of 6-6. The Hornets' other 1sts were in the 440, 880, mile and sprint medley relays. Washington and McIntire ran on all four relays, Franklin ran on the 440, 880 and mile relays, Certain joined these three on the 440 relay, Jim Walker replaced Certain on the 880 team, Hicks filled out the quartet in the mile relay, and Clarke and Javier joined the two mainstays on the sprint medley team. The 440 and sprint medley teams posted new meet records while the mile team tied the existing mark.

> **Gonzalo Javier: NCAA Champion**
> Gonzalo Javier was the NAIA National Champion in the 1500 meters outdoors in 1960. He was also a member of the Hornet national championship cross country teams in 1958 and 1959.
>
>

The next stop on the relay circuit was at the Texas Relays, where Fordham placed 2nd in the high jump and Certain took 5th in the broad jump in the university/college division open events. Three Hornet relay teams earned places in the college division, the two-mile team of Hicks, Matheson, Clarke and Javier placing 2nd, the mile team of Washington, Hicks, Clarke and Franklin taking 4th, and the 880 team of Washington, Walker, Certain, and Franklin placing 6th.

Emporia State dominated the Emporia Relays a week after Texas, winning the 880, mile, two-mile, sprint medley and distance medley relays. Washington and McIntire placed 1st and 2nd respectively in the 100-yard dash, while McIntire also took 3rd in the discus and 5th in the shot. The next weekend at the Arkansas Relays, McIntire starred in the same events. He reversed the finish of the 100 from the Emporia Relays in winning over Washington with the wind-aided time of 9.5 seconds, placed 4th in the discus with the school record toss of 162-5, took 5th in the shot put with a toss of 49-5, threw 180-0 in the javelin, and finished out his busy day running a 49.5 second split on the 3rd place mile relay team with Washington, Certain, and Clarke. One other school record fell during the meet when Bill Favrow threw the shot 51-7 to place 2nd and erase John Kuck's mark set in 1926. Other Hornet place winners were Tom Fincken, 5th in the discus with a toss of 160-7 to also break the old school record, the two-mile relay team of Hicks, Matheson, Clarke, and Javier in 3rd, and the 3rd place distance medley foursome of Washington, McIntire, Hicks, and Clarke.

Tom Fincken: Super Bowl Official
Tom Fincken competed in track and field at ESU, winning a conference championship in the discus as a senior, setting a school record and finishing 5th at the NAIA national meet in 1960. He worked as an NFL official and officiated Super Bowls XXX, XXXII, and XXXV. He also worked college basketball and officiated at the 1986 NCAA Final Four to become one of only two people to officiate in the Final Four and the Super Bowl.

The Hornets won two events at the Kansas Relays the next weekend, but the outstanding performance for KSTC was the non-winning long jump turned in by Noel Certain. Certain leaped 25-5, the third best mark posted in the United States during the 1960 season, to place 2nd in the university/college division event. The victories were earned by Fordham with a 6-5 ¾ leap in the high jump, and the distance medley foursome of Franklin, Hicks, Matheson, and Javier. The two-mile relay team of Hicks, Clarke, Matheson, and Javier placed second, as did the sprint medley team of Clarke, Washington, Franklin, and Javier. Third place was earned by the 440 relay quartet of Walker, Certain, Franklin, and Washington and the mile relay team of Washington, Certain, Franklin, and Clarke. David Ohlde placed 4th in the open 5000-meter run to earn the Hornets' final points.

Emporia State swamped the competition at the 1960 CIC outdoor meet, winning 11 of 14 events in setting an all-time CIC point total of 114 3/10, and also breaking three conference records, establishing one in a new event, and tying another. Washington turned in an outstanding performance, tying the conference mark of 9.7 seconds in winning the 100-yard dash, setting a CIC mark of 21.7 seconds in the 220-yard dash, which was run around the curve for the first time, and running a leg on the winning mile relay with Bill Certain, Franklin, and Clarke, which set a CIC record of 3:16.0. Other record breakers for KSTC were Favrow with the throw of 53-0 in the shot put, and freshman Charles Richard, who upset teammate Fordham to win the high jump with the leap of 6-6 ½. Also garnering victories for the Hornets were Javier in the mile and 880, Oden in the pole vault, Franklin in the 440, Certain in the long jump, and

Ohlde in the two-mile. Once again, McIntire was a workhorse for KSTC despite not winning an event, taking 2nd in the low hurdles, 3rd in the shot put, the 100 and the 220, and 5th in the discus.

Two weeks after the conference victory, several of the CIC champion Hornets competed in the Missouri Valley AAU meet. Fordham defeated teammate Richard to win the high jump with a leap of 6-5 ½, and Oden won the pole vault with a jump of 13-11. Seconds were earned by Favrow in the shot, Javier in the 1500-meter, Certain in the broad jump, and Franklin in the low hurdles. Franklin also placed 3rd in the 440. McIntire did not compete in this meet because he was preparing for the MVAAU Open Decathlon Championships to be held at Emporia State two days after the MVAAU track meet. The event was designed to help men qualify for the National Decathlon Championship Olympic Trials, which were held in conjunction during this Olympic year. McIntire easily met the Olympic Trials standard of 6750 points, scoring 6926 points while winning six of 10 events. Hornet Dale Greiner also turned in a solid performance, placing 3rd with 5299 points.

Emporia State's next competition was at the NAIA Championships, where the Hornets finished a disappointing 5th. Gonzalo Javier continued the KSTC domination of the mile event, winning the metric version in 3:52.8, while Bob Oden won his second consecutive pole vault title, tying for 1st with a jump of 14-¼. Other place winners for KSTC were Charles Richard and Monroe Fordham in a nine-way tie for 3rd in the high jump, Landis Franklin with a 4th in the low hurdles, another 4th by Russ Miller in the javelin, and Certain taking 6th in the long jump.

One week after the NAIA meet, Certain and Javier competed in the Meet of Champions at the University of Houston, Texas. Certain returned to his usual standards after his disappointing NAIA performance, jumping 24-3 ¾ to finish 2nd in the long jump. Javier placed 4th in the 1500-meter, finishing in the time of 3:47.7, which was the second fastest metric mile ever recorded by a Hornet runner, 2nd only to Bill Tidwell's 3:45.2 in 1956. McIntire's chance to qualify for the U.S. Olympic team came in early July when he competed in the Olympic Trials decathlon, and, since the event combined the National AAU championship and the Olympic trials, foreign athletes were allowed to compete. After the first day of competition, McIntire had 4251 points to stand as the 5th American and 6th overall. His first day performances had been his best ever in decathlon competition. Unfortunately, McIntire fell off the pace during the second day and finished as the 8th American and 9th overall with 6921 points. His biggest disappointment during the second day of competition came in the discus, where his best mark was over 20 feet under his personal best. Rafer Johnson of the United States won the event, setting a new world record of 8683 points, and Chuan-Kwang Yang, a citizen of Taiwan, finished 2nd. These men finished 1st and 2nd, respectively, in the 1960 Olympic Games decathlon, both smashing the old Olympic record.

1960 Women's Olympic Team trains in Emporia

In the middle of July of 1960, the U.S. Women's Olympic track and field team came to Emporia State to train for the Games, and stayed until August 15th when they left for Rome. While here, the women lived in Morse Hall and worked out on the stadium field under the direction of Fran Welch, who was an Olympic assistant coach. Wilma Rudolph was one of these athletes, and this young lady went on to win the 100-meter, the 200-meter, and anchor the United States winning 4 x 100-meter relay at the Rome Games.

> **Success in the 60s**
> During the 1960s decade, Emporia State athletes would win six conference indoor championships, capture seven conference outdoor track titles while finishing 2nd in the other three, and win one NAIA track title, finishing lower than 6th in the national team standings only twice. Hornet thinclads broke 23 of 34 school records at least once during the decade and garnered All-America honors 36 times. Hornet harriers were just as successful during the period, winning four conference titles and finishing 2nd three times, claiming two NAIA cross country titles, and finishing in the top 10 in the NAIA six other times. KSTC cross country runners earned All-America honors 14 times during the period.

1961

There was no falling off for KSTC's track squad in 1961, as the Hornet thinclads were stronger despite the graduation of national champs Javier and Oden and decathlete McIntire. Rex Ressler returned to give the Hornets an extremely potent sprint squad, with the Hornets other strength in the field events.

The Hornets opened the year at the International Meet of Champions in Winnepeg, Canada. The auditorium at Winnepeg was large enough to allow the discus to be thrown indoors, and Bill Favrow won the event with a toss of 133-11, grabbing a 2nd in the shot put as well. Eddie Washington garnered the Hornets other 1st, winning the 60-yard dash in 6.3 seconds, while John Evely and Matheson took 3rd and 4th respectively in the three-mile.

KSTC repeated as CIC indoor champs in 1961, although not as dominantly as the previous year, winning six events and breaking four records. Eddie Washington had a successful, yet unsuccessful, day, setting a record of 6.3 seconds in the 60-yard dash prelims then losing in the final to Roger Sayers of Omaha, and winning the 440-yard dash only to be disqualified in the event. KSTC's Frank Hicks benefited from Washington's misfortune in the 440 to win the event. Other records were set by Certain in the long jump, Richard in the high jump, and the mile relay team of Washington, Melvin Mayo, Hicks and Certain. The final Hornet victories were taken by Matheson in the mile and Favrow in the shot put. The Hornets ended the indoor season by again winning the college division of the KSU Indoor Relays.

The Hornet sprinters took over with the opening of the outdoor season, winning the 440, 880 and sprint medley relays, and finishing 3rd in the mile event at the Oklahoma State Relays. Certain, Mayo, Fessler and Washington formed the 440 quartet, Franklin replaced Certain in the 880 relay, and Hicks joined Franklin, Mayo and Washington in the medley event. Besides running on the winning 440 team, Certain finished 2nd in the long jump with the leap of 24-10 ½, close to his school record that still stands, his 25-5 jump at the 1960 Kansas Relays being wind-aided. Richard and Fordham tied for 1st in the high jump at 6-5 with Brady of Oklahoma, and Richard also placed 2nd in the high hurdles. The final Hornet place was earned by Tom Fincken with a 3rd in the discus.

The speedsters turned in another memorable performance at the Texas Relays. The team of Mayo, Ressler, Washington, and Franklin won the 880 relay with the time of 1:25.8 to set a school mark, and the mile relay team of Mayo, Hicks, Washington, and Franklin posted a second relay victory with the time of 3:16.3. Two other Hornet relays garnered 4ths: the 880 relay foursome running in the 440 relay, and the sprint medley team of Franklin, Ressler, Washington, and Hicks. Individually, Fordham turned in an outstanding jump to win the university class high jump with the height of 6-6 ¼, while Richard finished in a three-way tie for 2nd in the event. Rounding out the Hornet scoring was James Howell with a tie for 4th in the pole vault, and Certain with a 5th place in the long jump.

One week after the Texas Relays, Fordham leaped 6-8 at the Emporia Relays to set a new meet and school record, and post the second best jump in history by a Kansan. He continued the noteworthy

Monroe Fordham: School Record Holder
Fordham jumped 6-8 to set the school record. Note the straddle style of jumping and the sawdust pit in which he landed.

performances at the second stop on the Midwest relay circuit, tying for the Kansas Relays high jump crown with teammate Richard and Curtis of Baylor University at 6-6. The mile relay team garnered another title for KSTC, the foursome of Mayo, Franklin, Certain, and Washington running the superb time of 3:12.2 to post a new KU Relays and school record. Unfortunately, Ressler had injured his leg in a dual win over Fort Hays, and his loss prevented the Hornet sprint relays from achieving the success that had been realized at Oklahoma and Texas. Other KSTC place winners were the two-mile and sprint medley teams in 4th, Certain finishing 2nd in the long jump with a leap of 24-8, and Dale Greiner in 5th in the decathlon with 5170 points.

The Hornets met with limited success on the final leg of the relay circuit. Fordham was upset in his bid for the triple crown in the high jump with a 2nd place finish at Drake, and a 4th in the sprint medley and 5ths in the two-mile and distance medley relays were the only other places managed by the KSTC However, Welch sent most of his field competitors to the Colorado Relays instead of to Drake, and these men had a great deal of success in Boulder. Fincken and Favrow took 1st and 2nd, respectively, in the discus, then reversed their order to place 3rd and 4th in the shot put. Jim Howell earned another victory for the Hornets, finishing in a five-way tie for 1st in the pole vault, while Russell Miller took 2nd in the javelin to round out the place winners.

The Emporia State trackmen erased their year old CIC scoring record in the 1961 meet, racking up 119 ½ points to win by over 70 points. This feat was accomplished despite the absence of Ressler and the disqualification of KSTC's winning mile relay. Conference records were set by Miller with a toss of 223-8 ½ in the javelin, Fincken in the discus with a throw of 166-11 ½, and Fordham with the leap of 6-7 ½ in the high jump. The 440 relay team of Alex Czencz, Mayo, Franklin and Washington established a mark of 41.9 seconds in the event. Other winners for the Hornets were Matheson in the mile and two-mile, Clarke in the 880, Mayo in the 440, Franklin in the 220 yard low hurdles, Certain in the long jump, and Favrow in the shot put.

The Hornets again had a disappointing finish in the NAIA meet, taking 6th place as a team. KSTC's team chances were hurt by the continued absence of Ressler, who, since his freshman year in 1958 when he had established himself as one of the top sprinters in the country, had missed every NAIA meet with injuries. Leading the Emporia State effort at the NAIA meet was a trio of javelin throwers. Russell Miller, Kenny Oard, and Kent Hurn placed 2nd-3rd-5th, respectively, in the event, with Miller and Oard earning All-America honors. Fordham was defeated in the high jump for only the second time during the season, taking 4th, and was followed by Richard who finished in a four-way tie for 5th. Also earning 5ths for KSTC were Tom Fincken and Bill Favrow in the discus and shot put, respectively.

The Emporia State thinclads ended the season with a 3rd place finish in the NCAA Small College Midwest Regional meet, taking six 1sts and setting four records. The records were set by Favrow in the shot, Fincken in the discus, Fordham in the high jump and Richard in the high hurdles. Richard also won the low hurdles and tied for 2nd in the high jump. Miller was the final Hornet winner, taking 1st in the javelin.

The Hornets added an outstanding runner in 1961 that would add to their already-established distance legacy. Ireland Sloan had transferred to KSTC in the spring of 1961 from Morehead State, Kentucky. He had never run competitively before enrolling at Morehead in the fall of 1960, but was so outstanding that Dr. Nolan Fowler, the coach at Morehead, suggested that Sloan transfer to a larger school. Fowler recommended Houston, Oregon and KSTC, and Sloan chose Emporia State because of the size of the school. Sloan was not the first outstanding runner sent to Emporia by Dr. Fowler, as he had also sent Paul Whiteley a few years earlier. Sloan ran unattached in meets during the 1961 spring and fall seasons, turning in some outstanding performances, the best of which was a 6th place finish overall, and the second American, in the National AAU 10,000-meter during the 1961 summer. Sloan and Camien combined over the next several seasons to form one of the most potent distance duos in the history of the NAIA.

1962

The Hornets' potent sprint teams of previous seasons were no longer in evidence during the 1962 track season, with Ressler, Hicks, Franklin, and Certain graduated, and Mayo missing most of the season with an injury. Freshman Richard Vininski showed a great deal of promise in winning the 60-yard dash in 6.2 seconds at the International Meet of Champions in Winnepeg, tying the meet record held jointly by Charlie Tidwell and Bob Smith of KU. However, Vininski was injured in the first outdoor meet and missed the rest of the season, leaving the strength of the 1962 team in the distance runs and the throwing events. Besides Vininski's victory in the 60 at Winnepeg, the Hornets picked up one other 1st and four 3rds. The mile relay team of Vininski, Clarke, Washington and John Calderon provided the first, winning in the time of 3:24.0. The 3rds were earned by Washington in the 60-yard dash at 6.3 seconds, John Camien in the mile at 4:19.8, Sloan in the three-mile at 14:13.6, and the two-mile relay team of Chuck Atkins, Leon Storck, DeWolf Roberts, and Camien.

At the Kansas State Relays, the team of Melvin Mayo, DeWolf Roberts, John Calderon, and Eddie Washington set a new school record mark of 3.18.3 in the mile relay.

The Hornets claimed a third consecutive CIC indoor title in 1962, winning easily over the 2nd place Hays Tigers. KSTC thinclads won seven events, setting meet records in every event they won. Camien and Richard were double winners, Camien taking the mile in 4:19.9 and the 880 in 1:58.2, while Richard won the 60-yard high hurdles in 7.6 seconds and the high jump at 6-5. Sloan won the two-mile with a time of 9:15.0, while freshman Bill Goldhammer upset favored teammate Favrow to win the shot put at 52-11. Later in the indoor season at the Kearney dual, Goldhammer set an indoor school record in the shot put of 54-9 ½. The Hornets final victory was earned by the mile relay team of Alex Czenz, Roberts, Mayo and Calderon. Besides running on the victorious mile relay, Calderon set a CIC record of 50.7 seconds in the prelims of the 440 but managed only a 3rd place finish in the final.

KSTC returned to Canada for the second time during the 1962 indoor season to participate in the Royal Canadian Legion Indoor meet, and the Hornet trackmen earned three 2nd places. Camien finished 2nd in the mile at 4:13.5, one-tenth of a second behind Bruce Kidd of Toronto, while Sloan took 2nd in the two-mile at 9:12.6. The Hornets' other 2nd place was garnered by the two-mile relay team of Atkins, Storck, Roberts, and Camien.

Injuries plagued the Hornets through much of the outdoor season, with Richard, Sloan, Calderon, Washington, Vininski, Clarke and Mayo all missing parts of the year. The injury problems greatly diminished KSTC's success on the relay circuit. The Emporia State trackmen also suffered their first dual loss in five years, a 19-point loss to Kearney State when almost all of the above mentioned athletes were on the injured list. Despite these setbacks, the Hornets did have several individuals place well at the Texas

Relays, in particular John Camien. Camien turned in a very strong performance to win the 1500-meter run with the time of 3:53.5. Also placing for KSTC were Richard and Hurn with a 4th in the high hurdles and a 6th in the javelin, respectively, and Goldhammer with a 2nd in the freshman division shot put with a 54-2 ½ toss. However, the injuries took a toll at the last two stops on the Midwest circuit, and the Hornets were able to pick up only two places, a 2nd by Camien in the Kansas Relays' Glenn Cunningham mile, and a 3rd place finish by the sprint medley team at Drake.

Despite the injuries, Emporia again won the CIC outdoor crown although they did not challenge their scoring mark, piling up 98 points to 54 ½ for 2nd place Hays. Richard set a CIC mark of 14.4 seconds in winning the high hurdles, and also won the high jump. Favrow was a double winner as well, setting a meet record of 54-9 in the shot put and winning the discus with a 148-8 ½ toss. Goldhammer also broke the old CIC shot put mark in finishing 2nd. Camien and Sloan rounded out the Hornet victories, winning the mile and two-mile, respectively.

> **Ed Fletje**
> Ed Fletje was a hurdler on the ESU teams, graduating in 1964. However, his biggest impact on ESU was he served as the interim president for ESU for five months in 2011.
>
>

Emporia State served as host for the NCAA small college regional meet during the last weekend in May, but unfortunately, Camien and Goldhammer were eliminated from the competition because of a rule prohibiting freshman from colleges with an enrollment over 750 students from participating. Despite this loss of points, KSTC won the meet, scoring 79 ½ points. Favrow and Sloan were outstanding, Favrow winning the shot and discus with throws of 52-6 ½ and 158-4 ½, respectively, while Sloan won the mile and three-mile, posting times of 4:17.2 and 14:26.5, respectively. Seconds were earned by Ed Flentje in the 440 hurdles, Washington in the 440 dash, Clarke in the 880, and Richard in the high jump. Rounding out the Hornet scoring were 3rds by Richard in the high and low hurdles, James Howell in the pole vault, and Atkins in the 880.

> **John Camien: National Champion**
> John Camien competed from 1961-1965 for the Hornets. He won an amazing five national championships, including the 1500 meters four straight years. He won 18 conference titles and was a two-time time NAIA cross country national champion.
>
>

After the NCAA regional meet, the Hornets took 2nd in the NAIA national meet on the strength of the distance runners and the field event men. Camien was the only individual winner for KSTC, continuing E-State domination of the mile run by winning the event in 4:09.7. Sloan finished 3rd in the three-mile and 6th in the mile with times of 14:13.5 and 4:17.2 respectively, while Richard Woelk took 6th in the three-mile in 14:51.3. Richard finished 2nd in the high jump with a leap of 6-7 and took 6th in the high hurdles, while Kent Hurn earned All-America honors with a 2nd place in the javelin. Favrow placed 3rd in the shot put with the toss of 53-10 to edge Goldhammer, who finished in 4th. Goldhammer also picked up a 6th place in the discus to round out the Hornet scoring.

1963

The 1963 Hornet track squad retained the characteristic strength in the distances and throws, despite the loss of top weight men Favrow and Goldhammer. KSTC opened the season with the CIC indoor meet, again edging Fort Hays while winning their fourth consecutive title. Charlie Richard was the Hornets' top performer, breaking two meet records and tying another while winning three events. His new marks were 6-6 ½ in the high jump and 7.5 seconds in the 60-yard high hurdles, and he also tied the low hurdle mark of 6.9 seconds in upsetting defending champ and record holder Roger Sayers, a national sprint champion. Other record setters for KSTC were Camien, with marks of 4:14.7 in the mile and 1:54.9 in the 880, and Sloan with a time of 8:58.7 in the two-mile, the latter also a new school record. Steve Mitchell rounded out the Hornet victories, winning the pole vault at 13-0.

Fayetteville, Arkansas, home of the Arkansas Relays, was the first stop of the outdoor season for the Hornet thinclads. Winners for KSTC included Kent Hurn with a throw of 224-3 in the javelin, Richard Vininski in the 100-yard dash with a time of 8.7 seconds, and the distance medley team of Vininski, Clarke, Camien, and Sloan in 10:07.0. Also earning places were Sloan with a 2nd in the two-mile at 9:14.6, Ken Oard placing 3rd in the javelin, and Bill Eikermann taking 5th in the discus.

One week after Arkansas, Camien stole the show at the Texas Relays, blazing into national prominence in winning the mile run over a star-studded field. Although Camien was the defending champion in the event, the KSTC sophomore was not considered a favorite in the race that included Dyrol Burleson, the intercollegiate record holder at 3:57.6, and Bill Dotson, the former KU great who had a career best time of 3:59.0. However, Camien blistered the final 110 yards of the event to upset the favorites and win with the time of 4:02.6. This time was the best intercollegiate mark posted to that point in the season, a KSTC school record, and the third best mark ever posted by a Kansas miler. Sloan, running in the 1500-meter, finished 4th in 3:56.7, and the distance medley team took 3rd.

The next weekend at the Kansas Relays, Camien finished 2nd to Rob Lingle of Missouri in the Glenn Cunningham mile, Camien's time of 4:05.1 was only three-tenths of a second behind the winner. Sloan took 2nd in an AAU invitational 10,000-meter run, finishing in 31:57.9, while Hurn placed 4th in the javelin. The next weekend, Welch split the Hornet squad, sending some to the Colorado Relays and some to the Drake Relays. At Colorado, Hurn set a meet record of 203-9 in winning the javelin, while Ken Hawkinson placed 2nd in the discus and Mitchell took 4th in the pole vault. The distance medley team of Roberts, Clarke, Sloan and Camien placed 3rd at Drake, running 9:56.5.

The Emporia State trackmen won a fifth consecutive CIC title in 1963 to maintain the longest domination of the conference meet since Pittsburg's winning streak in the 1930s. The Hornets finished 1st and 2nd in the three distance runs to pick up a major number of points, from Camien and Clarke, respectively in the 880, Camien and Sloan, respectively, in the mile, and Sloan and Woelk, respectively, in the two-mile. Richard repeated in the high jump, but was a disappointment in the high hurdles, not placing in the event despite being the defending champion. Earl Kjekstad and Hawkinson provided surprises by winning the shot put and discus respectively, both upsetting favorite Chancellor of Pittsburg State. KSTC also scored heavily in the javelin, with Mike Pitko, Hurn, Oard and Lou Frohardt placing 2nd through 5th respectively.

While the balance of the squad participated in the Missouri Valley AAU meet in Kansas City, Camien went to the Modesto Relays in California. The Hornet star placed 5th in the mile event won by Peter Snell, the 1960 Olympic 800-meter champion, with Camien posting a time of 4:00.7 to set a school record and record the fastest collegiate mile of the year. The Hornets competing at the Valley meet were also successful, with 1sts earned by Richard in the high hurdles, Hawkinson in the discus, and Sloan in the three-mile, the latter with a meet record time of 14:15.8. Woelk finished 3rd in the three-mile run to earn the Hornets' final points.

On the strength of the distance runners, the KSTC trackmen placed 4th in the NAIA Championships. Camien repeated in the mile, setting an NAIA record of 4:04.3, and Sloan earned 3rd place in the three mile and 4th in the mile. With Camien's new record in the mile, Hornet runners held NAIA records in the 800-meter, 1500-meter, mile run and two-mile run. Also earning points for E-State were Richard with a 4th in the high hurdles and a 5th in the high jump, Pitko with a 6th in the javelin, and Hawkinson with a 6th in the discus.

The Hornets two distance stars, Camien and Sloan, continued competition into the summer of 1963 with very successful results. Camien ran at the United States Track and Field Federation Meet in Houston, Texas, and placed 2nd in the mile at 4:02.9. Next, he and Sloan went to the NCAA meet in Albuquerque, New Mexico, where Camien finished 4th in the mile with a time of 4:06.2. Sloan, despite spending time in the hospital with a stomach infection, took 4th in the six-mile run in 30:49.4, only 17 seconds behind the winner. The weekend after the NCAA championships, Camien went to St. Louis, Missouri, to compete in the National AAU meet and placed 5th in the mile at 4:01.2. Sloan was not able to compete due to the illness that had afflicted him at the NCAA meet. For his AAU performance, Camien was chosen to compete in 15 meets throughout Europe during the summer.

1964

Once again, the strength of the 1964 Hornet track squad was in the distances and weights. Camien and Sloan were among the best in the nation in their respective events, and with the addition of John McDonnell, Ireland's steeplechase champion, KSTC boasted a formidable distance squad. The Hornets also had outstanding depth in the throwing events, particularly in the javelin and discus.

Camien, Sloan, and McDonnell renewed the tradition of Hornet participation in the major indoor meets throughout the nation, meeting with outstanding success. Camien ran the mile at the Los Angeles Indoor Invitational in mid-January of 1964, finishing 2nd in 4:06.2 behind Jim Grelle of the LA track club. The week after the LA meet, at the International Meet of Champions in Winnepeg, Canada, Camien won the mile event in 4:05.2 while competing against some of the top milers in the U.S. and Canada. Sloan, running 9:09, placed 2nd in the two-mile behind Chris Williamson of New Brunswick University, and McDonnell finished 5th in the same event.

Competing in the Wanamaker Mile at the Millrose Games in New York, Camien finished in 2nd place with a time of 4:02.6, 12 yards behind Tom O'Hara of Loyola. O'Hara and Camien met again one week later in the New York Athletic Club Games, with Camien again finishing 2nd. Camien led the first eight laps of the race, setting a strong pace, but O'Hara surged ahead in the final three laps to set a new indoor world record of 3:56.6 while the Hornet star faded to 4:06.9. Sloan also placed at the Millrose Games, finishing 6th in the three-mile, but he and McDonnell were unable to place in the New York Club Games.

Camien picked up his second victory on the indoor circuit three days after pacing O'Hara to the world record, winning the Mason-Dixon Games mile in 4:01.9. After withdrawing from the NAAU indoor meet because of bronchitis, Camien entered the Milwaukee Journal Games, which had been designated as the USTFF Indoor Championships. Camien won the mile, running a time of 4:02.7, and McDonnell placed 5th in the same event. The most noteworthy performance, however, was turned in by Sloan, who set a new USTFF and school record of 8:57.2 in winning the two-mile run.

After the Milwaukee meet, the Hornets' three distance stars rejoined the team for the CIC indoor meet, and KSTC scored a narrow victory over Fort Hays to take their fifth consecutive title. Camien was a double winner, taking the 880 in 1:54.0 and the mile in 4:11.9, both new CIC records. Other winners for KSTC were Sloan in the two-mile, Earl Kjekstad in the shot put, DeWolf Roberts in the long jump, and C. R. Robe and Steve Mitchell tied in the pole vault.

The Hornets opened the outdoor season at the Arkansas Relays, and once again, the distance men provided the highlights. The foursome of Richard Woelk, Sloan, McDonnell and Camien set a Relays and school record of 17:13.0 while winning the four-mile relay. Sloan added a second victory in winning the two-mile with the time of 9:13.5. Also placing for the Hornets were Bill Eikermann with a 2nd in the discus, Kent Hurn and Mike Pitko finishing 2nd and 4th, respectively, in the javelin, and Roberts taking 3rd in the triple jump.

Former Hornet John McDonnell: Winningest Coach in NCAA History
Coach John McDonnell of the Arkansas Razorbacks became the winningest coach in NCAA history, all sports, with 40 national titles in cross country and track and field. McDonnell, a native Irishman, had started his illustrious career running for the Hornets in 1964, earning double All-American honors at the NAIA National Championships, placing 2nd in the 1500 and 3rd in the 3000 meter steeplechase. He ran one semester before transferring to Southwestern Louisiana.

The KSTC trackmen continued this success into the Midwest relay circuit. The distance medley team of Roberts, Burton Wolfson, McDonnell, and Camien had given a glimpse of what was to come in winning the event in the Kansas State Indoor meet with the fast time of 9:58.3, and this team was particularly outstanding on the relay circuit. The foursome won at Texas, Kansas and Drake to garner a Grand Slam in the event, Setting meet records of 9:57.8 at Texas, 9:48.4 at Kansas, and 9:51.9 at Drake. The mark set at KU was the fifth best posted in the nation during the 1964 season, and still stands as the Emporia State school record.

The Hornet thinclads also met with success in individual events. At Texas, Camien won his third consecutive title in the mile, while Sloan finished 2nd in the three-mile with a time of 14:01.6 and 6th in the mile. Hurn added a 2nd in the javelin. At Kansas, Pitko turned in a strong performance to win the javelin with a toss of 221-8 ½, while Sloan placed 2nd in the steeplechase in 9:04.4. Sloan finished 2nd again at Drake, although in the three-mile, to Geoff Walker of Houston. Sloan's three-mile time of 13:57.4 was the second best posted in the nation, while his time in the steeple set at KU also placed him among the top 10 in the nation. At Drake, Camien appeared to have finally defeated rival O'Hara in the mile, but the Loyola star burst past Camien in the final 100 yards of the race to win in 4:01.1 while the Hornet miler finished in 4:01.6. Camien's time also placed him among the nation's best, earning him a 3rd place ranking on the NCAA top 10 listing. Rounding out the Hornet scoring at Drake were McDonnell placing 4th in the mile in 4:08.6, and Pitko placing 3rd in the javelin.

While KSTC's top performers were competing at the Drake Relays, the remainder of the Hornet squad went to the Southwest Missouri Relays, where Richard Woelk was chosen "Outstanding Athlete" of the meet for his efforts. He won the mile, the three-mile, and anchored the distance medley team of Ron

Cluts, Dave George and Bob Finger to victory to earn the honor. Other winners for E-State were C. R. Robe in the pole vault, Hurn in the javelin and DiPaola in the shot put.

The Emporia State trackmen won their sixth consecutive conference crown in 1964, scoring a 13-point victory over runner-up Pitt State. Camien was a double winner, breaking Bill Tidwell's 1957 CIC mark in the mile with a time of 4:09.4 and winning the 880, and Sloan broke Archie San Romani's 26-year-old mark in the two-mile while winning the event. Eikermann and Hurn won the discus and javelin respectively to lead strong Hornet finishes in the events, as KSTC weight men took 1st, 2nd and 5th in the javelin and 1st, 2nd, 3rd and 5th in the discus. Other winners for the Hornets were DiPaola in the shot put and Robe in the pole vault.

Camien received recognition as one of the top milers in the country when he was invited to compete in the California Relays at Modesto, a meet in which only the best in the country competed. Camien placed 5th in the mile event with a time of 4:02.2. An interesting feature of this race was that one of the men who defeated Camien was Jim Ryun, the 17-year old Wichita East High School miler, who was to become the greatest miler in the world later in the decade. The remainder of the Hornets competed in the USTFF meet in Kansas City, which was held on the same day as the Missouri Valley AAU, the meet KSTC had traditionally participated in. Hurn and Pitko finished 1st and 2nd, respectively, in the javelin, while McDonnell placed 2nd in the 880 and mile runs. Second places were earned by Mitchell in the pole vault and Ken Hawkinson in the discus, and 3rds were taken by DiPaola in the discus and John Swaim in the intermediate hurdles.

The greatest achievement of the season came early in June, as the KSTC thinclads scored 60 points to win the NAIA National Track and Field crown. Camien was chosen "Outstanding Performer" of the meet on the basis of his efforts. He upset defending champion Jim Keefe in the 5000-meter run, sprinting ahead on the final curve to win and set an NAIA record of 14:25.0. Camien also set an NAIA record of 3:48.3 in winning the 1500-meter, breaking the old mark set by Tidwell in 1956. In addition to the two victories, Camien posted the third fastest qualifying time in the 800-meter preliminaries, but did not run in the final because of a slight injury. The Hornets had wrapped up the team title by the 800 finals and Welch did not want to risk having his star performer further irritate the injury. Sloan posted a third NAIA record for the Hornets, winning the steeplechase with a time of 9:09.1, as well as placing 4th in the 5000-meter run. McDonnell earned All-American honors in two events, finishing 2nd in the 1500-meter in 3:49.6, a time also under Tidwell's old mark, and placing 3rd in the steeplechase. Hurn and Pitko placed 3rd and 4th, respectively in the javelin, and DiPaolo took 5th in the discus to earn the Hornets final points. With the addition of the two new records, Emporia State athletes held the NAIA track records in the 800-meter, the mile, the 1500-meter, the two-mile, the 3000-meter steeplechase, and the 5000-meter.

Camien's next goal was to qualify for the U.S. Olympic Trials. At the NCAA and NAAU meets on the last two weekends in June, he ran two of the fastest races of his career to meet the qualifying standards in both meets. Camien ran 3:41.0 in the 1500-meter at the NCAA Championships to finish 3rd in the event behind Morgan Groth of Oregon State, who set a collegiate and meet record of 3:40.4, and Archie San Romani, Jr. of Oregon. The weekend after the NCAA meet, at the National AAU, Camien finished 5th in the 1500-meter in running the school record time of 3:39.9. Tom Hara won the event in the new American record time of 3:38.1, while the next three finishers, Dyrol Burleson, Jim Grelle and Jim Ryun, were all under the old mark of 3:39. 3.

The Olympic Trials were the next stop for Camien. The meet, held in New York, was not the final Olympic Trials, as only the winner of each event automatically qualified for the U.S. team. The next five finishers in each event had to compete in Los Angeles on September 12th and 13th to determine the final two places on the Olympic team. The New York winner would also have to run in LA, but only to prove that they had maintained themselves in top condition. Camien qualified for the 1500-meter final in the relatively slow time of 3:54.9. In the final, the runners set a slow early pace, with no one willing to go out fast and risk not having a kick at the end. Burleson took advantage of the slow pace and blazed a 52.5 second last 440 to win the event, and, unfortunately, Camien could manage only an 8th place finish and did not qualify for the Los Angeles meet. However, Camien was chosen by the AAU to participate on a competitive tour in Europe, the second consecutive summer he had received this honor.

1965

The 1965 track squad was without many of the outstanding performers who had helped win the NAIA title in 1964, as graduation had claimed distance men

1964 Track and Field: National Champions
KSTC thinclads scored 60 points to win the NAIA National Track and Field crown. Camien was chosen as the "Outstanding Performer" of the meet on the basis of his efforts. This is the only national track and field title Emporia State has ever won in their 100 plus years history.

Sloan and Woelk and javelin throwers Hurn and Oard. Also gone was javelin thrower Mike Pitko, who was playing professional baseball, and John McDonnell who transferred to Southwest Louisiana. Despite these losses, KSTC retained a strong team, but did not enjoy the dominance of the past seasons. John Camien, Bob Camien, and C. R. Robe competed in the International Meet of Champions in Winnepeg to open the 1965 season. John Camien, the defending champ in the mile, moved up to the two-mile and won the event with a time of 9:01.0, while Robe took 3rd in the pole vault, and Bob Camien (John's brother) placed 5th in the mile. John's next appearance was at the USTFF meet in Seattle, Washington, where he posted the best indoor mile time of the season in winning the event in 4:01.7. John competed in two more major indoor events during the season, the first at the New York Athletic Club meet where he was just nosed out of 1st by Jim Grelle, running 4:07.2 to Grelle's 4:07.1. At the second event, the Milwaukee Journal Games, Camien matched his nation's best mark of 4:01.7 in winning the mile. John had hoped to crack the four-minute barrier in the meet, and Bob Camien was in the race to act as a rabbit for his brother. Bob led through the quarter in 58 seconds and the half at 2:00 minutes, then John surged ahead and passed the three-quarter mark in 3:01.4. Unfortunately, John was unable to run the last lap fast enough and finished at 4:01.7.

Hornet Domination
The first 13 years of NAIA competition was dominated by Hornet distance runners. After the 1964 season, Emporia State athletes held the NAIA track records in every distance event: the 800-meter, the mile, the 1500-meter, the two-mile, the 3000-meter steeplechase, and the 5000-meter.

The Hornets ended the indoor season scoring a tight victory over Fort Hays to take their sixth consecutive CIC indoor title. With the low hurdles and mile relay remaining to be contested, KSTC was trailing Hays by two points. However, the four Hornet qualifiers in the low hurdles scored 10 points to none for Hays to provide E-State with an insurmountable margin. Camien was a double winner, taking the mile and two-mile, and would have added a third victory in the 880 except for the actions of a Fort Hays runner. Camien was severely elbowed by a Tiger runner while attempting to pass on the last lap of the half-mile and was forced to run wide. The man who committed the foul won the event, while Camien finished 3rd.

However, the Fort Hays man was disqualified because of the foul and Camien was moved up to 2nd. Wayne Rogers was also a double winner for the Hornets, taking the broad jump and the triple jump while setting a CIC and fieldhouse record of 44-3 ¾ in the latter. Robe added another CIC and fieldhouse record, winning the pole vault at 14-5 ¾. Vininski rounded out the Hornet winners, taking the 60-yard dash in 6.4 seconds.

Because of bad weather, the Hornets withdrew from the Arkansas Relays, so the first big relay meet attended by KSTC was the Texas Relays. In the distance medley event, the team was different from 1964 but the result was the same, as the foursome of Vininski, Bob Finger, Bob Camien and John Camien won the event and broke the meet record set by the 1964 Hornet team with a time of 9:54.4. John Camien also became the only man to ever win the mile run at Texas four times, taking the title with a time of 4:08.6. Another member of the medley quartet, Richard Vininski, turned in a strong individual performance, finishing 3rd in the 100-yard dash while tying the school record of 9.6 seconds for the second time in his career. Unfortunately, the Hornets' hopes for a second consecutive Triple Crown in the distance medley were devastated one week later when the day before the Emporia Relays, John Camien was hospitalized with a throat infection that turned out to be mononucleosis. Camien's loss severely limited the Hornets success on the remainder of the relay circuit, and Vininski earned KSTC's only place at KU, taking 5th in the 100-yard dash. The Hornets were unable to place at Drake.

The Hornets were favored to win their seventh consecutive CIC crown in 1965, but the illness to Camien proved disastrous. Camien could manage only a 5th place in the three-mile and a 3rd in the 880, and he dropped out of the mile. The lost points allowed Fort Hays to stay close to the Hornets, and with a victory in the mile relay the Tigers pulled off the upset by the score of 90 ⅕ to 87. Camien was not the only Hornet handicapped by health problems, as C. R. Robe, the defending champion in the pole vault, competed despite a broken jaw but could manage only a 2nd place finish. Winners for KSTC were Eikermann in the discus, Vininski in the 100-yard dash, Earl White in the 220-yard dash, Valgene Schierling in the high hurdles, and the 440 relay team of Greg Nunn, Vininski, James Whitcomb, and White. Eikermann's winning toss of 171-1 in the discus set a CIC and school record, and Vininski tied the CIC mark of 9.7 seconds in the 100. Wayne Rogers earned a sixth victory for the Hornets as he tied for 1st in the long jump, but he was officially given 2nd on the basis of the second best jump.

The Hornets' next competition was at the Midwest Federation meet in Kansas City, and Vininski turned in a strong performance in winning the 100 in 9.7 seconds and the 220 in 21.1 seconds to set new meet records in both events. Eikermann placed 2nd in the discus, and 3rds were earned by Valgene Schierling in the high hurdles and the intermediate hurdles, and by the 440-relay team.

The KSTC track squad ended the 1965 season at the NAIA Championships, slipping to 6th in the team standings. John Camien turned in his final performance as a Hornet, overcoming the effects of his long illness to win a fourth consecutive mile title in 4:10.1. Since his graduation from KSTC, Camien has been honored by induction into the NAIA Track and Field Hall of Fame for his outstanding performances in the NAIA meet during his career. Eikermann was KSTC's only other All-American, placing 3rd in the discus with a throw of 163-3, and Vininski earned the Hornets' final point with a 6th in the 220-yard dash.

Fran Welch Era

The 1965 track season capped the long and successful coaching career of Francis G. Fran Welch. Welch's accomplishments in his 38 years as head coach rank him as one of the outstanding track coaches in the United States. His Emporia State teams claimed eight conference cross country crowns, six indoor track conference titles, 12 outdoor track conference crowns, four NAIA cross country championships, one NCAA small college cross country title, and one NAIA track and field title. In NAIA competition, Welch-coached athletes won 18 individual titles, more than any other school through 1965. Welch coached international teams that represented the United States abroad, including the 1960 Women's Olympic track team. He was honored in 1960 when the Emporia State stadium was renamed Welch Stadium, and he was a charter inductee into the NAIA Hall of Fame and the Emporia State Athletic Hall of Honor. His contributions to the Hornet track and field program have been unmatched by anyone in the history of the University.

1966

Philip Delavan became the ESU head track and field and cross country coach in the fall of 1965.

In January of 1966, the NAIA added the National Indoor Track and Field meet to its schedule, and Delavan entered the Hornets in the first annual meet. KSTC came away with a 4th place finish in the meet, as Richard Boehringer won the long jump with a leap of 23-2 and teammates Wayne Rogers and Ira Gardner placed 4th and 5th respectively in the event. Placing 3rd to gain All-American honors along with Boehringer were Bill Fraley in the 600-yard run, Bob Camien in the mile, and Clarence Robe in the pole vault. Albert Burnes and John Swaim placed 5th in the 880 and 1000-yard runs, respectively, while the mile relay team placed 5th and the two-mile relay team took 4th to round out the Hornet scoring. Delavan's track team was also very young, and most of the men winning places were freshmen and sophomores.

Bob Camien received an honor when he was invited to compete in the Toronto Maple Leaf Indoor meet in Toronto, Canada, and he finished 4th in the mile run while his brother, former Hornet star John, won the event. KSTC concluded the indoor season at the Kansas State Relays, and the Hornets unveiled another strong representative in the distance medley relay, winning the college event in 10:07.3 with the team of Burnes, Fraley, Brinsko, and Camien. Camien also placed 3rd in the open mile. However, the Hornets were unable to defend their six consecutive CIC indoor titles, as the meet had been discontinued.

Opening the outdoor season at the Arkansas Relays, the Hornet thinclads turned in some strong performances, the most notable by sophomore Rich Boehringer. Boehringer won the triple jump with a leap of 50-2, the third best mark posted in the nation during the 1966 season and a school record. He also placed 2nd in the long jump with a leap of 23-9. Gaining 3rds for the Hornets were Val Schierling in the 120 high hurdles and the 440 hurdles, Richard DiPaola in the shot put, and the Hornet 880 and distance medley relay teams. Tom Jones also turned in a noteworthy performance, setting a meet record of 6-6 in winning the freshman division high jump.

Once again, the Hornets had a strong distance medley team on the major relay circuit. The foursome of Burnes, Fraley, Brinsko, and Camien placed 4th at the Texas Relays in 9:55.8 and placed 2nd at the Kansas Relays in 9:54.8. The Hornets gained a 3rd place finish from the 440-relay team at KU, but it is not known who composed the team. It would probably have been four of the following; Ron Cluts, Orville Brown, Fraley, Jim Whitcomb or Jim McClanahan. These five men combined at other meets during the season to form strong 440 and 880 sprint teams. Boehringer earned another 3rd at the Kansas Relays, leaping 48-7 ½ in the triple jump. Schierling rounded out the Hornet place winners at Lawrence, taking 4th in the 440-yard hurdles with a time of 53.4 seconds. Janell Smith, the coed speedster, won the women's open 100-yard dash in 11.1 seconds at the Kansas meet. The Hornet relay teams were unable to continue this success at the Drake Relays the following week, however, and KSTC did not earn a place at the third stop on the relay circuit.

Philip Delavan: Coach

Philip Delavan became the ESU head track and field and cross country coach in 1965. He had served as head track coach at Central Missouri State University from 1963 to 1965, previous to which he had been an assistant at Baylor University for one year and an assistant at Iowa State University for two years. Delavan had attended school at Iowa State from 1955-1959, during which time he was one of the best shot putters in the nation. In 1957, he placed 1st in the shot put in the Kansas Relays, and during the same year placed 6th in the finals of the NCAA shot put.

Richard Boehringer: National Champion

In January of 1966, the Hornets competed in the first NAIA National Indoor Track and Field meet held in Kansas City, Missouri. KSTC's Richard Boehringer won the long jump. Boehringer was also an outstanding triple jumper, jumping 50-2, an ESU record that stood for 42 years. He finished 2nd in the NAIA outdoor triple jump in 1967.

Janell Smith

Representing Emporia State in the NAIA Indoor, although unofficially, was a freshman coed named Janell Smith. Smith, from Fredonia, Kansas, was one of the top female track stars in the world, and at the age of 17, she had represented the United States in the 1964 Olympic Games. In the semifinals of the Olympic 400-meter, in which she just missed qualifying for the final, Smith set an American record of 54.5 seconds. Later that same year, she set the world indoor mark of 54.0 seconds in the 400-meter, and in 1965, Smith lowered her outdoor American record to 53.4 seconds. Smith had twice been named to the All-American Women's Track and Field team by the AAU. At the 1966 NAIA indoor meet, Smith won the 60-yard dash in 7.0 seconds and the 440-yard dash in 57.9

For the previous few seasons, the Emporia Relays, sandwiched between Texas and Kansas on the circuit, had been attracting a very strong field of college and university teams. The Hornets picked up three victories in their home Emporia Relays meet, Boehringer in the triple jump, and the 440, and 880 relay teams.

For the second consecutive year, Fort Hays came from behind to nip Emporia in the CIC meet, as the Tigers scored 35 ½ points in the final four events to finish 10 points ahead of the Hornets. Co-captain Wayne Rogers was a double winner for KSTC, setting a CIC record of 47-6 in an upset win over teammate Boehringer in the triple jump, and taking the long jump with a leap of 22-9. Freshman Bill Fraley won the 100-yard dash in 9.6 seconds, a time that bettered the conference mark but was not allowed because of an excessive tailwind. The 440-relay team of Cluts, Brown, Fraley, and Whitcomb won, as did DiPaola in the discus and Dean Woodson in the javelin. The victory by Woodson was a pleasant surprise for Delavan, as Woodson had been out for track for only two weeks. Despite the lack of practice, Woodson uncorked a throw of 220-3 ¼ to win the conference title. Val Schierling was the Hornets' top performer in the Missouri Valley meet and the NAIA nationals, winning the Valley title in the high hurdles in 14.2 seconds and tying for 1st in the 400-meter hurdles with Wally Young of Pittsburg. Schierling ended the Hornets' season by placing 5th in the intermediates and 6th in the highs at the NAIA Championships to earn KSTC's only places in the meet. The 1966 season was the only time during the decade that Emporia State failed to place in the top 10 teams at the NAIA outdoor meet.

1967

With the addition of a strong group of freshmen, headlined by Allan Feuerbach, the 1967 Hornet track team returned to the dominance enjoyed earlier in the decade. KSTC thinclads competed in the NAIA Indoor meet, where the Hornets finished 7th on the strength of Bob Camien's 2nd place in the mile behind John Mason of Fort Hays, and Camien's anchor carry on the 3rd place two-mile relay team.

Ryun goes sub-4 at Welch Stadium

The feature of the 1966 Emporia Relays was the entry of Kansas University's freshman team, starring Jim Ryun. Ryun anchored the KU four-mile relay team to a national freshman record of 16:53.9, running a split of 3:58, the only sub-four minute mile ever run in Welch Stadium. Ryun's presence in the competition drew one of the largest crowds in the history of the Relays.

Freshman Doug Caywood earned the final place, taking 6th in the pole vault, while Feuerbach just missed earning a point for KSTC, finishing 7th in the shot put.

Valgene Schierling: Outstanding Hurdler
During his collegiate career, Schierling won four conference hurdle championships and set school records in the short and long hurdles, as well as the indoor 600-yard run. Schierling continued his association with ESU as the head coach of the women's basketball team, becoming at the time the winningest women's basketball coach in school history.

Despite many outstanding performances by Hornet trackmen on the outdoor relay circuit, the efforts of junior Val Schierling were undoubtedly the most noteworthy. Schierling opened the outdoor season at the Arkansas Relays, setting a meet record of 53.2 seconds in winning the 440-yard intermediate hurdles and winning the high hurdles in 14.2 seconds. He had a very busy day at the Texas Relays one week after Arkansas, running a 53.2 second time in the 440 hurdles prelims, a 48.9 440-yard split on the non-qualifying mile relay team, 14.3 seconds in the high hurdles prelims, and winning the 440 hurdles in 51.7 seconds to top the day off. Schierling's time of 51.7 was the fastest recorded in the United States to that point in the season. Next, Schierling set a meet record of 52.9 seconds in his specialty at the Emporia Relays, then moved on to the second stop on the Midwest circuit. He gained his second victory toward the Triple Crown while setting a Kansas Relays record of 52.6 seconds in the 440 hurdles. Unfortunately, Schierling was upset in his bid for the Grand Slam when he finished 4th at the Drake Relays, again running 52.6 seconds. Besides placing 4th in the intermediates at Drake, Schierling ran on the Hornet mile relay team with Ron Cluts, Pando Markuly, and Bill Fraley that placed 5th in 3:17.5.

Two other Hornets, both competing in the freshman division, set Arkansas Relays records. Caywood posted a mark of 13-7 in the pole vault, and Feuerbach set a shot put mark of 52-8 ½. Feuerbach also won the freshman division discus, while 2nds in the varsity division were earned by Dean Woodson in the javelin and the distance medley foursome of Fraley, Roger Bruning, Bill Jacobs, and Camien. With Frank Hensley running in place of Bruning, the medley team placed 4th at Texas. Camien turned in a superb anchor on this relay, running a 4:07 mile split to pull the Hornets from 12th to 4th, and then came back to win the university/college division mile run in 4:09.9, churning a 57 second last quarter to run away from the field. Feuerbach won a third Texas Relays title for the Hornets, taking the freshman division shot put with a throw of 54-1.

At the Kansas Relays, Feuerbach again won the freshman division shot put, setting a new meet record of 54-5 ½. The Texas Relays medley foursome placed 4th at both Kansas and Drake, with times of 10:03.6 and 10:06.9, respectively. KSTC's javelin throwers were also successful on the circuit, as Marty McGlinn and Woodson placed 4th and 5th, respectively, at Kansas, and Woodson finished 4th at Drake a week later. McGlinn and Feuerbach competed at the Southwest Missouri Relays rather than at Drake, and McGlinn won the javelin while Feuerbach set a meet record of 53-10 in winning the shot put.

The Hornets ended the regular season by regaining the CIC championship after a two-year drought, scoring 113 points, the third highest point total in conference history, to upend defending champion Fort Hays State. Rich Boehringer, Schierling and Camien were the workhorses for Emporia. Boehringer, as expected, won the triple jump and long jump, posting a new CIC record of 49-3 in the triple jump. He provided a pleasant surprise, however, in also winning the high jump. Schierling set a conference record of 52.8 seconds in winning the 440 hurdles, won the 440-yard dash in 49.0 seconds, and placed 2nd in the high hurdles to Young of Pitt. Although Camien did not win an event, he had an outstanding two-day effort. On Friday, Camien finished 2nd in the three-mile run in 14:25.5, then came back on Saturday to earn 2nds in the mile and 880 with times of 4:16.7 and 1:53.9, respectively, and place 3rd in the steeplechase. Camien ran 9:16.4 in the steeple, but the race did not include any water barrier jumps, a standard part of the steeplechase event. Other 1sts were earned by Feuerbach in the shot put with a school and conference record throw of 55-1 ½, Woodson in the javelin, Caywood in the pole vault, and Fraley with his second consecutive victory in the 100-yard dash.

Two weeks after the CIC victory, Schierling won two of the three Hornet 1sts at the Missouri Valley AAU meet. He won the intermediate hurdles with a Valley record of 52.9 seconds, and won the high hurdles in 14.5 seconds. Boehringer provided KSTC's other victory, winning the triple jump, while Caywood placed 2nd in the pole vault and Camien earned a 3rd in the mile.

Emporia State scored 28 points to place 6th in the 1967 NAIA Outdoor Championships. Feuerbach gained a major portion of these points in winning the shot put, his toss of 56-2 ¼ smashing his three week old school record by over one foot. Boehringer leaped 48-4 ¼ to place 2nd in the triple jump and earn All-American honors, while Schierling rounded out KSTC's All-Americans, taking 3rd in the 440 hurdles with a personal best time of 51.4 seconds. Schierling also placed 5th in the high hurdles, and Camien picked up another 5th for the Hornets, running 9:29.2 in the steeplechase.

Schierling ended the 1967 season competing in the National AAU meet. He ran the high and intermediate hurdles, but did not qualify for the finals in either event. At the conclusion of the season, Schierling was chosen the 1967 "Outstanding Male Track Athlete" in the Missouri Valley Association of the AAU. The Missouri Valley Association included all the colleges and universities in the Midwest, so this was a great honor for Schierling and KSTC.

1968

The 1968 season was the final year of competition in the Central Conference. Starting in the spring of 1969, the Hornets would be members of the Rocky Mountain Athletic Conference, consisting of schools from New Mexico, Colorado, Utah, Nebraska, and Kansas. KSTC was to compete in the Plains Division of the RMAC along with all the other members of the old CIC. The Hornets won the last CIC track meet, scoring 102 points to outdistance Pittsburg State by 12 points. Bob Camien repeated his previous year's performance, finishing 2nd in the three-mile, the mile, and the 880, and taking 3rd in the steeplechase with times of 14:10, 4:11.9, 1:53.6, and 9:35.8, respectively. Schierling lowered his conference record in the intermediate hurdles by .7 of a second, and tied the CIC mark of 14.1 seconds in the high hurdles while winning both events. Two other Hornets set new conference marks, Feuerbach erasing his own record in the shot put with a winning throw of 56-5, and Caywood setting a record of 14-6 ¼ in winning the pole vault. Fraley won his third straight 100-yard dash title, tying the conference mark of 9.7 seconds, while Tom Jones placed 1st in the high jump and the 440-relay team of Pando Markuly, Ira Gardner, Fraley and Hilo Smith won.

During the 1968 season, the Hornet thinclads also earned honors at the Indoor Nationals, the Arkansas Relays and the "big three" - Texas, Kansas, and Drake. In the NAIA Indoor meet, Camien took 3rd in the mile run to earn All-American honors, his time of 4:10.6 breaking the NAIA record for the event. Fourths were earned by Feuerbach in the shot put, the mile relay team, and the two-mile relay team. Also earning points for KSTC were Jones in a tie for 5th in the high jump and Schierling in 6th in the 600-yard run. These efforts earned Emporia State 6th place as a team in the NAIA Indoor. Camien continued his noteworthy performances during the remainder of the indoor season, winning the mile at the State

Federation meet and the Kansas State Relays, as well as anchoring KSTC's winning distance medley relay at K-State. Jim Doyle, Fraley, and Brinsko joined Camien on this team that posted the outstanding time of 10:01.8. Feuerbach raised his school record at both meets, throwing 56-5 in the Federation meet and 56-8 ½ at K-State.

Opening the 1968 outdoor season, the Hornets won two events at the Arkansas Relays. Feuerbach won the shot put with a 56-foot throw, and the four-mile relay team of Dennis Delmott, Bob Szymanski, Brinsko and Camien won in 17:46.1, defeating Drake University by one second. Seconds were earned by the distance medley team of Jim Hensley, Fraley, Brinsko and Camien, and Doug Caywood in a tie for 2nd in the pole vault. Earning 3rd place for the Hornets were Jim Correll in the javelin and Schierling in the 440-yard hurdles.

Asphalt Track
Emporia State's track facility was greatly upgraded during the fall of 1967. A new track surface, consisting of two inches of asphalt covered by one and one-half inches of a special rubberized surfacing, was laid down, replacing the cinders. This new track gave the Hornets one of the best outdoor facilities in the state. In this picture, Coach Philip Delavan and former coach Fran Welch observe the new asphalt being laid.

Schierling had been trying for some time to convince Coach Delavan that he could run a competitive 880, but Delavan had remained skeptical. After the 1967 track season Schierling ran a half-mile on his own to prove to Coach Delavan that he could run it well. His performance was so noteworthy that Delavan consented, and when Schierling was not allowed to run the intermediate hurdles at Texas because of the four-year rule, Delavan ran him on the two-mile relay and added him in place of Frank Hensley on the 880 carry of the distance medley. Delavan's decision was highly rewarded, as the distance medley foursome placed 2nd in 10:04.0 despite Schierling getting knocked down on the lead-off carry and losing several yards on the field. This misfortune prevented the team from winning the Triple Crown in the event. The two-mile relay team, with Brinsko, Szymanski, and Hensley joining Schierling, placed 6th in 7:49.0. Feuerbach was KSTC's only winner at Texas, setting a school record of 57-2 in winning the shot put. Camien, the defending champ in the mile run, slipped to 5th in the event in 4:08.9.

However, Camien won the Wes Santee mile the next week at the Kansas Relays, running 4:18.4 on a very muddy track. Feuerbach picked up his second win of the Triple Crown, taking the shot put while extending his school record by one-fourth of an inch. The Hornets' third victory at KU was earned by the distance medley team, the same foursome that competed at Texas, running 9:59.2 to win the event. Camien ran a strong anchor to come from behind and catch the Loyola of Chicago anchorman. In addition to running a 1:52.2 split on the winning distance medley, Schierling finished 3rd in the 400-meter hurdles in 52.8 seconds. The two-mile relay team placed 4th, and Dennis Delmott took 5th in the 5000-meter run to round out the Hornet scoring.

The distance relay teams turned in two memorable performances the next weekend at the Drake Relays. The best effort was by the two-mile relay team of Hensley, Camien, Brinsko, and Schierling, which set a school and Drake Relays record of 7:30.0 in winning the event. Camien and Schierling both ran 1:50 splits on their respective carries. These two came back in the distance medley, along with Brinsko and Fraley, to win the event in 9:51.1, the second fastest time ever recorded by a Hornet team in the event. Camien turned in a 4:07 mile split to run down Loyola College for the second consecutive week. Feuerbach broke his school record in the shot for the fifth time during the season with a toss of 57-5, but placed only 3rd. Dean Woodson also placed 3rd with a toss of 220-10 in the javelin.

After the CIC victory, the KSTC trackmen attended the Missouri Valley AAU meet. Rich Boehringer, after missing much of the season with an injury, took 1st in the triple jump with a leap of 47-6. Roger Bruning had the Hornets' only other victory, winning the 880 in 2:09.0 on a track so muddy that the athletes could hardly run, making all the times ridiculously slow for the caliber of competition. Feuerbach finished 3rd in the shot and 2nd in the hammer, while Tom Jones placed 4th in the high jump.

Emporia State finished in a tie for 5th with St. Cloud, Minnesota, in the 1968 NAIA National Outdoor meet. Feuerbach took two 2nds, losing to James Bagby of Prairie View, Texas, in the shot put, and finished as runner-up in the hammer throw, a new event in the NAIA meet. Thirds were earned by Camien in the 1500-meter run in 3:48.9 and by Schierling in the 400-meter hurdles in 51.6 seconds. Schierling had set an NAIA record of 51.2 seconds in the semifinals, but could not repeat the performance in the finals. Boehringer rounded out the Hornet scoring, finishing 4th in the triple jump.

Schierling and Feuerbach went on to compete in the USTFF National Championships in Houston, Texas. Feuerbach took 3rd in the shot put with a toss of 56-5 while Schierling finished 4th in the 440-yard hurdles, running 51.1 seconds to set a school record that still stands. This meet ended Feuerbach's season, even though he had qualified for the U.S. Olympic Trials with his 2nd place finish in the NAIA Championships. Schierling, however, had not yet qualified for the Trials and was attempting to meet the standard in the National AAU meet in California. Unfortunately, he finished 11th overall and as the 7th American in the 400-meter hurdles to just miss qualifying. However, the day after the AAU, as Schierling and Coach Delavan were preparing to leave for home, they were informed that Schierling had been chosen by the Olympic committee to fill the final spot in the 400-meter hurdles at the Olympic Trials being held the next weekend in Los Angeles. Sixteen men qualified for each event, and the standards for qualifying were top six in the NCAA and the NAAU championships, top two in the NAIA, and 1st in the Armed Service Championships. The final qualifier was chosen by the Olympic committee, and Schierling was the entry chosen for the 400 hurdles.

Schierling stayed out in Los Angeles and trained during the week between the AAU meet and the Trials. The Los Angeles meet was the first Olympic Trials, with the top 10 in each event qualifying for the high altitude training camp in Colorado. The eight athletes who qualified for the finals in each event at Los Angeles automatically gained a berth at the high altitude camp, while the eight who were not in the finals ran a second heat to determine the final two men to attend the Colorado camp. Schierling did not qualify for the finals, and in the second heat he just missed a berth on the training team finishing 3rd in 51.3 seconds. The meet was Canada's Olympic Trials and Schierling defeated all the athletes who made the Canadian team.

1969

Because of the loss of many of the outstanding performers who had helped lead KSTC to two consecutive conference track titles, Coach Delavan termed the 1969 track season a rebuilding year. However, he had a solid base upon which to rebuild, including the broad shoulders of junior Allan Feuerbach. Feuerbach opened the indoor season by winning the shot put at the NAIA National Indoor meet, his winning toss of 57-5 ½ setting new NAIA and KSTC records. Brinsko placed 3rd in the mile at 4:15.8 and Darrell

Patterson took 3rd in the 1000-yard run in 2:14.4 to both earn All-America recognition. Fourth places were taken by Jim Kisel in the high jump, by the mile relay team, and by the two-mile relay team. Emporia State placed 4th as a team in the meet on the strength of these efforts.

Cloud 9
In the 1960s and early 70s, the Cloud 9 airbag was used. It was inflated by a fan. Fortunately the pit had a short history as athletes often penetrated to the bottom of the bag or bounced off.

Feuerbach added more than one foot to his school record when he threw 58-7 in the Kansas State-Oklahoma indoor dual, in which he entered as a practice meet. Feuerbach concluded the indoor season setting a meet record of 58-1 ¾ at the Kansas State Relays. He continued this success during the outdoor season, although the record-breaking spree ended temporarily. Feuerbach again won the Arkansas Relays shot title and finished 2nd in the discus. Dean Woodson was also a winner at Arkansas, taking the javelin with a toss of 230-7 with teammate Jim Correll finishing 2nd behind him. Thirds were earned by Kisel in the high jump at 6-7 and by the four-mile relay team of Nee, Delmott, Patterson, and Thomas.

Delmott's performance in the three-mile run was the highlight for KSTC at the Texas Relays. Although he finished 8th, Delmott ran the noteworthy time of 13:57.9 to post the second best time ever run in the event by a Hornet. Feuerbach and Correll did not make the finals in their respective events. While these men competed at Texas, another group of Hornets entered the Oklahoma Invitational. Kisel came away with a victory in the high jump with a school record leap of 6-8 ½, and Woodson won the javelin. Kisel's victory in the high jump led a Hornet sweep in the event. Tom Jones and Ed Glover finished 2nd and 3rd, respectively.

In Lawrence, at the second stop on the relay circuit, Feuerbach took 2nd in the hammer throw and teammate Gary Lawrence finished 3rd. Feuerbach could manage only a 5th place in the shot, finishing behind KU's outstanding trio of shot putters, Karl Salb, Steve Wilhelm, and Doug Knop. The three Jayhawks had taken the top three places in the NCAA indoor meet earlier in the season. Delmott finished 4th in the six-mile, running a time of 30:10.3, and the Hornets' mile and distance medley relay teams finished 5th. Dropped batons cost KSTC potential places in both the sprint medley and 880 relays.

Two Hornet relay teams, the distance medley and the 880, both earned 4th place at the Drake Relays. The weather was wet and miserable, and the rain-slicked track caused many falls. One occurred in the finals of the 440 relay when the runner in lane two fell and ended up out in lane five, knocking down Chester Bluett of KSTC. The weather conditions also affected the placing of Delmott, who fell in the three-mile.

Fort Hays regained the conference title in 1969, defeating runner-up Emporia State by 33 points in the first Rocky Mountain conference meet. The Hornets' strength was in the throwing events, as Feuerbach won the shot put, Woodson and Correll placed 1st and 2nd, respectively, in the javelin, and Ray Rodman led a 1-2-3-5 Hornet finish in the discus. Rodman pulled off the upset of favored teammate Feuerbach with a personal best throw of 170-2, one of the best throws posted in the NAIA during the season. Rodman, a senior transfer, had started the season as KSTC's fourth best thrower. However, by the middle of the season, he had progressed to the second best position behind Feuerbach, and Rodman defeated his celebrated teammate for the first time at the Kansas Relays. His second victory over Feuerbach earned

Rodman a conference title. Ted Potts ran 9.6 seconds in the 100-yard dash to win the event and tie the school record, while Bill Fraley, the three-time defending champ in the event, finished 3rd. Jim Kisel rounded out the Hornet champions, winning the high jump and extending his school record to 6-9.

The Emporia State trackmen earned two victories in the 1969 Missouri Valley meet. Dennis Nee won the 10,000-meter run in 32:16.2, and Feuerbach won the hammer throw. Feuerbach added a 2nd place in the shot put and a 4th in the discus, while Bluett took 2nd in the 440-yard hurdles. Adding 3rds to the Hornet effort were Patterson in the mile run and Rodman in the discus.

The Hornets ended the season placing 5th in the NAIA National Outdoor on the strength of the weight team. Feuerbach led the effort with three places, taking 2nd to Bagby in the shot put, 5th in the discus, and 5th in the hammer. Other KSTC place winners were Lawrence, who took 2nd in the hammer while setting a school record of 150-10 and Woodson, who placed 3rd in the javelin with a toss of 218-5.

1970

During the initial years of the decade, the KSTC track program carried a strong flavor of the sixties, because many of the top performers were carryovers from those very successful years. The 1970 track season, though, was dominated by Allan Feuerbach. When Feuerbach came to E-State from an Iowa high school in the fall of 1966, he carried only 180 pounds on his six-foot frame, and despite being a 60-foot thrower in high school, Feuerbach was considered too small to be an outstanding college shot putter. However, he was committed to making himself a national and world class shot putter, and through intensive weight workouts and training, he steadily improved his performances during his first three seasons at ESU. During his senior year in 1970, with his weight up to 235 pounds and his strength greatly improved, he became one of the top throwers in the country.

Feuerbach opened the indoor season with his first 60 foot throw as a collegian, winning the Drake Federation meet with a meet and school record toss of 61-5 ½. He bettered the mark a few weeks later at the NAIA Indoor meet, setting a meet record of 62-8 ¾ to win "Outstanding Performer" honors. Feuerbach's teammates Darrell Patterson and John Wilson earned 3rds in the 1000-yard run and the long jump respectively to garner All-American recognition along with Feuerbach. These three athletes led Emporia State to a 5th place team finish in the NAIA indoor meet.

Seven days after his NAIA performance, Feuerbach threw 62-11 ¼ at the Oklahoma City Invitational to set an indoor school record that still stands. He finished 2nd in the meet to the American record toss of 66-10 by Karl Salb of KU, but defeated Wilhelm and Knop of the Jayhawks. These three KU stars scored a second consecutive 1-2-3 finish at the NCAA Indoor meet later in the 1970 season. Feuerbach continued his outstanding throws through the remainder of the indoor season, tossing 62-11 at KU, 62-6 ¼ to set a meet record at the Iowa Federation indoor, and throwing 62-11 at the National AAU meet to place 4th.

At the Arkansas Relays Feuerbach was voted "Outstanding Performer" for the second time during the season, earning the honor by throwing 63-8 ½ to win the shot and set a school and meet record, and throwing 171-9 to win the discus. This mark in the discus was also a new school record. Feuerbach's winning toss in the shot ranked as the third best throw in the United States throughout the regular season. Freshman Larry Hynek made a clean sweep of the throwing events for the Hornets, winning the javelin with the toss of 209-4.

KSTC's star shot putter was unable to compete at the Texas Relays because he was a fourth year trackman, an NCAA rule that had handicapped the Hornets' top performers since the early days of the program. However, the Hornets did manage to earn a place at Texas, the sprint medley team taking 3rd due to the brilliant 1:50.9 anchor half-mile by Patterson. Patterson was in last place when he received the baton, but he pulled the team of Ted Potts, Wilson, and Chester Bluett up to 3rd for the Hornets' only points. The E-State relay teams were unsuccessful at Kansas, but several individuals picked up the slack and placed well. Feuerbach, competing in a special invitational shot put event against the best throwers in the world, placed 3rd behind Randy Matson, the world record holder, and Salb of KU. In the university/college division, Hynek placed 3rd in the javelin, Gary Lawrence placed 4th in the hammer, Ed Cox took 5th in the shot put, Patterson placed 5th in the mile, and Wilson finished 6th in the long jump. Dennis Delmott did not place in the six-mile, but ran the outstanding time of 29:24.0 to set the school record.

Al Feuerbach: National Champion
Al Feuerbach won NAIA shotput titles outdoors in 1967 and 1970 and indoors in 1969 and 1970. He also had four 2nd place showings at national meets in the shot put and hammer throw. He set both NAIA records in the outdoor and indoor shot put.

Coach Delavan decided to by-pass the final stop on the Midwest circuit and entered the full team in the Southwest Missouri Relays. The Hornets picked up four victories: from Feuerbach in the shot put with a meet record throw of 62-8 ½, Wilson in the long jump, Dennis Nee in the three-mile and the sprint medley team of Bluett, Ira Gardner, Potts and Patterson. KSTC's next two competitions were dual meets and several school records were the distinguishing features of these meets. Feuerbach upped his own discus record to 178-3 in the meet against Central Missouri, and senior Doug Caywood pole vaulted 14-8 ½ in the same meet to break C. R. Robes' school record mark. The next week against Pittsburg State, Feuerbach rested while Caywood set a vault record of 15-4.

The Hornets ended the season in fine fashion, upsetting defending champion and favored Fort Hays by 34 points to win the RMAC title. Wilson and Feuerbach were double winners for KSTC, Wilson taking the long jump at 24-9 ½ and the triple jump at 46-8, while Feuerbach won the discus and shot put with marks of 169-0 and 60-9 ¾ respectively. Also winners for the Hornets were Lawrence in the hammer with the meet record throw of 149-8, Potts in the 100-yard dash at 9.9 seconds, and Bluett in the 440-yard hurdles with a time of 54.0 seconds. The Hornets' strength in the weight events and good depth offset Hays' dominance in the distance events to provide the Hornets with victory.

As a senior, Feuerbach won the NAIA shot put title with a toss of 61-4 ¾ to regain the title he won as a freshman, and also placed 5th in the discus with a toss of 161-10. Wilson added a 3rd place finish in the long jump to earn All-American honors and help lead KSTC to a 9th place team finish. Wilson's jump of 24-9 ½, the same mark he had posted in winning the event in the RMAC, moved him into second in school history behind Noel Certain's 1960 school record.

Although this was the last time Feuerbach officially represented KSTC, his greatest achievements were yet to come. Later in the summer of 1970, while competing for the Southern Cal Striders, Feuerbach posted the two best marks to that point of his career, throwing 64-1 ½ in the Orange County Invitational and 65-0 in placing 3rd at the National AAU. By placing in the AAU meet, Feuerbach earned a trip to go Europe for AAU sponsored meets in France, Germany, and Russia.

1971

The 1971 Hornet track squad was without three of the five 1970 conference champions, with Feuerbach lost to graduation, Ted Potts passing up his last year of eligibility to work in the KSTC counseling department, and Chester Bluett severely injured in an automobile accident in February. Conference champ and All-American John Wilson was one of several strong individuals who returned, but the losses left KSTC without the team depth of previous years.

The Hornets did not experience a great deal of success during the indoor season, with junior Dennis Nee garnering most of the honors. Nee placed 5th in the two-mile at the NAIA Indoor meet, running 9:18.7 to earn honorable mention All-American honors, then won the two-mile in the RMAC Plains Division Indoor meet. Due to bad weather, only three teams competed in the first and only attempt at an RMAC indoor meet, and results showed Pittsburg State to be a clear winner over E-State and host Omaha. Nee's victory was the only 1st earned by a Hornet thinclad.

The Hornets' strengths during the 1971 outdoor season were in the distances, led by juniors Nee and Patterson, and in the javelin, led by sophomore Larry Hynek and senior Jim Correll. Hynek was outstanding during the regular season, winning his second straight javelin title at the Arkansas Relays with a toss of 229-9, placing 2nd in the Emporia Relays at 237-10, and taking 4th at KU with a throw of 235-7. Hynek's mark in the Emporia Relays set a new KSTC school record, surpassing the mark of 231-3 set in 1963 by Kent Hurn, who coached Hynek in high school. Correll, overshadowed by his teammate during the regular season, came up with two notable efforts in the RMAC regional qualifying meet and the RMAC championships to defeat Hynek. In the region meet, which was a new event that qualified the top three individuals and relays for the RMAC meet, Correll threw 228-1 to win the javelin. The following weekend at the RMAC championships, Correll came up with the greatest effort of his career to win the event and set a new conference and school record of 247-8. Hynek, after 3rd place finishes in the two RMAC meets, regained the upper hand in the NAIA nationals with a toss of 229-10 to take 6th, defeating Correll by seven feet.

Nee and Patterson helped form another in a long line of strong KSTC distance medley teams in 1971. These two, joined by Mark Sevier and Jim White, formed a team that won at the Arkansas Relays in 10:17.9 when the initial winning team was disqualified, won at the Emporia Relays, and placed 2nd at the Kansas Relays in 9:58.0. Patterson turned in a superb third carry for the Hornet team at KU, running his 1320-yard leg in 2:57.9 to bring KSTC's team from 5th to 1st. Nee turned in a game effort on the anchor, but lost on the finishing kick by .8 of a second. Patterson also earned an individual place at KU, running the fast time of 4:07.0 to take 5th in the mile. Because of his strong performances during the season, Patterson was a heavy favorite to win the RMAC mile title. However, due to an unfortunate set of circumstances in the RMAC regional meet, Patterson failed to qualify for the conference championships.

In the region meet, Patterson was leading the mile at the end of the third lap when he was bumped into the curb. By the time he regained his stride, he was in 4th place, and despite a strong finish, he ended in that position two-tenths of a second behind the winner. Nee, after a 2nd place finish in the three-mile run in the conference qualifying meet, came back to win the event at the RMAC and defeat Mike McDonald of Adams State, who had posted the top mark in the event in the NAIA during the 1971 season. The only other conference winner for KSTC was Mike Sharp, who won the discus with the toss of 157-5. The defending team champion Hornets fell to a disappointing 5th in the RMAC meet due to the failure of several key performers to qualify and the disappointing finishes of several individuals in the conference meet, most notably John Wilson. Wilson, the defending RMAC champion in the long jump and triple jump, garnered only a 4th place finish in the long jump in the conference meet to cap off a season well below the standard of performance that had come to be expected of him. The reason for the lack of results from Wilson is unknown, although he may have been injured during the season.

1972

Al Feuerbach: World Record Holder

In his career, Al Feuerbach set new indoor and outdoor world records for the shot put, setting an indoor mark of 68-11 in 1971 and extending it to 69-5 ¾ in 1973, and setting an outdoor record of 71-7 in 1973 while becoming only the second man in history to break the 70-foot barrier. Feuerbach also represented the United States in two Olympic Games, placing 5th in the shot in 1972 and 4th in the event in 1976, thus becoming only the fourth KSTC athlete to compete in the Olympics. In addition, Feuerbach qualified for the 1980 United States Olympic team but did not get to compete in the Moscow Games because of the United States boycott.

Since his graduation from Emporia State, Feuerbach has been honored with induction into the ESU, NAIA, Drake Relays, and Kansas Sports Halls of Fame. His accomplishments, both as a Hornet and after his graduation, rate him as one of the greatest track and field performers in Emporia State's rich history.

Coach Delavan predicted a good year for the 1972 Hornet track squad despite the fact that it was also a young team, with Nee and Patterson once again the only seniors on the squad. This prediction proved to be correct as the young Hornets improved steadily and wound up the season in the runner-up spot in the RMAC behind the Tigers of Fort Hays. Nee and Patterson capped very successful seasons by winning conference titles in the three-mile and one-mile runs, respectively. Patterson set a new conference record of 4:09.6 in the mile at the regional meet the week prior to the conference championships. Other Hornet winners in the RMAC competition were Art Peals in the high hurdles, Larry Hynek in the javelin, and Jerry Hinson in the discus. Hinson also placed 2nd in the shot put. Hays won only three individual titles but won the team crown with characteristically outstanding depth.

The 1972 track season opened with Nee and Patterson earning places in the NAIA Indoor nationals, finishing 4th in the two-mile and 5th in the 1000-yard run, respectively. In the outdoor opener at Arkansas, Nee earned KSTC's lone victory, winning the university division two-mile in 9:07.6, while the Hornets outstanding pair of weight men, Hynek and Hinson, also posted noteworthy performances. Hynek placed 2nd in the javelin, while Hinson took 2nd in the discus and 3rd in the shot put. The distance medley team of Jim White, Ron Wynn, Tom Quammen and Patterson finished a disappointing 5th due to a dropped baton.

At the Texas Relays, the Hornets picked up two 5th places, from Hynek in the javelin with the throw of 239-4, and the distance medley team with the time of 10:04.6. Nee, running the three-mile at Texas, could manage only a 9th place finish with the time of 14:10.5. However, Nee came back one week later at the Emporia Relays to run the outstanding time of 13:55.0 in the three-mile, setting a new school and Relays record. The Hornets attended the Kansas Relays the weekend after the E-State Relays, but were unable to score in the meet. Because of the lack of results at KU, Coach Delavan decided to bypass the Drake Relays, entering the Hornets in the SW Missouri Relays. Nee responded with another meet record, winning the three-mile with the time of 13:57.7. Other KSTC winners at Missouri were Hinson in the shot and discus, and Ben Pierce in the triple jump. Nee ended the 1972 season and his outstanding career placing 2nd in the 5000-meter run at the NAIA Outdoor meet, running the time of 14:37.6. Nee was the only Hornet place winner in the 1972 national outdoor competition.

1973

Because there were few outstanding individuals who could score in the big relay carnivals during 1973, Delavan began to put more emphasis on depth. Top performers for the Hornets that year were senior tri-captains Jerry Hinson, Larry Hynek and Art Peals, all three returning conference champs and all among the best in the NAIA in their respective events. Hynek posted the best results, placing 4th in the javelin at the Texas Relays with a PR of 242-1, and 4th again at the Kansas Relays with a 240-4 toss. In 1973, the Hornets were members of the Great Plains Athletic Conference, which consisted of the same teams that had comprised the Plains Division of the old Rocky Mountain Conference. Hynek won the javelin in the initial conference meet with the toss of 239-3, and ended his last year as a Hornet placing 2nd in the javelin at the NAIA meet with the toss of 237-9. That effort earned him All-American honors for the first time in his career despite the fact that he had been one of the top throwers in the NAIA during his four years of competition.

Peals also had an outstanding last year, posting a new meet record of 14.2 seconds in the high hurdles at the Emporia Relays, defending his conference title in the highs with the time of 14.4 seconds, and placing 6th in the event at the NAIA national meet to earn honorable mention All-American recognition. Hinson opened the outdoor season very impressively, posting two of the top marks in the NAIA with throws of 54-4 ½ in the shot put and 174-0 in the discus during the Fort Hays dual. Unfortunately, a wrist injury incurred during the Emporia Relays kept him out of competition for most of April. Hinson returned to action in time for the GPAC meet but, still bothered by the injury, he could manage only 3rd place finishes in the shot and discus with marks well below his season's bests. Despite a third individual conference title won by Arnold Sams in the high jump, the Hornets finished a disappointing 4th in the first GPAC meet behind Hays, Northern Colorado, and Pittsburg State.

1974

In February of 1974, the name of KSTC was changed to Emporia Kansas State College. The Hornet thinclads had a new look in addition to the new name, fielding an extremely strong sprint team for the first time since the early 1960s and for one of the few times in the history of the program. The first indication of the strength of the Hornet speedsters came in the District 10 indoor meet at Fort Hays, where the EKSC trackmen won six events and set five meet and fieldhouse records to finish 2nd as a team behind Fort Hays. Alan Johnson had a hand in three of the records, tying the mark of 6.2 seconds in winning the 60-yard dash, setting a mark of 32.6 seconds in winning the 300-yard dash, and teaming with Jimmie Cook, Ron Wynn, and Mark Sevier to win the one-mile relay with the record time of 3:25.3. The other records were set by Sevier in winning the 440-yard dash and Ed Edgerson in winning the triple jump. Gale Knight earned the Hornets' final victory, winning the 176-yard intermediate hurdles in 20.5 seconds. The EKSC trackmen concluded the indoor season at the NAIA national meet, placing 5th in the mile relay with the team of Don Wynn, Ron Wynn, Johnson and Sevier, and taking 6th in the two-mile relay with the team of Dwight Linder, Art Millikin, Steve Mosteller, and Rick Tyler.

A highlight of the 1974 outdoor season came at the Abilene Christian College Relays when the Hornets scored 50 points in the final four events to nose the host Wildcats by two points for the team title. Sevier won the Hornets' only individual title, taking the 440-yard dash in 48.9 seconds, but EKSC's win was due to good depth in the sprints and hurdles.

In addition, the Hornet sprinters led EKSC back to its traditional prominence on the relay circuit. The 440 relay team of Edgerson, R. Wynn, Sevier, and Johnson placed 4th at Kansas in 42.2 seconds and 6th at Drake in 42.3 seconds, despite Wynn pulling a muscle just before the handoff to Sevier at Drake. Johnson turned in a superb individual performance at the Kansas Relays, running a wind-aided 9.46 seconds in the semi-finals of the 100-yard dash. Unfortunately, this time did not qualify him for the finals.

The Hornet trackmen dominated the sprints and hurdles in the evening session of the GPAC meet, but weakness in the weights and distance events put EKSC too far behind, and they ended up in 4th place, one point behind Northern Colorado. Johnson had an outstanding day, setting conference records of 9.5 seconds and 21.2 seconds in winning the 100 and 220-yard dashes, respectively, anchoring the winning 440 relay team of Edgerson, R. Wynn, and Sevier in the GPAC record time of 41.6 seconds, and running on the winning mile relay team with Cook, D. Wynn, and Sevier. Rounding out the winners for Emporia State were Sevier in the 440-yard dash with the time of 48.1 seconds and Gale Knight in the high hurdles with the time of 14.5 seconds. The Hornet sprinters and relay teams went on to compete in the NAIA nationals and, despite posting some noteworthy times (Johnson ran 9.6 and 21.5 in the 100 and 220 respectively and Sevier ran 48.0 in the 440), EKSC thinclads were unable to earn a place in the meet.

1975

The Hornet sprint team was even stronger in 1975 with the return of Alan Johnson, Mark Sevier, Jimmie Cook, Ed Edgerson and Terry Wallace. The addition of junior transfer Dave Neufeldt and Tyrone Grey, a fleet Floral Park, New York freshman, helped replace the graduated Wynn brothers. These speedsters provided the strength upon which EKSC placed a close 2nd to Pittsburg in the indoor District 10 meet. Grey, Edgerson, and Wallace placed 1-3-4 respectively in the 60-yard dash and Sevier, David Thompson, and Neufeldt took 1-3-4, respectively, in the 440-yard dash. Grey and Johnson both tied Pitt State's fieldhouse record of 6.2 seconds in the 60, Grey in the finals and Johnson in the semis, but Johnson was disqualified in the final for a false start. Other Hornet winners were Mark Stanbrough, a sophomore transfer, in the 880-yard run; John Browne, in the two-mile walk; and Arnold Sams, in the high jump. Sams had won the GPAC high jump title in 1973 as a freshman, and after sitting out of competition in 1974, he returned in 1975 to add depth to the Hornet squad.

The Hornets' entry in the 1975 Kansas Relays was highlighted by EKSC's first victory on the major relay circuit since 1968. The win was provided by the 880-yard relay team of Grey, Neufeldt, Sevier, and Johnson in the time of 1:27.4. The Hornet speedsters added two 2nd place finishes, both behind Lincoln University, Missouri, in the mile relay with the time of 3:14.6 and in the 440 relay with the time of 42.1. The mile relay team consisted of the same foursome that won the 880 relay, and Edgerson replaced Neufeldt on the 440 relay. The Hornet sprint teams continued the success at the Drake Relays with the same combinations that had competed at KU. The 440 relay foursome again placed 2nd, running a time of 42.0 seconds, while the 880 and mile relay teams slipped to 4th in 1:26.8 and 3:15.0 respectively. The mile relay quartet got a scare just before the preliminary race when Grey got a cramp in his hamstring, but Stanbrough ran in his place to help the Hornet team qualify for the finals.

Ending the season at the 1975 GPAC meet, the EKSC trackmen scored 103 ½ points to finish a disappointing 3rd, 25 points behind champion Fort Hays. Again, the strength of the team was the sprints. Unfortunately, the Hornet speedsters were unable to duplicate the spectacular results of the previous year despite posting some outstanding times. Mark Sevier, defending 440 champ, and Alan Johnson, defending champ in the 100 and 220, were upset in their specialties, both placing 2nd. In finishing 2nd, though, Sevier broke the school record in the 440 held jointly by Eddie Washington and Melvin Mayo with the time of 47.8 seconds. The Hornet 440 relay team, also the defending champ, finished 2nd with the team of Edgerson, Grey, Sevier and Johnson setting a school record of 41.4 seconds. The only EKSC victory was turned in by the mile relay team of Neufeldt, David Thompson, Johnson, and Sevier in the time of 3:19.2. A pleasant surprise was the 38 points picked up in the field events on the strength of a 2nd in the discus and 3rd in the shot from Chuck Coblentz, and a 2nd in the javelin from Ross Meeker.

1976

Hurt by the loss of most of the strong sprint squad from the previous two years (Alan Johnson and Mark Sevier had graduated, while Tyrone Grey and Ed Edgerson transferred) the Hornet men lacked the strength and depth to field a contending team.

> **Leonard Hall: World Record for Deaf**
> Leonard Hall set a new world record in the three-mile run for a deaf runner of 14:20.2 at the Central Missouri Invitational, shattering the old mark of 14:34.0 held by a Swedish runner. Later that same year, at the U.S. Deaf Olympic tryouts, Hall set an American deaf record of 15:00.1 in winning the 5000-meter run, and also won the 10,000-meter run.

The 1976 indoor season included a 3rd in the shot by Chuck Coblentz at 51-0, a 4th in the mile by Rick Tyler in 4:18 and a 6th in the 1000 by Milliken in the USTFF Championships. At the District 10 meet, no team scores were kept but 2nds were captured by Dave George in the 600, Milliken in the 1000, Tyler in the mile, the mile relay of Neufeldt, George, Bob Ginavin, and T. Wallace and the two mile relay of Milliken, Tyler, Stanbrough, and Jamie McPhee. Coblentz picked up a 3rd in the shot as did Ginavin in the 176 hurdles and the 300.

EKSC opened the outdoor season at the Arkansas Relays, where three Hornets were able to place 3rd: Chuck Coblentz in the discus, Warren Fore in the javelin, and Steve Henry in the long jump. However, this success was marked by the loss of Terry Wallace, one of the few returning sprinters, with a pulled muscle.

The Hornets finished a disappointing 6th in the final GPAC meet with only 29 points, the lowest point total scored by a Hornet team in the conference meet in many years. The highest EKSC finisher was sophomore transfer Kim Bahner, who placed 2nd in the javelin. Emporia State became a member of the newly formed Central States Intercollegiate Conference after the 1976 Great Plains meet, along with Fort Hays State, Pittsburg State, Washburn, Kearney State Nebraska, Wayne State Nebraska, Missouri Southern and Missouri Western. The new conference was formed to reduce the travel costs incurred when competing with the westernmost members of the old GPAC.

1977

The men's track team rebounded from the disappointing 1976 season to post a very successful year in 1977. The indoor season was highlighted by several strong performances in the NAIA national meet and the District meet. These included a 6th place finish in the nationals by the distance medley team of Mark Stanbrough, Brad McKaig, Jamie McPhee and Greg Purkeypile; a 1st place in the district meet by the two-mile relay team of Tom Noonan, McPhee, Rick Brading, and Gary Plank; and Purkeypile's 9:15.1 two-mile in the district meet to earn 2nd place.

The Hornets opened the 1977 outdoor season at the Arkansas Relays, picking up four places. Sam Wilson, Craig Briggs and Kim Bahmer earned 5ths in the shot put, 100-yard dash and javelin respectively, while the 440-yard relay team of Steve Henry, Doug Ray, Briggs and McKaig sprinted to a 6th place finish. The Emporia thinclads turned in another strong performance two weeks after the Arkansas meet, garnering seven 1sts at the Central Missouri State Springfest. The victories were taken by Henry in the 220-yard dash, McKaig in the 440-yard dash, Stanbrough in the 880-yard run, Bahner in the javelin, Wilson in the shot put, the 440 relay team of Henry, Briggs, Ray and McKaig, and the mile relay foursome of Briggs, McKaig, Stanbrough, and Mike Beatty.

The regular season ended with an outstanding effort at the first CSIC meet, described by Coach Delavan as the best effort he had ever seen by a Hornet track team. Fort Hays, with their astounding depth, won the meet easily, but the Hornets put up a fierce battle with Pittsburg State for 2nd and came up just 2 ½ points short, finishing 3rd in the seven team field. Greatly enhancing Emporia State's effort were victories earned by freshman Briggs in the 100-meter with a time of 10.7 seconds, senior Stanbrough in the 800-meter in 1:52.2, the 440 relay team of Henry, Ray, Briggs, and Terry Wallace with the time of 42.0 seconds, and the mile relay team of McKaig, Stanbrough, Beatty, and Henry in a time of 3:16.6. Also helping the Hornet cause were 2nd places gained by Wilson in the shot put and discus, and by Brading in the 400-meter hurdles.

Stanbrough, Brading, and Purkeypile went on to compete in the NAIA national meet in Arkadelphia, Arkansas, and turned in strong performances despite not placing. Stanbrough qualified for the 800-meter finals with an outstanding time of 1:50.9 in the semis, but was able to place only 8th in the final. Brading and Purkeypile came close to personal bests in the 400 hurdles and 5000-meter respectively, but did not make the finals.

Phil Delavan Era

Phil Delavan, Emporia State's track and cross country coach since 1965, resigned in late August of 1978 to become the head women's track and cross country coach at the University of Texas. Delavan posted a very successful career as the head coach of Emporia State's teams, coaching champions Richard Boehringer, Allan Feuerbach, and Kathy Devine, as well as numerous All-Americans. Delavan had been widely recognized among his peers, having served as President of the NAIA Track Coaches Association and the NAIA Cross Country Coaches Association. He had also been selected a member of the high altitude training staff for the 1968 U.S. Olympic team, had served as a coach for the 1970 World University Games United States team and as manager for the 1973 World University Games US. Team, and had served as field coach for the 1972 United States Women's Olympic track team.

1978

The highlight of the men's indoor season was provided by Steve Henry and Tom Noonan, who won the 600-yard run and 1000-yard run, respectively, at the District 10 meet. The Hornet men's squad was decimated by illness at the NAIA indoor meet, with five men unable to attend because of the flu and the three who did compete handicapped by the illness as well. The Hornet men picked up four 6ths in the Arkansas Invitational to open the season: Sam Wilson in the shot put, Rick Brading in the 400 hurdles, Steve Henry in the long jump, and the 440 relay quartet of Henry, Doug Ray, Kent McCray, and James Wells.

The Kansas Relays college divison and women's division were held at Emporia State due to renovation at Memorial Stadium. Kim Bahner was the Hornets' top place winner, taking 3rd in the javelin with a 211-7 toss. Wilson and Mike Williams placed 4th and 5th, respectively, in the shot put, while Henry rounded out the E-State point winners placing 6th in the long jump. The men's team finished 4th in the conference meet behind Hays, Pittsburg, and Kearney. Henry was lost to the Hornets early in the meet when he pulled a muscle in the prelims, costing E-State valuable points. Despite this loss, the Emporia thinclads were leading Kearney by a ½ point going into the mile relay when ESU's leadoff man jumped the gun and the Hornets were disqualified, giving Kearney 3rd in the meet just by finishing the relay. However, Sam Wilson was a bright spot for Emporia State, winning the shot put with a conference record toss of 52-8 ¼ and taking 1st in the discus with a throw of 153-1.

1979

The 1979 men's track team placed 4th in the CSIC meet for the second consecutive year, behind Pitt State, Hays and Kearney. Sam Wilson failed to repeat as conference champ in the shot and discus, and his 2nd place in the shot was the highest placing earned by a Hornet thinclad. However, Wilson rebounded from this disappointment to place 5th in the shot put in the NAIA national championships to earn All-American honors, tossing the shot 53-10 ½. Wilson's NAIA performance was not the only highlight of the season, though. Four Hornets won indoor District 10 titles: Wilson in a tie for 1st in the shot put, Greg Topham in the mile, Rob Harber in the two-mile, and Kevin Byrne in the 1000-yard run. Another Hornet, senior Tom Noonan, just missed earning All-American honors during the indoor season, finishing 7th in the 1000-yard run in the NAIA indoor nationals. Freshman Wayne Defebaugh also performed well in the NAIA indoor meet, placing 11th in the high jump with a leap of 6-6.

Dennis Delmott: Coach
Dennis Delmott, the former Hornet distance runner and Delavan's graduate assistant was hired to coach the cross country and track teams on an interim basis for the 1978-1979 year. The school record holder at 6 miles, he finished among the top 25 runners at the 1976 Olympic Trials in the marathon.

1980

The 1980 track season was one of considerable contrast. The men's season was not without its highlights, but overall the team lacked the depth to be a force in any of the meets attended. Several strong performances were turned in at the outdoor District 10 meet, as Wayne Defebaugh won the high jump and Greg Topham, Evan Yoder and Kevin Byrne placed 1st-2nd-4th, respectively, in the 1500-meter run. Topham set a District 10 record of 3:57.3 in winning the event. Defebaugh had a strong outdoor season, consistently jumping around 6-8 to win at the Bethany Relays and the Emporia Relays, but despite another 6-8 jump at the CSIC meet, he was upset, finishing 2nd. Topham, a favorite in the conference 1500-meter, was also upset as he finished 3rd in the event. The Hornet thinclads picked up only a 5th and a 6th to round out their scoring, and finished last in the CSIC meet.

1981

Highlights from the 1981 season included the meet at Fort Hays with 2nd place finishes from Steve Beamon in the 100 meter hurdles in 16.7 and 3rds from Mike Moore in the 100 and Kevin Byrne in the 1500, and a 4th in the 1500 from Steve Hawkins. Todd Bays also captured a 4th in the long jump and high jump. At the Arkansas Relays, Wayne Defebaugh high jumped 6-6 and Moore posted quality marks in the 100 and 200.

The Hornets did improve their CSIC placing from the previous year, taking 5th in a six-team field. Senior Martin Moore picked up Emporia State's highest places, taking 3rd in the 200-meter and 400-meter dashes to account for most of the Hornets' 26 points. Moore was competing in track on the college level for the first time and had a very successful season despite the inexperience. Besides his high places in the conference meet, Moore was the only Hornet trackman to compete in the NAIA Outdoor nationals, qualifying for the semifinals in both the 200-meter and 400-meter dashes before being eliminated.

1982

The 1982 Emporia State track team was greatly strengthened by the addition of sophomore transfer Mike Cole from Panhandle State, Oklahoma. Cole twice set field house records at Pittsburg State in the 60-yard high hurdles, and lowered the Fort Hays Gross Coliseum record and ESU school record in the event to 7.36 seconds in winning the NAIA Indoor District 10 title.

Bill Tidwell: Coach
Bill Tidwell became the head track and field/cross country coach in 1980. Tidwell coached the ESU through the 1984 season. One of the top distance middle distance runners in the 1950s, he was a four-time NAIA champion in the 880 and the mile. He has been inducted into numerous athletic Halls of Fame including the NAIA Hall of Fame and the Kansas Sports Hall of Fame. His amazing 800 record of 1:47.61, set in 1955, still stands over 60 years later.

The outdoor season opened with Cole tying the E-State school record in the 200-meter dash during the Emporia State triangular, as well as winning the 110-meter hurdles. Three days later, Cole placed 2nd in the 110-hurdles at the Arkansas Relays. Cole continued his success in the high hurdles throughout the season, winning the event at Kansas Wesleyan, Central Missouri State, Southwestern, the District 10, and tying for the CSIC title with Ed Blackburn, Wayne State's, All-American hurdler. Cole advanced to the finals of the NAIA Outdoor Nationals high hurdles event, but finished 7th in the final, just missing All-American recognition. Also experiencing success for the men's team was senior Wayne Defebaugh. Defebaugh regained the form he had enjoyed as a sophomore to win the CSIC high jump at 6-8, and he set an ESU school record of 6-10 in the event at the district meet. Defebaugh's record leap was good for 2nd place, while Todd Bays added a district title in the triple jump to help the Hornets finish 5th in the 12 team field. The Hornet men also earned a 5th place finish in the six-team conference meet.

1983

Mike Cole, Emporia State's outstanding hurdler, advanced to the semifinals of the 60-yard high hurdles in the national indoor championships, but was edged out of the finals and did not place. Despite this disappointment, Cole had quite a successful indoor season. He placed 2nd in the 60-yard hurdles at the Oklahoma Track Classic in Oklahoma City, won the event at Pitt State and Hays, and repeated as district champ in the high hurdles while lowering his district, Pitt Coliseum, and school records to 7.29 seconds.

The 1983 men's outdoor track team held a great deal of promise at the opening of the season, but injuries took a serious toll. Because of cancellations due to bad weather, the season began at the Emporia Relays, and the Hornet men scored a surprising win in the 440-yard relay with the team of Cole, Steve Reichardt,

Hezekiah Conway, and Stuart Holmes. This same foursome was leading the 880 relay when Conway pulled up with a hamstring injury, denying the Hornets a second home relay victory and costing them a top performer for much of the season. Reichardt was lost later in the season to a hamstring injury, and Todd Bays, the defending outdoor district triple jump champ, was unable to reach his past form because of a badly bruised heel.

The top two performers, Mike Cole and Bernie Gardenhire, were injured late in the season. Gardenhire, a local freshman, had been an outstanding addition to the squad. After a late start in the program, he had set a school record of 10.6 seconds in the 100-meter dash at the Central Missouri Relays and had won the 100-meter dash at the Southwestern Relays in 10.8 seconds. In the CSIC championships, Gardenhire won the long jump on his first attempt with a leap of 23-5 ½. Unfortunately, during the approach on his second jump, he injured a hamstring and was unable to compete in the remainder of the meet. The injury also forced him out of the district and NAIA championships. Cole went unbeaten in the high hurdles through the outdoor season, including a repeat victory at the Central Missouri Relays. However, Cole was hampered in the CSIC by a back injury sustained during the week prior to the meet, and Russ Jewett of Pitt State (who would go on to have a highly successful career as the head coach at Pittsburg State) just nipped him in the 110-meter hurdles with both men timed in 14.34 seconds. The injury kept Cole from defending his district title in the hurdles and from attending the nationals.

1984

Mike Cole concluded the men's 1984 outdoor season by becoming the first Hornet men's All-American since 1979. Cole earned this honor by placing 4th in the 110-meter hurdles at the NAIA outdoor meet with the time of 14.35 seconds. Cole began the year very successfully, winning the 60-yard high hurdles in the Kansas University indoor meet with the school record time of 7.2 seconds, setting a Coliseum record of 7.3 seconds at Hays, placing 4th in the 60 hurdles at the Oklahoma Track Classic, and winning the indoor district titles in the 60 hurdles and the 176-yard intermediate hurdles. Cole missed the first half of the

Bill Tidwell Years
The 1984 season also marked the end of Bill Tidwell's career as head coach of the Hornet teams. Tidwell moved back into an administrative position left vacant by a retirement. During his five years as coach, the women's program had blossomed into one of the strongest in the NAIA, as evidenced by high team places in the national meets and 19 All-Americans in track and cross country.

outdoor season with a leg injury, but returned in time to win the CSIC and district titles in the 110-meter hurdles and earn a place in the national meet. However, he was the only Hornet individual to have much success during the season.

The 1984 season was one of many endings. Bill Tidwell ended his career as the head coach of the Hornet teams. Also, the E-State connection with the east coast had been dying out for several years and Kevin Dickerson's graduation marked the end of an association that had supplied the Hornet track program with some of their top performers since 1939.

1985

The 1985 track and field season was one of change for the Hornets. Mark Stanbrough took over as head track and field coach from Bill Tidwell. Justin Combes was the lone men's qualifier for NAIA Nationals in Municipal Auditorium in Kansas City, Missouri, competing in the two-mile run, but failing to place.

The 1985 outdoor season saw the Hornets place 4th of five teams in the CSIC meet, won by Pittsburg State. Highlights for ESU included a 3rd by Scott Tiffany in the 400 and a 3rd by the 4 x 100 relay team. The Hornets placed 9th of 13 teams at District 10. Tiffany ran 50.34 for 4th in the 400, Don Funke placed 5th in the pole vault at 13-6, and Jeff Becker was 6th in the discus at 137-8.

Other noteworthy performances in the 1985 season included Bernie Gardenhire winning the Emporia All-Comers meet 100 in 10.74 and the 200 in 21.72. Gardenhire competed in the 100 meters at the NAIA National Outdoor Track and Field Championships, but did not qualify for the final. Hezekiah Conway won the 400 in 49.72 at the McPherson Invite with teammate Tiffany behind in 49.98 and Becker posted a 145-8 discus throw to win.

Mark Stanbrough: Coach

Mark Stanbrough was the sixth coach in ESU men's cross country history. Stanbrough had competed in cross country and track and field for the Hornets from 1977 under Coach Phil Delavan. After graduation, he was an ESU graduate assistant in track and cross country, then taught and coached at Glasco High School for two years. He obtained his Ph.D. in exercise physiology from the University of Oregon. While in Oregon, Stanbrough competed for Athletes In Action and the Oregon Track Club.

Emporia hosted the Emporia Developmental track meet, which featured Harry Butch Reynolds who was running for Bud Light. Reynolds ran 48.0 to win and later went on the set the world record for 400 meters at 43.29. The old world record had stood for 20 years, set by Lee Evans in the 1968 Olympic Games. Reynolds' world record stood for over 11 years and was broken by Michael Johnson, running 43.18 in 1999.

1986

With the addition of several new recruits, the 1986 season was highly anticipated. One of the top recruits was Roger Jennings from Phillipsburg. Jennings was a high school state placer at Phillipsburg placing 2nd in the 3A 3200 meters. His top high school time in the 1600 was 4:28, but as he matured as a runner he would eventually lower his time to the equivalent of a sub-4 minute mile (1500 conversion) while at ESU. Jennings arrived as a raw runner with tremendous potential. His dad was the long-time coach/manager of the Pacific Coast Track Club (one of the top clubs in the U.S. with Dwight Stones and Al Feuerbach as athletes) and his step dad was the legendary John Mason who ran for Fort Hays and later the Pacific Coast Club. Mason ran numerous miles under 4 minutes and won two NAIA National Cross Country titles and eight NAIA National Track and Field titles. A factor in Jennings attending ESU was the fact that he was familiar with Feuerbach as a member of the Pacific Coast. Feuerbach won four NAIA National Championships while at Emporia State and later went on to become a two-time Olympian and world record holder in the shot put.

Indoors, the men garnered 1sts from Tod Johnson in the shot put at 45-3 and a first from Dennis Cargill in the 1000-yard run in 2:24.37 at the Alex Francis Invitational. ESU claimed two indoor district titles. Roger Jennings won the mile (4:21.5) and Cargill the 1000 (2:21.83). Mike Baumann was a national qualifier in the indoor 600 and the men's distance medley ran to an 11th place national finish at the NAIA National Indoor Track and Field Championships.

Highlights of the 1986 outdoor season included a 1500-meter win at Bethany by the freshman Jennings in 4:08.1. Jennings continued his success at home by winning the Emporia Twilight mile (4:23.0) and the 800 (1:58:5). Johnson captured the shot (45-3) and Tiffany (who was the only senior on the team) the 200 meters (22.7).

At the ESU Relays, Jason Schenck took a steeplechase title in 10:04.46, the distance medley of Paul Weidenbach, Scott Starks, Cargill, and Jennings won, as well as the two-mile relay of Baumann, Cargill, Weidenbach, and Jennings.

ESU finished 4th of 5 teams in the CSIC meet. Jennings ran 3:55.1 to take the 1500 title and Weidenbach took the 800 in 1:56.4. Jennings improved upon his time in the 1500 later in the year, taking the District 10 title in a meet record of 3:53.77. The team moved up to a 6th place finish at District 10, improving upon the 9th from the previous year and scoring 25 points, 15 more than the previous year.

1987

Roger Jennings started off the 1987 indoor season by claiming a victory in the mile at the Kansas Invitational, running 4:14.45. The men set three school records at the Central Missouri State Relays with Eric Boldridge shattering the triple jump record with a leap of 45-11 ¾ breaking a 22 year old record of 44-5 ¾ set in 1965 by Wayne Rogers. Junior transfer Lennie Allen established an ESU best of 6-9 in the high jump in his first meet as a Hornet. The old record of 6-8 was set by Wayne Defebaugh in 1980. Ted Methvin, a freshman competing in his first meet for ESU, set a pole vault record of 14-7. The old record of 14-6 was set by Dennis Webb in 1974. The three records in one meet was a unique accomplishment as only three school records had been set in the previous 12 years.

Jennings won the John Mason mile in 4:17.6 at the Alex Francis Invitational at Hays. The event was named after Roger's stepfather, a former sub 4-minute mile great at Fort Hays State. Jennings posted a new school record in the 1000-yard run at Kansas State, running 2:12.84. The previous record had lasted 20 years, held by Bob Camien, running 2:14.4 in 1967.

The 1987 District 10 meet conflicted with the Oklahoma Classic Track meet. Since the Oklahoma meet was run on a board track similar to the NAIA National Indoor, Stanbrough elected to take his top athletes to run at Oklahoma. No team scores were kept at District 10, was 3rd in the shot at 46-9 ¼ and Schenck captured 2nd in the two mile at 9:53.77. At Oklahoma, Jennings placed 2nd in the mile at 4:09.0 and the distance medley of Weidenbach, Crabtree, Byron Fick, and Jennings ran 10:21.0.

Jennings came up just short of a NAIA national championship, finishing 2nd in the mile at the 1987 NAIA National Indoor Track and Field Championships in 4:13.60. The winner, Brian Williams of Anderson, Indiana, finished less than a second ahead in 4:12.66. ESU was 9th in the distance medley at 10:38.21, with Weidenbach, Tom Crabtree, Byron Fick, and Jennings. Methvin also competed in the pole vault, but was unable to clear a height. ESU finished in a tie for 15th place in the team standings.

In the outdoor 1987 season, ESU continued to build upon the success of the previous season. Jennings and Crabtree were double winners at the ESU Developmental. At the Swede Invitational, the men got wins from Methvin in the pole vault, double wins from Jennings in the 1500 and 5000, and a 1-2-3 sweep of the steeplechase, led by Schenck in a 15-second PR. At the Southwestern Invitational, Tom Crabtree won the 400 in 48.6, came back 20 minutes later to run a 47.9 on the sprint medley relay, and he finished his day with a 48.4 split on the 4 x 400 relay.

Jennings set a PR and finished 7th in the 1500 meter run at the Drake Relays, running 3:48.5. His earlier PR of 3:52.05 was set in the summer of 1986 in an international meet in Helsinki, Finland. He won the Wes Santee 1500-meter run at the KU Relays earlier in the year, finishing in 3:52.52 and defeated an NCAA field that included sub-4 minute miler Glenn Klassa of Ohio State. Jennings pulled away from the field over the last 500 meters, opening up a lead of 7 meters on the field and holding it all the way to the line, running 55 seconds over the last 400 meters, an amazing feat, considering his best open 400 meters at the time was 53 seconds.

At the 1987 CSIC meet, the men finished 3rd. The major scoring event for ESU was the 3000-meter steeplechase, as the Hornets swept the first three places with Schenck the winner in 9:58.3 followed by Jim Robinson and Steve Peterson. ESU went 1-2 in the pole vault with Methvin winning at 14-0 and Dave Aleman finishing 2nd. Jennings captured the 1500 in 3:53.1 and Crabtree took the 400 in 49.3. ESU doubled their District 10 point total from the previous season, scoring 73 points and finishing 4th, with Jennings the lone winner as he defended his District 10 title at 1500 meters in 3:54.61.

Emporia State finished in a tie for 53rd place at the 1987 NAIA Outdoor Track and Field Championships with 4 points scored on the legs of Roger Jennings who placed 5th in the 1500 meters in 3:45.23. Crabtree finished just out of the top eight with a 9th place finish in the decathlon, scoring 6332 points.

1988

The Hornet men earned three All-American honors in the 1988 NAIA National Indoor Championships, their best national finish in 18 years as they finished 13th with 12 ¼ points. Jennings led the men with a 2nd place finish in the mile (4:13.27), marking the second year in a row he finished as national runner-up. Freshman Shawn Brewer ran his way to a 4th place finish in the 600-yard run (1:14.6) and Allen finished in a 6th place tie in the high jump at 6-9 to tie his school record.

Four men earned District 10 individual titles: Johnson in the shot (44-10 ½), Kirk Wyatt in the long jump (21-10), Funke in the pole vault (14-6) and Jennings in the 800 (1:58.9). Funke set a new school record of 15-6 in the pole vault earlier in the indoor season at Pittsburg State.

In the 1988 outdoor season, the men finished 3rd in the CSIC and 4th in the District 10 Championships. Jennings was the CSIC champion in the 800 meters at 1:54.5 and also won the 1500 meters in 4:02.0. Cargill followed Jennings in 2nd in the 15000 at 4:03.6 and 3rd in the 800 at 1:56.0. Brewer picked up a 2nd in the 400 at 49.7. District 10 champions were Jennings in the 800 at 1:52.79 (a new District 10 record) and 1500 at 4:02.7. Cargill was 2nd in the 1500 behind Jennings in 4:04.7. Methvin won the pole vault, Allen added a 2nd in the high jump at 6-8 and Johnson was 2nd in the shot at 48-6. The men continued their gradual improvement by winning the Fort Hays Dual, Swede Invitational and the Park College Relays.

At the 1988 National Outdoor Championships, Jennings raced to a 1500-meter National Championship in 3:47.64, covering the last 400 meters in 56.4 seconds. Methvin set the school record at 15-7 and placed 8th at nationals with a pole vault of 15-3 ¾. The men finished the team competition in 28th place, their highest national finish since Al Feuerbach won the shot put for the Hornets in 1970. Feuerbach's history at ESU was a factor in the recruiting process with Jennings and ironically, Jennings was the next national champion after Feuerbach in the ESU history books.

Jennings would compete internationally in the summer of 1988, traveling with his father and the Pacific Coast Club. He posted an outstanding time in the 1500 at the Bern International meet, running 3:41.47 to move to second on the all-time ESU 1500 list behind the legendary John Camien, who posted the school record of 3:40.04 at the Compton Relays in California in 1963.

1989

David Kipelio, a native of Kenya, transferred from Southwestern Louisiana to ESU in 1989. As Kipelio began to accumulate a good foundation

Roger Jennings: National Champion

Roger Jennings competed in track and cross country from1985-1989. He was a six-time All-American winning national outdoor championships in the 1500 meters and the indoor mile. He also placed second twice in the indoor mile. He won six conference eand district titles at 800 and 1500 meters and was the conference cross country champion in 1987.

He currently operates FlashResults and has been the head timer at the Olympic Trials and U.S.A. Track and Field Championships.

of training miles and gain confidence, he would become a major factor in re-writing the ESU history books. The E-State two-mile relay team placed 1st at the 1989 Jayhawk Invitational and shattered a 24-year school record by over four seconds with a time of 7:42.02. Jennings, Scott Starks, Kipelio, and Brewer ran on the relay. Mark Majors reset his own school record in the 35-pound weight throw with a toss of 44-7, and Jennings posted an outstanding early season time of 4:07.73 in the mile at the Dartmouth Relays.

E-State picked up five District 10 individual titles with Montgomery in the pole vault (14-6), Jennings in the 1000-yard run (2:16.3), Brewer in the 880 (1:54.61) and Kipelio in the mile (4:15.3). The two-mile relay of Rob Reynolds, Fick, Clint Burkdoll, and Scott Starks won in 8:11.4.

At the 1989 National Indoor Championships, Jennings lined up in the mile with confidence after he had won the National Outdoor 1500 championship and finished 2nd in the mile at the previous two National Indoor Championships. After slipping on the start and having the race re-called, Jennings took the lead from the gun and controlled the mile leading from start to finish and kicking strong over the last 440 to win by almost three seconds. Jennings told the Emporia Gazette, "I've never led a whole race like that before. I thought I was going slow and I felt if they were going to give it to me, I'd take it." Jennings became ESU's first ever national champion in the indoor mile. Jennings' stepfather, John Mason, won the first three NAIA indoor mile championships. The two-mile relay of Brewer, Starks, Jennings, and Kipelio finished 3rd in 7:52.4. Kieplio also picked up more All-American honors with a 6th place finish in the two-mile run at 9:09.51. Montgomery in the pole vault (15-0) and Boldridge in the triple jump (45-2) did not place.

Emporia State cracked the top 10 at the national meet with a 10th place finish.

A special highlight of the 1989 outdoor season was competing in the Drake Relays. The Hornets ran the 4 x 800 relay of Shawn Brewer, Scott Starks, David Kipelio and Roger Jennings. ESU ran with the leaders over the first three legs and as Jennings took over for the anchor, was sandwiched between Cal-Poly Pomona and South Dakota State. The three anchors battled down the final straightaway and despite an outstanding 1:50.5 anchor leg by Jennings, Cal-Poly pulled off the win in 7:34.75. South Dakota's outstanding anchor, Rodney Dehaven (who would later make the U.S. Olympic team in the marathon), moved his team slightly ahead of ESU with the Hornets third in 7:35.46, less than a second off the win. The next day in the distance medley relay, Jennings gave the Hornets a 30-meter lead in the race with a 1200 lead-off leg of 2:59.2. Brewer split 48.5 for 400 meters and the Hornets held the same advantage before Starks ran 1:57.9, surrendering the lead. Kipelio anchored the relay and his 4:12.1 time for 1600 meters got ESU close to first place Cal Poly Pomona. Kipelio inched ahead down the final straightaway but could not hold off the Cal Poly anchor. Cal Poly finished in 9:57.48 and ESU ran 2nd in 9:57.63. ESU came within a combined time of less than one second of winning both relays, and the close finishes would provide motivation to set the stage for wins in both the distance medley and the 4 x 800 relay the next two years.

David Kipelio
David Kipelio was a three-time NAIA National Champion, twice in the steeplechase and one in the indoor two mile. He was a nine-time All-American in track and once in cross country. He set four school records, the indoor 3000 and 5000 and the outdoor steeplechase and 5000 meters.

Kipelio also broke a 25-year-old school record with a time of 9:02.84 in the 3000-meter steeplechase. The old mark of 9:04.54 was set by Ireland Sloan in 1964. Kipelio was on pace to break 9 minutes, but with a lap to go, he fell over a barrier, which moved him back to 5th. He was able to bounce back and still take 3rd.

Kipelio would gain another opportunity in the steeplechase at the 1989 NAIA National Outdoor Championships. He raced to a 3000-meter steeplechase national title, winning in 9:00.58. Jennings, the defending national champion in the 1500 meters ran into a strong field and finished 7th in 3:53.89. The men with 11 points finished in 19th place, their best placing in over a decade.

The men enjoyed their best CSIC and District 10 finishes ever, finishing 3rd in both meets. Conference individual champions were Jennings in the 800 (1:53.94) and 1500 (3:56.4), Kipelio in the 3000 steeplechase (9.22.4) and 5000 (15.17.9) and Mark Majors in the hammer (143-1). Seconds were picked up by Montgomery in the pole vault going 15-0, Brewer who went 49.0 in the 400 meters, Brad Wecker in the 10,000 at 31:46.9 and Kipelio who finished behind Jennings in the 1500 (3:58.1). District 10 champions were Montgomery in the pole vault in 15-6, Jennings in the 1500 (with a new meet record of 3:50.36) and the 800 in 1:53.82, and Kipelio in the 5000 (14:35.3). Kipelio also finished behind Jennings in the 1500 for the second week in a row, running 3:53.18. John Byfield added to the Hornet point total with a 2nd in the 400 hurdles in 54.80.

1990

The men finished 10th at the national indoor meet with 20 points, the second year in a row they finished in the top 10 in the nation. Kipelio led the men's track and field team at the NAIA National Indoor Championships by winning the 2 mile running 8:48.73, a new school record. Kipelio won by over 100 meters and finished only one second off of the meet record. He came back to finish 3rd in the mile (4:12.67) and anchored the distance medley relay. The men's distance medley relay that finished 4th in 10:21.6 was composed of Brewer, John Byfield, Matt Hertig, and Kipelio. Other outstanding performances were turned in by Rick Boyle, who placed 7th in the 2 mile (9:17.60), and Brewer, who was 9th in the 880 (1:58.96). The men's two-mile relay team had the second fastest time in the nation entering the race but a dropped baton forced them to settle for 7th place.

At the District 10 meet, the Hornets finished 2nd to Southwestern. The well-balanced team scored in every event except the high jump. District 10 Championships were won by Kipelio in the mile at 4:11.4 and 1000 meters in 2:29.4, Brewer in the 800 at 1:54.6 and Boyle in the 2 mile at 9:21.9.

Besides Kipelio's school record indoor 2-mile in his national win, he also set the 3-mile run indoor record during the season, running 13:44. 26. Mark Majors also added a school record in the weight throw at 48-6.

The 1990 outdoor team finished 16th at the NAIA National Outdoor Track and Field meet in Stephenville, Texas. The men were highlighted by Kieplio, who successfully defended his national steeplechase title. His winning time of 9:04.07 won by over 12 seconds in the hot, humid conditions. Earning All-American honors, in the hammer throw was sophomore Mark Majors. Majors' toss of 167-5 established a new school record and placed him 4th. Senior Stacy Montgomery also garnered All-American honors placing 6th with a vault of 15-3 ¼. Montgomery's performance was impressive considering it was his first competition in a month due to a broken metatarsal. Montgomery spent the month cross training and doing pool workouts. He was medically cleared just before the NAIA National Outdoor meet. Because he was a senior and he had qualified for the national meet, he made the travel squad despite not having vaulted in a month. As the competition began, several vaulters passed at earlier heights, but Montgomery entered the competition at the first height and was able to work his way up to and clear 15-3 ¼. Disappointed with the result, Montgomery returned to the campus dorms where ESU was staying. As Montgomery spent his time lamenting what might have been if he had not been injured, a major thunderstorm hit and the meet was delayed. When competition resumed, the conditions were not conducive to pole vaulting as it was wet and windy. Several of the vaulters who had earlier passed at lower heights, began to no-height. A very surprised Montgomery was summoned from the dorms and told to report to the awards stand to receive his All-American honor. ESU's three All-Americans were the most for the men since 1969.

The men's 2nd place district finish was their best district finish ever. Kipelio won individual titles at District in the 1500 (3:53.34) and 5000 meters. Second places finishes came from Brewer in the 800 (1:53.3), Byfield in the 400 hurdles (54.8), and Brian Martin in the 200 (21.80), Thurston in the discus at 155-3 ½, and the 4 x 400 (3:17.84).

A highlight of the season was the men's team winning at the prestigious Drake Relays for the first time in 22 years, winning the 4 x 800 in 7:32.88 and the distance medley in 9:57.73. After finishing 3rd in the 4 x 800 the previous season and missing winning by four-tenths of a second, three of the four relay runners returned with a goal of mounting the top step of the podium and seeing the winning team's picture in the program the next year. The 4 x 800 team started the meet with a relay victory, consisting of Brewer (1:53.3), Starks (1:55.4), Hertig (1:51.1), and Kipelio (1:52.9). The men's distance medley, 2nd the previous year by only seven-tenths of a second, followed the next day. Hertig's lead-off 1200 leg of

3:03.5 put the Hornets' distance medley in contention. John Byfield followed with a 49.2 400-meter split and Brewer put ESU in the lead with a 1:52.4 800-meter leg. Kipelio brought home the victory with a 4:10.5 1600 anchor leg as ESU ran 9:55.72 to win in front of the 18,000 fans.

Kipelio went on a watch binge, winning the 1500 in 3:48.24 and the 5000 in 14:30.09 at the KU Relays and then anchored the two winning relays at Drake. Two new school records were established during the 1990 outdoor season: Majors in the hammer throw at 167-5, and Kipelio in the 5000 at 14:03.0.

1991

The 1991 indoor season was highly successful with the men finishing 7th in the NAIA National Indoor Track and Field Championships by scoring in eight events (the most events scored in by any men's team at the 1991 nationals) and seven men earning All-American honors. Hertig earned All-American honors with a 6th in the 880 in 1:55.99. Kipelio finished 2nd in the 2 mile in 9:02.66 and then came back to finish 4th in the mile in 4:15.68. Hornet Gary Lyles was 5th in the 3 mile at 14:25.98. The two-mile relay of Brewer, Kevin Williams, Hertig, and Kipelio finished 2nd in 7:52.15 and the distance medley relay finished 4th in 10:21.0 with Brewer, Pierre, Hertig, and Kipelio. Majors was 4th in the 35-pound weight throw with a school record toss of 52-9 ¾ and Jesse Gadison was 4th in the long jump with a 23-4 ½.

The men captured their first ever District 10 Indoor title in 1991, running away to win by 34 points. Kipelio picked up three wins at Districts, winning the mile (4:15.0), 1000 meters (2:28.3), a new district record, and the 800 meters (1:55.5). Gadison added victories in the long jump (23-4 ¼) and 55-meter dash (6.24, a new district record). Lyles added a win in the 2-mile (9:31.4) and the 1600-meter relay team of Brewer, Gadison, Hertig, and Pierre won in 3:21.4.

Alberto Lopez: Olympian
Alberto Lopez ran for the Hornets in 1991. A transfer from Blinn Community College, Lopez ran for his native country of Guatemala in the 1984 Olympic Games in Los Angeles. Lopez ran the 400, clocking a 52.21 for 8th in his heat and the 800 meters, where he ran 1:54.19 and finished 6th in his heat. Lopez was a national junior college champion at two miles. Lopez ran on two victorious relays at the Drake Relay, anchoring the distance medley.

As in the previous two seasons, the Hornets were competing at the prestigious Drake Relays in front of 18,000 fans. In 1990, the Hornets had won both the 4 x 800 relay and the distance medley relay, anchored by multiple national champion David Kipelio. They returned to the 1991 Drake Relays minus the superstar Kipelio and duplicated the feat winning both relays again. Brewer led off the winning 4 x 800 in 1:53.0, followed by Kevin Williams in 1:53.7, and Alberto Lopez in 1:54.7. The Hornets had the lead heading into the anchor leg, but a quick opening 400 by David Symonsbergen of Doane, an eight time NAIA All-American and two-time NAIA national champion, put the Hornets in 2nd down the final backstretch. However, an outstanding anchor leg by Hertig in 1:51.0 gave the Hornets the win in 7:33.13. Hertig came back the next day in the distance medley relay and led off with another outstanding 1200-meter leg of 3:04.7 to put the Hornets in contention. Desmond Pierre ran the 400 in 49.3, Brewer split 1:51.1 in the 800 and the Hornets had the lead. Alberto Lopez, an Olympian from Guatemala anchored the Hornets in 4:16.4 and to the victory in 9:59.50.

The 4 x 400 team of Brewer, Williams, Hertig, and Pierre ran the fastest 4 x 4 time for ESU in 16 years as they placed 4th in 3:15.75 at Drake.

With consecutive year wins in both the 4 x 800 and the distance medley, ESU added to the history books. The Hornets had captured five 4 x 800 relay victories at the Drake Relays, winning in 1933, 1936, 1968, 1990, and 1991. ESU posted their fourth win in Drake Relays history in the distance medley relay, winning in 1964, 1968, 1990, and 1991.

> **Double Back to Back Wins at Drake**
> In 1989 the Hornets ran two national champions (Jennings and Kipelio) on the 4 x 800 relay and the distance medly relay and missed winning both by a total of less than one second. The motivation of coming close inspired the Hornets for the next two years. The winners of a relay at Drake get their individual pictures in next year's program and the Hornets returned with a goal in mind. In 1990, running without one of the great distance runners in ESU history, Roger Jennings, the Hornets pulled off the distance double and indeed the pictures were in the Drake program the next year. However, three-time national champion David Kipelio, was gone the following year. Undeterred, the Hornets pulled the distance double again in 1991.
>
> **DRAKE** RELAYS
> *america's athletic classic*

Outdoors, the men had to overcome several injuries to finish 2nd in the District 10 meet. Lyles overcame the heat and humidity to win the 3000 meter steeplechase (9:46.49) and the 5000 meters (15:28.57), Jesse Gadison won the long jump (23-4 ½), Majors the hammer throw (177-9) and Thad Thurston the discus (156-8). Brewer ran a noteworthy 1:52.82 to finish 2nd in the 800 and Gadison clocked a 10.61 100 meters to finish 2nd. The Hornets went 1-2-4 in the 5000 with Boyle and Lopez, finishing behind Lyles.

Throwers Majors and Thurston led the men to a 20th place finish at the NAIA Nationals. Majors exploded for a school record in the hammer throw (180-3) to capture 2nd. It marked the third consecutive national meet that Majors had set a personal record, school record and earned All-American honors. Thurston closed out his outstanding career on a high note, earning All-American honors with a discus throw of 158-0. Lyles finished 10th in the 10,000 and set a PR to finish 12th in the 5000 at 14:53.24. Brewer advanced to the semis in the 800 running 1:52.04.

1992

The 1992 men were out to defend their District 10 indoor title and came from 60 points down to take the team lead with two events to go. In a competitive finish, the Hornets were passed by both Fort Hays and Southwestern, but hung on for 3rd. The men were led by Gadison who won the long jump (23-9 ¼) and 55-meter dash (6.50), Major's win in the weight throw (54-4 ½, a new district record) and Shawn Thomas with wins in the mile (4:16.8) and 2 mile (9:31.9). Richard Mick placed 2nd in the mile, only one-tenth of a second behind Thomas, and was also 2nd in the 1000 (2:32.1). Brian Martin picked up a 2nd in the 400 (50.9) and Gadison added a 2nd in the 300-yard dash (31.7).

> **Mark Stanbrough Era**
> While head coach from 1984-1992, the track and field teams won nine district titles. He coached 28 athletes to 60 NAIA All-American Honors, including 11 National Champions. He coached 10 teams that finished in the top 10 in the nation and 22 teams that finished in the top 20 in national competition. The top national finishes for Stanbrough teams were the 1986 women's cross country team finishing 2nd, the 1991 men's cross country team finishing 5th, the 1991 and 1992 women's indoor teams both finished 6th at nationals, and the men's 1991 indoor team finished 7th.
>
>

The team finished 9th in the team standings at the NAIA National Indoor Championships, finishing in the top 10 for the fourth consecutive year. Gadison improved on his 4th place finish from the previous year to finish 2nd in the long jump, going 23-4 ½, only 4 inches from the national championship. Thomas placed 4th in the 3 mile (14:06.72) with a big personal improvement and moved to 2nd on the all-time ESU list. Mark Majors picked up his fourth All-American honor by placing 5th in the weight throw. He set a school record in the weight throw at 54-4 ½ earlier in the year.

> **NCAA**
> After 35 years, ESU also moved to the NCAA Division II level of competition and joined the Mid-America Intercollegiate Athletics Association.
>
>

The Hornets finished 3rd at their final District 10 NAIA Outdoor Championships. Majors took the hammer in a district record of 182-6, Thomas won both the 3000 steeple (9:22.6) and the 5000 (15:31.66), and Gadison won the long jump (24-2 ½), and finished 2nd in the 100 (10.6).

ESU took nine men to the 1992 NAIA National Championships held in Abbotsford, Canada. It was ironic that the NAIA National Championships were held in Canada, but Simon-Fraser University, Canada, was an NAIA member and hosted the meet in the beautiful and scenic British Columbia Province. The ESU men tied for 37th place. Majors placed 5th in the hammer at 182-6, and Thomas placed 9th in the 5000 in 15:05.12. Gadison competed in the long jump but struggled and fouled all three attempts. Andrew LaRouche competed in the marathon, finishing in 14th, running 2:42.40. Jesse Griffin also competed in the marathon but did not finish. Martin in the 200, Shane Meyer in the 400 hurdles, Mick in the 1500, and Thomas in the 5K and 10K completed the Hornet national entries in 1992.

As ESU was returning to fly home from the meet out of the Vancouver airport, the first 21 ESU men and women had boarded, but LaRouche was not allowed to board the plane. LaRouche had dual citizenship in Africa and Canada and his student visa papers were not in order. Not wanting to leave LaRouche alone, Stanbrough stayed over with him and two days later his paperwork was straightened out and both flew home.

1993

The 1993 season was one of transition from the coaching staff of Stanbrough to David Harris. The men finished 8th in their first MIAA Indoor Track and Field Championships held in Warrensburg, Missouri. Gadison captured the MIAA long jump in 24-6 ½ inches to win by nearly a foot. He also placed 6th in the 200 and accounted for more than half of the Hornets' team points.

> **David Harris: Coach**
> David Harris was hired to lead the ESU program. Harris came to ESU after a seven-year stint as an assistant coach at the University of Nebraska where he coached 31 All-American and three Olympians. Harris received his bachelors' degree in physical education/social science and a master's degree in athletic administration from Northeast Missouri State University. While competing for the Bulldogs, he was a four-year letterman in cross country and track and field.
>
>

Gadison capped his collegiate career by placing 5th in the NCAA long jump with a 23-10 leap. Gadison's two points put ESU in a tie for 24th place as a team.

Jonathon Oshel led the men in the outdoor season as he won the javelin at the Gorilla Relays, throwing 203-6 and placed 3rd in the MIAA at 194-11. Josh Baxter also picked up a win in the Baker Twilight running 51.87 for the 400.

The men finished 8th in their first MIAA Outdoor Track and Field Championships, also held in Warrensburg, Missouri.

1994

Highlights of the 1994 indoor track and field season included Jermaine Mitchell, a Jamaican who transferred from Butler County Community College, running 4:13.07 for 3rd in MIAA in the mile. He also ran quality 5000s with a season best of 14:36.79 at the Husker Twilight, an MIAA 1st in 14:51.89, and a 7th in the NCAA National Indoor in 14:47.08 to earn All-American honors. Mitchell ran 3:52.98 in the prelim and 3:55.15 for 7th in final at the NCAA Indoor 1500.

Kirk Mensah ran the 55-meter hurdles in 7.68 to finish 2nd in the MIAA and also captured a win in the Mule Relays. Tim Vietti long jumped 23-¾ to finish 2nd in the MIAA and also won the KU Invite pentathlon with 3430 points. The Hornets won the 2 mile relay at the MIAA with Josh Baxter, Garth Briggeman, Ryan Kaberline, and Chad Brecheisen. Jason Stuke picked up a 3rd in the MIAA shot at 52-10. Other season highlights included Kaberline running 1:13.1 to win the 600-yard run at the Mule Relays.

Rick Ginter: Throws Coach
Ginter was a vital factor in ESU continuing to excel as an outstanding throws program. He coached eight NCAA DII National Champions.

The Hornets finished 3rd in the MIAA indoor.

The 1994 outdoor track and field team was led by an outstanding group of throwers. Stuke came up big in his freshman year at the NCAA Outdoor Track and Field Championships, placing 3rd in the shot put at 56-4 ¾ and 5th in the discus at 168-8. His shot season best of 56-6 ½ was a 1st place finish at the ESU Classic and he also picked up titles at KT Woodman, the SW Invite, and the ESU open. His discus PR was set at Fort Hays with a 176-10 in a winning effort. He captured the MIAA discus title in 162-8 and also won the Southwestern Invite, ESU Qualifier, the ESU Open, the Intercollegiate Classic, and the KT Woodman.

Jonathon Oshel added to the throw strength with his 208-10 javelin throw that won the MIAA championship and he finished 10th at the NCAAs with a 194-10. His season best of 216-10 was accomplished at the ESU Open. David Wells supplemented javelin points, finishing 2nd in the MIAA, throwing 196-11. Rick Ginter was 2nd in the MIAA hammer throw at 155-1 and threw a season best of 169-2 to win the ESU Qualifier. He also won at the Baker Relays, ESU Classic, and the FHSU Last Chance.

The versatile Vietti posted 6091 points for an 11th place national finish in the decathlon, setting his season best of 6708 for a 5th place finish at the Arizona Decathlon. Vietti finished 6th in the Texas Relays decathlon scoring 6598 points. Vietti also long jumped, going 24-6 at the FHSU Lance Chance, winning the ESU Classic and placing 4th in the conference.

Kaberline supplied middle distance points, finishing 2nd in the MIAA 800 in 1:53.11. Kaberline won the 800 at the ESU Open and ESU Spring Twilight and took the 400 in 49.61 at the ESU Classic. Jermaine Mitchell was outstanding. His 3:58.86 won the MIAA 1500, his 14:54.5 took the MIAA 5000 title, and his 32:15.32 took the MIAA 10K title. Mitchell just missed All-American honors, finishing 9th in the NCAA 5000 in 14:45. He posted a season best in the 1500 at KT Woodman in 3:53.90 and 5000 in winning the KU Relays in 14:27.40.

Shawn Thomas returned from an injury red-shirt year and enjoyed a tremendous season in the steeplechase placing 2nd in the MIAA in 9:17.69 and 9th in the NCAA championships in 9:16.91. Thomas ran his best time at the K.T. Woodman in 9:13.8 and also won the ESU Open.

The Hornets finished as the runner-up in the MIAA Outdoor Track and Field Championships.

1995

ESU fielded a strong team in the 1995 indoor season, finishing 3rd in the conference meet. Jermaine Mitchell continued to build upon his impressive credentials, winning the MIAA 1000 in 2:30.45 and the 5000 in 14:47.1. Mitchell posted his best 5000 time of the season at the NCAA Indoor Championships running 14:25.7 for 3rd place to earn All-American honors as ESU tied for 14th place as a team.

Kaberline took the MIAA 600 in 1:11.53 and also won the Mule Relays in that event. Brian Gomez won the MIAA 200 in 22.11, a new school record. Kirk Mensah took 2nd in the 55-meter hurdles at the MIAA meet in 7.69. Stuke put the shot 56-7 ½ at MIAA for 2nd. His indoor season best was a quality mark of 57-5 ¾ for 4th at Husker Invite. David Wells also posted a quality mark of 52-7 ½ in the weight throw to win the CMSU Invitational. The Hornets placed 3rd in the MIAA Championships.

Emporia State hosted their first NCAA DII National Track and Field Championship in 1995 at Welch Stadium. Stuke, Mitchell, and John Corwin were the headliners for the 1995 outdoor season. Stuke placed in the national meet in both the shot and discus. His put of 56-9 ½ placed 3rd and his discus throw of 163-7 placed 5th. Stuke's season best was 60-2 in the shot to win the ESU open. He also added titles in the KU Relays, KU Woodman, ESU Twilight, and the Fort Hays Triangular. He placed 2nd in the MIAA with 55-11 ¾. Stuke flung the discus 179-6 to set his season best in a win at the ESU Twilight and added titles at Fort Hays, the KU Relays and the ESU open. His throw of 168-4 gave him the MIAA Championships.

John Corwin threw a school record 241-10 in the javelin to place 2nd at the National Championships. Earlier in the year he threw 241-0 to win the ESU Twilight with a school record performance. Corwin led a 1-2-3 javelin sweep at MIAA winning in 228-1, with Oshel 2nd and Stuke 3rd. Oshel earned All-American honors by placing 7th in the NCAA with 213-11 and threw a best of 222-8 at the ESU Twilight.

Jermaine Mitchell supplied the firepower on the track from 1500 meters to 10,000 meters. He ran nearly identical times in winning the MIAA 10K (30:46.21) and placing 2nd at NCAA Nationals in 30:46.15. Mitchell placed 11th in the NCAA 5000 final in 15:13.40. He also added the 1500 and 5000 MIAA titles. As a native of Jamaican, Mitchell was eligible for the Jamaican national meet, and he finished 2nd in the Jamaican National Relays 1500 with a time of 3.53.45. Mitchell's season's best of 14:31.1 won the ESU Open 5000, and he also captured the KU Relays title.

Brandon Masters set a pole vault school record of 16-1 at KT Woodman and tied the record later in the year at the ESU Twilight. His vault of 15-7 won the KU Relays and he vaulted 16-0 ¾ to win the MIAA Decathlon.

Brian Gomez set an ESU 200 record of 20.90 at Southwestern and won the MIAA in 21.69. Kaberline posted good marks in the 800 running 1:51.25 for 2nd in the ESU Twilight. His 1:51.42 was 5th in the NCAA prelim but he did not advance to the final. His 1:53.78 was 2nd in the MIAA. Bill Lemaster was 2nd in the MIAA 100 hurdles in 14.84.

It was an outstanding year as the Hornets won their first MIAA Outdoor Championship. Behind the big points of Stuke, Corwin and Mitchell, the Hornets placed 9th in the National Outdoor Championships.

1996

Jason Stuke continued his great career with a 3rd in the NCAA Indoor shot at 58-7 ¾ and an MIAA win in 57-2 ¼. Jermaine Mitchell posted 2nds in both the mile (4:16.26) and 5000 (14:56.89) at the MIAA indoor but failed to qualify for nationals.

Bill Lemaster posted a 2nd place MIAA finish in 7.65 for the 55-meter hurdles. He also won the KSU Invite, Wildcat Invite, and CMSU Invite. Tamas Molnar, a 1992 Hungarian Olympian in the 400 meters, transferred from the University of Nebraska and ran 22.23 to place 2nd in the MIAA 200 and finished 4th in the 400 at 49.4. Cory Cole captured a 2nd in the 600 at 1:13.29. Brandon Masters set a season best 16-2 ¾ in the vault at CMSU to win.

The men finished 2nd at the 1996 MIAA Indoor Championships and 19th at the national indoor meet. The 1996 season was an excellent one for ESU. Corwin added to his impressive resume in the javelin with a 2nd place finish at NCAA's

Tamas Molnar: Olympian
Tamas Molnar competed in the 1992 Olympics games held in Barcelona, Spain. Molnar represented his native country of Hungary in the 400-meter dash, but did not qualify past the first round. Molnar transferred to ESU from the University of Nebraska in 1996.

in 233-8. He also added wins at the Texas Relays (234-5) and the MIAA title (226-7).

Stuke finished 2nd in the shot at NCAA's with a 57-8 ½. He also captured the MIAA title in 57-7 ½. He kept quite busy at the NCAA meet, as he also competed in the discus and javelin. His throw of 174-4 was 3rd in the NCAA discus and he won the conference meet in 173-2. He added discus wins at the KU Relays, MIAA, NCC, and ESU Twilight. Stuke also picked up an MIAA 2nd place in the javelin, throwing 210-2 and qualified for nationals, where he placed 10th with 183-2. Emporia State's throwers added to their impressive finish at the conference meet when Scott Campbell (175-6) and Mike Miller (166-1), went 2nd and 3rd, respectively in the hammer throw.

Mitchell continued to amass gold and add to a stellar career, winning the 10K in the MIAA and placing 6th at nationals with a 30:55.35. Mitchell won the KU Relays 5000 in 15:06.46 and placed 2nd in the conference 1500. Cole added one of the fastest 800's in school history, running 1:51.62 at the ESU Twilight to qualify for nationals. Here, he posted the 15th fastest time in the prelims by running 1:54.41, but did not advance to the final. Behind the running of Travis Powell, Molnar, Cole, and Kaberline, the sprint medley relay team ran 3rd at Drake in 3:24.67. Masters jumped a noteworthy 16-1 to win the ESU Invite pole vault. The men were unable to defend their conference title in 1996, finishing 2nd. They displayed their strength at the NCAA meet finishing in the top 10 at nationals for the second year in a row by placing 7th.

1997

Brandon Masters furnished the highlight in the 1997 indoor season, pole vaulting a school record 16-8 ¾ at the Nebraska Open as he improved upon his own school record. He cleared 16-0 ¾ to place 6th and earn All-American status at the NCAA DII Championships. Masters also cleared 15-5 to finish 2nd in the MIAA. Garth Briggeman picked up a 2nd in the MIAA, running 1:56.35 in the 800. ESU finished 3rd at the conference meet and 26th place at Nationals.

Masters continued to go higher in the 1997 outdoor season, setting and re-setting school records, going over 17 feet in five meets. His 17-4 ½ vault earned him a 4th place national finish, while his season best of 17-6 ½ gave him the MIAA title. Masters also won at the ESU Relays, KU Relays, and the ESU Last Chance.

Campbell and Mike Miller repeated their 2-3 MIAA finish from the previous season's hammer throw with Campbell 2nd in 177-0, and Miller 3rd at 174-10. Pat Schroeder went 6-8 ¼ to win the MIAA high jump, Briggeman was 2nd in the 800 at 1:56.35, Travis Powell 3rd in the 400 at 48.39, Brie Ary 3rd in the shot put, Dan Van Duren 2nd in the discus, and Bill Griffith 3rd in the javelin. ESU ended the season with a 3rd place finish in the MIAA and a tie for 26th place.

Of note, senior Josh Baxter clocked 1:56.10 for the 800 meters in 1977. Baxter, from Olpe, had a connection with ESU. His father, John was the athletic trainer at ESU for 46 years.

John Baxter: Long-time Athletic Trainer
When he attended the University of New Mexico in Albuquerque, Baxter was offered a student training position by the head athletic trainer at the school. After graduating from UNM, Baxter went on to the Army and was appointed as an assistant athletic trainer at West Point Academy. Baxter found his way to Emporia when he finished his stint in the U.S. Army and after teaching and coaching public school in Albuquerque, New Mexico. He was offered the job as athletic trainer at ESU by Joe Pease, who was athletic director at that time. "Doc" Baxter became a legend in his 46 years of service and helped thousands of athletes.

When John Baxter arrived at ESU in 1966, only men's athletics existed. When he retired in 2012, after 46 years, he had touched the lives of thousands of young people throughout his more than four decades at ESU. Baxter was an educator, mentor, friend, and father figure, who was recognized as one of the nation's outstanding collegiate athletic trainers and teachers. He was elected to the NAIA's Hall of Fame in 1986, the highest honor given by that association and also honored in the Emporia State Athletic Hall of Honor and the Kansas Athletic Trainers Society Hall of Fame. Baxter represented ESU for 20 years as the coordinator of the athletic training facilities at the NAIA National Basketball Tournament in Kansas City. He also served in that capacity at the NAIA National Indoor Track & Field Championships for four years. Baxter was awarded the National Athletic Trainer's Outstanding Service Award in 1992 and the Award of Excellence from the city of Emporia in 1990. Baxter's students have worked in high schools, universities, professional organizations, and sports medicine clinics as athletic trainers, physical therapists, and sports medicine administrators.

1998

Jason Stuke was back for his final season (after sitting out the 1997 season) as a Hornet and it was special. He put the shot 59-3 to place 2nd at the 1998 NCAA Indoor Championships. However, in three meets, he threw over 60 feet, winning at KU and Nebraska before hitting his indoor PR of 62-2 ½ to become an MIAA champion again.

Joseph Herron, from nearby Waverly, Kansas, represented the Hornets at the NCAA Indoor Championships, finishing 5th in the long jump at 23-5 ½. Herron won the MIAA in 24-0. Mike Giardine took a 3rd at the KSU meet in the 35-pound weight throw setting a PR and school record of 58-3 ½ and placed 2nd in the MIAA.

Bill Lemaster ran to 2nd place conference title in the 55-meter hurdles running 7.55, but his 7.65 did not advance him past the first round in the NCAA meet. The Hornets were strong in the middle distance events, with Cory Cole winning the conference 600 in 1:12.40 and Smitheran 3rd in 1:13.54. Josh McCleary ran an MIAA 2nd in 4:17.74 in the mile. The trio helped the two-mile relay win the MIAA championship. Cole posted a very fast 1:52.90 at the Cyclone Classic on the oversized 300-meter track at Iowa State.

ESU ended the season with a 2nd place finish in the MIAA, but did not qualify anyone for the NCAA Indoor Championships.

The 1998 outdoor season featured the ESU throwers. Stuke, in his last outdoor season won the NCAA Championship at 59-9 ¾ in the shot, the MIAA at 61-9 ½ and was 2nd at Drake in 61-10 ½. He also captured shot titles at Missouri Southern, the DII challenge, the ESU Relays, and the Pomona Invitational. Stuke finished 2nd in the discus at nationals throwing 189-4. His best throw of the year was a 199-10 at the MSSC Last Chance. He was 2nd in the MIAA and won the Florida Invite. Stuke's third event, the javelin, was pretty good also. He finished with an MIAA 2nd in 208-2 and an NCAA 10th place finish of 188-0.

> **Jason Stuke: National Champion**
> Jason Stuke was ESU's first NCAA DII male national champion, winning the outdoor shot put title in 1998. He was a 10-time All-American and seven-time MIAA champion. He still holds the school record in the discus.
>
>

In an impressive display of strength and power, ESU went 1-2-3-4 in the shot at MIAAs. Behind Stuke was Jim Riedesel, Giardine, and Brett Ary. Riedesel finished 9th in the NCAA meet in 52-2 ¾, with his season best of 55-6 ¼ coming at the ESU Last Chance Giardine was also 2nd in the conference hammer (193-3) and finished 11th in the NCAA meet. Miller finished behind Giardine at MIAA in 3rd place, but ahead of him at nationals, finishing 5th in the hammer at NCAA Nationals in 189-6.

Masters began to focus on the decathlon and posted 6692 points for a 2nd place finish in the MIAA. He also vaulted to a 5th place finish in the NCAA Championships with a 16-¾. His season best was 16-8 ½ and he won the MIAA in 16-4 ¾. Herron also picked up All-American honors with a 5th place NCAA finish at 23-10 ¼ in the long jump. Herron leaped to a PR of 25-1 ¾ at the DII challenge to win that event. Cole ran noteworthy 800 times of 1:52.4 at Mt Sac Relays and 1:52.89 at the Long Beach Invitational and ran 2nd in the MIAA with 1:54.77.

ESU ended the season with a 4th place finish at the MIAA and a top 10 national finish, placing 10th.

1999

Cory Cole continued to improve in the middle distance events, running 1:11.40 to win the KU Invite 600-yard run and set the 800 indoor school record, running a blistering 1:51.07 on the oversized 300 meter oval at Iowa State. Cole finished 3rd in the NCAA indoor meet in 1:53.39 after winning the MIAA in 1:54.03. Another school record was added by Paul Weldon, who triple jumped 50-11 at Kansas State and later placed 5th in the MIAA. Jim Riedesel threw 54-4 for 3rd in the MIAA.

Thrower Mike Giardine placed 3rd in the NCAA weight throw at 59-11 ¼ after winning the MIAA, with teammate Robert Wilmott finishing 2nd at conference. Riesdesel placed 3rd with a throw of 54-4.

Other noteworthy efforts in the 1999 indoor season included David Humbarger high jumping 6-11 at the KU Invite, and Bill Lemaster winning the 55-meter hurdles at the KU Invite and University of Central Missouri. Nathan Peck pole vaulted 15-1 ½ to finish 2nd in the MIAA. The two-mile relay team won the MIAA indoor in 7:51.10.

ESU finished 4th in the MIAA indoor meet and placed 5th at the national indoor meet, their highest NCAA DII finish in history.

The indoor success continued into the outdoor season as ESU won the MIAA outdoor title, their second in history, defeating Central Missouri. With the women also winning the MIAA, ESU became the first team in six years to capture both titles at the meet. Giardine was a horse, scoring 30 points in winning the discus (156-2) and hammer (179-4), then placing 3rd in the javelin (182-6) and 5th in the shot put. Other MIAA champs included Cole in the 800 (1:53.35), Riedesel in the shot (51-5 ¼), and Shane Osterhaus in the 1500 (3:58.04). Brent Smitheran (48.23) also posted a good meet, taking 2nd in the 200 (21.26) and 3rd in the 400 meters. David Humbarger added a 2nd in the decathlon scoring 6898 points and a 2nd in the high jump.

The 1999 NCAA DII Outdoor Track and Field Championships were hosted by Emporia State and the men supplied a few highlights for the home crowd. Riesedel placed 5th in the shot with a mare of 54-1 ¾. The most exciting moment occurred in the 4 x 400 relay. The team of Shawn Fairbanks, Brent Smitheran, Cole, and Luke Pickett ended the meet on a positive note by finishing 2nd. ESU hung near the lead for the first three legs and Pickett dropped from 2nd to 4th early in the anchor leg. However, a burst of speed moved ESU past Abilene Christian by a mere .07 seconds. The Hornet time of 3:08.89 still stands as a school record. ESU scored 12 points and finished 19th in the NCAA meet.

ESU hosted the 1995 NCAA DII National Outdoor Track and Field Championships at Welch Stadium.

2000

During the 2000 indoor season, ESU continued their legendary tradition in the throws with Wes Hill winning the MIAA shot at 52-0 and Riedesel placing 2nd in the weight throw at 49-11.

The 55-meter hurdles was a strong event for ESU. Bill Lemaster ran 7.64 to win the MIAA championships, with Dustin Brock 3rd in 7.69. The 600 was another strong event for ESU with Shawn Fairbanks 2nd in 1:12:18 in the MIAA Championships and Smitheran following him in 3rd in 1:12.75. Nick Beck added another strong 600 run during the season in 1:12.94. Smitheran Beck, Pickett, and Justin Stigge combined to win the MIAA 4 x 400 in 3:19.29, and ran even faster at the Cannon Classic held in Indianapolis in 3:15.95 to a set a new indoor school record. The strong collection of 400-800 runners also took the MIAA 4 x 800. Smitheran set a 400-meter school record of 48.94 at Iowa State and broke it again at the Cannon Classic in Indianapolis in 48.87.

ESU ended the season with a 3rd place MIAA indoor finish, but failed to score at the NCAA meet.

ESU added another prestigious Drake Relays title in 2000, winning the 4 x 400 relay with Fairbanks, Beck, Smitheran, and Pickett running 3:10.34 to win in the second fastest time in school history, highlighted by the smoking 46.0 carry by Smitheran. The same four runners ran 6th in the sprint medley at 3:23.63.

The 2000 MIAA Outdoor Championships featured an ESU 1-2-3 sweep in the 110-meter hurdles with Fairbanks (14.50), Lemaster (14.57), and Brock (14.70). Fairbanks was a double winner, taking the 400 hurdles in 52.34 and the 4 x 400, which ran 3:10.64 to tie the MIAA meet record. Picking up 2nd place finishes in the MIAA were Wes Hill in the shot at 49-2 ¼ and the javelin throw of Bill Griffith in 184-1. The Hornets placed 3rd in the MIAA meet

ESU scored a single point in the 2000 National Outdoor Track and Field Championships to place 52nd. Fairbanks picked up the point and All-American honors by placing 8th in the 400 hurdles, running 54.15 after running faster (52.52) in the preliminaries to qualify for the final. Smitheran qualified for the nine-man final by running a 47.49 400 in the prelims and returned to run 48.16 to place 9th. The 4 x 400 ran a very fast 3:11.50 to qualify for the final but could only post a 3:17.10 to place 9th in the final.

2001

Hurdler Dustin Brock highlighted the 2001 indoor season placing 3rd in the NCAA National Indoor Championship and ran a season best of 7.37 in the NCAA prelims. The ESU men placed 17th at the national meet.

John McGinty emerged as another great thrower in the long line of great ESU throwers in winning the MIAA indoor weight throw in 56-10 ¼. Wes Hill threw 52-11 to place 3rd in the MIAA shot put. The ESU men placed 3rd in the MIAA aided by the 2-3 finish of Nick Beck and Shawn Fairbanks in the 600.

Brock duplicated his 3rd place national indoor finish with a 3rd place national outdoor finish in the 2001 DII National Outdoor Championships with a school record of 13.98 in the 110-meter hurdles. He also captured the MIAA title in 14.19. Herron took 2nd (10.64) in the MIAA 100 ahead of teammate Eric Smith

The throwers had another highly successful season. Javelin thrower Ryan Sparks picked up All-America honors with a 4th place NCAA throw of 203-6, as well as capturing an MIAA championship. McGinty placed 11th in the NCAA, throwing 167-8 in the discus. McGinty took the MIAA title in 165-10 and threw 178-9 at the DII challenge.

Herron earned All-American honors with a 7th in the NCAA long jump. He jumped 24-5 ¾ at the ESU Spring Twilight and placed 3rd in the MIAA. Fairbanks picked up an MIAA title in 51.75 for the 400 hurdles. ESU featured a strong 1600 relay team consisting of Fairbanks, Justin Stigge, Carlson, and Beck. They ran a season best of 3:12.15 to place 6th at Drake, finished 2nd in the MIAA and 8th in the NCAA Championships. The 3200 relay of Beck, Stigge, Harris, and Eric Meyer ran 4th in the 4 x 800 relay at Drake.

The team finished a strong 2nd in the MIAA Outdoor Championships and tallied 17 points to finish 17th in the NCAA meet.

2002

ESU finished 6th in the 2002 MIAA Indoor Championships with 55 points. MIAA champions were Ron Hunter in the high jump at 6-10 ¼ and the 4 x 4 of Kip Wilson, Will Hill, Carlson, and Tanner Gassman ran 3:21.22. Brock was 7th in the 60-meter hurdles at the NCAA Championships in 8.07, although he ran a faster 7.94 in the prelims. Hunter jumped a season best and new school record of 7-1 at the KSU Open and finished 6th in the NCAA meet at 6-9 ¾. ESU's points at the National Indoor Championships earned the team a 28th place finish and their 55 points were good for 6th in the MIAA.

The javelin throwers led by Danny Bartlett shone in the 2002 outdoor track and field season. Bartlett had a season best 221-11 at the Spring Twilight and placed 15th at NCAA nationals. Sparks threw 212-01 and placed 9th at NCAA. Herron picked up an NCAA 11th in the long jump at 24-8 ½.

Brock took the MIAA 110 hurdles in 14.46 and the 4x 400 relay of Waller, Herron, Smith and Jon Dickson won the MIAA in 41.16. Smith added 2nds in both the 100 (10.58) and the 200 (21.32) in the MIAA and Wilson added a 2nd in the 400 (47.78), with Gassman close behind in 3rd. The 4 x 400 relay of Wilson, Demetri Jackson, Will Hill, and Gassman ran a noteworthy 4 x 400 relay of 3:13.50. Hunter also posted quality marks, high jumping 6-10 ¼ to win the ESU Relays and placing 4th in the MIAA at 6-9. ESU took 5th in the MIAA with 97 points but failed to score at the national meet.

2003

The men finished in 5th place in the MIAA 2013 Indoor Championships with 65 points. They fielded two MIAA champions in Corey Seachris in the 400 in 49.48 and Stigge in the 600 in 1:12.52.

The outdoor team also finished 5th in the MIAA Outdoor Championships with 76 points. Aiding the Hornet cause was Stigge with a 2nd in the 800 at 1:54.33 (he ran a season best 1:53.26 in the DII challenge). Jilka also placed 2nd in 400-meter hurdles in 54.47. Javelin thrower Danny Bartlett won the MIAA in 201-10, and earned All-American honors with an NCAA 6th in 206-2. Bartlett's season best throw came in the Spring Twilight at 211-1. Larry Randle placed 3rd in the MIAA in the triple jump and just missed All-American honors with a 10th place NCAA finish. Randle had a season best of 49-1 ½. Bartlett's three points in the javelin earned ESU three points and a 40th place national finish.

The ESU sprint relay teams were outstanding in 2003. The 4 x 100-meter relay ran 40.97 to set a school record, finishing 4th at the Pomona Pitzer Invitational, running with Luke Waller, Shane Grosdidier, Seachris, and Dickson. The 4 x 1 team was only 4th at the MIAA meet but also claimed a high finish of 4th at the always-fast Drake Relays. The sprint medley of Waller, Grosdidier, Hill and Stigge also placed 4th at Drake in 3:26.44. The 4 x 400 posted a very quality time of 3:13.83 at the Last Chance meet but did not qualify for the national meet.

2004

The 2004 team was led by hurdlers, multi-athletes, and the legendary throws program. Hurdler Dustin Brock ran 8.13 to win the 2004 Indoor MIAA, and posted an even faster 8.00 in the MIAA semis. Cameron Babb picked up a 3rd in the high jump and Tyler Witt added a 3rd in the weight throw with a 55-7 ¾ as the Hornets finished 5th in the MIAA. Brock competed at nationals but did not advance out of the prelims as ESU failed to score at the national meet.

ESU fielded a quartet of outstanding javelin throwers in 2004. The quartet of Vogelsberg in 1st (207-7), Bartlett in 2nd, Allen in 3rd, and Stroda in 7th scored 26 points for ESU at the conference meet. Vogelsberg was 3rd at the NCAA meet, throwing a 211-1, off his season best of 223-0 at the KSU Throwers Open. Vogelsberg competed at the USATF Junior meet and placed 3rd in 209-2, which qualified him for the IAAF Junior World Championships in Grosetto, Italy, where he threw 198-10. Stroda threw 211-3 at the Emporia Last Chance meet and was 16th at Nationals. Tyler Wilt added to the throwing strength when he won the discus in 185-6 in the MIAA meet and placed 15th at the NCAA meet.

Babb also competed in the USATF Juniors in the decathlon, placing 11th with 5933 points. His 6247 point total was good for 4th in the MIAA. Tyson Allen added a 3rd place finish in the MIAA decathlon. Brock finished 2nd in the MIAA in the 110-meter hurdles at 14.60, after running a season best at the DII Challenge with a 14.46. ESU finished 4th in the MIAA outdoor meet with 91 points and 32nd in the NCAA meet with 6 points.

2005

ESU finished 3rd in the 2005 MIAA Indoor Championships, scoring 86 points and finishing behind team champion Central Missouri. Chris Peoples, a transfer from TCU who also played football at ESU, had qualified and competed at the NCAA DI National Championships in Sacramento earlier in his career. Peoples won the conference high jump at 6-7 ½, was 2nd in the long jump at 23-10 ½, and 4th in the triple jump. Peoples placed 7th in the NCAA Championships in the long jump at 22-9 and placed 12th in the high jump.

Eric Hoffman set the school record in the 35-pound weight throw and became the first ESU athlete to break the 60-foot barrier when he threw 60-7 ¼ at K-State. Eric Wellman enjoyed a very successful 2005 indoor campaign, as he finished 2nd in the 3000 and 3rd in the mile at the MIAA meet and had a quality performance in winning the Nebraska Holiday Invite 3000 in 8:39.65.

Javelin thrower Andy Vogelsberg emerged as one of the top javelin throwers in the nation, placing 4th in the NCAA with a throw of 210-3. Vogelsberg threw a career best of 228-3 in the MIAA Championships but had to settle for 2nd as Missouri Southern's Mik Alahaivala won at 229-10. Vogelsberg won the javelin at Drake with a throw of 214-8, the first of three straight years of winning at the Drake Relays. Eric Hoffman placed 2nd in the MIAA hammer at 185-5. Peoples won the conference high jump at 6-10 ¼, after earlier in the season setting a school record at 6-10 ¾, and finished 2nd in the long jump at 24-¾. Eric Wellman was the MIAA 5000 champion in 14:53.1 and placed 2nd in the 1500, and Andrew Bird won the 10K in 31:26.71

The conference team title was extremely tight with ESU finishing 2nd to the host, Pittsburg State. The top four team scores were as follows: PSU 124, ESU 123, UCM 121, and Missouri Southern 119. The Hornets had a shot at winning when the meet entered the final event, the 4 x 400 relay. The ESU team of Braden Lysen, Modesto Gilstrap, Tanner Gassman, and Jeremy Rusco ran 3.5 seconds faster than they had ran all year to finish 2nd with a 3:15.97. However, the Pittsburg State anchor was able to edge out Missouri Southern at the line for 3rd place, thus giving the team title to the Gorillas by a single point.

The Hornets finished 21st in the NCAA Outdoor Championships with 10 points behind Vogelsberg's 4th in the javelin at 210-3, People's 8th in the long jump at 23-10 ¾, and Hoffman picking up All-American honors by placing 5th in the hammer, throwing 190-3.

Andy Vogelsberg: National Champion
Andy Vogelsberg won the 2006 NCAA National Outdoor Track and Field Championships in the javelin throwing 245-03, the second longest throw in NCAA DII history. Vogelsberg won three MIAA and Drake Relays titles.

2006

Eric Wellman had an outstanding 2006 indoor season running an excellent time in the mile, winning at Iowa State in 4:08.85. Wellman placed 12th in the NCAA mile in 4:10.33 and won the MIAA mile. Wellman also captured the 3000 in MIAA meet record time of 8:24.27 and anchored the distance medley relay of Shea Camien, Rusco, and Jonathon Heinicke which won in meet record time of 10:18.37. ESU placed 3rd in the MIAA Indoor Championships but did not qualify anyone for the NCAA Indoors.

Javelin thrower Andy Vogelsberg earned a national championship winning the 2006 NCAA National Outdoor Championships with a school record of toss of 245-3. Vogelsberg captured the Drake Relays winning in 215-6, and the MIAA in 211-1. Trent Olivier threw the shot 51-5 ¾ to win the MIAA and added a discus title. Olivier earned All-American honors with a 7th at NCAAs and threw a season best of 174-5 at the DII challenge.

Wellman won the MIAA outdoor 1500 in 3:50.54, and Cameron Babb captured the decathlon with 6595 points and followed that performance up to finish 8th at NCAA Nationals. The Hornets were 4th in the MIAA Outdoor and were 23rd at the NCAA National Outdoors.

2007

Wellman continued his improvement in the 2007 indoor season, running 4:10.98 for the mile at the Notre Dame Meyo Invitational. He ran 2nd in the MIAA mile at 4:15.44 and 2nd in the 3000 at 8:36.66. At the NCAA Indoor Championships, Wellman finished 13th in the mile in 4:18.24. Olivier placed 13th in the NCAA shot at 51-8 ½ after throwing the shot in the MIAA for 4th in 53-9 ¼. Dustin Andrews placed 10th in the high jump at 6-6 ¾ at NCAA Nationals. Andrews also played on the ESU basketball team and as soon as he finished high jumping at nationals he flew from Boston to Missouri and played nine minutes in the Hornets loss to Southeastern State in ESU's first round NCAA basketball game the next day. Andrews was 3rd in the MIAA in 6-10 ¼. Babb picked up a 2nd in the long jump in 23-¾.

ESU's second high jumper, Craig Saalfeld set a new indoor school record of 6-11 to win the ESU Last Chance and qualify for nationals, where he placed 15th at 6-6 ¾. However, Saalfeld could only place 6th in the MIAA meet.

The ESU legendary throws program continued to produce outstanding throwers. Vogelsberg placed 4th at the National Championships, throwing 210-0. His outstanding season included winning the MIAA at 232-10, the Drake Relays, the DII Challenge, and the ESU Relays. ESU went 1-2 in the MIAA javelin with Tyson Allen capturing a 2nd with a throw of 216-11. ESU added a 2-3 in the conference discus with Olivier 2nd in 172-9 and Damon Birk 3rd in 167-8.

Craig Saalfield

The Deaf Olympics requires its participating athletes to have a hearing loss in their better ear of more than 55 decibels. The Deaf Olympics is an international event recognized by the International Olympic Committee.

ESU track and field athlete Craig Saalfeld competed in the 2009 Deaf Olympics Games and picked up a pair of silver medals. He finished 2nd in the decathlon and ran on the 4 x 400 relay that finished 2nd. He also finished 5th in the high jump at 6-6 1/4.

Olivier became a two-time All-American in the discus, throwing 164-7 to place 8th.

The ESU men placed 5th in the MIAA Indoor Championships and 6th in the MIAA Outdoor Championships. The men were 16th at the NCAA DII Outdoor Championships.

2008

Sprinter Kenton Lonberger burst onto the scene in 2008. Lonberger won the MIAA 60, setting a school record of 6.81 and also placed 2nd in the 200 in 21.90. ESU jumpers were the class of the MIAA field with Saalfeld jumping 6-11 ½ to win the MIAA, followed by 2nd place Andrews in 6-10 ¾ and 4th place Alex Pyle in 6-10 ¾. Triple jumper Josh Honeycutt supplied the horizontal jump power, tripling 48-10 ¾ to win conference. The Hornets were 3rd in the MIAA Indoor meet and 14th in the NCAA Indoor Championships.

Lonberger kept up the speed during the 2008 outdoor season, sprinting a 10.29 wind-aided 100 meters at the Emporia Relays for a new school record. He was 3rd in the MIAA and 12th in the NCAA at 10.62. Lonberger also placed 3rd in the MIAA 200 at 21.16 but ran his best when it counted, hitting a PR 20.95 to place 4th at the NCAA meet. The 4 x100 relay team of Larry Beamon, Josh Schuler, Travis Lee, and Lonberger ran a very fast 40.98 at the Emporia Last Chance meet.

Honeycutt continued to score big for the Hornets. His triple jump of 50-7 set a new school record and meet record at the DII challenge. He won the MIAA and finished 10th at nationals, jumping 48-2 ½. Matt Koelling finished 12th at nationals in 47-9. Honeycutt long jumped 23-10 for a season best at the ESU Relays. Skyler Delmott was also an individual champion in the 3000-meter steeplechase at 9:25.01, while Wellman was 2nd in the 5000 at 15:09.89.

The 2008 ESU high jump crew was also outstanding in the outdoor season. Saafeld placed 2nd at the NCAA meet, jumping 6-10 ¾. Andrews cleared a season best of 6-10 ¾ at the ESU Relays and Pyle jumped 6-9 ¾ at the Last Chance meet. The trio finished 1-2-3 at the MIAA meet with all three jumping 6-09 ½ in this order: Saalfeld, Pyle, Andrews. Damon Burk posted noteworthy throws in the shot put, throwing 53-7 ¾ at the DII Challenge and the discus, throwing 159-10 at the ESU Relays.

ESU finished 3rd in the conference and 18th at the National Outdoor Championships.

2009

Josh Honeycutt emerged as an outstanding horizontal jumper in 2009. Honeycutt tripled to an NCAA Indoor championship, jumping 50-5 ½ and also placed 9th in the NCAA long jump at 23-2 ½. Honeycutt captured both the MIAA long and triple jump titles. Sam Williams emerged as a top sprinter for the Hornets during the 2009 indoor season. Williams won the MIAA in 6.82 and ran an 8th place finish at the NCAA meet in 6.89.

Josh Honeycutt: National Champion

Josh Honeycutt won the 2009 NCAA Division II Indoor National Championship in the triple jump and helped lead the Hornets to a fourth place finish at the 2011 Outdoor National Track & Field Championships. Honeycutt earned five All-American honors in the triple jump.

Sam Williams

Sam Williams starred on the ESU track teams in the sprints. A walk-on from the Ivory Coast in Africa, he earned All-Amercian honors in the 60 meters, the 200 meters and anchored the 400-meter relay team that broke the school record. His meteoric rise to sprint stardom was tragically cut short, the victim of a fatal motorcycle accident in November of 2009.

Williams also placed 2nd in the MIAA in 21.92. Vincent Howze captured an MIAA title in the 400, and Alex Pyle led a 1-2 ESU finish in the high jump. Pyle cleared 6-8 ¾ with teammate Craig Saalfeld jumping the same height at 6-8 ¾, but taking 2nd on more misses. Saalfeld scored an MIAA record 5715 points in winning the heptathlon. Adam McGovern took 2nds in both the 800 (1:55.34) and the mile (4.15.78). The Hornets finished 2nd at the MiAA, their best finish in 10 years matching their 2nd place finish in 1998. They were 14th at Nationals behind Honeycutt's National Championship.

Honeycutt triple jumped to a school record at 53-9 ¼ to win ESU Relays. He won the MIAA in 50-4 ¾ and led a 1-2-4 finish with Koehling and Doug Marshall behind him. Honeycutt long jumped 24-4 ½ at the ATG Qualifier and was 2nd in MIAA at 23-9.

Sprinter Sam Williams sprinted to a 7th place finish in the NCAA with a 21.11 200 meters and posted a school record 20.99 in the prelims. Howze added a 400-meter hurdle MIAA title in 52.36. The sprinters were outstanding. The team of Derwin Hall, Schuler, Longberger, and Williams set a school record of 40.01 in the prelims of the NCAA National Outdoor championships. In the final, they ran 40.74 to place 5th. The 4 x 100 won the ESU qualifier, the VS Athletic Beach and Brian Clay Invites.

Pyle took the MIAA high jump title at 6-7 ½, but three-sport letter winner Dustin Andrews jumped 6-10 ¾ to qualify for nationals.

The MIAA 3000 steeplechase featured three ESU athletes scoring who were all teammates at Emporia High School coached by former ESU coach Mark Stanbrough. Delmott was 2nd in 9:23.59 followed by his brother, Asher Delmott in 4th, and Andrew Wayman in 8th. Skyler Delmott was a state cross country champion while Asher Delmott and Andrew Wayman ran on cross country teams that won a state championship and finished 2nd three times in their high school career.

ESU finished at 3rd in the MIAA and 14th at National Outdoors.

2010

Josh Schuler and Josh Honeycutt led the Hornets in 2010. Schuler set an indoor school record at the Husker Invite at 200 meters, running 21.35 for 2nd place. He would run almost as fast, but with more on the line at the NCAA Championships as he blazed to a national runner-up finish in 21:37. Schuler placed 7th in the 60 meters at NCAA Indoors. Schuler also captured both the 60 and 200-meter titles in the MIAA.

Honeycutt, the defending NCCA DII Indoor champ in the triple jump, finished 6th at NCAAs in 49-11 ¾ and 2nd in the MIAA at 51-10. Honeycutt jumped 23-10 ¼ to win the MIAA long jump. Matt Koehling added a triple jump 9th place national finish in 47-11 ¾, after setting a PR of 49-1 at Wichita State earlier in the year. High jumper Briar Ploude earned All-American honors in the high jump, placing 6th at NCAA's in 6-10 ¼. Ploude cleared 7-2 in high school, one of only 10 Kansas high schoolers to jump that high. Briar Ploude high jumped 6-11 at WSU and pole vaulter Zach Rosenberger vaulted 16-2 ¾ at Missouri Southern. Howze set a 400-meter school record in the Husker Invite at 48.80.

The men finished 4th at the MIAA meet and 9th at the NCAA DII Indoor Championships.

Honeycutt placed 4th at the NCAA Outdoors Championships triple jump with 50-8 and 9th in the long jump at 23-6 ¾. He won the MIAA triple at 52-1 ¾ and the long jump in the MIAA in 23-10 ¼ with teammates Koehling (48-11) and Marshall (48-4) going 3-4. Pole vaulter Zach Rosenberger went 16-4 to place 3rd in the NCAA meet after winning the MIAA in 16-6.

David Harris Era
Emporia State won 10 MIAA team championships under Harris and had 20 runner-up finishes. The ESU women swept both the indoor and outdoor MIAA championships in 2001 and 2002. The ESU women earned the school's first top four NCAA finish nationally with a 4th place finish at the NCAA Outdoor Championships in Emporia in 1999 It was the second of three national championship meets at Witten Track/Welch Stadium held under Harris' leadership. The ESU men's track team also finished 4th at the NCAA's in 2011.

Schuler ran a wind-aided 10.47 in the 100 meters at KT Woodman to finish 2nd and placed 4th in the MIAA at 10.58. He added a wind-aided 2nd place MIAA finish in the 200 in 21.02. Howze ran 52.17 in the 400-meter hurdles to win the MIAA and also win the KT Woodman and ESU Relays.

The 4 x 100 relay continued their outstanding success from the previous season. The team of Derwin Hall, Schuler, Howze, and Richardson placed 9th in the 4 x 100 at the NCAA meet in 40.81, just missing the final by .01, and picked up a 2nd place finish at the Drake Relays in 40.97.

MIAA champion Briar Ploude cleared 6-10 ¼ to win the high jump, but teammate Dustin Andrews had the top ESU mark of the season of 6-11 to win the ESU Relays.

Saalfeld posted a decathlon score of 6888 points for 2nd in the MIAA and earned All-American honors with a 7th in the NCAA meet, scoring 6620 points.

The Emporia High School trio of Skyler Delmott, Asher Delmott and Wayman almost pulled off the scoring triple from the previous year in going 3-8-9, respectively, in the 3000-meter steeplechase.

The ESU team finished 3rd in the MIAA with 141 points and 22nd in the NCAA meet.

2011

The 2011 season became the Josh show-with Josh Schuler and Josh Honeycutt. Schuler finished 4th in the NCAA 60 at 6.72. He also claimed a 4th in the NCAA Indoor in the 200 at 21:14. Schuler captured both the 60 and 200 titles at the conference meet.

Steve Blocker: Coach

Steve Blocker was hired as the head track and field coach at Emporia State in 2011. Blocker had served as assistant coach since 2009 with ESU. Blocker previously was the first head coach at Culver-Stockton after the program was reinstituted in 2007 after a 30-year absence. Blocker spent the 2006-07 season as an assistant coach at Santa Barbara City College in Santa Barbara, California. Blocker's first coaching stop was at his alma mater, the University of Northern Iowa, where he served as a volunteer assistant while earning his master's degree. He competed as a hurdler while at UNI.

Honeycutt picked up another 2nd place finish at the national indoor meet for ESU in the triple jump, leaping 51-5 to go with his MIAA title at 50-0 ¾. The 2nd place showing at the NCAA meet continued with Andrew Etheridge placing 2nd in the 60-meter hurdles in 7.94 at the NCAA meet, after capturing an MIAA title.

Ploude captured the MIAA high jump title at 7-2 ½ and finished 9th at nationals in 6-9. Ploude won the Wichita State and Central Missouri meets with clearances over 6-10.

Zach Rosenberger set a new school record at 16-10 ¾ to place 3rd in the vault, after placing 2nd in the MIAA at 16-¾. Other outstanding MIAA indoor performances included Adam McGovern in the 800 at 1:55.0, and William Hohmeier 3rd in the mile at 4:19.92.

The ESU men finished 2nd in the MIAA meet and 5th in the NCAA National Indoor Championships, the highest ESU finish ever in NCAA DII. The MIAA flexed their power with Lincoln finishing 3rd, and Central Missouri finishing 4th.

ESU claimed another individual national championship with Andrew Etheridge winning the 100-meter hurdle titles at the 2011 NCAA National Outdoor Championships in 14.02. Etheridge was 2nd in the MIAA in 14.13. Sprinter Josh Schuler ran 10.26 to set a school record in finishing 2nd in the NCAA National Championships. Schuler also ran 20.75 (another ESU record) in finishing 2nd in the 200 to earn his second All-American honor of the meet. Schuler's successful year also included winning the ESU Relays, the ESU Open and the Sam Williams Qualifier. Tony Granillo scored 6832 points to earn a 3rd place national finish and improve one place on his 4th place MIAA finish of 6529 points. Kevin Roulhac placed 14th at the NCAA meet throwing 161-09 in the discus. The 4 x 100 of Hall, Schuler, Etheridge,

Andrew Etheridge: National Champion
Freshman Andrew Etheridge capped off an outstanding freshman year by winning the 2011 NCAA National Outdoor championships in the 110-meter hurdles. Etheridge finished 3rd in the 2012 National Indoor Championships meet in the 60-meter hurdles.

and Richardson ran a blistering 40.04 to place 2nd in the MIAA meet and place 3rd at nationals with a 40.70.

ESU went 1-2 in the MIAA long jump with Honeycutt at 23-9 ½ and Dwayne Wall at 23-3 ½. Honeycutt won the MIAA triple jump in 52-9 ½ and was 2nd in the Drake Relays at 51-5 ¾. Honeycutt finished off his outstanding career by placing 4th in the triple jump at the NCAA Outdoor Championships in 50-4 ½.

For the first time in school history, the Emporia State men were on the podium at the end of the NCAA Division II National Outdoor Track and Field Championships with a 4th place finish in Turlock, California. The performance marked the best team finish for the Hornets as a Division II school with the previous outdoor best being 7th in 1996.

In the MIAA, Schuler picked up big points in the 200 in 20.82 and finished 2nd in the 100 at 10.32. Etheridge took 2nd in the 110 hurdles and added a 4th in the 400 hurdlers at 55.3. Ploude added high jump points going 6-9 ¾ for 3rd. ESU finished 4th at the MIAA outdoor meet.

NCAA DII Podium
For the first time in NCAA DII history, the Hornets made the podium in 2011, finishing fourth at the national meet.

Another highlight of the season included the distance medley relay team of McGovern, Cortez, Miller, and Hohmeier running 10:04.10 to place 2nd in the prestigious Drake Relays.

2012

Andrew Etheridge continued to make ESU history in the 2012 season. He finished 3rd in the NCAA Indoor Championships in the 60-meter hurdles, running 7.90 in the final, but ran a slightly faster 7.78 in the prelims. After winning the MIAA championships as a freshman, he had a bad start to his sophomore year and failed to qualify for the finals of the 60-meter hurdles at the 2012 MIAA Indoor Championships. Briar Ploude continued his amazing high jumping as he set the indoor school record at 7-2 ½ at the Jayhawk Classic, adding to the mark he had established a week earlier of 7-1 ¾ at the Central Missouri Invite. His 6-10 ¾ placed him 2nd in the MIAA. Cody Miller picked up a 3rd place MIAA finish in the 600 at 1:14.32.

The Hornets finished 4th in the conference meet and the Hornets were 21st with 10 points at the NCAA outdoor meet.

Junior Vincent Howze's sprinting abilities were on display as he earned All-American honors by placing 6th in the NCAA National Outdoor Championships in the 200 meters. He placed 2nd in the 200 meters (21.16) and also added a 2nd in the 400 meters at the MIAA in 47.75. Howze saved the best for last for ESU turning in the second fastest 200-meter time in school history to earn All-American honors. His time of 20.86 was good for 6th in the event and 2nd in ESU history to Josh Schuler's 20.75 set at the previous year's national championships. It was his second All-American honor after finishing 7th in the 400 meter hurdles in 2009.

At the National Outdoor Championships, defending national champion Etheridge clipped a hurdle early and was not able to finish his prelim in the 110 hurdles. Andrew Wilcox competed at nationals and finished 17th in the long jump going 23-2 ½. The Hornet men finished 41st in the team standings, the 10th straight year they had scored at the national meet and the 18th time in the last 19 years they had scored.

Briar Ploude: School Record Holder
All-American Briar Ploude set the school indoor high jump record at 7-3 ¾ and the outdoor record at 7-2 ¼.

ESU finished in 6th place at the conference outdoor championships. Etheridge posted his fastest time of the year in the prelims of the 110 hurdles in the MIAA meet, running 14.09 but had difficulty in the final and finished 8th behind teammates Tyler Swalley and Gannon Mack in 5th and 6th. Witt won the hammer throw and Miller took a 2nd in the 800 at 1:53.88 in the conference meet. Asher Delmott picked up a 3rd in the 3000 steeplechase, as did the 4 x 400 of Miller, Frankie Cortez, Mack and Kyle Downing, running 3:15.60. Wilcox added a long jump 3rd in 24-6 ¼. The men's sprint medley consisting of Ryan Dickson, Etheridge, Howze, and Miller ran 3:27.08 to finish 4th at the Drake Relays.

2013

The Emporia State Hornet men placed 4th in the MIAA Indoor Championships. Ploude earned an individual championship when he set an MIAA record in winning the high jump. He cleared 7-2 ½ to break Kevin Dotson of Missouri Southern's record of 7-2, set in 1999. Marcus Calleja placed 4th with a 6-8 ¼ to give Emporia State 15 points in the high jump. Earlier in the year, Ploude jumped an outstanding 7-3 ¾ to set the ESU record, which also bettered the outdoor record. Ploude's jump at the Jayhawk Classic was the 19th best all-time in DII competition. The Hornets other individual championship came in the 60 hurdles as Emporia State took three of the top four spots. Gannon Mack won his first MIAA Championship at 8.04 while Swalley ran 8.06 and edged out Etheridge by .006 seconds for 3rd. In addition, Emporia State turned in three runner-up performances led by Lucas San Martin's personal best effort in the men's weight throw. He threw 59-1 ½ to place 2nd and move to 3rd on the Emporia State all-time list. Howze had a part in two 3rd place finishes. He was 3rd in a time of 21.95 in the 200 and joined Mack, Ashton Proctor, and Miller in a 3rd place finish in the 4 x 440 relay. Payson Maydew gave the Hornets a jumpstart on the meet with a 4th place finish in the heptathlon by scoring 5108 points.

Maydew started the 2013 NCAA DII National Indoor Championships off with a top 10 finish in the men's heptathlon. The only freshman in the field scored 5066 points in the seven events to place 10th. Etheridge earned his third All-American honor in the 60 hurdles. He ran an 8.00 to place 5th in the event.

Derwin Hall matched the second fastest time in school history with a 6.74 in the 60 to qualify for the finals with the second fastest time in the field. His time was just off Josh Schuler's 6.71 at the 2011

NCAA Championships. Hall ran 6.80 to earn his first individual All-American honor with 6th place finish in the 60 final. Mack barely missed the finals in the 60 hurdles, running 8.09 and placing 10th. Howze turned in the third fastest 200 meters indoors in Emporia State history at 21.86 to place 19th overall. Ploude entered the high jump competition with the top mark in the nation at 7-2 ½. However, he struggled, clearing 6-8 ¾ but taking three attempts at each of the first two heights to place 13th on misses. Teammate Calleja jumped up in the men's high jump to clear 6-8 ¾ to finish in a tie for 7th and earn All-American honors. The Hornets finished 21st in the national competition.

The Hornets moved up one spot from their MIAA Indoor finish to place 5th at the MIAA Outdoor Championships. Ploude won his 2nd MIAA Outdoor Championship and matched his indoor conference performance by clearing 6-11 ¾ in the high jump. Calleja also picked up points in the high jump, clearing 6-7 ½ to place 6th.

Payson Maydew: School Record Holder
All-American Payson Maydew established multi-event school records in both the heptathlon and decathlon. He became the first Hornet to surpass 7000 points in the decathlon.

The Emporia State "hurdle crew" had an outstanding MIAA outdoor meet with five different athletes scoring points. Etheridge broke his own school record by running 13.97 in the prelims of the 110 hurdles. He came back to lead a 2-3-4 sweep by running 14.23, while Mack ran 14.32 to just edge Swalley, who finished in 14.38. Mack and Michael Child both qualified for the finals in the men's 400m hurdles. Mack ran 52.68 to place 4th on the Emporia State all-time list. Child finished in 5th place.

Howze placed 4th in the 200-meter dash and ran a leg on both relays. He ran 21.51 in the finals after running a mark of 21.27 in the prelims. He joined Hall, Etheridge, and Richardson to run a 41.02 to finish 3rd in the 400 meter relay. He combined with Mack and John Thurston to place 4th in the 1600 relay with a time of 3:14.01. Richardson ran a season's best 10.44 in the prelims and turned in a 10.48 to place 3rd in the men's 100-meter dash final. Maydew scored a career-high 6615 points to place 3rd in the decathlon in an extremely talented field.

The Hornets notched a 15th place team performance at the 2013 National Outdoor Championships. A highlight for the 2013 season for the Emporia State men came from the 4 x 100 meter relay team. The foursome of Hall, Howze, Etheridge and Richardson entered the championships ranked 13th after running a 40.76 at the Drake Relays. They blew that away with a 40.07 that ranked third all-time at Emporia State in the prelims. The two teams in front of them both ran sub-40 seconds. The men's 4 x 100 relay team of Hall, Howze, Etheridge and Richardson placed 5th in the final with a time of 40.16 to earn All-American honors for the third time in five years.

Maydew competed in three decathlons in three weeks as he attempted to qualify for the national meet. He barely made the qualification, turning in a personal best 6719 points at the OBU Last Chance Meet to qualify 14th in the decathlon, as the last person to get into the competition. The freshman from Pratt was sitting in 12th place after the first day of national competition and started the second day with a personal best in the 110 hurdles. He finished with a 4:35.08 1500 to move all the way up to 6th place overall. He ended with a personal best of 6809 points to rank fifth all-time at Emporia State.

The men's high jump began during the running of the decathlon 1500. Within minutes of Maydew finishing his All-American performance in the decathlon, both Ploude and Calleja cleared 6-10 ¾ to ensure their own All-American status. The MIAA Indoor and Outdoor champion Ploude, cleared 7-½ and finished 4th in the competition. Calleja's personal record of 6-10 ¾ put him in a tie for 7th after being ranked last in the national field of 21 in the high jump.

Former national champion Etheridge had the highlight with a preliminary run. After nearly falling coming out of the blocks in the 110 hurdles, he recovered to run a school record 13.85 and qualify for the finals. After winning the national championship as a freshman in 2011 in Turlock, Calif., Etheridge had clipped a hurdle in Pueblo in 2012 and failed to make finals. But in 2013, Etheridge earned his second outdoor All-American honor in the 110 meter hurdles with a 14.04 to place 6th.

In his first national championship outing, Wall went 47-3 ½ to place 17th in the triple jump. Teammate Mack ran 14.15 to place 12th overall in the 110 hurdles and placed 18th in the nation after running 54.11 in the 400-meter hurdles. Donald Wilcox was another Hornet that just missed the finals. He went 24-11 ¾ on his final jump of the prelims to finish 11th with nine jumpers going to the finals. After anchoring the 4 x 100 relay, Richardson ran 10.49 in the open 100 meters to place 17th in the nation. It was the fifth straight race under 10.50 for Richardson, who had not cracked that mark prior to the MIAA Championships.

2014

Payson Maydew was the lone MIAA indoor champion in 2014, setting a Missouri Southern building record and Emporia State school record of 5305 points in the heptathlon. He also placed 6th in the 60 hurdles with a time of 8.52 in the finals. Samuel Saidi scored in two events for the Hornets. He was 2nd in the high jump (6-9 ¾) and 8th in the triple jump (46-2 ¾). Duke Tibbs ran 49.29 for 3rd in the 400 and Jordan Manning cleared 6-8 to tie for 3rd in the men's high jump. The ESU men finished 6th in the MIAA indoor meet.

Maydew competed in the 2015 NCAA National Indoor Track and Field Championships in the heptathlon and finished 5th, scoring 5247 points. ESU finished in a tie for 34th place at the 2014 indoor nationals.

Emporia State All-American Maydew followed up on his indoor success and punched his ticket to the NCAA Division II Outdoor Track & Field Championships, as he became the first Hornet to surpass 7,000 points in winning the decathlon at the ESU Combined Multis at Welch Stadium. He amassed 7202 points to shatter Tim Vietti's school record of 6913 points set at the 1995 College Station Relays. Maydew was in 2nd place, 226 points behind the first day leader Nathan Hancock of Minnesota State-Mankato after five events. The second day was Maydew's strong suit and after finishing 2nd in the 110-meter hurdles at 14.93 to open the second day, he had the top mark in the discus (122-10) and pole vault (14-3 ¼) to move into 1st place. Maydew had the second best javelin throw at 172-6 ¼ and then dominated the field in the 1500, with a time of 4:26.79 to win by over 15 seconds.

The men finished 7th in the MIAA 2014 Outdoor Championships. Both men's relay teams finished in the top four for Emporia State. A.J. West, Tibbs, Brady Huckaby, and Dickson were the runners up in the 400-meter relay in 41.16. The 1600 relay team of Dickson, Ashton Proctor, Jordan Smith, and John Thurston ran 3:14.49 to place 4th. The Hornet men picked up 12 points in the high jump, led by Ploude with a 6-9 ¾ to place 4th. He was followed by Grady Derryberry in 5th and Jordan Manning in 6th. The men's javelin had two Hornets place in the top seven with Pfizenmaier placing 4th at 195-07, while Alex Linsey threw 188-1 to place 7th in a career best. Nick Klenda continued a late season surge on as he placed 5th in the discus. Tibbs broke the 48-second barrier for the first time, running 47.94 to finish 5th in the 400. Dickson also scored for the Hornets by placing 4th in the 100-meter dash.

The Sam Williams Qualifier hosted by ESU had some outstanding relay performances. The 4 x100 relay of A.J. West, Duke Tibbs, Brady Huckaby and Ryan Dickson ran a 40.65 and Dickson and Tibbs then teamed with Proctor and Smith to run 3:11.30 in the 4 x 400 relay.

The men finished 19th at the NCAA Outdoor Track and Field Championships. Maydew and Ploude both garnered 3rd place finishes to earn All-American honors. In one of the toughest decathlons in NCAA Division II Championship history, Maydew shattered his own school record with 7413 points to finish 3rd overall. For the first time in the 21st century the top eight finishers all scored at least 7000 points as Chico State's J. Patrick Smith claimed his third straight national championship with 7645 points.

Maydew opened the day with a 14.93 in the 100-meter hurdles that was just .02 off of his personal best. A throw of 119-5 in the discus placed him 11th in that event for his lowest placing in the 10 events. He came back and cleared 15-1 in the pole vault and threw 162-8 to place 6th in the javelin and move up to 5th in the overall competition. After nine previous events in two days, Maydew came through with a personal best of 4:25.97 in the 1500 to break his own school record by 206 points.

Ploude entered his third and final outdoor championship ranked 12th in the field of 20 jumpers. He had placed 4th the previous year, but the top five competitors returned to compete in 2014. He made the first three heights on his second attempt and cleared the fourth bar, 6-11 ¾, on his third and final attempt to wrap up a 3rd place finish. Saidi was the other Hornet to compete in the high jump but failed to clear his opening height.

The men's 4 x 400 relay team of Dickson, Proctor, Smith, and Tibbs ran 3:13.39 to place 12th overall, but failed to qualify for the final. The Hornet 4 x 400 relay team had been met with much success at NCAA nationals. They entered the competition having placed in three of the previous five years. However, they had no one returning from the previous year's All-American performance. The all-new foursome of A.J. West, Tibbs, Huckaby, and Dickson ran 40.77 to finish 8th and earn All-American status for the men's 4 x100 meter relay team for the second straight year and fourth time in the last six years. Kyle Pfizenmaier placed 16th in the men's javelin at 195-5.

2015

The 2015 indoor season saw the Hornets place 5th in the MIAA Indoor Championships. Two Hornets that redshirted the previous indoor season saw their efforts pay off with conference championships. Etheridge ran a 7.99 to win the 60-meter hurdles and Wilcox long jumped a PR of 24-1 ¾ to win by 6 inches. Etheridge also anchored the 4 x 400 meter relay team of Ryan Dickson, Cody Miller, and Colin Coleman to a 2nd place finish in 3:21.54.

Maydew totaled 5363 points to finish 2nd in the heptathlon and set a new ESU standard. His old record of 5305 points was set as he won the 2014 MIAA Championship. Maydew was sitting in 4th place after the first four events but had the best marks in the field in the 60 and 1000 on the second day to move into 2nd place. Freshman Wyatt Sander scored 4592 points to finish in 8th place and pick up a point in the team standings for the Hornets. Earlier in the season at the Kansas State Invitational, Maydew had a breakthrough in the open pole vault, clearing 16-¾ for the third best vault in Emporia State indoor history.

Saidi cleared 6-11 ½ to give the Hornets another MIAA individual champion after finishing 2nd the previous season. He actually won the event on his first jump, clearing 6-8 on his first attempt of the competition while Kevin Schultz of Northwest Missouri took all three attempts to clear it before going out on the next bar. Dickson was a placer in two individual events for the Hornets. He was 5th in both the 60 and 200-meter dashes. He ran a 6.94 in the 60 and 22.23 in the 200. Miller placed 5th with a time of 1:14.82 in the 600 yard run. Jacob Bull ran 4:20.91 to place 6th in the mile run and Jordan Smith and Daniel Classen rounded out the men's scoring for the Hornets by placing in the 800. Smith ran 1:56.45 to place 6th, while Claassen ran 1:57.96 to finish 8th. The Hornet men competed without 400-meter star Duke Tibbs.

At the NCAA National Indoor Championships, the men finished 28th, led by Etheridge who earned his fourth All-American honor in four trips to the Indoor Championships in the 60 meter hurdles. His time of 8.16 was good for 7th overall. Bad luck struck in the heptathlon as Maydew did not finish the event. In the first of the second day, the 60 hurdles, he hit a hurdle and nearly went down to the track. As he recovered, he knocked down the next hurdle and his time was disqualified. He came back to clear 15-1 in the pole vault to finish 3rd in that event, but with no chance to move up into the scoring, he elected to not run the 1000 meters. The men placed 28th at the national meet.

The MIAA Outdoor Championships saw the Hornets place 6th, but only two points out of 4th in a tight team competition. Maydew began the competition with a 4th place finish in the decathlon. His total of 6941 points was one of nine provisional marks in the extremely strong decathlon competition. Kyle Pfizenmaier got the Hornets started at the MIAAs by winning the men's javelin. His toss of 221-01 ranked fifth on the ESU all-time list. Saidi cleared the seven-foot mark for the first time in 2015 to win the men's high jump title. He matched his personal best of 7-¼ set at the 2014 Kansas Relays. Etheridge picked up the Hornets lone win on the track. He ran a time of 14.28 to win his first MIAA Championship in the 110 hurdles to compliment his national championship in the event his freshman year. Tibbs, hampered by a hamstring injury for most of the outdoor season, ran his season's best performance in the prelims (his 47.56 was the second best in ESU history) and followed that with a runner-up finish in the finals of the 400. Wilcox also had a 4th place finish long jumping 24-3 ½. Smith and Thomas LaRoche both scored in the 800 for the Hornets. Smith placed 3rd in 1:52.76, while LaRoche ran a 1:55.39 to finish in 5th place. Tre Dickerson had a personal best mark 47-11 ¼ to place 4th in the men's triple jump.

The Hornets posted a couple of quality marks at the Sam Williams Qualifier with the men's 4 x 400 relay team of Dickson, Coleman, Miller and Sanders running 3:11.99 to place 5th on the Emporia State all-time list. Smith finished 2nd with an excellent time of 1:51.70 in the men's 800.

At the 2015 NCAA DII Outdoor Track and Field Championships, the Hornets finished 32nd in the competition, marking the 13th straight year the Emporia State men scored at the national meet and the 21st time in the last 23 years they scored at nationals. Maydew earned All-American status with a 3rd place showing in the decathlon scoring 7222 points and Wilcox placed 7th in the long jump at 24-5 ½. Etheridge ran 14.34 to place 9th in the 110-meter hurdles. Pfizenmaier threw 203-2 to place 12th in the men's javelin and Saidi cleared 6-6 ¾ in the men's high jump to finish in 15th place.

Epilogue

Emporia State's legendary track and field program began in 1902 and with the exception of two years during WWII, has continued for over 110 years. ESU has won one national track and field championship, winning the 1964 NAIA National Outdoor Track and Field Championship. Athletes from Emporia State University have set national and world records, won national championships and attained numerous All-American honors. ESU athletes have participated in the Olympic Games and one emerged as an Olympic champion. The coaches at ESU have also been honored with inductions into National Track and Field Halls of Fame and have helped coached United States Olympic and international teams.

ESU has had an amazing eight different athletes set World Records plus a distance medley relay team that set a World Record! John Kuck, a Hornet in the 1920's, won the gold medal in the shot put at the 1928 Olympic Games. Archie San Romani competed in the 1936 Olympic Games while still competing for Emporia State and finished fourth. After his career at Emporia State, Allan Feuerbach had 4th and 5th place finishes in the 1972 and 1976 Olympics. The ESU men have won an outstanding 39 individual national championships

The Hornets have competed in both NCAA and NAIA national competitions and in several different conferences in their 100 plus years of competition. The current MIAA conference is an outstanding track and field conference with consistent high national individual finishes and conference teams competing for national championships. Track and field has been successful at Emporia State through the determined efforts of athletes and coaches who have overcome major challenges such as lack of facilities, scholarships and funding. Emporia State has not only risen to the challenge but has thrived to become one of the legendary track and field programs in the history of collegiate track and field.

Women's Track and Field
Introduction

The history of women's track and field in the United States began in 1895, when the women of Vassar College Athletic Association inaugurated the first field day for women in the United States. By 1922, track and field for women was fashionable in colleges around the nation. Dr. Harry Stewart organized a competition to select a United States team to compete internationally in the Women's World Games in Paris. The competition was highly successful for the United States. However, Stewart was highly criticized by leaders of physical education of women, who sought to protect girls from the "evils of competition." Track and field for women suffered. Schools responded to the pressure and slowly track and field competition for women died, with only a few women's athletic clubs offering track and field. However, in 1962 the success of Wilma Rudolph inspired a joint effort of the Olympic Committee and the physical education association to help develop women's track and field once again in the schools. There have been many significant setbacks and victories throughout the years. By 1980, because of Title IX, rewards for athletic achievement were being shared with women. With many outstanding opportunities and the strong development of women's track and field competition, the women have caught up to their male counterparts.

Emporia State officially began women's track and field in 1976. However, its history begins before then. In 1960, the women's Olympic team trained in Emporia for 6 weeks to prepare for the 1960 Olympic Games. Coach Fran Welch was chosen as one of the coaches for the 1960 United States Women's Olympic Track and Field Team. Welch was recognized by his peers as one of the top track coaches in the United States, as demonstrated by his selection as an Olympic coach. In 1958, Welch had charge of a group of AAU stars that toured Europe, and he was also named field coach for the 1959 Pan American Games team. Welch had been president of the Missouri Valley Association of the AAU and was a member of the National AAU Track and Field Committee, as well as being one of the original inductees into the NAIA Track and Field Hall of Fame in 1954.

1960 Women's Olympic Team trains in Emporia

In the middle of July of 1960, the U.S. Women's Olympic track and field team came to Emporia State to train for the Games, and stayed until August 15th when they left for Rome. While here, the women lived in Morse Hall and worked out on the stadium field under the direction of Fran Welch. Wilma Rudolph was one of these athletes, and this young lady went on to win the 100-meter, the 200-meter, and anchor the United States winning 4 x 100-meter relay at the Rome Games.

Front row from left: Martha Hudson, Barbara Browne, Karen Anderson, Ernestine Pollards, Willye White, Pam Kurrell and Lucinda Williams
Back row from left: Ed Temple (coach), JoAnn Terry, Barbara Jones, Earlene Brown, Pat Daniels, Marie Wagner (chaperone), Jean Gaertner, Wilma Rudolph, Shirley Crowder, Anne Smith, Neomia Rogers, Irene Robertson, and Fran Welch (field coach)

The 1960 Women's Olympic Track and Field team was coached by Ed Temple of the Tennessee State Tigerbelles and featured Wilma Rudolph. Rudolph had overcome childhood polio and after being told she may never walk again, she bounced back to win the 100 and 200 meter dashes, as well as anchor the winning 4 x 100 meter relay team to victories in the 1960 Rome Olympics.

Emporia had their own Olympian Janell Smith. Smith, from Fredonia, KS, was one of the top female track stars in the world, and at the age of 17, she had represented the United States in the 1964 Olympic Games. In the semifinals of the Olympic 400-meter, in which she just missed qualifying for the final, Smith set an American record of 54.5 seconds. Later that same year, she set the world indoor mark of 54.0 seconds in the 400-meter, and in 1965, Smith lowered her Outdoor American record to 53.4 seconds. Smith had twice been named to the All-American Women's Track and Field team by the AAU. She was featured on the cover of Sports Illustrated as she prepared for the 1964 Olympics. Janell Smith attended Emporia State after the 1964 Olympics as a student. The school did not officially offer a women's track program, but Smith continued to compete. As a freshman, Smith represented Emporia State in the 1966 NAIA Indoor, although unofficially. She won the 60-yard dash in 7.0 seconds and the 440 dash in 57.9 seconds. Smith also competed in some collegiate meets, winning the open 100-yard dash in 11.1 seconds at a University of Kansas meet.

Janell Smith: Olympian
Representing Emporia State in the NAIA Indoor, although unofficially, was a freshman coed named Janell Smith. Smith, from Fredonia, KS, was one of the top female track stars in the world, and at the age of 17 she had represented the United States in the 1964 Olympic Games. In the semifinals of the Olympic 400-meter, in which she just missed qualifying for the final, Smith set an American record of 54.5 seconds. Later that same year, she set the world indoor mark of 54.0 seconds in the 400-meter, and in 1965 lowered her American outdoor record to 53.4 seconds.

1976

For the first time in the history of the school, in 1976, Emporia Kansas State College (EKSC) fielded an intercollegiate women's track and field team during the 1976 season. The first year women's team, led by San Diego, California, freshman Kathy Devine, stole the headlines from the established men's program. As a junior in high school, Devine had set a national high school record of 51-1 for the eight pound shot put to establish herself as one of the top women shot putters in the country. She chose to attend EKSC because of Coach Phil Delavan's reputation as one of the top weight coaches in the United States, and because of the success Hornet grad Allan Feuerbach was enjoying on the world track circuit. Devine made an immediate impact on the program and firmly established her potential in her first college appearance, setting the best national shot put mark of the young season with a 50-9 toss at the KU indoor meet. The following weekend, Devine placed 2nd in the National AAU indoor championships with the toss of 49-10 ¼. This performance at the AAU meet earned Devine the right to join an AAU team for a dual meet in March against the Russian team in Leningrad, but she declined because of school commitments.

Philip Delavan: Coach

Philip Delavan became the ESU head track and field and cross country coach in 1965. He had served as head track coach at Central Missouri State University from 1963 to 1965, previous to which he had been an assistant at Baylor University for one year and an assistant at Iowa State University for two years. Delavan had attended school at Iowa State from 1955-1959, during which time he was one of the best shot putters in the nation. In 1957, he placed 1st in the shot put in the Kansas Relays, and during the same year placed 6th in the finals of the NCAA shot put.

Devine continued her outstanding success during the 1976 outdoor season, garnering "Outstanding Woman Athlete" honors at the Arkansas Relays by winning the shot put, discus and javelin with marks of 50-1, 146-5 and 129-8, respectively. The mark in the discus set a meet record. Finishing 3rd for the Lady Hornets at Arkansas were Becky Armstrong in the two-mile and the 440 relay team of Karen Lane, Pat Roberts, Kim Haines and Lorye Nielson. One week after Arkansas in the Emporia Invitational, Devine turned in her most spectacular result of the young season, throwing the shot 52-4 ½ to establish a new National Women's Intercollegiate record and erase the mark of 52-0 ¼ by Maren Seidler of San Leandro State set in 1972. In 1976, Seidler was the American record holder for the shot put at 56-0.

Devine rolled through the remainder of the schedule unbeaten in the shot, setting meet records of 51-5 at the Kansas Relays and 49-3 ½ at the Wichita State Relays, winning the AIAW Region Six title in St. Cloud, Minnesota, with a toss of 49-10 ½, and extending her national collegiate record to 53-1 in winning the AIAW National shot put title. Devine was also successful in the discus, winning at the Wichita meet with the record toss of 146-3, finishing 2nd at KU at 145-0 while breaking the old meet record, and finishing 2nd at the AIAW Region Six. Devine concluded her phenomenal season by winning the U.S. Track and Field Federation shot title, then qualifying for the Olympic trials by placing 2nd at the AAU outdoor meet to Maren Seidler. Devine again placed 2nd to Seidler in the Olympic trials shot final with the toss of 51-0, but unfortunately, to qualify for a trip to Montreal she would have had to either win the event or throw 54-6 in placing 2nd or 3rd, so Devine was not eligible to compete in the 1976 Olympic Games.

Kathy Devine: Collegiate Record

Kathy Devine was one of the premier throwers in the United States during her time at Emporia State. She set the national collegiate record in the shot put four different times. She earned two 1st place finishes and one 2nd place finish at nationals in the shot put. She held the school record in the shot put and javelin. Also an outstanding volleyball player, Devine participated in the 1976 and 1980 U.S Olympic Trials.

1977

The 1977 Lady Hornet track squad was strengthened by the addition of two outstanding freshmen, Brenda Short and Pam Bulson. The addition of these two, combined with the return of sophomore All-American Kathy Devine, gave E-State three top quality performers. However, the Lady Hornets did not have the depth necessary to contend for the conference title in the first year of the women's event, and they finished a distant 2nd to Kearney State in the CSIC meet. Devine won the conference shot, discus and javelin titles, a feat she performed quite regularly during the season, with marks of 50-10 ½, 140-1, and 139-5, respectively. Short and Bulson accounted for the bulk of the remaining Hornet points, Short taking 2nd in the long jump, 3rd in the 100-meter dash and 4th in the 200-meter dash, and Bulson placing 2nd in the high hurdles and the high jump and 4th in the long jump.

> **Patricia Roberts: U.S.A. Olympian**
> EKSC was officially represented in the Montreal Olympics, although not in track and field competition. Pat Roberts, an outstanding player on the Lady Hornet basketball team and a very good high jumper on the 1976 track and field team, was selected to play on the United States women's basketball team which won a silver medal in the 1976 Olympic Games in Montreal. Roberts missed the latter half of the track season because of the tryouts and subsequent practice by the Olympic team. Following the Olympics, Roberts transferred to the University of Tennessee to play for her Olympic coach, Pat Summitt.

This outstanding trio of Lady Hornets began the 1977 season quite impressively at the Missouri Women's Indoor Invitational, with Devine and Bulson winning the shot put and high jump, respectively, while Short placed 2nd in the 60-yard dash and the long jump. Devine continued her winning ways during the outdoor season while competing in the major meets in the Midwest. Opening at the Arkansas Relays, she won the shot, javelin and discus, setting meet records in the first two, to win "Outstanding Woman Performer" for the second consecutive year. Moving on to the Wichita Relays, Devine won the same three events while setting a meet and school record of 152-5 in the discus. The next major meet for the Lady Hornets was the Oklahoma State Invitational, where Bulson, Devine and Short garnered four 1sts, all with meet record performances, to lead EKSC to a 5th place finish in a predominantly major college field. Devine won the shot put and discus with marks of 49-11 and 14-7, respectively, while Bulson tied for 1st in the high jump at 5-5 and Short won the long jump at 18-2 ½.

The team moved next to the Midwest relay circuit, and Devine won the shot put and discus and placed 2nd in the javelin at the Kansas Relays. At the Drake Relays, the final event before the CSIC meet, Devine won the shot put with a meet record throw of 50-4 ½. After leading Emporia State to the 2nd place finish in the CSIC meet, Devine,

> **Kathy Devine: National Champion**
> Kathy Devine was a two-time national champion for the Hornets. She won the national championships in 1976 and 1977 while Emporia State competed in the AIAW. In 1976 her winning throw of 53-1 was a new collegiate record. In 1978 Devine finished 2nd in the AIAW shot put.

Short, and Bulson competed in the AIAW Region 6 meet. By placing 1st in the shot, 4th in the long jump, and 2nd in the high jump respectively, all three Lady Hornets qualified for the AIAW National meet to be held the following weekend. At the AIAW Championships, Devine successfully defended her national title by winning the shot put with a toss of 51-4 ½, but neither of the other Lady Hornet performers were able to place. Devine continued her season-long unbeaten streak in the shot put by winning the event at the USTFF meet in Wichita, throwing 50-9 but, as in 1976, Devine suffered her first loss at the National

AAU meet, placing 3rd behind Maren Seidler, the American record holder, and Jane Frederick, respectively. Seidler extended the American shot put record to 62-7 ¾ in 1979, while Frederick was the American record holder in the heptathlon.

1978

Kathy Devine provided most of the excitement in the 1978 indoor track meet, setting an indoor school record of 52-5 ¾ in the shot put during a practice meet at Pittsburg and again winning the shot at the Missouri Invitational with a toss of 50-5 ½. Freshman Judy Becker also provided a victory in the Missouri indoor meet, winning the high jump with the school record leap of 5-4. Most of the Lady Hornets other top performers were involved with other winter sports, such as basketball and swimming, and did not make an impact on the indoor season.

> **KU Relays at Emporia State**
> A portion of the Kansas Relays, typically held in Lawrence, Kansas was held at Welch stadium on the ESU campus in 1978. Renovation of Memorial Stadium caused the meet to be transferred to four regional locations, including Emporia, which hosted the men's small college and women's divisions.
>
>

Devine opened the outdoor season in usual form, winning the three throwing events at the Arkansas Relays for the third consecutive year while extending her own meet records to 50-6 in the shot put, 148-1 in the discus, and 150-11 in the javelin. The latter mark was also a new ESU school record. Other Lady Hornets placing at Arkansas were Pam Bulson with a 2nd place in the high jump, Brenda Short with a 3rd place in the long jump, and Judy Becker with a 6th place in the high jump.

Two weeks after the season opener at Arkansas, while the men's team competed in the Emporia Relays, the Lady Hornets traveled to Stillwater to participate in the Oklahoma State Invitational and picked up a 2nd place team finish, losing to Southwest Missouri by only five points. Devine provided her usual three victories, winning the shot put, discus and javelin, while Becker won the high jump at 5-8 and placed 2nd to Devine in the discus. Short also picked up a victory for E-State, winning the long jump with a leap of 18-8. Rounding out the Hornet scoring were seconds by Laura Schroer in the javelin and Dorothy Frey in the high jump. The Lady Hornets were without Bulson at the OSU meet, costing them valuable points and possibly the team title. The Hornet performers were very successful against some strong competition at the Kansas Relays, which were held in Emporia in 1978. Devine led the way with three victories and a national intercollegiate record, extending her shot put mark to 53-3 ¾, as well as winning the discus and javelin. Becker and Frey finished 2nd and 4th, respectively, in the high jump while Short placed 3rd in the long jump. Fifths were earned by Schroer in the shot put and by the 440 relay team of Leslie Whitsitt, LaDonna Dearing, Karen Lane, and Short.

Devine continued her superb performances the next weekend at the Drake Relays, bettering her week-old national record and her Drake Relays record with a toss of 53-7 ¾. Also placing at Drake were Short with a 4th in the long jump and Becker with a school record leap of 5-8 ¼ to place 6th in the high jump. Unfortunately, this success was tainted by an injury Devine sustained to her throwing hand, which kept her from competing in the CSIC meet and hindered her performances during the remainder of the season. However, even with Devine, the Lady Hornets could not have challenged the powerful Kearney State team for the CSIC title, as the Antelopes won by more than 200 points over the 2nd place Hornets. Devine's absence was not the only disappointment of the CSIC meet, as the Emporia State women who did compete failed to win an event, turning in performances well below their normal standards.

Devine was able to throw the shot put the weekend after the CSIC meet in the AIAW Region 6 meet, but the injury prevented her from throwing the discus and javelin, and her winning toss of 49-1 ¾ in the shot was well below her usual standards during the season. Frey and Becker placed 1st and 2nd, respectively in the high jump, both clearing 5-2, and Short placed 3rd in the long jump. Rounding out the Hornet scoring was a 5th in the shot and a 6th in the javelin by Laura Schroer, and a 5th by the 440 relay team of Whitsitt, Dearing, Lane, and Short. Despite being the pre-meet favorite to win a third consecutive national shot put title, Devine was upset in the event, finishing 2nd to Jennifer

> **Delavan Era**
> Coach Philip Delavan coached 35 All-Americans including seven national champions in his 12-year tenure at ESU. His teams consistently placed in the top 10 at the NAIA championships and he was the coach of the first ESU Women's track and team. He also coached the field events for the 1972 U.S. Women's Olympic team and served as a coach for the 1970 and 1973 United States track and field teams at the World University Games.
>
>

Smith of the University of Texas-El Paso. Devine ended her season by repeating her 1977 placing in the National AAU meet, taking 3rd with a toss of 50-10. Maren Seidler again won the event.

1979

Much of the flair of the previous three track seasons was lost when Kathy Devine transferred to the University of Texas after the 1978 fall semester, following Coach Delavan, who had taken the head women's track position at Texas in August. Despite the absence of Devine, the women maintained a solid program due to several outstanding performers, most notably Brenda Short, Dorothy Frey, and Judy Becker. Short and Frey picked up 3rd and 5th place finishes in the long jump and high jump, respectively, at the Arkansas Relays to open the outdoor season. Again, the lack of indoor results was because most of the top performers participated in other winter sports. Short played a big part in the Lady Hornets' victory in the Central Missouri State Invitational, winning the 100-yard dash, 220-yard dash, the long jump, and anchoring the winning 440 relay team. Also picking up victories for E-State in the CMSU meet were Frey in the 100-yard hurdles, Becker in the high jump, Cheryl Phares in the 880, Nancy Davidson in the mile, and the mile relay team.

> **Dennis Delmott: Coach**
> Two-time cross country All-American Dennis Delmott took over on an interim basis for one year when Coach Delavan accepted the University of Texas head women's coaching position. The school record holder at 6 miles, he finished among the top 25 runners at the 1976 Olympic Trials in the marathon.
>
>

Frey earned Emporia State's only place on the major relay circuit with a 5th in the high jump at the Kansas Relays with a personal best leap of 5-7. Short, although not placing at Kansas, qualified for the AIAW Region 6 meet and set a new school record with a 12.1 second 100-meter.

Despite these strong performers, a lack of depth caused the Lady Hornets to slip to 3rd place in the CSIC behind perennial champ Kearney State and Fort Hays State. Short garnered the only Emporia State victories in the conference meet, winning the 100 and 200-meter dashes as well as placing 2nd in the long jump. Short also accounted for the Lady Hornets' only 1st in the final competition of the season, the AIAW Region 6 meet, winning the long jump with a leap of 18-2 ½. Short added a 5th in the 200-meter, while Frey and Becker placed 2nd and 4th, respectively, in the high jump.

1980

The 1980 track season was one of considerable contrast. The women's team was still small in numbers but maintained the tradition of strong individuals who placed well in the meets.

Led by seniors Brenda Short and Dorothy Frey, the 1980 Lady Hornets maintained a strong program, winning the Bethany Relays, placing 3rd in the CSIC, and finishing 13th in the AIAW Region Six meet. Highlighting the indoor season was the women's participation in the NAIA indoor meet, although it was not an official national competition for the women. In the meet, Short and Patty Herrick placed 3rd in the long jump and mile run, respectively, Cindy Edgerton took 4th in the 880-yard run, and Cheryl Phares and Shirley Thompson earned 6th places in the 600-yard run and the 440-yard dash respectively. Short, Edgerton, Herrick and Phares combined to form a mile relay team that took another 3rd place at the NAIA meet, covering the distance in 4:29.0. Also highlighting the women's indoor season was the school record leap of 19-1 ½ in the long jump by Short at the Pittsburg dual.

> **Bill Tidwell: Coach**
> Bill Tidwell coached the ESU men's and women's teams from 1979 to 1984. One of the top distance middle distance runners in the 1950's, he was a four-time NAIA champion in the 880 and the mile. He has been inducted into numerous athletic Halls of Fame including the NAIA Hall of Fame and the Kansas Sports Hall of Fame. His amazing 800 record of 1:47.61, set in 1955, still stands for over 60 years.
>
>

The women's victory in the Bethany Relays to open the outdoor season was accomplished on the efforts of Short, Judy Becker, and an outstanding group of young distance runners. Short won the 100-meter, 200-meter and long jump, a feat she performed regularly during the season, while Becker won the high jump and placed 3rd in the discus. Sophomore transfer Edgerton, sophomore Phares, and freshmen Herrick and Kay Hoffman finished 1st through 4th respectively in the 800-meter, while Herrick and Hoffman placed 1st and 2nd respectively in the 1500-meter, accounting for a large portion of the Lady Hornets' scoring. Many of these same individuals accounted for the bulk of the women's scoring in the CSIC meet. Short provided victories in the 100-meter, 200-meter, and long jump; Herrick won the 1500 and placed 3rd in the 3000-meter; and Becker placed 2nd in the high jump. Becker earned the same place in the high jump at the AIAW Region 6 meet, while Short placed 3rd in the long jump and 6th in the 100-meter, and Herrick placed 6th in the 5000-meter run.

1981

The Lady Hornet distance squad, after finishing 2nd in the NAIA National Cross Country Championships, was led by Lesha Wood. The team continued its outstanding success into the 1981 indoor track season. Wood established Coliseum records in the mile at Pittsburg and in the two-mile at Fort Hays, then placed 2nd and 3rd in the mile and two-mile, respectively, at the NAIA Indoor Championships to help lead E-State to a 4th place team finish in the women's division. Other place winners at the NAIA meet were Cindy Edgerton with a 3rd in the 1000-yard run, and the 2nd place two-mile relay team of Cheryl Phares, Darcy Mikesich, Nancy Gray, and Edgerton. All of the women earned All-America honors for their efforts in the meet. The Lady Hornets closed out the indoor season at the District 10 meet picking up three 1st places. Mikesich won the 600-yard run with the school record time of 1:30, Wood won the mile, and the two-mile relay team also won.

The Lady Hornets opened the outdoor season at the Arkansas Relays earning three places, Julie Burik taking 6th in the javelin, Patty Herrick finishing 5th in the 3000-meter run, and the two-mile relay team of Edgerton, Gray, Phares, and Mikesich running 9:47.04 while taking 2nd. The E-State women's strengths were in the distance events and the throwing events, and these strengths were highlighted at the Emporia Relays as the Lady Hornets won the two-mile relay, the distance medley relay, the shot put relay, and the javelin relay. This was the first time college women had ever participated in the Emporia Relays, as Coach Tidwell had redesigned the format to include women in the meet that had begun back in 1947. Another change instituted by Tidwell was that all the events were competed as relays, as had been done when Fran Welch began the annual event 34 years earlier. The practice of all relay events had ended in 1957 when open events were added to the meet

Lesha Wood
Lesha Wood was a standout in track and cross country from 1980-1984. She earned seven All-American honors and led three cross country teams to top 10 national finishes. Her highest national finish was a 2nd place runner-up in the 1500 meters.

The weekend after the Emporia Relays, freshman Carol Swaney turned in a noteworthy performance to win the Kansas Relays women's division marathon with a time of 3 hours, 39.28 minutes. Judy Becker also participated at KU, setting a school record of 4307 points in the heptathlon while placing 11th in the event. Two weeks later, Becker provided one of the Lady Hornets' four victories in the CSIC meet held in Joplin, Missouri, winning the high jump with a leap of 5-7. Wood won the 1500-meter and 3000-meter runs, setting a conference record of 10:30.1 in the latter, and Edgerton accounted for E-State's final victory winning the 800-meter in 2:19.9. The Emporia State women finished 3rd in the CSIC meet behind Kearney State and Fort Hays respectively.

Woods' performances at the 1981 NAIA Outdoor Championships, held at Houston, were outstanding. She placed 4th in the 1500-meter and 5th in the 3000-meter to earn All-America honors in both, and also ran a 2:16.5 leadoff 800-meter on the Lady Hornets 4th place 4 x 800-meter relay. Woods' times of 4:38.07 and 10:21.3 for the 1500 and 3000-meters, respectively, established school marks. Running on the relay with Wood was Darcy Mikesich, Nancy Gray, and Cindy Edgerton: the quartet setting a school record of 9:29.86. Also earning All-American honors was Judy Becker, although not in her specialty, which was the high jump. Becker was eliminated from the high jump at a height she normally cleared and one that would have placed her in the top five. While the high jump was still being contested, competition began in the women's javelin, an event Becker had also entered. Just minutes after being eliminated from the high jump, Becker was up in the javelin. Still upset by her performance in the high jump, Becker took out her anger by tossing the javelin 138-0, well beyond her previous personal best in the event, to place 3rd and earn All-American.

1982

The Hornet women placed 3rd in the seven-team CSIC field, as freshman Barb Knackstedt and senior Cheryl Phares won the shot put and 800-meter run, respectively. The next weekend in the district meet, the Lady Hornets finished 2nd out of eight teams. Four women earned victories, three of whom set new meet records. Edgerton set a record of 2:26.28 in the 800-meter, Burik set a mark of 122-0 in the javelin, and the 4 x 800-meter relay team of Phares, Cindy Edgerton, McCammon, and Mikesich set a record of 10:12.25. Rounding out the district winners was Michelle Augustyn in the 400-meter hurdles. The Lady Hornets ended the season with a great deal of success at NAIA nationals. All-American recognition was earned by Phares with a 3rd place in the 800-meter run in the school record time of 2:15.52, Michelle Augustyn with a 6th place in the 400-meter hurdles in the school record time of 1:04.77, and the two-mile relay team of Kelly McCammon, Lesha Wood, Phares, and Edgerton, placing 3rd while also setting a school record of 9:23.71. ESU scored 13 points at the national meet and placed 12th.

1983

Lesha Wood continued her success during the 1983 indoor track season. Wood won the mile run at Fort Hays, Central Missouri, and Pittsburg, before concluding the indoor season with a 5th place finish in the mile at the NAIA Indoor meet, setting a school record of 5:06.23. Wood was the only Hornet to earn All-American honors in the NAIA Indoor Nationals. The Lady Hornets tied for 14th in the meet standings.

The 1983 women's outdoor team was characterized by four outstanding individuals: Wood, Kelly McCammon, Michelle (formerly Augustyn) Orton, and Beth Shannon. These four accounted for a majority of the Lady Hornets' individual victories during the season, and were the only E-State entries in the NAIA National Outdoor meet. Shannon, a sophomore discus thrower, let loose a throw of 145-6 at the Southwestern Relays on April 29th to post one of the top marks in the event in the NAIA. Unfortunately, she was unable to repeat her performance in the NAIA championships and did not place. McCammon, also a sophomore, won the CSIC (2:23.85) and district (2:20.4) titles in the 800-meter run, but was unable to place in the event at nationals. Wood was also a conference and district champion, winning the 1500-meter title in both meets and setting a district record of 4:50.16. However, she also failed to place in the national meet. Orton recorded victories in the 400 hurdles at the CSIC and District 10 meets, setting a district record of 1:05.80 in winning that title. Orton was the only E-State performer to place in the NAIA meet, taking 6th in the 400-meter hurdles to earn her second consecutive All-American honors. Orton lowered her school record in the event to 1:03.40 in the national meet. ESU placed 4th in the CSIC meet.

> **Bill Tidwell Era**
>
> The five year tenure of Coach Bill Tidwell was characterized by starting one of the most successful women's cross country teams in the NAIA. He coached the very first women's cross country team at ESU and led the women to a national runner-up finish and two other finishes in the top 10 at nationals. Tidwell coached one All-American in cross country and nine All-Americans in track and field.
>
>

1984

With the addition of senior transfer Julie Browning, and the return of Beth Shannon, Lesha Wood, Kelly McCammon, and Michelle Orton, the 1984 Lady Hornet track team boasted a strong nucleus of performers. Browning opened the indoor season with a victory in the two-mile at the Kansas University All-Comers meet, then set a Coliseum record in the two-mile at Fort Hays. She also won the district indoor two-mile title, and then set a school record of 11:15.0 in the event while placing 10th at the NAIA indoor. McCammon also had an outstanding indoor season. She set a coliseum record in the mile at Fort Hays, placed 4th in the mile at the Oklahoma Track Classic, won the district indoor 880-yard and mile titles, and placed 3rd in the mile run at the NAIA Indoor Championships to earn All-American recognition. McCammon's time of 5:02.67, in addition to setting a new school record, broke the NAIA national record for the mile by two seconds. The Lady Hornets also earned a 4th place in the distance medley relay at the indoor nationals, with the team of Orton, McCammon, Wood and Browning turning in a school record time of 12:23.46.

Individual success was the keynote of the outdoor season, as the Lady Hornets lacked the numbers to challenge for team titles. In the CSIC meet, Wood won the 1500 at the CSIC and district (new record of 4:49.70), McCammon took the CSIC and District 10 800 (new record of 2:14.97) titles, and Orton won both the CSIC and District 10 titles.

Beth Shannon capped off her junior season with a 6th place finish in the discus at the NAIA outdoor championships to earn All-American honors, tossing the discus 135-0. Shannon had an inconsistent season up to that point, her biggest disappointment coming at the CSIC meet when she threw almost 30 feet below her usual standard and did not make the finals. However, her performance at the national meet made up for the disappointments. The 4 x 800-meter relay team of Dutton, Browning, Wood, and McCammon set a new school record mark of 9:16. 67.

1985

The 1985 women's season was one of transition. Coach Tidwell had resigned and Coach Mark Stanbrough inherited a small squad. The emerging star on the team, Kelly McCammon, was redshirted after suffering an achilles injury. Peggy Teichgraeber and Barb Knackstadt represented ESU at the NAIA National Indoor Championships in the mile and shot put, respectively, but failed to place in the top six.

The outdoor season highlights included wins at the Emporia Developmental by Teichgraeber in the 800 and Beth Shannon in the discus and javelin. Shannon also won the discus at the McPherson Invitational and was joined in the winner's circle by Knackstadt in the shot put.

The Lady Hornets, finishing 4th of 4 teams in the CSIC meet with only 8 points, all of which were scored in the throwing events. Shannon led the way with a CSIC record of 149-4 in winning the discus. Shannon finished 2nd in the discus at the District

> **Mark Stanbrough: Coach**
> Mark Stanbrough became the head track and field/cross country coach in 1984/85. Stanbrough had competed in cross country and track and field for the Hornets from 1977 under Coach Phil Delavan. After graduation, he was an ESU graduate assistant in track and cross country, then taught and coached at Glasco High School for two years. He obtained his Ph.D. in exercise physiology from the University of Oregon. While in Oregon, Stanbrough competed for Athletes In Action and the Oregon Track Club.

10 meet and Knackstedt added a 3rd in the shot at 38-8. The team finished 7th out of 11 scoring teams at Districts with 18 points. 3rd

Shannon duplicated her 6th place finish at NAIA Outdoor Nationals from the previous year as she threw 142-10 in the discus at Hillsdale, Michigan in the 1985 NAIA National Outdoor Track and Field Championships. Shannon's one point for 6th place gave ESU a tie for 38th place.

1986

The 1986 indoor season was one of much improvement for the Lady Hornets. Coach Stanbrough stepped up the recruiting and several newcomers made an immediate impact. After failing to score at the NAIA National Indoor Championships the previous year, the women capped off the much-improved season with a 9th place national finish. Kelly McCammon, after sitting out a redshirt season, won the 1986 NAIA National Indoor Championship in the mile in 5:02.01 at Municipal Auditorium in Kansas City. She set two District Indoor titles in record time, running the 800 in 2:21.6 and the mile in 5:06.4. By the end of the 1986 outdoor season, McCammon was the school record holder in an amazing eight events. All-American Susan Stine set a school record in her first indoor two mile (11:05.7) and improved upon it three times, as well as setting a district record in the 1000 yard run (2:51.4) and being named Outstanding Female Athlete at the Alex Francis Invitational. Stine finished 5th in the 2 mile run at the NAIA National Indoor Championships running 10:49.0 to re-set her record. The distance medley relay team of Jean Kolarik, Ann Stoll, Stine and McCammon placed 5th at nationals in 12:29.0. Kolarik established an indoor district mark in the 600 (1:30.2) and a school mark in the 176-yard hurdles at 23.70. Michelle Payne, the school's first women's triple jumper, steadily upped her school record mark to 35-3. The women's team of Kolarik, Stoll, Amy Potter, and McCammon established a new two mile relay indoor record of 9:41.02. Potter also won a district championship in the two mile.

The women's 1986 outdoor season began at home with the Emporia Twilight with the team winning 14 of 17 events. McCammon, fresh off a national championship in the indoor mile, captured the mile in 5:02.4. Payne won the 100, triple jump and also the long jump (18-2 ¼), winning by half an inch over teammate Kolarik (who won the 200). Stoll doubled in winning the 400 and 400 hurdles. Annette Noll captured the shot and Tammy Holdeman the discus. The Lady Hornet distance strength was evident in the 5000 meters as placers 1, 2, and 3 all broke the school record of 18:32.14 with Stine (17:34.2), McCammon (18:08.8) and Potter (18:18.9). Kolarik displayed her versatility as a multi-eventer in capturing the 400 hurdles in 1:06.7, winning the high jump at 5 feet even, taking 3rd in the 100 hurdles, and 2nd in the long jump. Kolarik would come back five days later and compete in the Central Missouri Multi and finish 3rd with 4232 points. Payne and Noll completed the Hornet domination winning the long jump and triple jump, respectively.

Kelly McCammon: National Champion
Kelly McCammon competed in track and cross country from 1982-1986. She was the NAIA national champion in the indoor mile in 1986. She earned six All-American honors, including one in cross country. Her finest hour as a Lady Hornet came when she set two new school records in the 1500 and 3000 meters, that still stand today, in the span of one hour, finishing 2nd and 4th respectively in those events at the 1986 National Outdoor Track and Field Championships.

McCammon continued her senior season at a torrid pace winning the 800 at Park, the 3000 at Bethany and the 1500 at the Emporia Relays in 4:42.12, a meet record. Kolarik continued to display her versatility winning the 800 at Bethany and the high jump at ESU. She would compete in the KU Relays heptathlon, scoring 4360 points. Payne also continued her sensational freshman season in winning the triple jump at Park and ESU, as well as the 100 meters in 12.74 at the ESU Relays. Annette Noll contributed for the throwers winning both the shot and discus at the Bethany Invite.

The ESU women dominated the relay events at the Emporia State Relays, winning the distance medley, sprint medley, two-mile relay, and mile relays. The sprint medley of Payne, Jan Peters, Kolarik, and McCammon established a school record in the 100-100-200-400 meter relay event. At the Southwestern Relays, Payne ran the 100 meters in 12.34 to set a meet record and Kolarik won the 400 hurdles in a meet record time of 1:04.99. McCammon ran the 1500 meters in 4:34.18, a meet record and school record, breaking the old school record of 4:38.07 set by Lesha Wood in 1981. McCammon also tied the meet record in the 800, running 2:18.5 and anchored a meet record 4 x 400, teaming with Kolarik, Stoll, and Peters. For her efforts in setting three meet records, McCammon was named female "outstanding athlete" of the meet.

At the CSIC conference meet, the ESU women finished 4th, only 4 points out of 2nd. McCammon again led the efforts with a win in the 1500 in a meet record time of 4:34.27 and a win in the 800 in 2:15.23. Stine won the 3000 in 10:16.22 to establish a new meet record and Kolarik picked up a win in the 400 hurdles in 1:05.19.

The 1986 Lady Hornet team was much improved over Coach Stanbrough's first team in 1985. With a highly recruited class of freshmen, the Lady Hornets had steadily improved over the season. They were anxious to demonstrate how much at the District 10 meet. The previous year, they had finished 7th with 18 points. However, this year, a two-hour rain storm delay almost canceled the entire meet. The Hornets were determined to stick it out and wait. Eventually, the skies cleared and it turned into a beautiful evening for track and field and the ESU effort matched the weather. The Lady Hornets ran away from the competition to finish 1st with 156.5 points, beating 2nd place Fort Hays by 33.5 points. Three Lady Hornets were brilliant, scoring a combined 103 points. McCammon scored 32.5 points, winning three national quality races and anchoring the 4 x 400 relay. Kolarik scored 34.5 points, winning both the 400 hurdles and the 400 meters, and placing in 7 events. Stine ran three national quality races in scoring 26 points. The eight new freshmen totaled 108.5 points.

McCammon's day consisted of winning the 1500 in meet record time of 4:34.46, winning the 800 in 2:16.11 and the 3000 in 10:05.68. Stine (17:55.2) and Potter went 1-2 in the 5000, with Stine finishing 2nd in both the 1500 and 3000 to McCammon.

The 1986 NAIA National Championships were held in Russellville, Arkansas. As she had done all year, McCammon was spectacular but would save her best performance for the last meet of her outstanding career. Both of McCammon's races were scheduled for the same evening and only 50 minutes apart. The first race, the 3000 meters, was ran at a fast pace. Ann Manning of Portland set a new national record of 9:34.00; however, McCammon gave her a good run finishing 2nd in 9:39.97. Forty minutes after finishing the fast paced 3000, McCammon lined up for the start of the 1500 meters. Fighting the fatigue associated with such a quick turn-around, McCammon battled to a 4th place finish in 4:26.20. Within 50 minutes, McCammon had pulled off the greatest feat in ESU women's distance running and established herself as one of the greatest female distance runners in ESU history. Her performances in both the 1500 and 3000 meters set school records that still stand over 30 years later. Many great ESU female distance runners would follow but none have come within with three seconds of McCammon's 1500 record.

McCammon would not be the only school record setter in Russellville that day, as freshman Stine ran a school record 17:10.49 to finish 3rd in the 5000 and fellow freshman Kolarik finished 7th in the heptathlon with 4372 points. Emporia State finished in a tie for 8th place in the national meet.

1987

The 1987 team was led by the distance runners who had completed an outstanding season in the fall of 1986 finishing 2nd in the NAIA National Cross Country Championships. The team was led by the All-Americans Susan Stine and Amy Potter who finished 14th and 16th, respectively, in the national competition. Stine added a school record in the 3000, running 10:09.26 in a tough field at the Oklahoma City Classic and also ran on the school record-setting 2-mile relay, teaming with Joni Dutton, Gloria Bates, and Jean Kolarik to run 9:40.17 at the Jayhawk invitational.

Marathon Co-Record Holders

The NAIA conducts a marathon in the national track and field championships. In December of 1986, Amy Potter ran the Dallas White Rock Marathon finishing 7th overall in the women's division with a time of 3:07.48. Her time qualified her for the 1987 NAIA Marathon. The following year in December of 1987, Mary Griebel, traveled to Dallas to attempt to qualify for the National Marathon Championships. Running the same course, but a year later, Mary ran 3:07.48, the exact same time to the second that Amy ran the year before. Over 26.2 miles and in an event that lasts over three hours, what are the odds that they would run the exact same time? Potter would finish her 1987 national marathon in 3:28.59 to finish 8th, Griebel would finish her 1988 marathon in 3:10.44 for 6th place.

Potter

Griebel

Freshman Clarissa Keeling started the 1987 indoor season off with a school record in the 60-yard hurdles in her first meet as a Lady Hornet, clocking 8.82 at the Kansas Invitational. Keeling improved upon her mark the following week with an 8.64, and lowered it even further the following week to 8.62 at the Jayhawk Invitational. Keeling would add a school record 300 yards in 38.6 at the K-State Invitational.

Trish Bahr, a junior college transfer from Butler County, jumped to a school record of 5-5 ¼ in the high jump at Oklahoma City. At the NAIA National Championships, she would improve that mark to 5-6 and tie for 2nd with another school record. The 1987 District 10 meet conflicted with the Oklahoma Classic Track meet. Since the Oklahoma meet was run on a board track similar to the NAIA National Indoor, Stanbrough elected to take his top athletes to run at Oklahoma. No team scores were kept at District 10. At the District 10 meet, Jennifer Strader won the 600 in 1:36.26 and the 1000 in 3:04.59. Noll was 2nd in the shot at 38-4 ½ and LeaAnne Snelling was 2nd in the triple jump at 30-6 ½. Griebel added 2nds in the mile at 5:32.01 and the 2 mile in 11:43.80. At Oklahoma City, Kolarik would compete in the seldom run 500 meters and run a new school record. Stine finished 7th in the 3000 in 10:09.26 to set a new school record as did Bahr in the high jump at 5-5 ¼.

Both the distance medley team of Kolarik, Gretchen Bohm, Trudy Searcy and Stine (12:38.21) and the 2 mile relay of relay of Bohm, Dutton, Bates, and Kolarik (9:44.14) would finish 4th at the NAIA Nationals. Stine would contribute with a 7th place finish in the 2 mile in 11:18.2. Kolarik in the 600 yard run (1:30.19), Searcy in the mile (5:13.56), Keeling in the 60-meter hurdles (8.63), and Potter in the 2 mile (11:27.66), would all compete but not advance to the finals. Emporia State finished 10th at the 1987 NAIA Indoor Championships.

ESU started the season the 1987 outdoor season with the ESU Developmental meet and took wins by: Keeling in in the 100 meter hurdles in 14.5, Bohm in the 400 in 59.6, Searcy in the 3000 in 10:39.6, Bahr in the high jump at 5-6, Kolarik in the long jump at 17-7 ½, and the mile relay of Kolarik, Strader, Keeling, and Bohm. The following week, Searcy would win the 1500 in 4:48.4, Stine the 5000 in 18:15 and Payne the triple jump. Stine continued her winning streak sweeping the 1500 (4:52.9) and the 3000 (10:26.4) at the Swede Invitational.

At the ESU Relays, Keeling picked up wins in both the 100 and 400 hurdles, Searcy captured the 1500, Stine the 5000, Bahr the high jump, Noll the shot put, and Payne both the long jump and triple jump. As they had done the previous year, ESU dominated by winning every relay, winning the 440, 880, mile, sprint medley and distance medley relays. In a further display of dominance, ESU ran two distance medley teams and finished 1st and 2nd.

The quality of the distance program was evident as four Lady Hornets ran the 10,000 meters at the KU Relays and they all broke the school record. Stine led the way, placing 7th as the top non-DI runner with a time of 36:53, followed by Griebel (37:12), Amy Potter (37:45), and Trudy Searcy (37:49). Bahr upped the school record to 5-8 and finished 3rd in the high jump. Kolarik, competing in the heptathlon, finished with the top heptathlon 880 time of 2:17.84.

The Lady Hornets' only win in the CSIC meet would be by Bahr in the high jump (5-7). Stine finished 2nd in the 1500 (4:48.1) and 2nd in the 3000 (10:45.9), with Greibel (10:48.6) and Potter (10:52.9) close behind in 3rd and 4th. Kolarik finished 2nd in the 800 in 2:21.0 and Payne 2nd in the triple jump at 36-1 as the Lady Hornets finished in 2nd place in the team results behind Kearney State.

The women defended their District 10 title winning by 70 points over Pittsburg State, with Potter a double winner in the 3000 in 10:31.56 and the 5000 in 18:25.95. Stine won the 1500 in 4:46.06, Strader the 800 in 2:21.7, and Kolarik the 400 hurdles in a meet and school record time of 1:03.68. The Lady Hornets again displayed their distance dominance by going 1,3,4,5, in the 800: 1, 2, 6 in the 1500; 1, 3, 4 in the 3000; and 1,2 in the 5000 for a total of 77 points from the distance runners.

The 1987 NAIA National Championships were held in Russellville, Arkansas for the second year in a row. The Lady Hornets finished in 14th place. Bahr continued to jump big when it counted the most in championship meets. Her 5-8 high jump earned her a 2nd place finish. ESU ran three runners in the 10,000 meters, with Searcy making a bold move to take the lead late in the race and then holding on for 4th place in 36:24.85, a new school record. Stine would finish 5th in 36:27.45 and Griebel 8th in 37:37.76. Potter ran the marathon in 3:28.59 to finish 8th and Kolarik added a 9th place finish in the heptathlon with a score of 4337 points.

1988

The Lady Hornets added a dominating runner in senior transfer Cindy Blakeley, from Ottawa for the 1988 season. Blakeley had started her career at the University of Kansas, then transferred to Ottawa University. She had finished in 36th place in the 1986 NAIA National Cross Country Championships while running for Ottawa, and then as a Lady Hornet, earned All-American honors at the 1987 NAIA National Cross Country Championships by placing 9th. She also won the CSIC and District 10 cross country titles for ESU.

Blakeley continued her outstanding ESU career in the 1988 indoor track season. Led by Blakeley and high jumper Trish Bahr, the Lady Hornets scored 18 points to place 8th at the 1988 NAIA Indoor National Track and Field Championships in Municipal Auditorium in Kansas City, Missouri. In Blakeley's only track and field national meet (she would miss the majority of the outdoor season with an injury) she finished 2nd in the mile (5:01.24) and broke former national champion Kelly McCammon's school record. Bahr finished 3rd in the high jump at 5-8 and improved upon her own school record. Blakeley also anchored the 2 mile and distance medley relays to 5th place finishes with the 2 mile relay (9:35.09) setting a school record. Both relays consisted of Kolarik, Bohm, Strader, and Blakeley.

Lisa Farris: National Champion
Back-to-back National Championships
Lisa Farris competed for ESU in 1988 and 1989. She was a two-time NAIA national champion for the Lady Hornets in the discus. She also won two All-American honors in the shot-put placing 2nd in the 1989 outdoor championships as well as winning five conference and district shot put and discus titles.

The Lady Hornets captured five individual District 10 titles in the non-scoring District meet. Blakeley won the mile and 1000 meters, establishing a new district record in the 1000. Strader won the 800, Lisa Farris the shot put, and Bahr the high jump. Kolarik set indoor records in the 440 in 60.84 and the 880 in 2:21.49 and anchored the mile relay (Bohm Strader, Blakeley, and Kolarik) that established a new indoor mark of 4:07.35.

In the 1988 outdoor season, Lady Hornets finished 4th in the CSIC behind individual championships Farris in the shot (44.4.5), Bohm in the 800 (2:21.6), and Brenda Cunningham in the javelin (134-5). Connie Maxwell picked up a 2nd in the 100 hurdles at 16.1, and Farris placed 2nd in the discus at 129-9. After dominating the District 10 track the previous two years, the Lady Hornets were hindered by injuries and slipped to 2nd. District champions were Farris in the shot (43-6) and discus (148-5), Bahr in the high jump (5-8), and Bohm in the 800 (2:20.74). Runner-up status went to Brenda Cunningham in the javelin at 126-11, Maxwell in the hurdles at 16.14, Kolarik in the 400 hurdles at 1:04.45, and the medley relay team in 1:52.40.

The highlight of the 1988 outdoor season occurred at the NAIA National Outdoor Championships in Azusa, California, with Lisa Farris claiming a national title in the discus with a throw of 146-2. The victory by Farris was the first national championship outdoors for the Lady Hornets since Kathy Devine won the shot put in 1977. The season best marks by Farris of 148-5 in the discus and 44-4 ½ in the shot put moved her to 2nd on the all-time ESU list behind former collegiate record holder Devine.

Bahr continued her amazing high jumping at national meets. For her fourth national meet in a row she placed in the top three, finishing 3rd with a school record leap of 5-8 ½. Griebel, (the co-school record holder in the marathon) finished 6th in the marathon in 3 hours 10 minutes and 44 seconds despite missing two months of track because of a stress fracture. Kolarik, who set the school record earlier in the season with 4669 points, finished 7th in the heptathlon with 4545 points.

The Lady Hornets finished in 11th place with 21 points at the 1988 NAIA National Outdoor Championships.

1989

The 1989 indoor track season saw newcomer Sandra Freeman, a transfer from Highland Community College and a Georgia native, make a big ESU debut by breaking the Hornet standard in the 60-yard dash, running 7.21 at Central Missouri. The former record was set by standout Brenda Short of 7.44 in 1978. Freeman doubled back to set another school record in the 300, running 38.11. Bohm lowered the school record to 1:28.61 in the 600-yard run at the Central Missouri Indoor, then lowered the 800 school record to 2:19.78. Deanna Tolin continued the record breaking assault taking the 400 school record to 59.93 and teaming with Bohm, Freeman, and Brenda Thompson to set a new 4 x 440 mark of 4:07.35 at the Oklahoma City Classic.

Lisa Farris repeated her District 10 indoor title in the shot put with a throw of 43-1 ½. Bohm won the 600 improving her school record to 1:27.8 and setting a new district standard. Freeman won establishing a new district record of 7.06 in the 60-yard dash. The mile relay of Tolin, Thompson, Freeman, and Bohm set a new district indoor record in their victory (4:12.6).

At the NAIA National Indoor Championships, the women finished 13th in the team standings, led by Sandra Freeman sprinting a blistering 7.02 to finish in 3rd place, only .04 off the winning time. Freshman Cecilia Gunn make an immediate impact placing 3rd in the shot at 43-9 with Farris back in 6th with a 43-2. Bohm lowered her own school record to 2:18.75 and finished 7th in the 880 final. Strader added to the Lady Hornet point totals by placing 7th in the NAIA Nationals 1000-yard run in 2:48.30.

The Lady Hornets finished 5th in the CSIC outdoor meet with Farris capturing a double championship in the shot (44-1 ¼) and discus (146-10). CSIC runner-up finishes were contributed by Gunn in the discus at 141-0 and shot put at 43-1 ¾. The women's 4 x 400 team of Thompson, Deanna Tolin, Strader, and Bohm established a new school record of 4:01.4 at the CSIC meet. The Lady Hornets finished 4th in the District 10 Championships, as Gunn added a championship in the discus (140-8) with Farris close behind in 2nd (137-4). The duo of Farris and Gunn went 2-3 in the shot at 42-10 ½ and 41-9, respectively. Bohm placed 2nd in the 1500 meters at 4:51.77.

Returning to the NAIA National Outdoor Track and Field Championships in Asuza, California, the same site where she won her first national championship, Lisa Farris claimed her second consecutive national title in the discus with a throw of 145-4 and placed 2nd in the shot put at 45-½. Gunn also claimed All-American honors with a 3rd place finish in the shot throwing a PR 44-6. The throwing efforts from the ESU women led to 24 points and an 11th place national finish.

1990

The 1990 indoor Lady Hornets won the District 10 title led by District 10 Indoor champions: Cecilia Gunn in the shot (44-3 ½), Ingrid Frazier in the mile (5:19.4) and 1000 meters (3:10.7), Deanna Tolin in the 600 (1:30.1), Bohm in the 800 (2:19.8), and Stine in the 2 mile (12:04.9).

At the National Indoor championships in Kansas City, senior Gretchen Bohm earned All-American honors with a 6th place finish in the 800 meters (2:18.33) in school record time. The women's two-mile relay, composed of Frazier, Katie Wheeler, Bohm, and Michelle Hebb, ran a school record (9:34.83) to place 5th and Cecilia Gunn finished 7th in the shot put (42-8 ¾). Teamwise, the Lady Hornets finished in 11th place.

With no outdoor conference meet, the Hornets focused on the District 10 meet for the team goal and they responded, vaulting from 4th the previous year to win by over 50 points. District champions for the

Hornets included Bohm, running a tremendous triple with wins in the 800 (2:17.75), 1500 (4:45.87), and 3000 (10:53.58). Hebb finished 2nd to Bohm in all three events. Other District 10 champions were Brenda Risner in the 100 (12.5), Michelle Tyrrell in the 5000 (19:37.00), and the 4 x 100 relay of Julie Hurt, Marcy Post, Tolin, and Risner (50.02). The women also established two new school outdoor records with a 9:15.67 in the 4 x 800 relay (Bohm, Frazier, Wheeler, Hebb) and a 12:17.3 in the distance medley (Bohm, Wheeler, Frazier, Hebb).

At the NAIA Nationals, the performance was highlighted by sophomore Cecilia Gunn. Gunn established a new school mark by placing 3rd in the discus with a throw of 157-2 to break the mark held by the legendary Kathy Devine. Gunn also set a personal best to place 2nd in the shot put 46-4 ¼ to lead the women's team, which finished in 16th place at the NAIA national meet in Stephenville, Texas.

1991

The 1991 women's team repeated their District 10 indoor team title and won nine events. Gunn captured the shot put (45-8 ¼), Amy Ayers the 55 meter hurdles (8.94), Sherlyn Weide the 55 meters (District 10 record of 7.13), Tolin the 600-yard run (1:29.4), Ingrid Frazier the 1000 meters (District 10 record of 2:18.5), Jennifer Mullen the 2 mile (11:31.5) and Hebb the mile (5:12.0) and 880 (District 10 record of 2:18.5). The distance medley of Wheeler, Cicely Moreland, Kerry Stine, and Maureen Fitzgerald (District 10 record of 13:15.3), as well as the 3200 relay (10:08.7) of Wheeler, K. Stine, Frazier, and Hebb also won. During the 1991 indoor season, Amy Huggins set a new school record in the 25-pound weight throw with a 20-10 ¾.

The women finished 6th in the NAIA National Indoor Championships led by Gunn capturing a 2nd in the shot at 44-0 ¾. Frazier was 6th in the 1000 yard run in 2:45.79. Mullen captured 3rd in the 3 mile in 17:08.32. The mile relay of Weide, Hebb, Brenda Bina and Tolin were 6th in 4:10.06. The two-mile relay of Frazier, Wheeler, Bina, and Hebb were 4th in 9:38.57 and the distance medley relay team of Frazier, Tolin, Hebb, and Mullen placed 3rd in 12:32.10.

Cecilia Gunn: National Champion
Cecilia Gunn was a three-time NAIA champion in the shot put and a ten-time All-American in the shot put and discus. Gunn won seven conference or district titles in the shot or discus. She set the school record in the discus.

The 1991 outdoor season saw Sherlyn Weide establish a school record of 11.99 in the 100 meters at the Gorilla Relays. The Lady Hornets successfully defended their District 10 outdoor track and field title by winning 13 of the 18 events overall and 10 of the 12 running events. For the second consecutive year, the women won Districts in cross country, indoor track and outdoor track. All-American Cecilia Gunn led the way picking up double wins in the shot (44-11 ¾) and discus (152-9). Behind Gunn in both events was Marla McTaggart who had personal bests of 40-5 ¾ to finish 4th in the shot and 138-9 to place 2nd in the discus. Mary Kerwin set a PR and won the javelin on her last throw of the competition in 137-6.

On the District 10 track, ESU was dominate with numerous double winners. Hebb took the 800 (2:19.91) and 1500 (4:56.21), Mullen the 3000 (10:33.09) and 5000 (19:00.00), and Weide the 100 (11.71) and 200 (25.49). Julie Hirt won the 400 hurdles (1:06.14) and Amy Ayers the 100 hurdles (15.38). ESU also captured the 4 x 100 and 4 x 400 relays (4:06.81).

Emporia State took 10 women to the national meet in Stephenville, Texas. Cecilia Gunn captured her first national title, throwing 46-0 ½ in the shot put, after finishing 2nd the two previous times. She also moved up a notch from her previous year place of 3rd in the discus throwing 153-6 to capture 2nd. Gunn led the Lady Hornets to a 12th place national finish. Also competing at the nationals in 1991 but not scoring were Maureen Fitzgerald and Michelle Tyrell running the marathon, Frazier in the 1500, Hirt in the 400 hurdles, Kerwin in the javelin, McTaggart in the discus, Mullen in the 5K and 10K, Weide in the 100 and 200, and the Lady Hornets fielded a 4 x 100 relay.

1992

The 1992 District Indoor Championships saw the Lady Hornets win 7 events, highlighted by three wins courtesy of Michelle Hebb, (5:09.5 in the mile, 1000 meters in 3:04.7, and the 800 in 2:19.5) and the double wins and school records in the 600 (1:27.0) and 300 (37.7) by Tolin. Gunn won the shot (48-1 ½) in a new district record and Mullen the two mile (11:48.7). Fort Hays won the district meet with ESU 2nd.

At the 1992 NAIA Indoor National Championships, the women finished 6th in the final team standings matching their 6th place finish of the previous season. Gunn won her second national title in the shot put, dominating the competition in winning by over three feet (48-5), and matching her personal best to earn her 8th All-American title.

Hebb raced to a PR and a 4th place finish in the women's mile (5:05.55), upholding the Hornet tradition in the mile. In each of the previous six years and nine of the last 10, Hornet milers had earned All-American honors. Included in the string were two national champions, three 2nd place finishes, and seven different All-Americans. Mullen earned her fourth All-American honor by placing 6th in the three mile run (17:11.72). For the second year in a row, the women's mile relay team scored at nationals with a major seasonal improvement. The team of Tolin, Julie Worley, Brenda Bina, and Laura Gerstberger placed 5th in 4:05.90.

Outdoor school records were set in 1992 by Tolin in the 400 meters at 57:13 and the 4 x 400 meter relay of Worley, Hebb, Gerstberger, and Tolin in 3:58.93, as well as the sprint medley relay of Gerstberger, Ayers, Worley, and Tolin (1:48.54).

The Lady Hornets won their third consecutive outdoor district title and their fifth straight district crown (indoor and outdoor) winning 11 of 18 events. Gunn set a new district record in the shot put throwing 49-9 ¾, to take the over the national lead. Double winners at the meet were Mary Bailey in the discus at 152-11 (the top throw in the nation at the time) and javelin (131-2); Mullen in the 5000 in 19:16.69 and the 3000 in 10:48.29; and Hebb in the 1500 (4:50.2) and the 800 (2:20.12). E-State's other District 10 champions were Tolin in the 400 (58.3), and Worley in the 400 hurdles (14.01). Both the mile (4:06.74) and sprint medley relays (1:48.8) were also champions. The team of Ayers, Gerstberger, Worley, and Tolin set a new school record in the sprint medley relay.

Gunn led the efforts at the 1992 NAIA National Outdoor Track and Field Championships in Abbotsford, British Columbia, Canada. It was ironic that the national meet was held in Canada, but the host, Simon Fraser University, was a member of the NAIA. Gunn defended her shot put title with a heave of 47-7 ¼ and also placed 3rd in the discus at 146-1. Bailey finished 5th in the discus at 144-4.

Mullen earned NAIA All-American Honors by placing 6th in the marathon in 3 hours, 11 minutes and 30 seconds. Teammate Maureen Fitzgerald placed 18th in 3:44.52. The marathon started in Canada, crossed the border into the United States and then went back into Canada to finish. Mullen had a tough double as she ran the 10K two days earlier, totaling 32.3 miles for the weekend. Mullen positioned herself into 6th place at the eight-mile mark of the marathon and held her position the rest of the way to claim All-American honors bestowed upon the top six finishers. Mary Dannels and Bailey both competed in the javelin, but did not place. E-State finished 8th with 23 points in the 1992 National Outdoor Championships.

1993

The 1993 track season was a transition year from Coach Stanbrough to Coach Harris. Indoor highlights included Worley taking the 400 in 59.92 at the Kansas State Invitational, Hebb winning the 800 at the Mule Relays, Ayers setting an school record in the 55-meter hurdles in 8.45, and Bina moving to 2nd on the all-time indoor high jump with a mark of 5-4 ¼.

> **Mark Stanbrough Era**
> While head coach from 1984 to 1992, the track and field teams won nine district titles. He coached 28 Athletes to 60 NAIA All-American Honors, including 11 National Champions. He coached 10 teams that finished in the top-10 in the nation and 22 teams that finished in the top 20 in national competition. The top national finishes for Stanbrough teams were the 1986 women's cross country team finishing 2nd, the 1991 men's cross country team finishing 5th, the 1991 and 1992 women's indoor teams both finished 6th at nationals, and the men's 1991 indoor team finished 7th.

The Lady Hornets competed in their first season in the MIAA Indoor Conference Championships in 1993. At the MIAA indoor meet, Ayers ran 7.63 to place 4th in the 60 hurdles. Hebb won a MIAA title in the 1000 meters in 3:00.67 (a MIAA indoor meet record), and Dana McIntyre won the shot in 44-5 ½, a personal best by almost 2 feet. The Lady Hornets finished in 5th place as a team in their first MIAA Championships.

> **David Harris: Coach**
> David Harris was hired to lead the ESU program. Harris came to ESU after a seven-year stint as an assistant coach at the University of Nebraska where he coached 31 All-American and three Olympians. Harris received his bachelors' degree in physical education/social science and a master's degree in athletic administration from Northeast Missouri State University. While competing for the Bulldogs, he was a four-year letterman in cross country and track and field.

For the first time ever, the ESU women competed in the NCAA DII National Championships. Hebb placed 8th in the indoor championships 1500 in 4:45.30 and McIntyre was 8th in the shot at 43-4 ½. As the top six places made All-American status and scored points, the ESU women did not score at the national meet.

Hebb continued to star in the outdoor season, taking the KT Woodman meet at Wichita State 800 in 2:17.7 and the 1500 in 4:48.9. Ayers added a 2nd in the Pittsburg State Gorilla Relays 100 hurdles in 14.88 and also won the Baker Twilight. Worley took the Baker Twilight 400 hurdles. Dannels captured the javelin title, throwing 128-11 at the Swede Invitational, and Maria Lunkwitz had a fine discus throw of 144-10 to finish 2nd in the Nebraska Twilight.

The Lady Hornets competed in their first MIAA Outdoor Championships held in Warrensburg, Missouri and finished 4th. Brenda Bina, who started her career as a middle distance runner for ESU, pulled off an upset by winning the MIAA high jump at 5-5 ¼. Hebb posted a 2nd place finish in the 1500 in 4:40.36 and added a 2nd in the 3000 in 10:34.11. Ayers added another 2nd in the 100 hurdles at 15.27, and Worley placed 2nd in the 400 hurdles in 1:02.43. The throwers added to the ESU point total, with Lunkwitz finishing 3rd in the discus in 144-7, and Laura Rand adding a 126-8 to place 8th. McIntyre finished 4th in the shot at 42-0, followed by Rand at 38-¾. Rand's performance is noteworthy, because she would make dramatic improvement and two years later become ESU's first female competitor to win an NCAA national title.

> **NCAA & MIAA**
> In 1993, ESU also moved to the NCAA Division II level of competition and joined the Mid-America Intercollegiate Athletics Association.
>
>

1994

The 1994 women's indoor season highlights included a 1000-yard win (2:42) by Amy Moore in the Kansas Invitational. Ayers continued her outstanding hurdling career by winning the University of Central Missouri Invite 55 hurdles in 8.25, the Mule Relays in 8.42 and the KU Invite. Bina continued to impress in the high jump clearing 5-5 at Central Missouri. Laura Rand added a 2nd place finish (43-1) in the shot put at the MIAA as the Lady Hornets finished 7th in the team standing

Ayers continued the 1994 outdoor season on record setting pace, placing 3rd in the 100-meter hurdles at the KU Relays to set a new ESU school record (14.54). Ayers won the SMU Invite, ESU Classic and the ESU Spring Twilight and finished 2nd in the MIAA. Gerstberger added to the ESU strength in the hurdles, winning the 400 hurdles at Southwestern.

The high jumpers contributed their share to the team with Jennifer Wolf jumping 5-6 to win at Baker and 5-5 to win at ESU. Bina added a 2nd place finish at ESU with her 5-5. Wolf placed 5th in 5-1¾ at the MIAA meet with Bina in 6th.

The highlight for the throwers was the emergence of Laura Rand. Rand threw 146-2 in the discus to win the FHSU Last Chance meet, as well as taking wins in the ESU Intercollegiate Classic, ESU Spring Twilight, ESU Open and finishing 4th in the MIAA with a 127-2. Rand improved dramatically in the shot put to throw 46-1½ for her season best at the ESU Intercollegiate. She also added wins at the Southwestern Invite, the ESU Spring Twilight, and KT Woodman Classic, and capped the season with a 2nd place finish (43-10) at the MIAA Championships.

The women finished 6th in the MIAA Outdoor Championships and tied for 42nd in the NCAA DII National Outdoor Championships, with Rand picking up All-American honors with an 8th place finish throwing 142-0 in the discus at Nationals.

ESU hosted the 1995 NCAA DII National Outdoor Track and Field Championships at Welch Stadium.

1995

The Lady Hornets finished 5th in the MIAA Indoor Championships. Bridget Clem posted the best placing by an ESU woman by finishing 3rd in the 600 with a time of 1:29:31. The mile relay also posted a 3rd place finish. Deandra Doubrava was the Hornets only multiple scorer, placing 4th in the 400 meters and 5th in the long jump.

The 1995 track season featured Emporia State hosting the NCAA DII National Outdoor Track and Field Championships at Welch Stadium. Three outstanding individuals led ESU. Laura Rand was a junior who had gradually improved and progressed. She threw 42-0 to finish 4th in the MIAA indoor shot put. Outdoors, she improved to win the MIAA with 46-0 and also won the ESU Twilight, Fort Hays Tri, and the Southwestern Invite. What she was about to do on May 27, 1995 would make ESU history. Throwing in her home ring, with the home crowd behind her, Rand responded with the best throw of her career, 47-9 ¾ to become the first Lady Hornet in any sport to win an NCAA Championship. Rand also starred in the discus, throwing 150-8 to win the ESU Twilight and 147-8 to become the MIAA discus champion.

Deandra Doubrava, from Scott City, Kansas, competed in track and also played volleyball. Doubrava would go on to be one of the greatest female athletes in ESU track history, and one of the best all-around athletes in school history, male or female. Named the Gatorade Kansas Girls High School Track and Field Athlete of the Year in 1994, she started the indoor season by placing 5th in the MIAA 400 in 59.94. She would lower her times considerably outdoors to win the MIAA in 57.42 she then ran 55.56 in the NCAA Outdoor Championships prelim and 55.68 in the final to place 5th and earn All-American honors. She posted her season best of 55.24 at the ESU Twilight, won five outdoor meets, and set the school record of 24.90 in the 200 meters. Doubrava also displayed her jumping abilities, long jumping 18-2 at KT Woodman and picking up wins in both the long and triple jumps at the Southwestern Invite and the ESU Twilights.

Laura Rand: National Champion
Laura Rand was ESU's first NAAA Division II women's national champion winning the shop put in her home ring as ESU hosted the 1995 national championships. She was a four-time All-American and three-time MIAA champion in the throws.

Joyce Burnett's accomplishments added to the list of outstanding individuals in the 1995 season. In the javelin, the Council Grove native threw an ESU record of 160-9 to win the ESU Twilight. She won the MIAA in 147-3 and added a 5th at the NCAA meet with 152-11. Burnett also picked up season wins at KT Woodman and the Fort Hays Triangular. The outstanding group of throwers was complemented by Kelly Hare, who threw the hammer 153-2 to win the MIAA meet.

The Lady Hornets finished 5th in the Outdoor Championships and tied for 13th in the NCAA DII Outdoor Championships.

1996

The 1996 indoor season again featured some of the top athletes in women's track history. Magali Schneider transferred from Wayland Baptist, where she had starred and would become an impact competitor at ESU. Her husband, Brandon, was the women's basketball assistant coach at ESU. Schneider teamed with Doubrava to become a dynamic duo. Schneider ran 55.70 in the 400 to place 6th in the

NCAA Indoor Championships. Doubrava ran an excellent 56.88 in the prelims but did not advance to the final.

Doubrava ran to an ESU indoor school record 55.45 400 meters in an NCAA Qualifier meet. Doubrava ran the 600 at conference in 1:27.00 to win. Schneider also won the NIAC Invite, the K-State Invite, and captured the MIAA title in 57.09. Schneider set the school record in the 200 at 25.06 by winning the Jayhawk Invite. Schneider added another school record in the 55-meter dash at 7.13 and won the MIAA title in 7.28. Schneider showed her versatility in running a blistering 1:22.77 600-yard run to win the Jayhawk Invite. The Lady Hornets were stacked with quality middle distance runners, as evidenced in the 600-yard run as Kari Pitman ran 1:27.98, Jessica Oberg 1:28.51, and Bridget Clem 1:30.88 for the season.

With the plethora of outstanding middle distance runners and sprinters, it was no surprise the Lady Hornets were outstanding in the mile and two mile relays. The team of Schneider, Oberg, Pitman, and Doubrava clocked a 3:47.72 in the NCAA Qualifier right before NCAAs for an indoor school record and then improved on the school record with a time of 3:47.38 in the NCAA meet to place 4th. The same team also captured the MIAA title, as did the 2-mile relay of Pittman, Oberg, Schneider, and Billi Jo Ross in 9:33.65.

Doubrava displayed her jumping abilities by tripling 38-3 for 3rd in the MIAA and placing 12th in the NCAA Championships at 36-8½. Angela Cathcart contributed on the distance side by placing 1st in the MIAA 5000 in 18:09.11.

The defending national champion in the outdoor shot put, Rand, placed 4th in the NCAA indoor meet in the shot at 47-5 ¼. ESU continued its dominance in the weight throw with a 1, 2, 3 sweep at the MIAA meet. Hare won in 46-8 ¾ and was followed by Lynda Barnard in 2nd and Rand in 3rd. Hare established an ESU record of 47-1 at the Central Missouri Invite.

The Lady Hornets were 2nd in the MIAA indoor meet and 13th at the National NCAA indoor meet.

The throwers continued to display their power prowess during the 1996 outdoor season. Hare added the outdoor hammer to her ESU record resume with a 165-10 at the MIAA Championships to win. Lynda Barnard finished 2nd to Hare at the MIAA throwing 160-11 then turned the table on her teammate by placing 5th in the NCAA's in 159-3. Hare earned All-American honors by placing 8th in the NCAA final with a 150-5. Barnard captured the hammer throw title at the U.S. Junior Nationals (athletes under the age of 20) held in Columbus, Ohio, becoming the first Hornet to capture a national junior title.

Burnett popped a javelin throw of 163-3 to finish 2nd in the NCAA Outdoor Championships, with Hare finishing 9th in 136-10. Burnett (149-9) took the MIAA title, and led her teammates Hare (141-9) and Barnard (117-5) to a 1-2-3 sweep in the event. Laura Rand added a MIAA discus title in 150-8 and went on to finish 9th in the NCAA Outdoor Championships in 142-6. Rand also won the KU Relays, the JCCC Relays, and the DII Challenge. Rand added shot put titles, winning the MIAA in 44-9, as well as a KU Relays title in 46-9 ½.

Speed was displayed in the form of Schneider, who won the MIAA 100 in 12.19 and finished 3rd in the NCAA meet with a 24.17 for 200 meters. Schneider was 2nd in the MIAA 200, won the ESU Invite, and the MIAA/NCC challenge. Schneider added another 3rd in the 400 at the NCAA National Championships, clocking a 53.33. She displayed her tremendous range, as she also posted the fastest ESU time of the year in the 800 meters with a 2:14.75 to win the ESU Open. She won the MIAA title in 2:16.79 and also added the DII Challenge 800 win. Doubrava was 3rd behind Schneider in the conference 200 and behind Schneider at the national 400, taking a 7th place finish in 54.81. The versatile Doubrava won the MIAA long jump at 19-4 and placed 6th in the NCAA National Championships (19-2) to go along with wins at the DII challenge and the ESU Twilight. Doubrava's triple jump skills earned her a 2nd at 38-0 at MIAAs. She also captured the heptathlon with 4795 points.

Doubrava and Schneider teamed with Pitman and Oberg to take 2nd in the NCAA 4 x 400 with a school record 3:42.94. The foursome had set the school record earlier in the year (3:48.27) in winning at the prestigious Drake Relays. The NCAA prelim time of 3:45.60 re-set the record before the team demolished the record in the final. The team showed their quality by winning at the MIAA, KU Relays, MIAA/NCC challenge, DII Challenge, and ESU Open. The relay success continued with the 4 x 800 relay taking a 1st at the KU Relays with Oberg, Pitman, Doubrava, and Schneider running 9:42.2. The distance medley relay also won at KU with Oberg, Ross, Cathcart, and Schneider in 12:33.30. The sprint medley added another championship relay title at Drake in 3:58.1 with Sharolyn Wilson, Bridget Clem, Doubrava, and Schneider.

Gillian Curtiss added an MIAA 2nd in the 400 hurdles, running 1:03.82 and also captured the DII challenge. ESU added distance points in the 10K with Michelle Daniel 2nd in the MIAA in 38:33.74 and capturing the ESU Twilight.

The Lady Hornets won the MIAA Outdoor Championships, their first ever MIAA title and placed 5th in the NCAA Outdoor Championships.

1997

The dynamic duo of Schneider and Doubrava returned in 1997. Schneider placed 8th in the NCAA DII National Indoor Championships 60 meter dash in 7:31 and demonstrated tremendous versatility by placing 6th in the NCAA 800 in 2:10.32. She also won the Cyclone Classic in 2:12.18 and then improved to 2:12.14 with a 5th at the Husker Invite. She captured the MIAA title in 2:17.73. Schneider's tremendous season continued with a 56.99 to finish 2nd in the MIAA and she ran a season best of 55.80 to win the Wildcat Invite. She added a blistering 1:22.50 to her season resume to win the Nebraska Invite 600.

Doubrava was just as outstanding, running 55.99 for 6th place in the NCAA Indoor Championships 400. She placed 1st in 1:25.38 to win the MIAA 600. Doubrava also added a pentathlon score of 3515 to win the Jayhawk Invite. Schneider and Doubrava formed half of the 4 x 400 relay with Jaylane Gerber and Pitman that ran 3:42.35 at Iowa State and placed 4th in the NCAA indoor meet in 3:46.93. The two mile relay of Doubrava, Adrienne Johnson, Oberg, and Pittman won the Jayhawk Invite in a season-best 9:35.47 and also captured the MIAA title. Nikki Runnebaum hurdled a noteworthy quality time of 8:30 in the 55-meter hurdles at Iowa State. The Lady Hornets were 2nd in the MIAA Indoor and 21st in the NCAA Indoor.

Schneider had used up her collegiate eligibility for the 1997 outdoor season and the spotlight would shine on Doubrava. She ran 57.31 in the 400 to win the ESU Twilight but began to shift her attention toward the heptathlon and the 400 hurdles, where she ran 1:01.49 at the Billy Hayes Invitational and 1:02.06 to win the MIAA meet. Teammate Gillian Curtiss was 3rd in the MIAA 400 hurdles and ran a season best of 1:02.28 at the ESU Last Chance.

Doubrava won the MIAA heptathlon with 4949 points and finished 3rd in the NCAA Outdoor National Championships with 5095 points. In the long jump she had a season best of 18-9 ½ to win the ESU Twilight, and also won the ESU Relays at 18-0 ½.

The relays were once again of high quality during the 1997 outdoor season with the team of Curtiss, Jalane Gerber, Pitman and Doubrava finishing 4th in the NCAA Championships in 3:43.65. The 4 x 800 relay team of Sarah Walter, Doubrava, Pitman, and Oberg ran 9:26.32 to win the KU Relays.

Joyce Burnett: National Champion
Joyce Burnett won the 1997 NCAA DII National Outdoor Championships title in the javelin. Her mark of 167-0 in the old javelin is an ESU record by over 16 feet. Burnett finished 5th in 1995, and 2nd in 1996, before capturing her title in 1997.

Burnett led a throwing trio that was of national quality. Burnett enjoyed the most successful javelin season in women's track and field history, capturing the NCAA National Championship title in the javelin throwing 157-8. She threw a season best of 167-0 at the ESU Twilight, captured the MIAA title at 159-5 and also won the ESU Twilight, ESU Relays, KU Relays, and finished 4th at the Drake Relays. Lynda Barnard was also outstanding in the hammer throw, placing 2nd in NCAAs with 185-0, a new school record. She captured the MIAA title in 181-3 and also won at the Drake Relays, KU Relays, ESU Relays, and the ESU Twilight. Barnard also threw 138-11 to earn All-American honors in the NCAA javelin by placing 7th. Barnard was challenged in the hammer by Laura Mayo, a transfer from Allen County, who placed 6th in the NCAA final in the hammer at 169-1 and 2nd in the MIAA in 163-7. Mayo also won the Southwestern and Baker Invitational.

The team captured 2nd in the MIAA Outdoor Nationals and 8th at NCAA DII National Outdoors.

1998

The 1998 indoor track and field season was highlighted by the senior season of Doubrava. She finished 4th in the NCAA indoor 400 in 55.23, while winning the MIAA in 56.79. She also added a 3rd in the MIAA 200 in 25.57. Doubrava continued to shine in the long jump at 19-0 ¾ to win MIAA and place 5th in the NCAA champs at 19-0. Doubrava posted the season's fastest 600-yard time of 1:23.66 to finish 2nd at the KU Invite. She did not run the 600 in the MIAA, but the Hornets didn't miss a beat with Pitman taking the title in 1:26.67 and Kristin Brune in 1:26.94 for 3rd. Pitman recorded an indoor season best 800 in 2:14.75 at the Iowa State Qualifier and competed in the NCAA DII championships (2:15.62) but did not advance out of the prelims. Wendy Duran ran 2nd in the MIAA 800 in 2:17.99, and the 2-mile relay won in 9:41.00. Senior Laura Mayo picked up a 2nd in the MIAA shot in 52-1.

The Lady Hornets finished 2nd in the MIAA champs and 10th in the NCAA DII National Indoor Championships.

The NCAA DII Outdoor Track and

Laura Mayo: National Champion
Laura Mayo won the 1998 NCAA DII National Championships in the hammer throw for ESU with a school record toss of 188-9. Mayo was a two-time All-American as she also placed 6th in the hammer in 1997.

Field Championships were scheduled to return to Emporia in 1999. With an eye on competing at home in her final season, Doubrava redshirted the 1998 outdoor season. Gillian Curtiss stepped up with an outstanding 400 hurdles performance at the NCAA meet to finish 2nd in 1:00.20. Curtiss ran 1:00.02 in the hurdles to win the MIAA and placed 2nd with a 56.09 in the open 400. She displayed her outstanding versatility, competing in the MIAA heptathlon, scoring 4076 points for 3rd. Nikki Runnebaum picked up a 4th with 4022 points.

The 4 x 400 relay team of Curtiss, Emily Bloss, Brune, and Pitman finished 6th in the NCAA Outdoor Championships final, running a season best of 3:49.97 in the prelims. They also won the MIAA Championship in 3:48.31.

Mayo, who had earned All-American honors by placing 6th the previous year in the hammer, made a significant improvement, by almost 20 feet. Mayo won the MIAA championship in 186-3 and then improved on that to become a national champion with a throw of 188-9 at the NCAA DII National Championships. Mayo also won the UMKC, Missouri Southern, and DII Challenge meets. Freshman Heather Leverington showed a preview of great accomplishments to come by winning the shot put at the UMKC, Missouri Southern, Mule Relays, and Baker Relays with a season best of 47-4 ½.

In 1998, the javelin specifications changed, shifting the weight distribution and making it harder to throw further. Amber Frese had the best ESU throw of the year in the Emporia Relays at 141-6 and therefore, she became the ESU school record holder in the new javelin. Joyce Burnett's throw of 167-0 stood as the old javelin school record.

The Lady Hornets placed 4th in the MIAA Indoor Championships and 10th in the NCAA National Outdoor Championships.

1999

The 1999 indoor season was highlighted by the emergence of Heather Leverington throwing over 50 feet and earning her first national title. Her 10 points gave ESU a 10th place team finish. It was the first ever DII Indoor National Championship and the first national title since Kelly McCammon captured the NAIA mile run back in 1986. The sophomore captured the

> **Heather Leverington: National Champion**
> Heather Leverington was a five-time national champion in the shot put, winning the indoor title three times, and the outdoor title twice. She holds both the indoor and outdoor shot put records and set the NCAA D-II National Outdoor meet record in the shot twice in her career. Leverington won nine MIAA champions in various throwing events.
>
>

MIAA shot title at 50-1 ¼ (an MIAA record) and then bettered that mark with a 50-2 ½ to become the NCAA Indoor champion. She also picked up wins at KU, KSU, Pittsburg State and Central Missouri. Tara Hudspeth picked up an 800 win in MIAA in 2:18.72 with Robin Childers 3rd in 2:19.87. The one-mile relay team (3:59.18) and two-mile relay team (9:34.65) both won MIAA titles, with the two mile relay also winning at the Jayhawk and KU Invites. Sprinter Tiffany Burden added a 55-meter title at the Kansas Invitational in a noteworthy 7.09.

The women placed 3rd in the MIAA Indoor Championships and 10th at the NCAA Indoors.

> **Deandra Doubrava: One Woman Scoring Machine**
> Deandra Doubrava scored an amazing 66 points in the 1999 MIAA Outdoor Track and Field Championships to lead ESU to a team title at home. She won four events: the triple jump, 200, 400, and heptathlon, and placed 2nd in the long jump and 100 hurdles. Her heptathlon score of 5219 points, included a 2:12.40 800 and was the top-ranked score in the nation.

The 1999 women's outdoor season was highly anticipated for two reasons. ESU was hosting the NCAA DII track and field championships for the second time (hosted the first time in 1995), and the return of Deandra Doubrava from a redshirt year. Coach Harris had pointed his athletes for a peak performance at the home national meet and his plan worked to perfection, as ESU had a record setting year. Doubrava was amazing in scoring 66 points by herself at the MIAA meet. She would finish 2nd in the 100 hurdles at 14.22, win the 200 in 24.80, the 400 in 55.90, the triple jump in 38-7 ¾, and the heptathlon (which included a blistering 2:12.40 in the 800) with 5219 points. The throwers were also a force in the 1999 season. Besides Leverington, Jody Wood emerged in the discus, winning the MIAA in 153-11, and Lynda Barnard won the hammer in 170-5. Led by Doubrava's big points, the Lady Hornets captured their second-ever MIAA Championship as a team.

Doubrava would see her finest hour as a Hornet at Welch Stadium in her final collegiate meet. She recorded a meet record 5394 points in the heptathlon to win her first NCAA championship. She trailed after six events and needed to beat Texas A & M-Kingsville's Anna Olason by nine seconds if she was to win. She did just that, winning with a time of 2:13.52, almost 33 seconds better than Olason.

> **Deandra Doubrava: National Champion**
> Deandra Doubrava was a 14-time All-American and two-time national champion for the Hornets. She won both the 400 hurdles and the heptathlon at the 1999 national outdoor championships to lead the Hornets to a 4th place team finish. She won an MIAA record setting 18 conference individual titles.
>
>

She followed that up with one of the most memorable moments in ESU track history, Doubrava and Curtiss-Masters both qualified for the 400-meter hurdle finals. Curtiss-Masters had finished 2nd at the national meet in the 400 hurdles the previous season and won the 1999 MIAA Championship in 1:02.20. For the final, she joined teammate Doubrava for a competitive run at a national title. The thrilling final saw the Emporia State teammates Doubrava and Curtiss-Masters storm down the final straightaway for a 1-2 national finish with the ESU faithful roaring. The final results: Doubrava 1st in 1:00.11, Curtiss-Masters 2nd in 1:02.08.

Doubrava's senior season of outstanding 400-meter hurdling also included a PR and school record of 59.67 at the ESU Last Chance, a 5th at the Drake Relays in 59.67, and 1st at the Mt. SAC Relays in 60:06.

> **1999 Team Women's Track and Field Team**
> **4th at NCAA Nationals**
> The ESU women's team finished 4th at the 1999 NCAA led by the National Championships of Deandra Doubrava and Heather Leverington.
>
>

Curtiss-Masters concluded her brilliant career by teaming with Doubrava, Celeste DeTiege, and Kristin Brune in the 4 x 400 relay to place 4th at nationals with a 3:43.49. Lynda Barnard added to the Hornet success by placing 5th in the hammer throw in 169-7.

As outstanding as Doubrava's heptathlon victory was, and as thrilling as the 400-meter hurdle final was, they were not the only memorable moments of the meet. Leverington came into the 1999 National Outdoor Championships as the MIAA shot put champion at 49-7 ½. She had also won the 1999 NCAA Indoor National Championship earlier in the year and she had added wins in the Spring Twilight, ESU Relays, DII Challenge, UMKC, and USTA meets. Leverington rose to the occasion in her home ring, winning the NCAA Championship in the shot put, throwing a personal record 52-6 ½ to become a two-time national champion. The outstanding efforts and high finishes enabled ESU to place 4th, earning their highest NCAA team finish in women's track and field history.

2000

The 2000 season featured the return of Heather Leverington for the indoor season. Leverington won the MIAA indoor shot in 51-11 ½ and placed 2nd in 51-5 at the NCAA Indoor Championships. Outstanding performances were ran in the 600-yard run at the MIAA championships, as Deneal Bedenbender won in 1:26.35 and Brune was 2nd in 1:26.89. The 4 x 400 meter relay team of Melissa Burden, Celeste DeTiege, Brune, and Bedenbender placed 5th in 3:51.25 at the NCAA Indoor Championships after winning the MIAA in 3:58.31.

The strength of the ESU throws core was evident during the indoor season. Besides standout Leverington, Kara Brockmeier placed 2nd (45-10 ¾) and Melanie Goetz 4th (42-4 ¾) in the MIAA shot put. Leverington placed 2nd in the weight throw at 54-10 ¾ in the MIAA Championships and 9th in the NCAA Championships at 51-2 ¼. ESU finished 2nd in the MIAA Indoor Championships with 131 points and 10th in the NCAA Indoor meet with 12 points. New school records were also set by Tara Hudspeth with a 1000-meter record at Iowa State in 2:59.84 and Laci Kirkaldie set a new pole vault record of 9-4 ½.

The 2000 outdoor Lady Hornets were without national champion Heather Leverington and finished 2nd in the MIAA meet held at Pittsburg State. The Burden sisters, Tiffany and Melissa led the sprint core. Tiffany won the 100 in 11.95 and was 2nd in the 200. Her sister Melissa ran 3rd in the 200 and led a 2-3-4 finish by Burden (57.57), Bedenbender (57.78), and Amy Allen in 57.95 in the 400 meters.

MIAA champions were Emilee Hamlin in the triple jump at 38-9 ¾, Kara Brockmeier in the shot at 47-7, Sara Weurtz in the heptathlon with 4533 points, and the 4 x 400 winning in 3:50.96. Other strong MIAA efforts included 800 runners Robin Childers and Wendy Duran, 2nd and 3rd at 2:14.9 and 2:17.4. Nikki Runnebaum was 2nd in the 100 hurdles at 14.29, Brockmeier, 2nd in the discus at 162-7, followed by teammates Sarah Collins in 3rd at 146-9 and Rachel Goetz 6th in 133-11. Wuertz added a 2nd in the javelin at 131-11 and Hamlin was a runner-up in the heptathlon with 4514 points.

ESU finished 2nd at the 2000 MIAA outdoor meet and placed 28th at Nationals with 8 points. Picking up national points for the Hornets was Brockmeier with a 7th in the shot at 47-7 ¼ and a 6th in the discus at 150-8. Wuertz tossed the javelin 143-4, good enough for 6th place.

2001

Heather Leverington returned for the 2001 indoor season, determined to win another NCAA title after winning two titles her sophomore season. She dominated the competition, winning her 3rd NCAA title at 52-6 ½ and winning the MIAA Indoor at 52-1 ¾. She threw an indoor season best 53-7 at Kansas State. ESU flexed their muscles at the MIAA meet. Behind Leverington's winning effort in the shot came the 2-3-4 placers, all from ESU; Sarah Collins (44-10 ¼), Brockmier (44-3 ¼), and Goetz (42-10 ¼).

Leverington added yet another MIAA championship, winning the weight throw in 53-0 ¼ and garnering a school record of 56-6 earlier in the year.

ESU romped to the MIAA team title with 159 points. Kristin Brune ran the 600 in 1:25.82 for 2nd, Childers ran 2:15.3 to win the 800 with Hudspeth 3rd. Nikki Runnebaum was 2nd in the 55-meter hurdles in 8.22, establishing a new school record. The relay teams upheld the strong ESU baton tradition by winning the 4 x 400 at MIAA with Bredenbender, Brune, Robin Childers, and Amy Allen, running 3:56.70 and the two mile relay also winning in 9:25.90, a new school record, with legs by Hudspeth, Childers, Duran, and Brune.

Emilee Hamlin made her presence known setting a school record in winning the MIAA triple jump in 39-6. Hamlin doubled up to win the MIAA long jump in 18-1. High jumper Sara Wuertz cleared 5-6 to place 2nd in the MIAA championships.

Leverington dominated the outdoor season in the shot, winning her 4th NCAA DII national title. Her put of 53-5 set a new national DII record. Her winning toss of 50-10 ¼ established a new MIAA shot put indoor record. She also earned All-American honors in the hammer throw placing 8th with a throw of 164-0, the same distance she threw to win the MIAA hammer.

The 2001 ESU throws group was one of the best in school history. Brockmeier placed 6th at NCAA nationals in the shot, throwing 47-9 ¼ and finished 2nd at MIAA. Brockmeier established a new school record in the discus throwing 163-6 at the DII Challenge and placing 6th in the NCAA Nationals. She captured the MIAA title in 152-2 and also won at the Twilight Qualifier, UMKC Invite, and the Cavalier Cup. ESU had the MIAA champion in the javelin in Kristi Smith, throwing 136-10, but the season best belonged to heptathlete Sarah Wuertz who threw 141-0.

In a new event for women, Tricia Kantack placed 4th in the MIAA steeplechase, setting a school record of 11:44.63. Another relatively new event saw Lacey Kirkaldie set an ESU standard by pole vaulting 10-11 ¾. ESU swept the MIAA multis with Hamlin scoring 4726 points, Wuertz 4599 points, and Runnebaum 3rd in 4296 points. The 24 points in the multis sent the Hornets well on their way to winning the MIAA Championships with 195 points. The Lady Hornets 20 points at the NCAA championship earned ESU a 13th place national finish.

2002

The 2002 indoor track and field season featured an outstanding distance runner from Estonia, Kadri Kelve. Kelve placed 7th in the NCAA Indoor Championships and set a new ESU mile record of 4:54.69. Kelve also finished 10th in the 5000 at the NCAA meet running 18:11.11, off her school record performance at MIAA when she finished 2nd in 17:22.55.

The field events were once again the strong suit in 2002 for ESU with Kara Brockmeier finishing 2nd at the NCAA national meet with a shot put of 47-10 ½, closely followed at nationals by Rachel Goetz in 3rd in 47-10 ½. They would also finish in that order at the MIAA going 1-2, but Goetz posted the season best indoor mark of 48-11 ¾. Goetz set a school record in the weight throw with a toss of 58-3 to finish 5th in the NCAA Championships and won the MIAA in a new meet record of 57-3.

Hamlin scored in the horizontal jumps with a 4th place NCAA finish in the triple jump in 39-7 at and a 7th place NCAA finish in the long jump at 19-2, a new school record. Hamlin captured both jump titles at the MIAA meet with her 40-7 ¾ triple jump at MIAAs, establishing a new school. Wuertz added to the jump party, clearing 5-8 in the high jump at the MIAAs to set school and meet records. She would follow that up with a 9th place NCAA National finish at 5-3 ¾.

Emporia State defended their MIAA Indoor conference title, scoring 120 points and placing 6th at the NCAA Indoor championships with 29 points.

The 2002 outdoor season featured one of the finest displays of shot putting in the long and storied tradition of the shot put at Emporia State. With shot put legends such as John Kuck, the Olympic champion; Al Feuerbach, the world record holder; and Kathy Devine, the American record holder, ESU's putting history is indeed legendary. Leverington entered her final season as a four-time national champion. She was throwing better than ever and had thrown her collegiate best at the Pomona-Pitzer Invitational in California. Her put of 54-2 ¾ established a new school record, which is still 3rd all-time in NCAA-II. She led an ESU shot put domination at the MIAA conference meet, with ESU taking the first four places, all with national qualifying marks. Leverington, as usual, led the way with a 53-9 ¼, a new MIAA record, Brockmier was 2nd (45-3 ½), Goetz 3rd (45-0 ½), and Collins 4th (44-8 ¾). Adrian Blewitt of Ashland University came into the NCAA DII national meet as the national indoor champion, as Leverington was out of indoor eligibility and did not compete in the 2002 indoor championships. Blewitt had been outstanding all year and before the NCAA meet, she was named the NCAA Div. II Female Athlete of the Year by the coaches of the 620 athletes competing. In an exciting back and forth competition, Blewitt and Leverington twice traded national meet records before Blewitt nailed the winning toss. Leverington's outstanding season also included wins at the Spring Twilight, JC Cavalier Cup, Drake Relays and the ESU Relays. The three other ESU shot putters competed in the national meet with Brockmeier (43-10 ½) placing 11th, Melanie Goetz (45-½) placing 16th, and Sara Collins (38-4 ¾) placing 14th.

Brockmeier captured the MIAA discus title in 163-10 for a new school record and finished 4th in the NCAA Championships throwing 156-2. Collins posted a quality mark in finishing 4th at MIAA in the discus at 151-1 and finished 10th in the NCAA meet. Leverington added MIAA points with a 5th in the discus and won the hammer in 173-8, an event she would place 11th in at nationals.

Sarah Wuertz led the javelin throwers, setting a new school record for the new javelin, throwing 146-6 to win the MIAA and place 5th at nationals at 138-8. Courtney Hurt picked up a 3rd in the MIAA and a 14th place national finish. Wuertz also became an All-American in the heptathlon, placing 7th with 4988 points after capturing the MIAA title with 4750 points, including a 5-7 high jump in the multi-competition. Hamlin earned All-American honors with a 6th place finish at the NCAA championships in the triple jump at 41-1 ½, after winning the MIAA top honor.

The middle distance crew of Kelve and Brune posted outstanding times in the 800 at Pomona-Pitzer with Kelve clocking 2:12.90 and Brune, 2:13.04. Brune won the MIAA 800 in 2.15.25 and Kelve took the 1500 in 4:38.10.

Emporia State was dominant in winning the MIAA title for the second consecutive year, scoring 161 points. The women scored 21 points to finish 17th at the NCAA National Outdoors.

2003

ESU's throwers were again outstanding in the 2003 indoor season. Kara Brockmeier (47-02 ¼) and Rachel Goetz (46-0) went 1-2 in the shot at MIAA's and then proceeded to pick up All-American honors at nationals with Brockmeier 6th in 46-0 ¾, and Goetz 8th in 45-6 ¼. Goetz added a 2nd in the weight throw at 56-5 ¾.

The 2003 indoor season also marked the emergence of distance runner Kadri Kelve. Kelve's outstanding season included a 6th place NCAA finish in the mile in 4:52.94. She posted an even faster school record time at the Nebraska Invite. Kelve was a warrior in winning four events at the MIAA indoor, taking the 800 in 2:15.2, the mile in 5:00.51, the 3000 in 10:16.66, and the 5000 in 17:57.17. Kelve also ran the 5000 at nationals and finished 12th in 17:26.96. Hamlin also picked up more All-American honors by placing 5th at the NCAA Indoors at 39-0 ¼ in the triple jump. She won the MIAA triple in 39-6 and was 2nd in the MIAA long jump at 18-3.

As a team, ESU finished 2nd in the MIAA Indoor with 114 points and 11th in the NCAA Indoor with 14 points.

The outdoor 2003 Lady Hornets were extremely well balanced, deriving points from sprinters, jumpers, throwers and distance runners. The distance firepower came in the form of Kelve, who ranged from the 800 to the 10K and included the steeplechase. At 800 meters, she ran 2:14.01 at the DII Challenge to finish 2nd. She won an amazing four distance events at the MIAA Outdoor Championships, winning the 3000 (10:19.26), 5000 (18:12.98) 10,000 (38:14.42), and 3000-meter steeplechase (11:19.05).

Kadri Kelve: National Champion
Kadri Kelve capped off her outstanding career at Emporia State by winning the 3000-meter steeplechase at the 2003 NCAA DII National Track and Field Outdoor Championships in meet record time. In her senior season of 2002-2003, she won an amazing eight MIAA individual track titles and the cross country title. She also became the first female runner from Emporia State to earn All-American honors in cross country at the NCAA DII level.

Kelve's first steeplechase of her career was at the ESU Relays, where she won in 10:56.7. She competed in her second steeple race of the season at the Mt. Sac Relays, where she placed 4th in 10:41.57 to set a new ESU school record and qualify for the national meet. Her third steeple was part of her historical four-win effort at the MIAA meet, winning in 11:19.05. The fourth steeple of her career came at the NCAA meet in the prelims, where she qualified for the final. As Kelve lined up for the 3000-meter steeplechase final, she was to begin only her fifth steeplechase ever, having been running the event less than two months. Kelve was outstanding as she ran and hurdled her way to the NCAA Championship in 10:22.81, setting a new school record and NCAA DII National Outdoor Championships meet record.

The sprint points came from Courtney Bruna who took a 3rd place finish in the MIAA at 12.23 and 21st place NCAA finish in 12.17. Ashley Melichar added a 2nd in the MIAA at 58.00 in the 400. 400 hurdler Kayla Pauly's time of 1:002.01 was 4th in the MIAA and her time of 1:00.10 earned her 11th at the NCAAs. The 400-relay of Bruna, Alicia Burns, Natasha Oakes, and Emily Watson ran 47.20 to win the Last Chance in school record time.

Pauly helped lead the jumpers as her 19-1 ½ long jump earned her the MIAA championship and she was followed by 2nd place finisher Hamlin in 18-11 ¼. Hamlin triple jumped at NCAA Nationals and her leap of 40-5 was good enough for All-American honors in 4th place. Hamlin also captured the MIAA title in 39-2.

Brockmeier and Goetz were dominant in the throws, going 1-2 in the shot at conference with Brockmeier1st in 46-7 ½ and Goetz 2nd in 45-9. Brockmeier added NCAA All-American honors with a 5th in 46-3 ½ and Goetz an 11th in 43-10 ¾. Goetz won the MIAA discus in 151-11, and Brockmeier was

2nd in 149-7, with Brockmeier posting a season best of 158-2 at the ESU Last Chance. Heptathlete Sarah Wuertz took the MIAA title with 4546 points and placed 13th in the NCAA's with 4626 points.

The Lady Hornets finished 1st in the MIAA (for the third consecutive year) with 189 points and finished in the top 10 at the national meet, placing 7th in the NCAA with 25 points.

2004

The Lady Hornets were led in the 2004 indoor season by thrower Rachel Goetz. Goetz continued the tradition of outstanding throwers by winning the conference shot in 46-7 ¼ and placing 5th in the NCAA Indoor Championships at 45-9 ¼. The Hornet throws program had produced an All-American at every national championship since the 1998 outdoor season for a total of 13 straight national championships. She added a 4th in the weight throw at nationals with a 57-7 ¾ and runner-up finish in MIAAs with a 56-04 ¾.

Rachel Goetz: National Champions
Rachel Goetz won the national championship in the outdoor shot put in 2004. Goetz was a nine-time All-American and still holds the school record in the indoor weight throw.

Sprinter Courtney Bruna captured the indoor conference title in the 200 in 25.11 and was 2nd in the 60-meter dash in 7.80. Jumpers Natasha Oakes and Alicia Burns both added conference seconds in the long jump (18-5) and triple jump (38-2 ¾), respectively. The women's 4 x 400 relay team of Daniele Sedivy, Burns, Jennifer Lawellin, and Oakes ran a quality 3:47.72 at the Last Chance meet.

The Lady Hornets finished 5th in the MIAA indoor and 15th at Nationals in 2004.

Goetz and Bruna continued to lead the team during the 2004 outdoor season. Goetz moved up from her 5th place indoor national finish to capture her first national title in the shot put with a 47-11 ¼. Goetz dominated the competition, also taking shot 1sts at the Mule Relays, ESU Last Chance, Missouri Southern DII Challenge, Spring Twilight, and the ESU Relays. Goetz doubled up at nationals to earn her second All-American honor of the outdoor season by taking 4th in the discus with a fling of 156-2.

Bruna sprinted to a 4th place national finish in the NCAA Championships establishing a new ESU school record with a time of 11.64. She had an outstanding day at the MIAA meet in winning three events and setting school records in all three. Her 100 time of 11.85 broke her own school record set earlier in the year. She added the 200-meter title, setting the school record of 23.83 in the 200. The old record was set in the 1996 NCAA Championships by Magali Schneider in 24.17. The sprint 4 x 100 relay team of Bruna, Burns, Oakes, and Lawellin captured the MIAA title in 46.50, setting a school record and finishing 10th at NCAA Nationals in 46.40. The 4 x 400 posted a school record at the ESU Last Chance meet with the team of Oakes, Lawellin, Burns, and Sedivy running 3:47.72.

Oakes had an off-day at the MIAA meet, finishing 11th in the long jump at 17-0 ½ but came back in a week and improved to 19-2 at the ESU Last Chance meet, putting her into the NCAA national meet where she placed 9th with a 17-0 ½.

Lawellin ran 1:02.24 in the 400 hurdle prelims at the MIAAs to finish 5th in 62.84 and followed that with a slightly faster time to place 14th in the NCAA Championships in 1:02.40.

The Lady Hornets were 5th in the MIAA Outdoor and 14th in the NCAA DII Outdoor.

2005

The 2005 indoor season saw the women place 2nd in the MIAA with 93 points in a meet that was won by Central Missouri. Krysta Fennewald captured the 800 in 2:17.04, Shannon Butler the long jump at 18-2 ½ and the distance medley relay of Fennewald, Jaclyn Sill, Jonel Rossbach, and Kristen Larson won in 12:23.82, as well as Alicia Burns in the triple jump at 38-6.75. Seconds were captured by Butler in the 60 with a school record tying 7.71, and Hurt in the shot in a PR 46-9. The mile relay of Burns, Ashley Melichar, Danielle Sedivy, and Fennewald won the MIAA title in 3:56.21 and ran a season best time of 3:46.52 for 7th at NCAA Indoor Nationals. Larson also set a school record in the 1000, running 3:01.01 at Kansas State. The women finished 2nd at the MIAA meet and 35th at the NCAA Indoor Championships.

The Hornet relay teams sparkled in the 2005 outdoor season. The 4 x 100 meter relay of Bruna, Burns, Melichar, and Butler placed 6th in the NCAA meet in a school record time of 46.39. The same team won at the prestigious Drake Relays and finished 2nd in the MIAA. The 4 x 400 relay team of Sedivy, Sill, Burns, and Melichar won the MIAA in 3:48.95. Butler added a school record in the long jump in winning the MIAA in 19-4 ¾.

In a display of javelin strength, Connie Phillips led a 2, 3, 4 MIAA finish, throwing 145-3. A few weeks later, Phillips upped that to 144-1 for 6th and All-American honors in the NCAA National Championships. Hurt threw 143-2 for 3rd in the MIAA and 11th at nationals in 132-6, with Allison Casey throwing 139-2 for an MIAA 4th and a 13th place national finish. Larson ran a 4:38.21 1500 meters for 2nd in the MIAA and ran to a 13th place finish (4:44.91) in the NCAA nationals. Fennewald posted a noteworthy time of 2:14.94 at the University of Texas Arlington Invite, and Bruna ran 11.95 for 3rd in the MIAA 100, and 24.89 for 4th in the MIAA 200.

The women finished 4th in the MIAA Outdoor with 83 points and 37th in the NCAA Outdoor with 6 points.

2006

The sprinters led the way for the 2006 women's team. Shannon Butler captured the MIAA 60 meter dash in a school record time of 7.66 and finished 12th in the NCAA National Indoor. She doubled winning the 200 at the MIAA meet and then ran 10th at NCAAs in 24.81. Kara Euler followed her in the MIAA 200 for a 1-2 ESU finish, running 25.62 and winning the 400 in 57.5. Butler also long jumped, blasting out to a school record 19-11 ½ in the long jump at the Nebraska Invitational. Butler earned All-American honors leaping to a national runner-up finish in 19-5 ½ and took the MIAA title in 18-10.

Sill posted a mark of 1:26.65 to win the MIAA 600. Rossbach ran 2:13.85 for the 800 at Iowa State to qualify for nationals where she placed 15th. Courtney Hurt placed 2nd at the MIAA in the shot, throwing 45-6 ¼. The women finished 3rd in the MIAA Indoor and 20th in the NCAA National Outdoor.

In the 2006 outdoor season the sprinters continued to post great times. Butler placed 9th at NCAAs running 11.90 in the 100, following up on her MIAA win in 11.96. Euler placed 19th at NCAAs in the 400 (56.59) and 23rd in the 200 (24.85). Earlier in the season, she took the MIAA title in the 400 in 55.82 and placed 2nd in the 200 in 24.54. The 4 x 100 of Euler, Sedivy, Melichar, and Butler ran to a 7th place finish at NCAAs running 46.18 in the final but posting an even faster time of 46.15 in the prelims, which was a new school record.

After setting the ESU long jump record indoors, Butler added the outdoor school record leaping 19-7 ½ in the DII Challenge hosted by ESU. Butler won the MIAA in 19-6 and earned yet another All-American honor by placing 7th at NCAA's in 19-3 ½.

ESU was represented by two distance runners in the national meet. Rossbach placed 12th in the 1500 in 4:55.7 after a 2nd place MIAA finish of 4:40.38 and a 2nd in the MIAA 800 in 2:15.28. Kristin Larson won the MIAA 3000 in 10:08.49 and finished 13th in NCAA 3000 in 10:43.6.

The women finished 3rd in the MIAA with 101 points and scored 4 points for a 44th place national finish.

2007

ESU finished 5th as a team in the 2007 MIAA Indoor Championships as Jonel Rossbach won MIAA titles in the 3000 (10:23.01) and the 5000 (17:41.08), and was 2nd in the mile at 5:06.68. Rossbach placed 4th in the mile at the DII National Championships in 4:50.65 to earn All-American track honors to go with her All-American cross country honor, as the Hornets finished 31st as a team. Rossbach's time broke the previous school record, beating Kadri Kelve's 2003 mark of 4:52.24 by nearly two seconds. Rossbach's performance gave ESU a 31st place national finish. Sill added a 600 win in the MIAA meet in 1:26.03 and Euler placed 2nd in the 400 at 58.79 and 3rd in the 200 at 25.54.

Sill, Euler, and Rossbach continued to lead the Hornets in the 2007 outdoor season. Sill took the MIAA 400 in 55.78 and placed 13th in the NCAA Championships in 55.70. Euler's 55.70 season best was ran at the ESU Last Chance. She also ran 2nd in the MIAA meet in 56.80 and 17th in the NCAA Championships in 56:43. Rossbach competed in the 1500 meters at nationals and placed 8th in 4:33.00. She had a monster conference meet, winning the 3000 in 10:40.60, the 5000 in 17:34.22, placing 2nd in the 1500 in 4:37.85, and 2nd in the 800 in 2:14.71. The 4 x 400 of Sill, Sedivy, Euler, and Rossbach finished 9th in the NCAA championship field, running 3:44.79.

The team placed 5th in the MIAA Outdoor and 58th at NCAA Outdoor.

2008

The 2008 indoor track season was a combination of speed, endurance and power Brooke Kent brought the speed, winning the MIAA 60 (7.70) and the 200 (25.7). Sill defended her 600 indoor conference title improving her time to 1:24.40. The 4 x 400 relay of Brandi Lundgren, Ashley Spencer, Chelsea Hughes-Stanton, and Sill ran 3:59.10 to win a conference title.

The power was supplied by the leaping ability of Jennifer Robinson and Kent. Robinson took the conference high jump title in 5-7 ¼ (and also finished 2nd in the long jump) and later finished 13th in the NCAA field in 5-5. Kent captured the MIAA long jump title in 18-11 ¾.

The endurance component came from the tireless legs of Rossbach. She finished 6th in the indoor NCAA 5000 running 17:16.91, took the MIAA 5000 title and established a school record of 16:51.62 at the Iowa State Classic. Rossbach also won the MIAA mile in 5:03.96 and ran a season best of 4:56.96. In addition, she won the 3000 in a meet record time of 10:02.17 but ran even faster in setting a new school record of 9:50.39 at the Iowa State Open. The old record of 9:59.36 set by Susan Stine in 1987 lasted 21 years.
The Lady Hornets finished 2nd in the MIAA Indoor and 23rd at the NCAA Indoor.

Rossbach continued to shine into the 2008 outdoor season. She dominated the MIAA meet, winning the 800 in 2:12.96, the 1500 in 4:39.85, the 3000 in 10:10 and the 5000 in 17:37.42. The 40-point effort was just a warm-up for Rossbach, as she won the NCAA 5000-meter run in 16:52.28, establishing a new school record. The old record stood for 22 years and was held by Susan Stine who ran 17:10.49 at the NAIA National meet in Russellville, Arkansas in 1986. Rossbach would double up at the National Championships in the 10,000 meters, finishing 2nd in 35:35.02. Her earlier time of 35.24.81 at the Mt. Sac Relays established a new school record, breaking a 21-year-old record, held by Trudy Searcy, set in 1987 of 36:24 at the 1987 NAIA Championships.

Jonel Rossbach: National Champion
Jonel Rossbach was the 2008 NCAA DII 5000-meter outdoor champion and was runner-up at 10,000 meters. Rossbach won an amazing 4 distance events at the 2008 MIAA meet winning the 800, 1500, 3000 and 5000. She won 12 MIAA titles and currently holds five school records.

Brooke Kent was a double winner in the MIAA Championships winning the 100 in 12.09 and 200 in 24.62. She placed 17th and 21st respectively in those events at the NCAA Championships. Sill added a win in the 400 in 56.33 at the MIAA and was joined by high jump champion Jennifer Robinson (5-8 ½), who also won the long jump (18-9 ¼). Kent earned All-American honors by long jumping 18-4 ¼ to place 6th. Robinson high jumped 5-8 to place 7th in the NCAA high jump and Phillips threw the javelin 138-2 to place 8th.

The women's team finished 3rd in the MIAA Outdoor Championships and 10th at the NCAA Outdoor Championships.

2009

The 2009 women's indoor saw Katie Mona win MIAA Freshman of the Year honors. She anchored the distance medley relay to a win with Kathryn Davison, Tiffany Baum, and Christy Weller, setting an MIAA record of 12:20.94. Mona also finished 2nd in the mile, 3rd in the 800, and 5th in the 3000. Kent defended her MIAA 2008 title by winning the long jump in 18-2 ½. The ESU women finished 8th as a team at the MIAA indoor and did not score at the national meet.

Mona continued her distance success outdoors, winning the MIAA 3000 in the MIAA in 10:03.04, and placing 2nd in the MIAA 1500. Her 1500 season best came in the ESU Last Chance meet with a 4:35.19, which put her in the national meet where she finished 14th in 4:41.09. Sill captured the conference 400 (56.30) title as she won her third straight 400-meter conference championship. She also placed 2nd in the 200 (25.08). Sill competed at nationals and finished 16th in the 400 at 56.35.

Kent earned All-American honors with a 7th place NCAA Outdoor National finish leaping 19-4 ¼ in the long jump after placing 3rd in the MIAA at 19-1 ¼. Phillips picked up another All-American honor with a 5th place NCAA finish in the javelin at 148-0. Phillips also won her first MIAA title in the javelin with a throw of 142-5.

The team finished 6th in the MIAA and 36th at nationals.

2010

In 2010, Jennifer Robinson continued to shine in the high jump, earning a silver medal at 5-8 ½ at the NCAA Indoor Championships. Robinson won the MIAA at 5-8 ¾, setting ESU school and MIAA meet records, and also picked up wins at the Kansas State and Wichita State meets.

> **Jennifer Robinson: National Champion**
> Jennifer Robinson was the 2010 NCAA DII Outdoor champion in the high jump, setting a school record of 5-9 ¼. She also placed 2nd at the 2010 Indoor Championships.
>
>

Brooke Kent captured the MIAA title at 19-03 ¼ in the long jump and added an NCAA 6th place finish at the national meet at 18-8. Kent added an 8th place finish at the NCAAs in the triple jump at 39-5 ¾, just off her season best 39-8 ¾ accomplished in a Wichita State win.

Katie Mona captured the MIAA mile title in 4:59.22 and pulled extra duty with a 2nd in the 800 (2:17.69), a 5th in the 3000 (10:17.68) and anchored the distance medley relay (12:29.27) with Davison, Jacobs, and Baum. ESU finished 4th in the MIAA Indoor Conference and 17th at the NCAA National Indoor meet.

Robinson would earn her highest honor as a Hornet in winning the 2010 Outdoor NCAA DII Track and Field Championships title in the high jump by clearing 5-9 ¼ (school record). Robinson also captured titles at the KU Relays and ESU Relays.

> **David Harris Era**
> Emporia State won 10 MIAA team championships under Harris and had 20 runner-up finishes. The ESU women swept both the indoor and outdoor MIAA championships in 2001 and 2002. The ESU women earned the school's first top four NCAA finish nationally with a 4th place finish at the NCAA Outdoor Championships in Emporia in 1999. It was the second of three national championship meets at Witten Track/Welch Stadium held under his leadership. The ESU men's track team also finished 4th at the NCAA's in 2011.
>
>

Kent tripled jumped to a school record 41-1 ¾ to place 2nd in the NCAA Championships. Kent also captured the MIAA in 40-7 ¾. Kent and Robinson posted the top two long jump performances of the season at the Tabor Invitational, with Kent posting a 19-7 ¾ for a school record and Robinson close behind at 19-5. However, the marks were wind-aided and did not get them into the national meet. Kent placed 2nd at the MIAA and Robinson 7th in the event. Deja Jackson led the throwing effort with the top shot put, discus, and hammer performances of the season for the Hornets.

The team finished 8th with 51 points at the MIAA Outdoor Championships and 14th in the NCAA National Outdoor Championships with the scoring efforts of Robinson's 10 points and Kent's 8 points.

2011

Katie Mona highlighted the 2011 indoor season with a 5th place finish at the NCAA Championships in the 800 meters. Mona ran 2:12.46 in the final, but ran slightly faster in the prelims (2:12.31) to qualify for the final. Mona added a MIAA mile title in 5:00.93, but posted her season best of 4:56.40 in Nebraska and her season best time in the 3000 of 10:36.27 at the University of Central Missouri Invitational. Mona had workhorse duties in the MIAA anchoring the team of Kathryn Davison, Marqueita Marisette, and Courtney Maddux to win the distance medley relay in 12:25.95. Mona did not compete in the 800 and Davison stepped in to finish 2nd in 2:18.39.

Indoors, the Lady Hornets placed 8th in the MIAA and 35th at Nationals.

Katie Mona qualified for the 2011 NCAA outdoor meet in the 800 with a 2:11.76, a school record, at the Sam Williams Qualifier. She lowered her school record in the next meet running 2:10.99 in the NCAA preliminary round. In the final, the race went out very tactical, with Mona leading at the 400-meter mark, but could not get separation as she finished with a time of 2:16.89 to finish 7th. Mona led a 1-2 finish in the MIAA 800 with Davison following. Mona was a double winner in the MIAA, winning the 1500 in 4:39.39, but ran her season best of 4:36.76 to win the KU Relays.

Jennifer Robinson was back for her final semester of eligibility and finished 11th in the NCAA Outdoor Championships in 5-5, the same mark, which earned her 5th in the MIAA meet. Robinson's top mark was posted at the ESU Spring Twilight at 5-7 ¾.

Alaina Fairbanks established a new school record for the pole vault, clearing 11-5 to garner 3rd at MIAAs. Deja Jackson posted noteworthy throws of 152-1 in the discus and 169-5 in the hammer throw. Javelin throwers Ashley Watkins and Elizabeth Stover also posted provisional NCAA qualifying marks by throwing 139-8 and 133-5, respectively.

The ESU women finished 6th at the MIAA and 55th at the national meet.

2012

Katie Mona returned for her final season as a Hornet in 2012 and placed 7th in the NCAA Indoor 800 in 2:12.04, posting a season best time of 2:10.71 at the Husker Invitational. Mona won an amazing three events at the MIAA Indoor Championships, leading the Hornets to a 5th place team finish in capturing the 800 in 2:14.99, the mile in 4:54.01, and the 3000 in 10:00.59. Mona set school records in the indoor mile (4:48.55) at the Iowa State Classic and the indoor 3000-meter run (9:47.15) at the University of Central Missouri Invite. Mona concluded her fantastic career as a three time All-American at the NCAA Outdoor Championships by placing 14th in the 1500 in 4:46.07. Mona posted a 4:29.00 personal record at the KU Relays to move to number two on the Hornet all-time list, behind the legendary Kelly McCammon. Mona also posted a season outdoor best of 2:12.79 in the 800, and finished 2nd in the 800 (2:13.90) and 1500 (4:36.44) at the outdoor conference meet.

Nikki Wetstein established a new school record in the 60-meter hurdles, posting an 8.95 in the prelims of the MIAA meet and came back to run 9.00 to finish 6th in the final. Wetstein would add another school record outdoors in the 100-meter hurdles. Her time of 14.10 at the Sam Williams Qualifier established a new school record. Sonya Schement set a new indoor school record at 11-5 ¾ in the pole vault, winning the University of Central Missouri Invite. Schement added the outdoor school record to her resume in clearing 11-9 ¾ at the ESU Spring Twilight. Maggie Wilson came within a fraction of an inch in taking the record by vaulting 11-9 at the Sam Williams Qualifier. Wilson finished 2nd at the MIAAs at 11-5.

> **Steve Blocker: Coach**
> Steve Blocker was hired as the head track and field coach at Emporia State in 2011. Blocker had served as assistant coach since 2009 with ESU. Blocker previously was the first head coach at Culver-Stockton after the program was reinstituted in 2007 after a 30-year absence. Blocker spent the 2006-07 season as an assistant coach at Santa Barbara City College in Santa Barbara, Calif. Blocker's first coaching stop was at his alma mater, the University of Northern Iowa, where he served as a volunteer assistant while earning his master's degree. He competed as a hurdler while at UNI.
>
>

Besides the vaulting success, two horizontal jumpers posted outstanding marks with Carmen King long jumping 19-2 ¾ and Wetstein triple jumping 39-3 ¾.

King also led the sprinters posting high caliber marks of 11.71 and 24.52, both times in the prelims of the MIAA meet. Marqueita Marisette posted a quick 55.98 400, but the quality of the MIAA field was so deep, it only netted a 5th place finish. King turned in her third sub-12 second race of the season at the NCAA meet, but it was not enough to make the finals in the 100 meters. She ran 11.96 to place 13th overall and was the second freshman finisher.

Sara Dunkin led the throwers with a 9th place showing at the NCAA Championships with a 144-9 in a competition that saw three of the top 10 marks in Division II history. The freshman finished 2nd at MIAAs and threw a season best of 149-9 at the ESU Spring Open. Her throw of 149-9, broke the 2009 ESU school record of 148-0 set at the NCAA championships by her event coach, Connie Phillips. Jackson threw outstanding season marks of 156-8 in the discus and 167-1 in the hammer. She qualified for nationals and threw 127-09 to place 19th in the women's discus. Valeria Jordan also posted a quality mark of 44-0 ¾ in the shot put.

The women's sprint medley relay of King, Jackie Jacobs, Marisette, and Mona finished 2nd with a time of 3:56.82 at the highly competitive Drake Relays. The women were 5th at the MIAA Indoor and 43rd at the NCAA Indoor Championships. The outdoor team tied for 3rd in the conference meet with Missouri Southern with 85 points. Sprint power Lincoln University ran away with the MIAA title, scoring 204 points. The ESU women had their string of 17 straight years scoring at the national outdoor meet snapped.

2013

In the 2013 MIAA Indoor Championships, King produced an 18-5 ¾ to place 2nd in the women's long jump while Dominique Staats placed 2nd in the women's 800 (2:18.60). Wetstein scored in three events with a 3rd place finish of 38-4 ¼ in the triple jump and was 4th at 8.61 in the 60 hurdles. Her final point came from an 8th place finish in the long jump. The 4 x 440 yard relay team of Marisette, Peyton Weiss, Lindsay Kunkel, and Jackie Jacobs ran 3:58.88 to place 5th and secure the 3rd place finish in the team standings. Fairbanks joined Wilson as the only two Hornets to clear 12 feet in the pole vault as she went 12-¾ to place 3rd. Wilson cleared 11-9 to place 6th.

At the 2013 NCAA DII Indoor Championships, the women's 4 x 400 relay team ran the third fastest time in Emporia State history to finish 11th overall. The foursome of Marisette, Weiss, Kunkel, and Jacobs clocked a 3:47.53. Wetstein tied her own school record with an 8.61 in the 60-meter hurdles to finish 12th in the NCAA meet. Marisette ran the second fastest 400 in Emporia State history to place 14th overall. Her time of 55.56 was just behind Deandra Doubrava's 55.23 set at the 1998 NCAA Championships.

The Lady Hornets finished 3rd in the MIAA indoors and 11th at the national indoor meet.

Outdoors in 2013, the ESU relay teams were even better, running a 4 x 400 relay school record of 3:42.80 to place 6th in the NCAA championships. They were 2nd in the MIAA and 4th at the Drake Relays. The team of Marisette, Jacobs, Weiss, and King ran a quick 46.56 4 x 100 meter relay to finish 10th in NCAAs.

King qualified for nationals with a 19-7 leap at the Sam Williams Qualifier and placed 3rd in the nation at 19-9 ¾. She won her first MIAA Championships long-jumping 19-1 ¼. Dunkin qualified for the NCAA meet for the second consecutive year and threw 140-5 for a 10th place finish, finishing in the top 10 in the nation for the second straight year. Wilson posted a MIAA 12-1 ½ to place 3rd in the vault, and Marisette posted a fine 55.76 400-meter time at the Sam Williams Qualifier. King captured her first MIAA Outdoor Championship to lead three Emporia State women in the top six of the women's long jump. King leapt 19-1 ¼ for the win, while Weiss finished 2nd at 19-½ and Wetstein jumped 18-8 ½ to place 6th and give Emporia State 21 points in the event.

Wetstein became the first Emporia State woman to crack the 14-second barrier and broke her own record in the 100 hurdles for women. She ran a 13.92 in the MIAA prelims and came back with a 14.43 to place 6th in the finals. She ran 14.05 in the prelims at the NCAA meet to place 18th. At the MIAA meet, Marisette placed 4th in the 200 (24.49), 5th in the 400 (56.03), and led off the runner-up 400 and 1600 relay teams. She was joined on the 4 x 400 relay team by Weiss, Kunkel, and Jacobs to run a 3:48.99 and place 2nd. Marisette teamed with Jacobs, Weiss, and King to run 47.31 and place 2nd in the 400 relay. Wilson cleared a school record 12-1 ½ to place 3rd in the pole vault.

The women finished in 4th place in the MIAA outdoor and placed 29th at the NCAA outdoor.

2014

At the 2014 MIAA Indoor Championships, the women were 7th. Alaina Fairbanks and Maggie Wilson both cleared 11-8 ½ in the pole vault, with Fairbanks getting 3rd on misses. Wetstein scored 3517 points in the pentathlon to place 4th and came back with an 8.62 in the finals of the 60 hurdles to place 4th. She jumped 18-3 to place 8th in the long jump. Morgan Brant high jumped 5-5 to place 7th and Kunkel ran a quick 1:26.50 in the 600 to place 5th.

Peyton Weiss: School Record Holder
Weiss became the first Lady Hornet long jumper to break the 20-foot barrier, going 20-1.

Wetstein had a season best and school record in the 60 hurdles running 8.56 at the University of Central Missouri. She qualified for the NCAA Indoor Championships and ran 8.82 in the 60-meter hurdles prelims but failed to make the finals. The Lady Hornets did not score at the national indoor meet.

Wetstein continued her outstanding hurdling year in the 2014 outdoor season, winning the ESU Relays, the KT Woodman, and the MIAA. Wilson won the MIAA pole vault in 12-2 ½, and the 4 x 100 of Morgan Flowers, Weiss, Wetstein, and King ran 47.03 to take an MIAA title. Sara Duncan threw 140-5 for the javelin to place 10th in the NCAA after throwing 140-3 for 4th in the MIAA.

The women finished 6th at the 2014 Outdoor MIAA led by the pole vault championship of Maggie Wilson clearing 12-2 ½ to better her own school mark of 12-1 ½. Fairbanks cleared 11-10 ½ to place 4th in the championships. Wetstein finished 3rd in the women's 100 hurdles improving her time to 13.93. Shelby Buster had a top three finish for the women. She threw 138-5 to place 3rd in the javelin. It was the first time of the track season that she competed in the javelin. Emporia State picked up 12 team points in the women's long jump, finishing 4th, 5th, and 6th in the event. Weiss went 19-2 to finish 4th. King went 18-9 ¾ and Wetstein jumped 18-8 ½ to place 5th and 6th, respectively. Sara Duncan threw 140-3 in the javelin for 4th.

Weiss became the first woman from Emporia State to break the 20-foot barrier in the long jump as she went a wind aided 20-1 to win the women's long jump at the KT Woodman classic. She broke Brooke Kent's Emporia State record of 19-7 ¾ set at the 2010 Tabor Invitational. Weiss also competed in the 400 hurdles and placed 7th with a time of 1:04.68 and was a part of the 4 x 100 meter relay team that ran 47.57 to place 7th as well.

At the Sam Williams Qualifier, Wetstein again broke her own school record with a 13.80 in the 100 hurdles. Marisette ran an outdoor personal best of 55.76 to move to 4th all-time at Emporia State in the 400 meters. Marisette, Jacobs, Weiss, and King ran the 4th fastest time in Emporia State history, 46.60, in the 4 x 100 relay. Two-time United States Olympian Muna Lee won the 100 and posted one of the fastest times ever ran in Welch Stadium with a time of 11.39 to break the meet record at the Sam Williams Qualifier.

Nikki Wetstein: School Record Holder
All-American Nikki Wetstein set both the indoor 60-meter hurdles and outdoor 100-meter hurdle school records.

The women finished 29th in the NCAA National Outdoor Championships. King entered the NCAA Outdoor Championships in the long jump ranked 14th in the nation. She started the prelims with a pedestrian jump of 18-3 ¾ and then went 19-2 ½ on her second jump. She exploded for a school record, wind legal leap of 19-9 ¾ on her final jump of the prelims to move into 2nd place headed into the finals. She ended the meet in 3rd place behind two jumps of over 20 feet, including a Division II meet record of 21-2 ¾ from champion Vashti Thomas of Academy of Art. The women's team of Marisette, Weiss, Kunkel, and Jacobs posted a school record in the 4 x 400 relay. Their time of 3:42.80 was good for a 6th place finish. Marisette ran in the women's open 400 in addition to the leg on the 400-meter relay. She ran 55.87 to place 14th after being the last entry into the field of 21 for the championships. The team of Marisette, Jacobs, Weiss, and King just missed the finals in the women's 4 x 100 meter-relay. They ran a season's best of 46.56 to rank 4th all-time at Emporia State and finish 10th in the nation, just missing the nine-team final.

Sara Dunkin finished in the top 10 in the nation for the second straight year in the javelin. She threw 140-10 to place 10th in the event. Misty Lowe was the other competitor in Pueblo, Colorado for the national meet representing the Hornets. Her mark of 42-5 ½ placed 20th in the shot put. Wetstein ran 13.85 in the women's 100 hurdles to place 8th. It was her first All-American performance in three trips to the outdoor national championships.

2015

ESU finished in 7th in the MIAA 2015 Indoor Championships. Morgan Brant finished 3rd in the high jump, clearing 5-9 ¼. Brant was the lone ESU female representative at the NCAA DII National Indoor Championships and earned All-American honors by finishing 5th, jumping 5-8. Brant's 5th place finish was worth 4 points and placed ESU 39th at nationals.

Other high performers at the MIAA Indoor included King who scored in three events. She was 5th in the 60 meters with a time of 7.84 and ran 25.92 to place 8th in the 200. She also long jumped 18-3 ¾ to place 6th. Weiss long jumped 18-3 ¾ and was able to place 5th in front of King based on her second best jump. Emily Schoenfeld placed 6th in the 5000 with a time of 18:10.00 that shaved over 15 seconds off of her previous career best and was the 4th best in school history.

The women placed 9th in the 2015 MIAA Outdoor Championships. Wilson had the best individual finish for Emporia State. She broke her own school record with a mark of 12-5 ¼ to finish 2nd in the pole vault. Field events were again a strength of the Emporia State women, as Buster threw 167-8 in the hammer for the 5th best mark in school history. Elizabeth Costello placed 5th in 133-4 and Sara Dunkin Beam 8th (128-9) in the javelin. Emporia State also got a pair of placers in the women's shot put. Morgan Gilliland finished 5th with a mark of 44-1 ¼, while Kayla Henault went 43-3 ¾ to place 6th.

Schoenfeld placed in her second event of the weekend when she ran 18:52.77 to finish 8th in the 5000 after running 39:16.93 to place 5th in the 10,000 meters. Both relay teams provided points on the track for Emporia State with a pair of 6th place finishes. The foursome of Flowers, Latiyera Yeargin, Weiss, and Wilson ran 47.75 in the 4x100 relay. Staats, Weiss, Sophie Hayes, and Elizabeth Blevins ran 3:53.74 in the 4 x 400 relay, bettering Emporia State's previous season's best in the event by 12 seconds.

The 2015 NCAA DII Championships were held in Allendale, Michigan. Wilson, the MIAA champion in the pole vault, qualified for nationals to become the first female vaulter at ESU ever to compete in a national championship. She cleared the opening height of 11-9 ¾ on her first try. She took three attempts to clear 12-1 ½ and was one of 14 vaulters to clear the second bar. She missed her first two attempts at 12-5 ½ and was down to her final jump of her collegiate career. Maggie vaulted over the moon on her third attempt to set a new ESU school record. Only three other vaulters cleared the next height, 12-9 ½, but the combination of misses kept Wilson in 11th place overall. Dunkin Beam was 15th in the women's javelin at 138-3 while Costello threw 120-2 to place 20th in the javelin. For Dunkin-Beam, the school record holder in the javelin (she threw 151-7 at the ESU Open in 2013), it was her fourth trip to the NCAA National Outdoor Championships.

Epilogue

The Emporia State Women's Track and Field program began in 1976 and was an early pioneer in women's sports. The program has achieved outstanding success over a 40-year history. The ESU women have won an amazing 21 individual national championships. Kathy Devine kick-started the program by setting collegiate and American records in the shot put for the Lady Hornets. The Lady Hornets have excelled in every domain, with All-Americans in the throws, distance, sprints, and jumps. The Hornets have competed in both NCAA and NAIA national competitions and in multiple different conferences in their 40 years of competition. The current MIAA conference is an outstanding track and field conference with consistent high national individual finishes and conference teams competing for national championships. Track and field has been successful at Emporia State through the determined efforts of athletes and coaches who have overcome major challenges such as lack of facilities, scholarships, and funding. Emporia State Women's Track and Field has not only risen to the challenge but established themselves as one of the outstanding track and field programs in collegiate track and field.

Hornet History

ESU National Championship Teams

1958 Men's Cross Country NAIA
1959 Men's Cross Country NAIA
1961 Men's Cross Country NAIA
1962 Men's Cross Country NAIA
1963 Men's Cross Country NCAA
1964 Men's Outdoor Track and Field NAIA

World and American Record Holders

Kathy Devine (1976-78)
Outdoor Shot Put
52-4 1/2	April 1976	College & AR
53-1	May 1976	College & AR
53-3 3/4	April 21, 1978	College & AR
53-7 3/4	April 28, 1978	College & AR

Leonard Hall (1973-76)
Outdoor 3-Mile Run
14:20.2	April 1976	WR/deaf runner

5000-meter run
15:00.1	June 1976	AR/deaf runner

Allan Feuerbach (1967-70)
Indoor Shot Put
68-11	1971	WR & AR
69-4 1/4	Jan. 20, 1973	WR & AR
69-5 3/4	Jan. 30, 1973	WR & AR

Outdoor Shot Put
71-7	1973	WR & AR

Archie San Romani (1935-37)
Indoor 3000-meter run
8:27.4	Jan. 1938	AR

Outdoor 2000-meter run
5:16.8	Aug. 26, 1937	WR

Distance Medley Relay
10.12.7	April 1936	WR

Duward Crooms, Norman Rhoads,
Paul Bridges, Archie San Romani

Robert Greenwade (1926-27)
Outdoor 400-meter dash
48.7	Aug. 1926	Tied WR

John Kuck (1925-26)
Indoor Shot put
49-0 1/4	Feb. 1926	WR
50-6 3/4	March 1926	WR

Outdoor Javelin
214-2 1/8	May 1926	College & WR

Shot put
48-11	April 1925	College & WR
51-1 1/2	April 1928	WR
51-2	May 1928	WR
52-0 13/16	Aug. 1928	WR & Olympic

Shot Put
68-7 5/8 (8lb)	June 1926	WR
57-9 3/4 (12lb)	June 1926	WR

Elijah Williams (1922-25)
Outdoor 100-yard dash
9.7	1923	Tie College AR

220-yard dash
21.8	1923	Tie WR

Earl McKown (1922-25)
Indoor Pole Vault
12-10	March 1923	WR

Outdoor Pole Vault
13-1	April 1923	Tie College AR
13-2 7/8	April 1925	College & WR

Harry Cole (1908-12, 21, 23)
Indoor Discus
140-9	1916	WR

Hornets in the Olympic Trials		
1924	Earl McKown 5th	Pole Vault
1928	John Kuck 1st	Shot Put
1936	Archie San Romani 2nd	1500-m Run
1956	Bill Tidwell 6th	800-m Run
1960	Paul Whiteley	5000-m Run
1960	Duane McIntire 8th	Decathlon
1964	John Camien 8th	1500-m run
1968	Val Schierling 11th	400-m Hurdles
1972	Allan Feuerbach 1st	Shot Put
1976	Allan Feuerbach 1st	Shot Put
1976	Dennis Delmott 31st	Marathon
1976 *	Kathy Devine 2nd	Shot Put
1980 **	Allan Feuerbach 2nd	Shot Put
1996	John Corwin 18th	Javelin
1996	Magali Schneider 2nd (Columbia)	400-m Run
2000	Heather Leverington 9th	Shot Put

Hornets in the Olympic Games		
1928	John Kuck 1st	Shot Put
1936	Archie San Romani 4th	1500-m Run
1972	Allan Feuerbach 5th	Shot Put
1976	Allan Feuerbach 4th	Shot Put
1984	Alberto Lopez (Guatemala)	400 and 800
1992	Tamas Molnar (Hungary)	400

* Did not meet qualifying performance standards for the Olympic Games.
** Feuerbach qualified for the Olympic Games in 1980, but was unable to attend because of the United States' boycott of the Moscow Games.

Hornet Track and Field All-Americans

Men

1923 to 1937 NCAA
1952 to 1992 NAIA
1993 to 2015 NCAA

- **Bold=National Champion**

1923
Earl McKown	Pole Vault	T 1st

1925
Earl McKown	Pole Vault	T 1st

1926
John Kuck	**Shot Put**	**1st**
	Javelin	3rd

1935
Archie San Romani	**Mile**	**1st**

1936
Archie San Romani	**1500**	**1st**

1937
Verne Sumner	220-y H	3rd

1952
Robert Klotz	100-y	2nd
Hugh Lewick	Javelin	3rd

1953
Wayne Goodell	**Shot Put**	**1st**

1954
Henry Thompson	**440-y**	**1st**

1955
Bill Tidwell	**880-y**	**1st**
	Mile	**1st**
Dick Utter	**Pole Vault**	**1st**
Reece Bohannon	Pole Vault	T 3rd

Henry Thompson	220-y H	3rd
1956		
Bill Tidwell	**800-m**	**1st**
	1500-m	**1st**
Dick Utter	Pole Vault	T 2nd
1958		
Rex Ressler	**220-y**	**1st**
	100-y	2nd
Paul Whiteley	Mile	2nd
1959		
Paul Whiteley	**Mile**	**1st**
	2-Mile	**1st**
	NCAA 3-Mile	**1st**
Bob Oden	**Pole Vault**	**1st**
1960		
Gonzalo Javier	**1500-m**	**1st**
Bob Oden	**Pole Vault**	**T 1st**
Charles Richard	High Jump	T 3rd
Monroe Fordham	High Jump	T 3rd
1961		
Russell Miller	Javelin	2nd
Kenny Oard	Javelin	3rd
1962		
John Camien	**Mile**	**1st**
Ireland Sloan	3-Mile	3rd
Charles Richard	High Jump	2nd
Kent Hurn	Javelin	2nd
Bill Favrow	Shot Put	3rd
1963		
John Camien	**Mile**	**1st**
Ireland Sloan	3-Mile	3rd
1964		
John Camien	**1500-m**	**1st**
	5000-m	**1st**
Ireland Sloan	**Steeple**	**1st**
John McDonnell	1500-m	2nd
	Steeple	3rd
Kent Hurn	Javelin	3rd
John Camien	**Mile**	**1st**
Bill Eikermann	Discus	3rd

1966 Indoor		
Rich Boehringer	**Long Jump**	**1st**
Bill Fraley	600-yd	3rd
Bob Camien	Mile	3rd
Clarence Robe	Pole Vault	3rd
1967 Indoor		
Bob Camien	Mile	2nd
	2-Mile Relay	3rd
1967 Outdoor		
Allan Feuerbach	**Shot put**	**1st**
Val Schierling	440-yd H	3rd
Rich Boehringer	Triple Jump	2nd
1968 Indoor		
Bob Camien	Mile	3rd
1968 Outdoor		
Bob Camien	1500-m	3rd
Val Schierling	440-yd H	3rd
Allan Feuerbach	Shot Put	2nd
	Hammer	2nd
1969 Indoor		
Allan Feuerbach	**Shot Put**	**1st**
David Brinsko	Mile	3rd
Darrell Patterson	1000-yd	3rd
1969 Outdoor		
Allan Feuerbach	Shot Put	2nd
Gary Lawrence	Hammer	2nd
Dean Woodson	Javelin	3rd
1970 Indoor		
Allan Feuerbach	**Shot Put**	**1st**
Darrell Patterson	1000-yd	3rd
John Wilson	Long Jump	3rd
1970 Outdoor		
Allan Feuerbach	**Shot Put**	**1st**
John Wilson	Long jump	3rd
1972 Outdoor		
Dennis Nee	5000-m	2nd
1979 Outdoor		
Sam Wilson	Shot Put	5th
1984 Outdoor		
Mike Cole	110-m H	4th

1987 Indoor
Roger Jennings | Mile run | 2nd

1987 Outdoor
Roger Jennings | 1500-m | 5th

1988 Indoor
Roger Jennings | Mile run | 2nd
Shawn Brewer | 600-yd | 4th
Lennie Allen | High jump | T 6th

1988 Outdoor
Roger Jennings | **1500-m** | **1st**

1989 Indoor
Roger Jennings | **Mile** | **1st**
Roger Jennings | 2-Mile Relay | 3rd
David Kipelio | 2-Mile | 5th
David Kipelio | 2-Mile Relay | 3rd
Shawn Brewer | 2-Mile Relay | 3rd
Scott Starks | 2-Mile Relay | 3rd

1989 Outdoor
David Kipelio | **Steeple** | **1st**

1990 Indoor
David Kipelio | **2-Mile** | **1st**
 | Mile | 3rd

1990 Outdoor
David Kipelio | **Steeple** | **1st**
Mark Majors | Hammer | 4th
Stacy Montgomery | Pole vault | 6th

1991 Indoor
David Kipelio | 2-Mile | 2nd
 | Mile | 4th
 | 2-Mile Relay | 2nd
Matt Hertig | 880-yd | 6th
 | 2-Mile Relay | 2nd
Mark Majors | 35# Weight | 4th
Jesse Gadison | Long Jump | 4th
Kevin Williams | 2-Mile Relay | 2nd
Shawn Brewer | 2-Mile Relay

1991 Outdoor
Mark Majors | Hammer | 2nd
Thad Thurston | Discus | 4th

1992 Indoor
Jesse Gadison | Long Jump | 2nd
Shawn Thomas | 3-Mile | 4th

1992 Outdoor
Mark Majors | Hammer | 5th

1994 Outdoor
Jason Stuke | Shot Put | 3rd
 | Discus | 5th

1995 Indoor
Jermaine Mitchell | 5000-m | 3rd
Jason Stuke | Shot put | 5th

1995 Outdoor
Jason Stuke | Discus | 3rd
 | Shot Put | 5th
John Corwin | Javelin | 2nd
Johnathon Oshel | Javelin | 7th
Jermaine Mitchell | 10,000-m | 2nd

1996 Indoor
Jason Stuke | Shot Put | 3rd

1996 Outdoor
Jason Stuke | Shot Put | 2nd
John Corwin | Javelin | 2nd
Jermaine Mitchell | 10,000-m | 6th

1997 Indoor
Brandon Masters | Pole Vault | 6th

1997 Outdoor
Brandon Masters | Pole Vault | 4th

1998 Indoor
Jason Stuke | Shot Put | 2nd
Joseph Herron | Long Jump | 5th

1998 Outdoor
Jason Stuke | **Shot Put** | **1st**
 | Discus | 2nd
Brandon Masters | Pole Vault | 5th
Joseph Herron | Long Jump | 5th
Mike Miller | Hammer | 5th

1999 Indoor
Cory Cole | 800-m | 3rd
Jim Riedesel | Shot Put | 3rd
Mike Giardine | 35# Weight | 3rd

1999 Outdoor
Luke Pickett	4 x 400	2nd
Shawn Fairbanks	4 x 400	2nd
Brent Smitheran	4 x 400	2nd
Corey Cole	4 x 400	2nd
Jim Riedesel	Shot Put	5th

2000 Outdoor
Shawn Fairbanks	110m H	8th

2001 Indoor
Dustin Brock	55m H	3rd

2001 Outdoor
Nick Beck	4 x 400 Relay	8th
Dustin Brock	110m H	3rd
Brandon Carlson	4x400 Relay	8th
Shawn Fairbanks	400m H	6th
	4 x 400 Relay	8th
Joseph Herron	Long Jump	7th
Ryan Sparks	Javelin	4th
Justin Stigge	4 x 400 Relay	8th

2002 Indoor
Dustin Brock	55m H	7th
Ron Hunter	High Jump	6th

2003 Outdoor
Danny Bartlett	Javelin	6th

2004 Outdoor
Andy Vogelsberg	Javelin	3rd

2005 Indoor
Chris Peoples	Long Jump	7th

2005 Outdoor
Andy Vogelsberg	Javelin	4th
Eric Hoffman	Hammer	5th
Chris Peoples	Long Jump	8th

2006 Outdoor
Andy Vogelsberg	**Javelin**	**1st**
Trent Olivier	Discus	7th

2007 Outdoor
Tyson Allen	Javelin	2nd
Andy Vogelsberg	Javelin	4th
Trent Olivier	Discus	8th

2008 Indoor
Alex Pyle	High Jump	3rd
Dustin Andrew	High Jump	4th
Kenton Lonberger	200-m	5th
Craig Saalfeld	High Jump	8th

2008 Outdoor
Craig Saalfeld	High Jump	2nd
Kenton Lonberger	200-m	4th

2009 Indoor
Josh Honeycutt	**Triple Jump**	**1st**
Sam Williams	60m	8th

2009 Outdoor
Josh Honeycutt	Triple Jump	6th
Sam Williams	200m	7th
	4 x 100 Relay	5th
Vincent Howze	400m H	7th
Derwin Hall	4 x 100 Relay	5th
Josh Schuler	4 x 100 Relay	5th
Kenton Lonberger	4 x 100 Relay	5th

2010 Indoor
Josh Schuler	60m	7th
	200m	2nd
Josh Honeycutt	Triple Jump	6th
Briar Ploude	High Jump	6th

2010 Outdoor
Zach Rosenberger	Pole Vault	3rd
Josh Honeycutt	Triple Jump	4th
Craig Saalfeld	Decathlon	7th

2011 Indoor
Josh Schuler	60-m	4th
	200-m	4th
Josh Honeycutt	Triple Jump	6th
Andrew Etheridge	60-m H	2nd
Zach Rosenberger	Pole Vault	3rd

2011 Outdoor
Andrew Etheridge	**110-m H**	**1st**
	4 x 100 Relay	3rd
Josh Schuler	100-m	2nd
	200-m	2nd
	4 x 100 Relay	3rd
Tony Granillo	Decathlon	3rd
Derwin Hall	4 x 100 Relay	3rd
Shjuan Richardson	4 x 100 Relay	3rd
Josh Honeycutt	Triple Jump	4th

2012 Indoor
Andrew Etheridge	60-m H	2nd
Briar Ploude	High Jump	8th

2012 Outdoor
Vincent Howze	200-m	6th

2013 Indoor
Andrew Etheridge	60-m H	5th
Derwin Hall	60-m	6th
Marcus Calleja	High Jump	T7th

2013 Outdoor
Andrew Etheridge	110-m H	6th
	4 x 100 Relay	5th
Briar Ploude	High Jump	4th
Marcus Calleja	High Jump	T7th
Payson Maydew	Decathlon	6th
Derwin Hall	4 x 100 Relay	5th
Vincent Howze	4 x 100 Relay	5th
Shjuan Richardson	4 x 100 Relay	5th

2014 Indoor
Payson Maydew	Heptathlon	5th

2014 Outdoor
Payson Maydew	Decathlon	3rd
Briar Ploude	High Jump	3rd
AJ West	4 x 100 Relay	8th
Dukiya Tibbs	4 x 100 Relay	8th
Brady Huckaby	4 x 100 Relay	8th
Jon Dickson	4 x 100 Relay	8th

2015 Indoor
Andrew Etheridge	60-m H	7th
Donald Wilcox	Long Jump	5th

2015 Outdoor
Payson Maydew	Decathlon	3rd
Donald Wilcox	Long Jump	7th

Women

1976
Kathy Devine	**Shot Put**	**1st**

1977
Kathy Devine	**Shot Put**	**1st**

1978
Kathy Devine	Shot Put	2nd

1981 Indoor
Cindy Edgerton	1000 yd	3rd
	2-Mile Relay	2nd
Lesha Wood	Mile	2nd
	2-Mile Run	3rd
Nancy Gray	2-Mile Relay	2nd
Darcy Mikesich	2-Mile Relay	2nd
Cheryl Phares	2-Mile Relay	2nd

1981 Outdoor
Lesha Wood	1500-m	4th
	3000-m	5th
Judy Becker	Javelin	3rd

1982 Outdoor
Cheryl Phares	800-m	3rd
	3200 Relay	3rd
Kelly McCammon	3200 Relay	3rd
Lesha Wood	3200 Relay	3rd
Cindy Edgerton	3200 Relay	3rd
Michelle Orton	400-m H	6th

1983 Indoor
Lesha Wood	Mile	5th

1983 Outdoor
Michelle Orton	400-m H	6th

1984 Indoor
Kelly McCammon	Mile	3rd

1984 Outdoor
Beth Shannon	Discus	6th

1986 Indoor
Kelly McCammon	**Mile**	**1st**
Susan Stine	2-Mile	5th

1986 Outdoor
Kelly McCammon	1500-m	4th
	3000-m	2nd
Susan Stine	5000-m	3rd

1987 Indoor
Trish Bahr	High Jump	T 2nd
Trudy Searcy	Mile Run	5th

1987 Outdoor
Trish Bahr	High Jump	2nd
Trudy Searcy	10,000-m	4th
Susan Stine	10,000-m	5th

1988 Indoor
Cindy Blakeley	Mile Run	2nd
Trish Bahr	High Jump	2nd
Sandra Freeman	60-y	3rd

1988 Outdoor
Lisa Farris	**Discus**	**1st**
Trish Bahr	High Jump	3rd
Mary Griebel	Marathon	6th

1989 Indoor
Cecilia Gunn	Shot Put	3rd
Lisa Farris	Shot Put	6th

1989 Outdoor
Lisa Farris	**Discus**	**1st**
	Shot Put	2nd
Cecilia Gunn	Shot Put	3rd

1990 Indoor
Gretchen Bohm	800-m	6th

1990 Outdoor
Cecilia Gunn	Shot Put	2nd
	Discus	3rd

1991 Indoor
Cecilia Gunn	Shot Put	2nd
Jennifer Mullen	3-Mile	3rd
	Dist. Medley	3rd
Ingrid Frazier	1000-y	6th
	Dist. Medley	3rd
Michelle Hebb	Dist. Medley	3rd
Deanna Tolin	Dist. Medley	3rd

1991 Outdoor
Cecilia Gunn	**Shot Put**	**1st**
	Discus	2nd

1992 Indoor
Cecilia Gunn	**Shot Put**	**1st**
Michelle Hebb	Mile	4th
Jennifer Mullen	3-Mile	6th

1992 Outdoor
Cecilia Gunn	**Shot Put**	**1st**
	Discus	3rd
Mary Bailey	Discus	5th
Jennifer Mullen	Marathon	6th

1994 Outdoor
Laura Rand	Shot Put	8th

1995 Outdoor
Laura Rand	**Shot Put**	**1st**
Joyce Burnett	Javelin	5th
Deandra Doubrava	400-m	5th

1996 Indoor
Deandra Doubrava	4 x 400 Relay	4th
Magali Schneider	4 x 400 Relay	4th
Kari Pitman	4 x 400 Relay	4th
Jessica Oberg	4 x 400 Relay	4th
Laura Rand	Shot Put	4th
Magali Schneider	400-m	6th

1996 Outdoor
Deandra Doubrava	4 x 400 Relay	2nd
	400-m	7th
	Long Jump	6th
Magali Schneider	4 x 400 Relay	2nd
	400-m	3rd
	200-m	3rd
Kari Pitman	4 x 400 Relay	2nd
Jessica Oberg	4 x 400 Relay	2nd
Laura Rand	Shot Put	7th
Joyce Burnett	Javelin	2nd
Lynda Barnard	Hammer	5th
Kelly Hare	Hammer	8th

1997 Indoor
Deandra Doubrava	4 x 400 Relay	5th
	400-m	6th
Magali Schneider	4 x 400 Relay	5th
	60-m	8th
	800-m	6th
Kari Pitman	4 x 400 Relay	5th
Jalayne Gerber	4 x 400 Relay	5th

1997 Outdoor
Joyce Burnett	**Javelin**	**1st**
Deandra Doubrava	4 x 400 Relay	4th
	Heptathlon	3rd
Kari Pitman	4 x 400 Relay	4th
Gillian Curtiss	4 x 400 Relay	4th

Jalayne Gerber	4 x 400 Relay	4th		**2002 Indoor**		
Lynda Barnard	Hammer	2nd		Kara Brockmeier	Shot Put	2nd
	Javelin	7th		Rachel Goetz	Shot Put	3rd
Laura Mayo	Hammer	6th			Weight Throw	5th
				Emilee Hamlin	Triple Jump	4th
1998 Indoor					Long Jump	7th
Deandra Doubrava	400-m	4th				
	Long Jump	5th		**2002 Outdor**		
				Kara Brockmeier	Discus	5th
1998 Outdoor				Emilee Hamlin	Triple Jump	6th
Laura Mayo	**Hammer**	**1st**		Heather Leverington	Shot Put	2nd
Kari Pitman	4 x 400 Relay	6th		Sarah Wuertz	Heptathlon	7th
Kristin Brune	4 x 400 Relay	6th			Javelin	5th
Gillian Curtiss	4 x 400 Relay	6th				
	400-m H	2nd		**2003 Indoor**		
Emily Bloss	4 x 400 Relay	6th		Kara Brockmeier	Shot Put	6th
				Rachel Goetz	Shot Put	8th
1999 Indoor					Weight Throw	6th
Heather Leverington	**Shot Put**	**1st**		Emilee Hamlin	Triple Jump	5th
				Kadri Kelve	Mile Run	6th
1999 Outdoor						
Deandra Doubrava	**Heptathlon**	**1st**		**2003 Outdoor**		
	400-m H	1st		**Kadri Kelve**	**Steeplechase**	**1st**
	4 x 400 Relay	4th		Kara Brockmeier	Discus	7th
Heather Leverington	**Shot Put**	**1st**			Shot Put	5th
G. Curtiss-Masters	400-m H	2nd		Rachel Goetz	Discus	5th
	4 x 400 Relay	4th		Emilee Hamlin	Triple Jump	4th
Lynda Barnard	Hammer	5th				
Celeste DeTiege	4 x 400 Relay	4th		**2004 Indoor**		
Kristen Brune	4 x 400 Relay	4th		Rachel Goetz	Shot Put	5th
					Weight Throw	4th
2000 Indoor						
Heather Leverington	**Shot Put**	**1st**		**2004 Outdoor**		
H. Bedenbender	4 x 400 Relay	5th		**Rachel Goetz**	**Shot Put**	**1st**
Kristen Brune	4 x 400 Relay	5th			Weight Throw	4th
Melissa Burden	4 x 400 Relay	5th				
Celeste DeTiege	4 x 400 Relay	5th		**2005 Indoor**		
				Alicia Burns	4 x 400 Relay	7th
2000 Outdoor				Ashley Melichar	4 x 400 Relay	7th
Kara Brockmeier	Shot Put	7th		Krysta Fennewald	4 x 400 Relay	7th
Sarah Wuertz	Javelin	6th		Danielle Sedivy	4 x 400 Relay	7th
2001 Indoor				**2005 Outdoor**		
Heather Leverington	**Shot Put**	**1st**		Courtney Bruna	4 x 100 Relay	6th
				Alicia Burns	4 x 100 Relay	6th
2001 Outdoor				Ashley Melichar	4 x 100 Relay	6th
Kara Brockmeier	Shot Put	6th		Shannon Butler	4 x 100 Relay	6th
	Discus	6th		Connie Phillips	Javelin	6th
Heather Leverington	**Shot Put**	**1st**				
	Hammer	8th		**2006 Indoor**		
Nikki Runnebaum	100m H	6th		Shannon Butler	Long Jump	2nd

2006 Outdoor
Shannon Butler   4 x 100 Relay   7th
Kara Euler   4 x 100 Relay   7th
Danielle Sedivy   4 x 100 Relay   7th
Ashley Melichar   4 x 100 Relay   7th

2007 Indoor
Jonel Rossbach   Mile Run   4th

2007 Outdoor
Jonel Rossbach   1500m   8th

2008 Indoor
Jonel Rossbach   5000m   6th
Brooke Kent   Long Jump   6th

2008 Outdoor
Jonel Rossbach   **5000m**   **1st**
                       10,000m   2nd
Brooke Kent   Long Jump   6th
Jennifer Robinson   High Jump   7th
Connie Phillips   Javelin   8th

2009 Outdoor
Connie Phillips   Javelin   5th
Brooke Kent   Long Jump   7th

2010 Indoor
Jennifer Robinson   High Jump   2nd
Brooke Kent   Long Jump   6th
                       Triple Jump   8th

2010 Outdoor
Jennifer Robinson **High Jump**   **1st**
Brooke Kent   Triple Jump   2nd

2011 Indoor
Katie Mona   800-m   5th

2011 Outdoor
Katie Mona   800-m   7th

2012 Indoor
Kaite Mona   800-m   7th

2013 Outdoor
Carmen King   Long Jump   3rd
                       4 x 400 Relay   6th
Marqueita Marisette   4 x 400 Relay   6th
Peyton Weiss   4 x 400 Relay   6th
Jackie Jacobs   4 x 400 Relay   6th

2014 Outdoor
Carmen King   Long Jump   3rd
Marqueita Marisette   4 x 400 Relay   6th
Peyton Weiss   4 x 400 Relay   6th
Lindsey Kunkel   4 x 400 Relay   6th
Jackie Jacobs   4 x 400 Relay   6th

2015 Indoor
Morgan Brant   High Jump   5th

Men's Indoor Track and Field Records

Event	Record	Athlete	Year
60m Dash	6.71	Josh Schuler	2011
200m Dash	21.14	Josh Schuler	2011
400m Dash	48.02	Dukiya Tibbs	2015
600yd Dash	1:11.34	Val Schierling	1967
800m Run	1:51.07	Cory Cole	1999
Mile Run	4:01.84	John Camien	1965
3000m Run	8:09.60	David Kipelio	1990
5000m Run	14:25.33	David Kipelio	1990
60m Hurdles	7.87	Andrew Etheridge	2012
High Jump	7-03.75	Briar Ploude	2013
Pole Vault	16-10.75	Zach Rosenberger	2011
Long Jump	24-10	Noel Certain	1960
Triple Jump	51-10	Josh Honeycutt	2010
Shot Put	62-11.25	Allan Feuerbach	1970
35# Wgt Throw	63-2.75	Kevin Roulhac	2011
4 X 400 Relay	3:15.72	Fairbanks, Stigge, Beck, Wilson	2001
2 Mile Relay	7:39.34 (m) 7:42.02 (y)	Jennings, Starks Kipelio, Brewer	1989
Distance Medley	9:54.97 (m) 9:58.44 (y)	McDonnell, Wolfson Camien, Sloan	1964
Heptathlon	5363	Payson Maydew	2015

Men's Outdoor Track and Field Records

Event	Record	Athlete	Year
100m Dash	10.26	Josh Schuler	2011
200m Dash	20.75	Josh Schuler	2011
400m Dash	47.12	Brent Smitheran	2000
800m Run	1:47.61	Bill Tidwell	1955
1500m Run	3:40.04	John Camien	1964
5000m Run	14:02.56	David Kipelio	1990
10,000m Run	30:11.04	Dennis Delmott	1970
110m Hurdles	13.85	Andrew Etheridge	2013
400m Hurdles	50.64	Val Schierling	1968
3000m Steeple	8:49.94	David Kipelio	1989
High Jump	7-2.25	Briar Ploude	2013
Pole Vault	17-06.50	Brandon Masters	1996
Long Jump	25-05	Noel Certain	1960
Triple Jump	53-09.25	Josh Honeycutt	2009
Shot Put	65-00	Allan Feuerbach	1970
Discus	199-10	Jason Stuke	1998
Hammer	193-3	Mike Giardine	1998
New Javelin (since 1986)	245-03	Andy Vogelsberg	2006
Decathlon	7413 pts.	Payson Maydew	2014
400-m relay	40.01	Hall, Schuler Lonberger, Williams	2009
1600-m relay	3:08.89	Fairbanks, Smitheran Cole, Pickett	1999

Emporia State Men's Indoor Top Five
(as of end of 2015 season)

60-METER DASH
6.71	Josh Schuler	NCAA Championships	2011
6.74	Derwin Hall	NCAA Championships	2013
6.74	Sam Williams	Mule Relays	2009
6.79	Kenton Lonberger	KSU All-Comers	2008
6.83	Shjuan Richardson	Jayhawk Classic	2012

200-METER DASH
21.14	Josh Schuler	NCAA Championships	2011
21.80	Kenton Lonberger	MIAA Championships	2008
21.86	Vincent Howze	NCAA Championships	2013
21.89	Duke Tibbs	Herm Wilson Invitational	2015
21.91	Sam Williams	MIAA Championships	2009

400-METER DASH
48.02	Duke Tibbs	Sevigne Husker Invitational	2015
48.80	Vincent Howze	Sevigne Husker Invitational	2010
48.87	Brent Smitheran	Cannon Classic	2000
49.18	Corey Seachris	Prairie Wolf Invitational	2004
49.30	Kip Wilson	Iowa State Open	2001

600-YARD RUN
1:11.34	Val Schierling	Kansas State Relays	1967
1:11.40	Cory Cole	KU Pre-Conference	1999
1:11.53	Ryan Kaberline	MIAA Championships	1995
1:12.18	Shawn Fairbanks	MIAA Championships	2000
1:12.22	Nick Beck	MIAA Championships	2001

800-METER RUN
1:51.07	Cory Cole	Iowa State Open	1999
1:52.09	Bill Tidwell	Kansas State	1956
1:53.70	John Camien	CIC at Omaha	1964
1:53.70	Garth Briggeman	Iowa State	1997
1:53.88	Roger Jennings	Oklahoma Classic	1989

MILE RUN
4:01.84	John Camien	USTAF at Seattle	1965
4:06.44	Bill Tidwell	Boston Games	1956
4:06.48	Roger Jennings	Dartmouth	1988
4:08.85	Eric Wellman	Iowa State Open	2006
4:08.90	David Kipelio	Oklahoma Classic	1990

3000-METER RUN
8:09.60y	David Kipelio	NAIA Championships	1990
8:17.58y	Ireland Sloan	USTAF at Milwaukee	1964
8:19.31	Jermaine Mitchell	Kansas	1994
8:21.10y	John Camien	Winnipeg	1965
8:22.02y	Bob Camien	Kansas State Relays	1967

5000-METER RUN
14:25.33	David Kipelio	NAIA Championships	1990
14:25.70	Jermaine Mitchell	NCAA Championships	1995
14:37.20	Shawn Thomas	NAIA Championships	1992
14:44.47	Ireland Sloan	Winnipeg	1962
14:56.46	Skyler Delmott	Iowa State Classic	2008

60-METER HURDLES
7.87	Andrew Etheridge	NCAA Championships	2012
7.94	Dustin Brock	NCAA Championships	2001
8.00	Gannon Mack	Iowa State Classic	2013
8.06	Tyler Swalley	MIAA Championships	2013
8.17	Vincent Howze	MIAA Championships	2009

4 x 400 RELAY
3:15.72	Fairbanks, Stigge, Beck, Wilson	Iowa State Open	2001
3:15.95	Smitheran, Beck, Pickett, Stigge	Cannon Classic	2000
3:17.34	Smitheran, Herron, Pickett, Cole	Iowa State Qualifier	1998
3:17.39	Cole, Smitheran, Pickett, Bieker	Iowa State Open	1999
3:17.59	Dickson, Proctor, Smith, Tibbs	Sevigne Husker Invitational	2014
3:17.59	Dickson, Miller, Etheridge, Tibbs	K-State Winter Invitational	2015

DISTANCE MEDLEY RELAY
9:54.97 (m) 9:58.44 (y)	McDonnell, Wolfson, Camien, Sloan		1964
9:58.93	McGovern, Miller, Cowing, Hohmeier	Husker Tune-Up	2009
10:16.09	Applegate, Baab, Stearns, Wellman	Iowa State Open	2005
10:17.13	Camien, Rusco, Heinicke, Wellman	Neb. Holiday Inn Inv.	2006
10:17.40 (m) 10:21.00 (y)	Brewer, Pierre, Hertig, Kipelio	NAIA Championships	1991
10:17.40 (m) 10:21.00 (y)	Weidenbach, Crabtree, Fick, Jennings	Oklahoma City	1987

HIGH JUMP
7-03.75	Briar Ploude	Jayhawk Classic	2013
7-01	Ron Hunter	KSU Open	2002
6-11.50	Samuel Saidi	MIAA Championships	2015
6-11.50	Craig Saalfeld	MIAA Championships	2008
6-11	Chris Peoples	Iowa State Open	2005
6-11	David Humbarger	KU Pre-Conference	1999
6-11	Dustin Andrews	Mule Relays	2008

POLE VAULT
16-10.75	Zach Rosenberger	NCAA Championships	2011
16-08.75	Brandon Masters	Nebraska Invitational	1997
16-00.75	Payson Maydew	KSU Open	2015
15-06	Don Funke	Pittsburg State	1988
15-03	Jeremy Swaim	MIAA Championships	2011

LONG JUMP
24-10	Noel Certain	Kansas State	1960
24-08.50	Jesse Gadison	Mule Relays	1993
24-01.75	Donald Wilcox	MIAA Championships	2015
24-00.75	Joseph Herron	MIAA Championships	1998
23-10.25	Chris Peoples	MIAA Championships	2005

TRIPLE JUMP
51-10	Josh Honeycutt	MIAA Championships	2010
50-11	Weldon Paul	KSU All-Comers	1999
49-01	Matt Koelling	WSU Varsity Apts. Inv.	2010
48-03.50	Ramel Williams	Wildcat Invite	2000
48-00	Doug Marshall	Mule Relays	2009

SHOT PUT
62-11.25	Allan Feuerbach	Oklahoma City	1970
62-02.50	Jason Stuke	MIAA Championships	1998
55-00.75	Jim Riedesel	MIAA Championships	1999
54-09.25	Bill Goldhammer	Kearney State	1962
54-08.75	Trent Olivier	Mule Relays	2007

35# WEIGHT THROW
63-02.75	Kevin Roulhac	MIAA Championships	2011
60-07.25	Eric Hoffman	KSU Open	2005
59-11.25	Mike Giardine	NCAA Championships	1999
59-01.50	Lucas SanMartin	MIAA Championships	2013
58-04.50	Trent Olivier	Jayhawk Invitational	2005

HEPTATHLON
5363	Payson Maydew	MIAA Championships	2015
5175	Craig Saalfeld	MIAA Championships	2009
4940	Tony Granillo	MIAA Championships	2011
4727	Grady Goff	MIAA Championships	2014
4592	Wyatt Sander	MIAA Championships	2015

Emporia State Men's Outdoor Top Five
(as of end of 2015 season)

100-METER DASH
10.26w	Josh Schuler	NCAA	2011
10.29	Kenton Lonberger	ESU Relays	2008
10.40	Shjuan Richardson	MIAA	2013
10.43w	Derwin Hall	Sam Williams Qualifier	2013
10.49	Jerry Bishop	Last Chance	1997

200-METER DASH
20.75	Josh Schuler	NCAA Championships	2011
20.92	Rex Ressler	CIC at Pittsburg	1958
20.95	Kenton Lonberger	NCAA Championships	2008
20.99	Sam Williams	NCAA Championships	2009
21.01	Vincent Howze	NCAA Championships	2012

400-METER DASH
47.12	Brent Smitheran	MIAA Championships	2000
47.56	Dukiya Tibbs	MIAA Championships	2015
47.66	Mark Sevier	GPAC at Pueblo, Colo.	1975
47.75	Vincent Howze	MIAA	2012
47.76	Eddie Washington	NCAA Regional	1962
47.76	Melvin Mayo	CIC	1961

800-METER RUN
1:47.61	Bill Tidwell	National AAU at Boulder	1955
1:50.40	John Camien	Pittsburg State Dual	1963
1:51.04	Mark Stanbrough	NAIA Championships	1977
1:51.24	Cory Cole	ESU Last Chance	1999
1:51.25	Ryan Kaberline	ESU Twilight	1995

1500-METER RUN
3:40.04	John Camien	Compton Relays, CA	1963
3:41.47	Roger Jennings	Bern International	1988
3:45.34	Bill Tidwell	Finland	1956
3:46.41	David Kipelio	Finland	1989
3:47.84	Gonzalo Javier	Meet of Champions, TX	1960

5000-METER RUN
14:02.56	David Kipelio	Finland	1990
14:25.14	John Camien	NAIA Championships	1964
14:25.21	Dennis Nee	Emporia Relays	1972
14:27.40	Jermaine Mitchell	Kansas Relays	1994
14:27.69	Ireland Sloan	Drake Relays	1964

10,000-METER RUN
30:11.04	Dennis Delmott	Kansas Relays	1970
30:44.68	Shawn Thomas	NAIA Championships	1992
30:46.00	Jermaine Mitchell	MIAA/NCC Challenge	1996
31:26.18	Dennis Nee	Kansas Relays	1971
31:26.71	Andrew Bird	MIAAChampionships	2005

110-METER HURDLES

13.85w	Andrew Etheridge	NCAA Championships	2013
13.98	Dustin Brock	NCAA Championships	2001
14.15	Gannon Mack	ESU Relays	2013
14.33	Tyler Swalley	MIAA Championships	2013
14.35	Mike Cole	NAIA at Charleston, W.V	1984

400-METER HURDLES

50.64	Val Schierling	USTAF at Houston, Texas	1968
51.75	Shawn Fairbanks	MIAA Championships	2001
52.17	Vincent Howze	MIAA Championships	2010
53.07	Gannon Mack	MIAA Championships	2012
53.14	Rick Brading	CSIC at Emporia	1977

3000-METER STEEPLECHASE

8:49.94	David Kipelio	Finland	1989
9:04.54	Ireland Sloan	Kansas Relays	1964
9:13.80	Shawn Thomas	K.T. Woodman Classic	1994
9:16.88	Skyler Delmott	VS Athl. Beach Invite	2009
9:23.74	Chuck Weston	CMSU	1975

400-METER RELAY

40.01	Hall, Schuler Lonberger, Williams	NCAA Championships	2009
40.03	Hall, Schuler, Etheridge, Richardson	MIAA Championships	2011
40.07	Hall, Howze, Etheridge, Richardson	NCAA	2013
40.65	West, Tibbs Huckabay, Dickson	Williams Qualifier	2014
40.79	Hall, Schuler Dickson, Richardson	NCAA Championships	2011

1600-METER RELAY

3:08.89	Smitheran, Cole, Fairbanks, Pickett	NCAA-II Championships	1999
3:10.34	Beck, Smitheran Pickett, Fairbanks	Drake Relays	2000
3:11.23	Mayo, Franklin, Certain, Washington	Kansas Relays	1961
3:11.30	Dickson, Proctor, Smith, Tibbs	Williams Qualifier	2014
3:11.99	Dickson, Coleman, Miller, Sander	Williams Qualifier	2015

HIGH JUMP

7-02.25	Briar Ploude	Drake Relays	2013
7-00.50	Samuel Saidi	KU Relays	2015
6-11.00	Dustin Andrews	ESU Relays	2010
6-11.00	Craig Saalfeld	ATG Sports Qualifier	2007
6-10.75	Chris Peoples	UT-Arlington	2005
6-10.75	Marcus Callaja	NCAA Championships	2013

POLE VAULT
17-6.5	Brandon Masters	MIAA Championships	1997
16-6	Zach Rosenberger	MIAA Championships	2010
15-7	Ted Methvin	Dist. 10 at ESU	1988
15-7	Nathan Peck	D-II Challenge	1999
15-7	Payson Maydew	ESU Multis	2015

LONG JUMP
25-5	Noel Certain	Kansas Relays	1960
25-1.75	Joseph Herron	DII Challenge	1998
24-9.50	John Wilson	RMAC Championships	1970
24-7	Anthony Wilcox	ESU Mid-week	2015
24-6.25	Eustace Shannon	Drake Relays	1935

TRIPLE JUMP
53-09.25	Josh Honeycutt	D-II Challenge	2008
50-2.00	Richard Boehringer	Arkansas Relays	1966
49-07.25w	Doug Marshall	KT Woodman	2010
49-06.50w	Dwayne Wall	Sam Williams Qualifier	2013
49-6.25	Ramel Williams	Kansas Relays	2000

SHOT PUT
65-0	Allan Feuerbach	AAU	1970
61-10.50	Jason Stuke	Drake Relays	1998
56-1.25	Jerry Hinson	Fort Hays Dual	1972
55-7.75	Jim Riedesel	ESU Last Chance	1998
54-9	Bill Favrow	CIC Championships	1962

DISCUS
199-10	Jason Stuke	MSSC Last Chance	1998
178-09	John McGinty	D-II Challenge	2001
178-03	Allan Feuerbach	CMSU Dual	1970
174-05	Trent Olivier	D-II Challenge	2006
174-00	Jerry Hinson	Ft. Hays Dual	1973

HAMMER
193-03	Mike Giardine	MIAAChampionships	1998
191-11	Mike Miller	MSSC Last Chance	1998
190-03	Eric Hoffman	NCAA Championships	2005
187-01	Scott Campbell	Southwestern Relays	1997
186-07	Kevin Rouhlac	MIAA Championships	2010

JAVELIN (New Javelin since 1986)
245-03	Andy Vogelsberg	NCAA-II Championships	2006
241-10	John Corwin	NCAA-II Championships	1995
222-08	Johnathon Oshel	ESU Spring Twilight	1995
221-11	Danny Bartlett	ESU Spring Twilight	2002
221-01	Kyle Pfizenmaier	MIAA	2015

DECATHLON (New Javelin 1986 Season)
7413	Payson Maydew	NCAA Championships	2014
6913	Tim Vietti	College Station Relays	1995
6898	David Humbarger	MIAAChampionships	1999
6888	Craig Saalfeld	MIAA Championships	2010
6832	Tony Granillo	NCAA	2011

Women's Indoor Track and Field Records

Event	Record	Athlete	Year
60m Dash	7.66	Shannon Butler	2006
200m Dash	24.81	Shannon Butler	2006
400m Dash	55.23	Deandra Doubrava	1998
600yd Run	1:22.50	Magali Schneider	1997
800m Run	2:10.32	Magali Schneider	1997
Mile Run	4:48.55	Katie Mona	2012
3000m Run	9:47.15	Katie Mona	2012
5000m Run	16:51.62	Jonel Rossbach	2008
60m Hurdles	8.56	Nikki Wetstein	2014
Pole Vault	12-1.50	Maggie Wilson	2013
High Jump	5-9.25	Morgan Brant	2013
Long Jump	19-11.50	Shannon Butler	2006
Triple Jump	40-07.75	Emilee Hamlin	2002
Shot Put	53-07	Heather Leverington	2001
20# Wgt Throw	58-03	Rachel Goetz	2002
4 x 400 Relay	3:42.35	Schneider, Gerber, Pitman, Doubrava	1997
2-Mile Relay	9:25.90	Hudspeth, Childers, Duran, Brune	2001
Distance Medley	11:59.94	Davison, Jacobs, Baum, Mona	2010
Pentathlon	3672	Deandra Doubrava	1998

Women's Outdoor Track and Field Records

Event	Record	Athlete	Year
100m Dash	11.64	Courtney Bruna	2004
200m Dash	23.83	Courtney Bruna	2004
400m Dash	53.33	Magali Schneider	1996
800m Run	2:10.99	Katie Mona	2011
1500m Run	4:26.20	Kelly McCammon	1986
3000m Run	9:37.90	Kelly McCammon	1986
5000m Run	16:52.28	Jonel Rossbach	2008
10,000m Run	35:24.81	Jonel Rossbach	2008
100m Hurdles	13.80	Nikki Wetstein	2014
400m Hurdles	59.67	Deandra Doubrava	1999
3000m Steeple	10:22.81	Kadri Kelve	2003
High Jump	5-09.25	Jennifer Robinson	2010
Pole Vault	12-5.5	Maggie Wilson	2015
Long Jump	20-01	Peyton Weiss	2014
Triple Jump	41-01.75	Brooke Kent	2010
Shot Put	54-02.75	Heather Leverington	2002
Discus	163-10	Kara Brockmeier	2002
Hammer	188-09	Laura Mayo	1998
New Javelin (since 1998)	151-7	Sara Dunkin	2013
Heptathlon	5394 pts	Deandra Doubrava	1999
4 x 100 relay	46.15	Euler, Sedivy, Melichar, Butler	2006
4 x 400 relay	3:42.80	Marisette, Weiss, Kunkel, Jacobs	2013

Emporia State Women's Indoor Top Five
(as of end of 2015 season)

60-METER DASH
7.66	Shannon Butler	MIAA Championships	2006
7.70	Brooke Kent	MIAA Championships	2008
7.76	Carmen King	MIAA Championships	2013
7.77	Marqueita Marisette	MIAA Championships	2013
7.78	Courtney Bruna	Prairie Wolf Invitational	2004

200-METER DASH
24.81	Shannon Butler	NCAA Championships	2006
24.96	Magali Schneider	Jayhawk Invitational	1997
25.05	Marqueita Marisette	Sevigne Husker Invite	2013
25.11	Courtney Bruna	MIAA Championships	2004
25.14	Jackie Jacobs	Iowa State Classic	2013

400-METER DASH
55.23	Deandra Doubrava	NCAA Championships	1998
55.56	Marqueita Marisette	NCAA Championships	2013
55.80	Magali Schneider	Kansas State	1997
57.01	Kara Euler	Iowa State Open	2006
57.31	Gillian Curtiss	Iowa State Qualifier	1998

600-YARD RUN
1:22.50	Magali Schneider	Kansas State	1997
1:23.66	Deandra Doubrava	KU Invitational	1998
1:24.40	Jaclyn Sill	MIAA Championships	2008
1:25.18	Kristin Brune	MIAA Championships	2001
1:25.55	Lindsay Kunkel	MIAA Championships	2013

800-METER RUN
2:10.32	Magali Schneider	NCAA Championships	1997
2:10.75	Katie Mona	Sevigne Husker Invitational	2012
2:13.86	Jonel Rossbach	Iowa State Open	2006
2:14.75	Kari Pitman	Iowa State Qualifier	1998
2:15.23	Robin Childers	MIAA Championships	2001

MILE RUN
4:48.55	Katie Mona	Iowa State Classic	2012
4:50.65	Jonel Rossbach	Notre Dame Invitational	2007
4:52.24	Kadri Kelve	Neb. Holiday Inn Invitational	2003
5:01.24	Cindy Blakeley	NAIA-Kansas City	1988
5:02.07	Kelly McCammon	NAIA-Kansas City	1986

3000-METER RUN
9:47.15	Katie Mona	UCM Invite	2012
9:50.39	Jonel Rossbach	Iowa State Open	2008
9:59.36	Susan Stine	Oklahoma City	1987
10:07.20	Kadri Kelve	MSSC Open	2002
10:10.83	Cindy Blakeley	Kansas Invitational	1988

5000-METER RUN
16:51.62	Jonel Rossbach	Iowa State Classic	2008
17:11.80	Kadri Kelve	Prairie Wolf Invitational	2003
17:45.01	Jennifer Mullen	NAIA Championships	1991
18:10.00	Emily Schoenfeld	MIAA Championships	2015
18:19.63	Angela Cathcart	Jayhawk Invitational	1996

60-METER HURDLES
8.56	Nikki Wetstein	UCMO Invite	2014
8.95	Nikki Runnebaum	KSU Open	2001
8.97	Emilee Hamlin	MIAA Championships	2003
9.12	Lindsay Poague	KSU Open	2015
9.15	Jodi Russell	MIAA Championships	2012

4 x 400 RELAY
3:42.35	Gerber, Schneider, Pitman, Doubrava	Iowa State Qualifier	1997
3:47.25	Curtiss, Brune, Doubrava, Pittman	Iowa State Qualifier	1998
3:47.48	Pitman, Oberg, Schneider, Doubrava	NCAA Championships	1996
3:47.53	Marisette, Weiss, Kunkel, Jacobs	NCAA Championships	2013
3:49.35	Fennewald, Melichar, Sill, Burns	Nebraska Invitational	2005

DISTANCE MEDLEY RELAY
11:59.94	Davison, Jacobs, Baum, Mona	Iowa State Classic	2010
12:04.00	Davison, Jacobs, Weller, Mona	Iowa State Classic	2009
12:15.45	Fennewald, Sill, Rossbach, Larson	Iowa State Open	2005
12:19.12(m) 12:23.46(y)	McCammon, Orton, Wood, Browning		1984
12:20.94	Davison, Baum, Weller, Mona	MIAA Championships	2009

HIGH JUMP
5-09.25	Morgan Brant	MIAA Championships	2013
5-08.75	Jennifer Robinson	MIAA Championships	2010
5-08.00	Sarah Wuertz	MIAA Championships	2002
5-08.00	Trish Bahr	NAIA-Kansas City	1988
5-06.00	Morgan Brant	KSU Open	2014

POLE VAULT
12-01.50	Maggie Wilson	Jayhawk Classic	2013
12-00.75	Alaina Fairbanks	MIAA Championship	2013
11-01.75	Catalina Bissett	MIAA Championships	2015
11-05.75	Sonya Schement	UCM Invite	2012
10-11.75	Jennifer Nemeth	KSU All-Comers	2001

LONG JUMP
19-11.50	Shannon Butler	Holiday Inn Invite	2006
19-03.25	Brooke Kent	MIAA Championships	2010
19-02.00	Emilee Hamlin	NCAA Championships	2002
19-01.50	Brenda Short	Pittsburg	1980
19-00.75	Deandra Doubrava	MIAA Championships	1998

TRIPLE JUMP
40-07.75	Emilee Hamlin	MIAA Championships	2002
39-08.75	Brooke Kent	WSU Varsity Apt.	2010
38-08.00	Deandra Doubrava	MIAA Championship	1998
38-06.75	Alicia Burns	MIAA Championship	2005
38-06.75	Nikki Wetstein	Iowa State Classic	2013

SHOT PUT
53-07.00	Heather Leverington	KSU All-Comers	2001
52-05.75	Kathy Devine	Pittsburg State	1978
48-11.75	Rachel Goetz	KSU Open	2002
48-05.50	Kara Brockmeier	MIAA Championships	2002
48-05.25	Cecilia Gunn	Jayhawk Invitational	1992

20# WEIGHT THROW
58-03.00	Rachel Goetz	NCAA Championships	2002
56-06.00	Heather Leverington	KSU All-Comers	2001
56-00.00	Morgan Gilliland	Missouri Southern	2014
55-07.00	Deja Jackson	MIAA Championships	2011
53-01.50	Melanie Goetz	MIAA Championships	2002

PENTATHLON
3672	Deandra Doubrava	KSU Winter Pentathlon	1998
3517	Nikki Wetstein	MIAA Championships	2014
3291	Brooke Kent	Robinson Pentathlon	2008
3288	Monica Howard	MIAA Championships	2014
3260	Sarah Wuertz	KSU Winter Pentathlon	2001

Emporia State Women's Outdoor Top Five
(as of end of 2015 season)

100-METER DASH
11.64	Courtney Bruna	NCAA Championships	2004
11.74w	Carmen King	MIAA Championships	2012
11.90	Shannon Butler	NCAA Championships	2006
11.95	Tiffany Burden	MIAA Championships	2000
11.99	Sherlyn Weide	Southwestern Invitational	1991
11.99	Brooke Kent	D-II Challenge	2012

200-METER DASH
23.83	Courtney Bruna	MIAA Championships	2004
24.17	Magali Schneider	NCAA-II Championships	1996
24.18	Marqueita Marisette	MIAA Championships	2011
24.48	Kara Euler	MIAA Championships	2007
24.52	Alicia Burns	MIAA Championships	2012

400-METER DASH
53.33	Magali Schneider	NCAA-II Championships	1996
54.81	Deandra Doubrava	NCAA-II Championships	1996
55.70	Kara Euler	ATG Sports Qualifier	2007
55.76	Marqueita Marisette	Sam Williams Qualifier	2013
55.77	Jaclyn Sill	Sooner Invite	2009

800-METER RUN
2:10.99	Katie Mona	NCAA Championships	2011
2:12.40	Deandra Doubrava	MIAA Multi Championships	1999
2:12.90	Kadri Kelve	Pomona-Pitzer Inv.	2002
2:12.96	Jonel Rossbach	MIAA Championships	2008
2:13.04	Kristin Brune	Pomona-Pitzer	2002

1500-METER RUN
4:26.20	Kelly McCammon	NAIA at Russellville, Ark.	1986
4:29.00	Katie Mona	KU Relays	2012
4:30.10	Jonel Rossbach	Bobby Lane Inv.	2008
4:32.21	Kadri Kelve	Pomona Pitzer Inv.	2003
4:38.07	Lesha Wood	NAIA at Houston, Texas	1981

3000-METER RUN
9:37.90	Kelly McCammon	NAIA at Russellville, Ark.	1986
9:56.05	Kadri Kelve	ATG Twilight Qualifier	2003
9:57.34	Susan Stine	Kansas Relays	1986
9:59.37	Jonel Rossbach	D-II Challenge	2008
10:03.04	Katie Mona	MIAA Championships	2009

5000-METER RUN
16:52.28	Jonel Rossbach	MIAA Championships	2008
17:10.49	Susan Stine	NAIA at Russellville, Ark.	1986
17:34.34	Trudy Searcy	Emporia Twilight	1987
17:43.34	Amy Potter	Emporia Twilight	1987
17:53.44	Mary Griebel	Emporia Twilight	1987

10,000-METER RUN
35:24.81	Jonel Rossbach	Mt. SAC Relays	2008
36:24.85	Trudy Searcy	NAIA at Russellville, Ark	1987
36:26.54	Jennifer Mullen	Texas Relays	1992
36:37.45	Susan Stine	NAIA at Russellville, Ark.	1987
37:12.00	Mary Griebel	Kansas Relays	1987

100-METER HURDLES
13.80w	Nikki Wetstein	Sam Williams Qualifier	2013
14.16	Nikki Runnebaum	NCAA Championships	2001
14.22	Deandra Doubrava	MIAA Championships	1999
14.42	Gillian Curtiss-Masters	MIAA Multi Championships	1999
14.54	Amy Ayers	Kansas Relays	1994

400-METER HURDLES
59.67	Deandra Doubrava	ESU Last Chance/Drake Relays	1999
1:00.02	Gillian Curtiss	MIAA Championships	1998
1:02.10	Kayla Pauly	NCAA Championships	2003
1:02.24	Jennifer Lawellin	MIAA Championships	2004
1:02.36	Julie Worley	Nebraska Twilight	1993

3000-METER STEEPLECHASE
10:20.81	Kadri Kelve	NCAA Championships	2003
11:44.63	Tricia Kantack	MIAA championships	2001
11:54.99	Emily Schoenfeld	ESU Relays	2015
12:02.94	Tiffany Lytle	ATG Twilight	2001
12:15.49	Taylor Stueve	KU Relays	2014

400-METER RELAY
46.15	Euler, Sedivy, Melichar, Butler	NCAA Championships	2006
46.39	Bruna, Burns Melichar, Butler	NCAA Championships	2005
46.50	Bruna, Burns Oakes, Lawellin	MIAA Championships	2004
46.56	Marisette, Jacobs Weiss, King	NCAA Championships	2013
46.66	Marisette, Jacobs Wetstein, King	MIAA Championships	2012

1600-METER RELAY
3:42.80	Marisette, Weiss, Kunkel, Jacobs	NCAA Championships	2013
3:42.94	Schneider, Pitman, Oberg, Doubrava	NCAA Championships	1996
3:43.31	DeTiege, Masters, Brune, Doubrava	NCAA Championships	1999
3:43.65	Curtiss, Doubrava, Gerber, Pitman	NCAA Championships	1997
3:44.79	Sill, Sedivy, Euler, Rossbach	NCAA Championships	2007

HIGH JUMP
5-09.25	Jennifer Robinson	NCAA Championships	2010
5-08.5	Trish Bahr	NAIA at Azusa, Calif.	1988
5-08.25	Judy Becker	Drake Relays	1978
5-08	Dorothy Frey	Kansas Relays	1979
5-07	Sarah Wuertz	MIAA Multi-events	2002
5-07	Morgan Brant	ESU Relays	2014

POLE VAULT
12-5.5	Maggie Wilson	NCAA Championships	2015
11.11.75	Alaina Fairbanks	Spring Twilight	2012
11-9.75	Sonya Schement	K.T. Woodman	2013
11-5.75	Catalina Bissell	KU Relays	2015
10-11.75	Lacey Kirkaldie	KU Relays	2001

LONG JUMP
20-01	Peyton Weiss	KT Woodman	2015
19-9.75	Carmen King	MIAA Championships	2015
19-07.75	Brooke Kent	Tabor Invitational	2010
19-07.50	Shannon Butler	D-II Challenge	2006
19-05	Jennifer Robinson	Tabor Invitational	2010

TRIPLE JUMP
41-01.75	Brooke Kent	NCAA Championships	2010
41-01.50	Emilee Hamlin	NCAA Championships	2002
39-07.25	Alicia Burns	ESU Spring Twilight	2004
39-7.25	Nikki Wetstein	MIAA Championships	2011
38-07.75	Deandra Doubrava	MIAA Championships	1999

SHOT PUT
54-02.75	Heather Leverington	Pomona-Pitzer	2002
53-07.75	Kathy Devine	Drake Relays	1978
49-00	Cecilia Gunn	Texas Relays	1992
47-11.75	Rachel Goetz	NCAA-II Championships	2004
47-09.75	Laura Rand	NCAA-II Championships	1995
47-09.75	Kara Brockmeier	NCAA-II Championships	2001

DISCUS
163-10	Kara Brockmeier	MIAA Championships	2002
160-01	Rachel Goetz	ATG Twilight Qualifier	2004
157-02	Cecilia Gunn	NAIA at Stephenville, Tex	1990
156-8	Deja Jackson	MIAA Championships	2012
155-07	Laura Rand	ESU Twilight	1996

JAVELIN (new javelin since 1998)
151-7	Sara Dunkin	ESU Open	2013
148-00	Connie Phillips	NCAA Championships	2009
146-03	Sarah Wuertz	MIAA Championships	2002
144-05	Elizabeth Costello	ESU Mid-week	2015
143-08	Courtney Hurt	MIAA Championships	2002

HAMMER THROW
188-09	Laura Mayo	NCAA Championships	1998
185-00	Lynda Barnard	NCAA Championships	1997
173-08	Heather Leverington	MIAA Championships	2002
169-05	Deja Jackson	KT Woodman	2011
167-8	Shelby Buster	Sam Williams Qualifier	2015

HEPTATHLON (New javelin rule 1999)
5394	Deandra Doubrava	NCAA-II Championships	1999
4988	Sarah Wuertz	NCAA Championships	2002
4726	Emilee Hamlin	MIAA Championships	2001
4586	Brooke Kent	MIAA Multi's	2008
4487	Monica Howard	MIAA Championships	2015

Top Performers Retired Events

Men's Indoor

300-yd dash
31.74	Eddie Washington	Kansas State Relays	1960
31.84	Jesse Gadison	Dist. 10 at K-State	1992
32.44	Mike Cole	Pittsburg State Univ.	1982
32.64	Shane Meyer	Dist. 10 at K-State	1992

1000-yd run
2:12.74	Bill Tidwell	AAU at New York	1955
2:12.84	Roger Jennings	Kansas State Univ.	1987
2:14.14	John Camien	Kansas State Univ.	1967
2:14.24	Darrell Patterson	NAIA at Kansas City	1970

1500-m run
3:52.98	Jermaine Mitchell	NCAA	1994

Men Outdoor
Mile run
4:00.2	Roger Jennings	Prefontaine, Oregon	1988
4:00.7	John Camien	Compton Relays, Calif.	1963
4:07.0	Darrell Patterson	KU Relays	1971
4:07.2	Archie San Romani	Princeton Invite.	1937

Two-Mile run
8:48.73	David Kipelio	NAIA	1990
8:57.34	Ireland Sloan	USTAF at Milwaukee	1964
9:01.14	John Camien	Winnipeg	1965
9:02.14	Bob Camien	Kansas State Relays	1967

Three-Mile run
13:55.26	David Kipelio	Jayhawk Invitational	1990
14:06.72	Shawn Thomas	NAIA at Kansas City	1992
14:13.74	Ireland Sloan	Winnipeg	1962
14:25.98	Gary Lyles	NAIA	1991

Marathon
2:36.51	Mark Feldkamp	Dallas White Rock	1986
2:42.40	Andrew LaRouche	NAIA at Abbottsford	1992

Old Javelin
247-8	Jim Correll	RMAC	1971
242-1	Larry Hynek	Texas Relays	1973
231-3	Kent Hurn		1963
230-7	Dean Woodson	Arkansas Relays	1969

Women's Indoor

300-yd dash

37.84	Deanna Tolin	Dist. 10 at K-State	1992
38.11	Sandra Freeman	Central Missouri	1989
38.32	Sherlyn Weide	Jayhawk Invitational	1991
38.84	Clarissa Keeling	Kansas St. University	1989

1000-m run

3:00.67	Michelle Hebb	MIAA Championship	1993
3:08.17	Katarina Nilsson	Central Missouri	1995
3:14.88	Olivia Fowler	MIAA Championship	1994

1000-yd run

2:40.34	Kelly McCammon	Fort Hays	1986
2:43.29	Ingrid Frazier	NAIA	1991
2:46.14	Cindy Edgerton	NAIA	1981
2:48.19	Michelle Hebb	Jayhawk Invitational	1992

1500-m run

4:45.30	Michelle Hebb	NCAA	1993

3-Mile run

17:08.32	Jennifer Mullen	NAIA	1991

Women Outdoor

Old Javelin (Before 1998)

167-00	Joyce Burnett	ESU Last Chance	1997
150-11.75	Kathy Devine	Arkansas Relays	1978
145-10	Kelly Hare	K.T. Woodman	1995
138-11	Lynda Barnard	NCAA	1997
138-04	Judy Becker	NAIA	1981

Marathon

3:07.48	Amy Potter	Dallas White Rock	1986
3:07.48	Mary Griebel	Dallas White Rock	1987
3:11.18	Trudy Searcy	Dallas White Rock	1992

Non-Championship Events School Records

Men Indoor

300-yd dash	31.74	Eddie Washington	1960
1000-yd run	2:12.74	Bill Tidwell	1957
2-Mile run	8:48.73	David Kipelio	1990
3-Mile run	13:55.26	David Kipelio	1990
176-yd hurdles	19.97	Mike Cole	1984
Pentathlon	3430	Tim Vietti	1994
2-Mile Relay	7:39.34	Jennings, Starks, Kipelio, Brewer	1964

Men Outdoor

Mile run	4:00.34	Roger Jennings	1988
Marathon	2:36.51	Mark Feldkamp	1986
4 x 800 relay	7:27.53(m) 7:30.14(y)	Camien, Brinsko Hensley, Schierling	1968
Dist. Medley	9:44.58(m) 9:48.54(y)	Roberts, Wolfson, McDonnell, Camien	1964

Women Indoor

300-yd dash	37.94	Deanna Tolin	1992
1000-yd run	2:40.34	Kelly McCammon	1986
2-Mile run	10:47.26	Susan Stine	1987
3-Mile run	17:08.32	Jennifer Mullen	1991
176-yd H	23.94	Jean Kolarik	1986

Women Outdoor

Marathon	3:07.48	Amy Potter	1987
	3:07.48	Mary Griebel	1988
4 x 800 relay	9:11.93(m) 9:15.67(y)	Bohm, Frazier Wheeler, Hebb	1990
Dist. Medley	12:13.16(m) 12:17.44(y)	Bohm, Wheeler Frazier, Hebb	1990

Men's All-Time Track and Field Participants

The listing of names is as complete and accurate as could be obtained from the sources used. There is a possibility that some who participated in track and field are not in this list.

Last	First	Yr 1	Yr 2	Yr 3	Yr 4	Yr 5
Acker	William	1927	1928			
Acton	Seth	2014				
Adams	George	1929				
Adams	James	1947				
Adams	Robert	1958				
Adell	Harry	1916	1920			
Agrelius	Clair	1920	1921	1922		
Agrelius	Ken	1921				
Akins	Robert	1981	1982	1983		
Aleman	Dave	1987	1988			
Allard	Joseph	1977	1978			
Allbaugh	Francis	1936				
Allen	Gerald	1977	1978			
Allen	Lennie	1987	1988			
Allen	Todd	1990	1993			
Allen	Tyson	2004	2005	2007		
Allen	Wade	2002				
Allen		1925	1926			
Allison	David	1957				
Altenroid		1916				
Ames	David	1973				
Ames	John	1932				
Ames	Warren	1932	1933			
Amos	Clarence	1940				
Andereck	Zach	2002				
Anderson	Brad	1972	1973			
Anderson	Carol	1936				
Anderson	John	1934				
Anderson	K.	1969				
Anderson		1922				
Andrews	Dustin	2007	2008	2009	2010	
Anthony	Monroe	2001				
Applegate	Mark	1979				
Applegate	Nolan	2002	2003			
Applegate	Tyler	2002	2003	2004	2005	2006
Armstrong	Jim	1954	1955			
Arnold	Dan	1964				
Arnold		1922				
Arnspiger	Harold	1924				
Arthur	Charles	1936				
Arthur	William	1932				
Ary	Brett	1997	1998			
Atkins	Charles	1960	1961	1962		
Auerbach	Neil	1958				
Augustyn	James	1980	1981			
Augustyn	Joseph	1978	1979			
Austin	Jackson	1925	1926			
Austin	Loren	1935	1936			
Austin		1972				
Avery	Frederick	2012	2013	2014		
Avery	Michael	1979	1980	1981	1982	
Ayers	Vern	1937				
Babb	Cameron	2004	2005	2006	2007	
Babinsky	Thomas	1932				
Bacon	William	1934	1935			
Bader	Virgil	1934	1935			
Bagley		1930				
Bahner	Kim	1976	1977	1988		
Bailey	Charles	1935				
Bailey	Lane	1971				
Bailey	William	1948				
Ball	Bruce	1935				
Ballou	Dan	1982	1983			
Baltz		1908	1909			
Banks	Andre	1995				
Bantz	Clinton	1934				
Barber		1916	1917	1920		
Barndt	George	1922	1924	1925	1926	
Barnett	Kevin	1997	1998			
Baronoski	Ted	1942	1947			
Barrier	Adam	2000	2001			
Barry	Harry	1910	1911	1912		
Barteley		1914				
Bartels	Joe	1962				
Bartlett	Danny	2002	2003	2004		
Bartlett	Glen	1915				
Bartz	Tim	1990	1991	1992	1993	1994
Basom	Merle	1938				
Bath	Bart	1984				
Bauersfield	Reid	1999				
Baugh	Clarence	1918				
Baugh		1910				
Baumann	Bob	1960	1961	1962	1963	
Baumann	Mike	1986				
Baustert	Jonathan	2013	2014			
Baxter	Josh	1993	1994	1995	1996	1997
Bay	David	1977				
Bayack	Robert	1977	1978			
Bayless	Marvin	1941				
Bays	Todd	1980	1981	1982	1983	
Beadles	Paul	2000	2001			
Beals	Ray	1927	1928			
Beamon	Larry	2007	2008	2009		
Beatty	Mike	1977				
Beauchamp	Mike	1971				
Beck	Nick	2000	2001			
Beck		1921				
Becker	Jeff	1984				
Beckman	Robert	1977				
Beecher	Tommy	1912	1913			
Beeman	Jon	1982	1984			

Beeman	Steve	1979	1980	1981			Bowlin	James	2015		
Belden	Roman	2009					Boyer	Ryan	1990	1991	1992
Bell	Chris	2001					Boyle	Rick	1988	1989	1990	1991	1992
Bellinder	Francis	1951					Boyle	Thomas	1927	1928	
Belscamper		1925					Braden	Prince	2005		
Belting		1938					Brading	Rick	1976	1977	1978	1979
Bender	Drew	2004	2005				Bradner	Fred	1920	1921	
Bennett	Bob	1932					Brady	George	1926	1927	1928	1929
Bennett	Greg	1975					Brammer	Scott	2002	2003	2004
Bennington	Sean	1994					Brandley	Delbert	1971	1972	1973
Benson	Jeffrey	1995					Brant	Robert	1994		
Bentz	George	1958					Branum	Larry	1981	1982	
Berger		1916					Braugh	Gerald	1936		
Berry	Ross	2003	2004	2006			Brazelton	Darnell	2007		
Bert		1902					Brecheisen	Chad	1993	1994	1995
Bertsche	Roger	2006	2007	2008			Brecheisen	Ken	1932		
Betty		1921					Breech	Garrett	2011		
Betz		1915	1916				Breithaupt	Sean	1989		
Bevan	Earl	1925	1926	1927	1928	1929	Brenneman	Amos	1911		
Bieker	Mark	1997	1998	199			Brewer	Shawn	1988	1989	1990	1991
Bilderback	Ted	1967	1968				Brewster	Joe	1933	1934	
Bilyieu	Darrell	1959					Brewster		1929		
Bird	Andrew	2001	2002	2003	2004	2005	Bridges	Paul	1933	1934	1935	1936
Birk	Damon	2005	2006	2007	2008		Briggeman	Garth	1994	1995	1996	1997	1998
Birkholz	Richard	1963					Briggs	Craig	1977		
Birnbaum	Jim	1971					Brigham	Tremayne	1934	1935	
Bishop	Jerry	1996	1997	1998	2000		Brinsko	David	1966	1968	1969
Bishop	Rick	1971	1972	1973	1974		Brock	August	1929		
Black	Yarber	1936					Brock	Dustin	2000	2001	2002	2004
Blackburn	Ted	1932					Brokaw	Trey	2010	2011	2012
Blair	Henry	1901					Brook	C.	1929		
Blair	Robert	1948					Brooks	Brian	1973	1974	
Bliss	Don	1958					Brough	Paul	1978		
Bliss	Richard	1953	1954	1957	1958		Broughton		1908		
Blow	Don	1954	1955	1956	1957		Brown	Alfred	1913		
Bluett	Chester	1969	1970	1971	1972		Brown	Bob	1938		
Blunt		1921					Brown	Charles	2001		
Blythe	Donald	1947	1948	1949	1950		Brown	Drake	2014	2015	
Bockus	Brad	1984					Brown	Ed	1922		
Boehringer	Richard	1965	1966	1967	1968		Brown	F.E.	1904	1905	1906	1907
Boeve	Brian	1988	1989				Brown	Franklin	1930		
Bohannon	Reece	1955	1956				Brown	Henry	1934	1935	1936	1937
Bohm	Matt	1989	1990	1991	1992		Brown	Ibra	1924		
Boldra	Bob	1981	1982	1983			Brown	Jimmy	1965		
Boldridge	Eric	1986	1987	1988	1989		Brown	Ken	1925	1926	1927	1929
Bolen	Steve	1970					Brown	M.	1926	1927	
Boles		1964					Brown	Marvin	1948	1949	1950
Boley	John	1989	1990				Brown	Orville	1966		
Boline	Duane	1960					Brown	Pete	1949	1950	
Bollin	John	1911	1912	1914	1915		Brown	Ron	1967	1970	
Bonar	Robert	1953					Brown		1919		
Bond	L.	1969					Browne	John	1973	1974	1975
Bond	Ryan	2011					Broyles	Wes	2002	2003	
Borgendale	Kevin	1975	1977				Brundage	Kurt	1999		
Borror	John	1914					Bruning	Roger	1967	1968	1969	1970
Bousom	Dave	1977	1978				Buck	Andy	1913		
Bowers		1910					Buck	Bob	1956		

Buck	Walter	1924				Carter	Paul	1918	1920	1921	
Buckly		1957				Carter	Tim	1964			
Bull	Jacob	2011	2012	2013	2014	2015	Cartwright	Russell	1932		
Burger	Greg	1986				Caselman	Wade	1988	1989	1990	1991
Burkdoll	Clint	1989				Casey	Michael	1994	1995		
Burnes	Albert	1965	1966			Cash		1903			
Burnett	Dale	1927	1928	1929	1930	Caywood	Doug	1967	1968	1969	1970
Burns	Cody	2008	2009			Caywood	Keith	1939	1940	1941	1942
Burris	Schyler	1925	1926	1927	1928	Certain	Noel	1958	1959	1960	1961
Burrows	John	1977	1978			Certain	William	1960			
Bursch	Charles	1914	1915	1916	1917	Chamberlain	Alla	1901			
Bursch	James	1918				Chapman	Larry	1983			
Burt	James	1971	1972	1973		Chauncy		1913			
Burton		1934				Cheatum	Marvin	1931	1933	1934	
Bush	Walter	1941				Child	Michael	2012	2013	2014	
Bushore	Steve	1969				Childress	Tracey	1988			
Bust		1941				Chiles	Cecil	1930			
Butterfield	Edwin	1937				Chiles	Kevin	1979			
Butterfield	Harold	1947	1948	1949		Christensen	Oscar	1916	1917		
Butterfield	Sam	1940	1941			Christenson	Bryan	1981			
Buyer		1916				Christian	William	1949	1950		
Byfield	John	1989	1990			Church	Winfred	1938			
Byrne	Kevin	1978	1979	1980	1981	Claar	Eric	1994			
Cagle	Gary	1973				Claassen	Daniel	2013	2014	2015	
Caine		1947	1948			Clark	H.	1918	1919		
Calderon	John	1962				Clark	Leland	1921	1922		
Caldwell	Walter	1901				Clark	Morris	1933			
Calleja	Marcus	2010	2011	2012	2013	2014	Clarke	Peter	1960	1961	1962	1963
Calloway	Autrey	1956	1957	1958		Clasen	Richard	1961			
Camien	John	1962	1963	1964	1965	Clewell	Harry	1903	1904		
Camien	Robert	1965	1966	1967	1968	Clouston	Laurel	1938			
Camien	Shea	2006	2007			Clum	Stephen	1990			
Campbell	Jewell	1929				Cluts	Ronald	1964	1965	1966	1967
Campbell	Jonathon	2000	2001	2002		Clyma	David	1988	1989		
Campbell	Max	1933	1934			Coats	Roy	1924			
Campbell	Raymond	1946	1947			Cobb	Henry	1947			
Campbell	Scott	1995	1996	1997	1999	Coberly	R.L.	1954			
Campbell	W.Roy	1907	1908	1909	1910	Coblentz	Charles	1973	1974	1975	1976
Campbell		1922				Coffey	George	1925	1926	1927	
Canse		1919				Coffman	Floyd	1937			
Cantril	David	1979				Coffman	Harold	1909	1913		
Cargill	Dennis	1986				Cohen	Edward	1960			
Carle	Clarence	1921	1922	1923	1924	Cole	Cecil	1934			
Carlisle	Darin	1993				Cole	Cory	1995	1996	1997	1998	1999
Carlson	Brandon	2000	2001	2002	2003	Cole	Harry	1908	1909	1910	1911	1912
Carlson	Shane	1999				Cole	Mike	1982	1983		
Carpenter	Clifford	1914	1915	1916		Cole	Preston	1929			
Carpenter	Custer	1937	1938			Cole	William	1929			
Carpenter	Elmer	1940	1941	1946		Coleman	Colin	2015			
Carpenter	Greg	1969				Coleman	Gary	1962			
Carr	Tom	1946	1947	1948		Collins	Bill	1977			
Carroll	Bernard	1935				Collins	Henry	1932			
Carroll	Jerome	1932	1933	1934	1935	Colton	Leo	1932	1933	1934	1935
Carson	Elmer	1942	1946			Combes	Justin	1984	1985		
Carson	Gilbert	1935	1936			Commotte	Dick	1971			
Carson	Zach	2000	2001			Concannon	John	1925	1926	1927	1928
Carson		1922				Conner	Quentin	1996			

Conroy	Russel	1965				Davis	Clint	2003			
Conway	Hezekiah	1983	1984	1985		Davis	Cole	2009	2010		
Cook	Harold	1934	1935	1936		Davis	Dale	1914			
Cook	Jimmie	1972	1973	1974	1975	Davis	Don	1921			
Cook	Ray	1918	1919			Davis	Eldon	1942			
Cook	Warren	1929	1930	1931	1933	Davis	Glen	1932			
Cooks	Jerome	2004				Davis	H.D.	1905	1906	1907	1908
Cooley	Tye	1996	1997	1998	1999	Davis	Jack	1947			
Coop	Forest	1937				Davis	Lynn	1960			
Cooper		1917				Davis	Mark	2013			
Cordrey	Bill	1973	1974			Davis	Russel	1994			
Corey	Jim	1947				Davis	Willard	1986			
Correll	James	1968	1969	1970	1971	Davis		1902			
Cortez	Frankie	2009	2011	2012	2013	Dawson		1925	1926		
Corwin	John	1995	1996			DeBauge		1920			
Corwin	Richard	1959	1960			Deck	Merrill	1953	1954		
Cosand		1920				Decker		1908			
Cowan	Arthur	1906	1907			Defebaugh	Cameron	2014	2015		
Cowdrey	Robert	1937				Defebaugh	Walter	1979	1980	1981	1982
Cowing	Dillon	2009	2010	2011		DeForest		1914			
Cox	Edward	1970	1971			Deinlein		1932			
Cox	Evan	2003	2004			Dellunto	Jerry	1962			
Cox	Richard	1983	1984	1985		Delmott	Asher	2009	2010	2011	2012
Cox		1912				Delmott	Dennis	1967	1968	1969	1970
Crabtree	Tom	1987				Delmott	Skyler	2007	2008	2009	2010
Craig	Roy	1933				DelRossi	Alfred	1978	1979	1980	1981
Creitz	Revel	1934				DeMott	Gail	1941	1942	1943	
Cremer	Bill	1941				DeMott	Ken	1935	1936	1938	1939
Cremer	Raymond	1917				Dent	Ellsworth	1920	1921	1922	
Cress	Alan	1983	1984			Denton	Chris	1996	1998		
Creyaufmiller	Gene	1953				DePass	Clifford	1966	1967	1968	1969
Criqui	Orville	1950				DePriest	Henry	1952			
Crist	Ted	1932				Derley	Jay	1995	1996		
Cristler	Stewart	1932				Derley	Troy	1994	1995	1996	1997	1998
Cromer	Meredith	1923				Derrick	Doyle	1930	1931		
Crone		1934				Derrine	Fred	1957			
Crooms	Duward	1933	1934	1935	1936	Derryberry	Grady	2014			
Cross	Elmer	1940	1946			DeWeese	Bill	1955	1956		
Cross	Guy	1916	1917	1924		Dewey	Delmar	1912	1913	1914	
Crumb	Jim	1972				Dick	Warren	1941			
Cruz	Nick	1977	1978	1979		Dickerson	Kevin	1981	1981	1982	1983
Culter	Harold	1913	1914			Dickerson	Tre	2013	2014	2015	
Cummings		1911				Dickey	Bill	1956			
Cuzzo		1973	1974			Dickinson	Guy	1909	1910	1911	
Czencz	Alex	1961	1962			Dickson	Jon	2001	2002	2003	2005
Daeschner	Richard	1934				Dickson	Ryan	2011	2012	2013	2014	2015
Dain	Todd	1991	1992	1993		Dieker	Stephan	1975			
Dains	Ben	2009				Diekman	Henry	1936			
Dalton		1921				Dierking	Troy	1989			
Daniel	Jerry	1985	1986	1987		Diggs	Welford	1912	1913		
Davenport	Chester	1925	1926	1927	1928	Dilks	David	1981			
David	Kirk	1976	1948			Dillon	Franklin	1920	1922		
Davidson	Aubrey	1906	1907	1908		DiPaola	Richard	1963	1964	1965	1966
Davidson	John	1940				Dirks	Aaron	2003	2004		
Davies	John	1902	1903			Ditmars	Tommy	1913	1922		
Davies	Walter	1953				Dittermeyer		1913			
Davis	Bill	1955	1956			Dittmer	Jared	2002			

Dixon	Avril	1929	1930			Eickermann	Homer	1936			
Dixon	Lynn	1935				Eikermann	William	1962	1963	1964	1965
Dixon	William	1950	1951			Eldersveld	Jim	1988			
Dobbs	Joel	1932				Eldridge	David	1960			
Dodd	Richard	1935	1936			Eldridge	Tom	1965			
Dodds		1921				Ellis	Clarence	1931			
Dodson	Marc	1978	1979			Ellwood	Scott	1996			
Doherty	Brian	1999				Elsbaugh		1925			
Doile	Glenn	1935	1936			Emmons	Travis	1995			
Dolan	Jason	2001	2002	2003	2004	Engle		1921			
Dolisi	Earl	1965				Enneking	Brian	1984			
Donaldson	Dave	1918	1919	1920	1921	Erbert	Collin	2012	2013		
Donnellan	Quentin	1938				Ericson	Ted	1970			
Doperalski	Ted	1969				Errett		1908			
Douglas	Roy	1934				Etheridge	Andrew	2011	2012	2013	2014	2015
Douglass	Aubrey	1909	1910	1912		Evans	Bill	1932	1933		
Downey	James	1957				Evans	Kyle	2015			
Downing	Gary	1965				Evans	Parker	2015			
Downing	Kyle	2010	2011	2012	2013	2014	Evans		1949			
Downs	Ted	1938	1939	1940	1941	Eve	Ted	1965			
Doyle	Tim	1966	1967	1968		Evely	John	1961			
Drake	Frank	1902	1904	1905		Ewed	J.S.	1902			
Dreiling	Jamie	2001	2002			Ewen	James	1904	1905	1906	1907
Dryer	Cecil	1934	1935	1936		Fairbanks	Shawn	1998	1999	2000	2001
Dudley	William	1950	1951			Fanning	Cleo	1936	1937		
Duer	Joe	1918	1920			Farleigh	Sam	2004			
Dummond	Ivan	1928				Farr	Randy	1977			
Duncan	Chester	1950				Farrow	Jimmy	1935	1936		
Duncan	Vernon	1947	1948	1949		Favrow	Bill	1958	1960	1962	1963
Duncan		1957				Feldkamp	Mark	1987			
Dunn	Artie	1956				Fergerson		1933			
Dunn	Eddie	1947				Feuerbach	Allen	1967	1968	1969	1970
Dunning	Robert	1921	1922	1923	1924	Fick	Byron	1987	1989		
Durbin	William	1968	1969			Field	Bruce	2010	2011		
Durham	Roy	1921				Fields	Carl	1930			
Durkin	John	1963				Fields	Myron	1935			
Dvorak	Chris	2008	2009	2010	2011	Filinger	William	1920			
Dwyer		1913				Finch		1902			
Dye	Max	1947	1948	1949		Fincken	Tom	1958	1959	1960	1961
Early	Ruben	1961	1962			Finger	Robert	1963	1964	1965	1966
Ebel	Clarmore	1926	1927			Finklea	Aaron	1925	1926	1927	
Eberhart	Jim	1937				Finklea	Raymond	1903			
Ecord	Floyd	1920	1921			Finley	A.W.	1918			
Edgar	Glover	1966	1967	1968	1969	Finney	Marshall	1933			
Edgerson	Edward	1973	1974	1975		Finnin	Laurence	1927	1928		
Edmonds	Roger	2000	2001	2002		Firestone	Frank	1909			
Edmonds	Tanner	2002				Fischer	Curtis	1942			
Edmonds		1940				Fischer	Darrin	1988			
Edwards	Donald	1952	1953	1954		Fischer	Jeramie	2014	2015		
Edwards	Jim	1931	1934			Fisher	Claude	1932	1933		
Edwards	Lloyd	1942				Fisher	D.C.	1901			
Edwards	Vaughn	1939	1940			Fisher	James	1951	1952		
Edwards		1917				Fisher	Joseph	1958	1959	1960	1961
Egbert	Gwynne	1920				Fitch	Lucas	2014			
Ehrlich	Harold	1951				Fitzgerald	Alfred	1950	1951	1952	1953
Eichenburg	Bra	2009				Fleming	Tyler	2009			
Eickenberg	Jon	2011				Fleming	William	1958	1959	1960	

Fleming		1909	1910		
Flentje	Edward	1961	1962	1963	
Fletcher	W.B.	1917			
Foncannon	Adrian	1912	1913		
Forde	Ed	1906	1907		
Fordham	Monroe	1958	1959	1961	
Fore	Warren	1976			
Forsythe		1934			
Foster	Eugene	1936			
Foster	Larry	1960	1961		
Fowler	Steven	1972	1973	1974	1975
Fowler	Troy	1989	1990		
Fowler		1937	1940		
Fox	Rudolph	1934			
Fraley	Bill	1966	1967	1968	1969
Fraley	Jim	1933	1934	1935	1936
Frame	Wendall	1935	1936	1937	1938
Frank	Garett	2004			
Frankenberger	William	1971	1972	1973	1974
Franklin	Landis	1958	1960	1961	
Freebourne		1914	1915	1917	
Freeman	Alfred	1939	1940		
Freeman	Claude	1929			
Freeman	Larry	1961	1963		
Freeman	Owen	1932			
French	Loren	1934			
Fridley	J.B.	1904	1905	1906	1907
Frisbie	Arthur	1927	1928		
Frohardt	Louis	1962	1963	1964	1964
Fry	Ken	1936			
Fulks	Willis	1976	1977		
Funke	Don	1984	1985	1986	1988	1989
Funke	Robert	1954			
Furman		1973			
Gaddis	H.L.	1903	1905		
Gadison	Jesse	1989	1990	1991	1992	1993
Galbraith	Claude	1916	1917	1921	
Gambill	Marcus	1909	1910	1914	
Gangel	Francis	1955	1956	1957	1958
Garcia	Alec	2014	2015		
Gard	Ernest	1907	1909		
Gardenhire	Bernie	1983	1985		
Gardner	Ira	1966	1968	1969	1970
Garner	Darius	2007			
Garrett	Ed	1951			
Garrett	Frank	1925	1926		
Garrett	Harley	1925	1926	1927	1928
Garrettson	Patrick	1970			1930
Garris	Jerry	1955			
Garrison	Arthur	1917	1921		
Garten	Harry	1923			
Gary	Prentice	1941	1942	1946	1947
Gasche	Lewis	1935			
Gassman	Tanner	2002	2003	2004	2005
Gaugh	James	1907			
Gellinger	Brian	2012	2013	2014	
George	Bill	1939			
George	David	1963	1964	1965	
George	David	1976	1977	1978	1979
George	William	1914			
Giardine	Mike	1998	1999		
Gibbs	George	1954	1955	1956	1957
Gibson	David	2007			
Gibson	R.	1969			
Giffin	Jason	1983	1984		
Gilbert	Otis	1922			
Gilbert		1925			
Gillispie	Cleve	1932			
Gilmore		1925			
Gilson	Aeron	2011			
Gilstrap	Modesto	2005	2006	2007	
Ginavin	Robert	1976	1977		
Ginter	Rick	1994	1995		
Gist	Ray	1905	1906		
Givens	Dick	1940			
Goff	Grady	2011	2012	2013	2014
Goldhammer	Bill	1962			
Goldsmith	Wayne	1939	1940	1941	1942
Goldsmith	Wendell	1938	1939		
Gomez	Brian	1995			
Gomez	Edward	1973	1974	1975	1977
Gonzalez	Jerry	1997			
Good	J.C.	1901			
Goodell	Wayne	1953			
Goodnature	Brennan	2012	2013		
Gordon	Edward	1926			
Goss	Richard	1975			
Gould	Alva	1933			
Goulden	Clyde	1955			
Goyer		1916			
Graber	Byron	1942			
Grady	Tom	1989	1990	1991	1992
Grafke	Ed	1952	1953	1954	
Graham	Kale	2004			
Grandfield	Derek	2002			
Granillo	Tony	2009	2010	2011	
Grant	Bernard	1930	1931	1932	1933
Grant	Ed	1929			
Grant		1949			
Gratto	Chuck	1977	1978		
Grayum	William	1910	1912		
Grecian	Larry	1974	1975		
Green	Curtie	1932			
Green	Gilbert	1951	1952		
Green	Michael	1959			
Greenly	Jesse	1932			
Greenwade	Robert	1926	1927		
Gregg	Eugene	1952			
Greiner	Dale	1960	1961		
Grella	John	1965	1967		
Grey	Tyrone	1975			
Griffin	Jesse	1992			
Griffin	Todd	1994			
Griffith	Bill	1998	2000	2001	

Surname	First	Y1	Y2	Y3	Y4	Y5
Griffith	Bob	1958				
Griffith	Jerry	1925				
Griffiths	Corey	1989				
Grigsby	Mark	2006				
Grimes		1920				
Grimm	Robert	1947	1948	1952		
Grimwood	Bill	1946				
Gritton		1955				
Gronquist	David	1970	1971			
Grosdidier	Shae	2003	2004			
Gross	Adam	1999				
Gross	Bret	2010	2011			
Grote	Curtis	2002	2003	2004	2005	2006
Groves	Harold	1930	1932			
Groves		1938				
Guberman	Erik	1996				
Guilford	Floyd	1930				
Gunderson	Mike	1998	1999	2000		
Gutierrez	Jose	2011	2012	2013		
Gwaltney	Ronald	1975				
Haddock		1964				
Hagan	Dan	1989	1990			
Hager		1925				
Hagg	Jason	1993				
Haggerty	Walter	1965	1967	1968		
Haggerty	Walter	1967				
Hagins	Austin	1932				
Hague	Lawrence	1936	1937	1938	1939	
Hahn	Ryan	2008	2009	2010	2011	
Hainline	Bob	1931				
Hainline	Menzo	1925	1926	1927	1928	
Haizlip	Alva	1930	1931			
Hakes	Milo	1908	1909	1910		
Hall	Derwin	2009	2010	2011	2012	2013
Hall	Dwayne	2010				
Hall	Leonard	1973	1974	1975	1976	
Hall	Wayne	1933				
Haller	Damon	2009				
Halley	Thomas	1911	1912			
Hamill	Lloyd	1916				
Hamilton	Gail	1940	1941			
Hamilton	Hugh	1925				
Hamman	Marvin	1941				
Hammond	James	1958				
Hampton	Robert	1959				
Hanhel		1957				
Hankenson		1932				
Harber	Robert	1977	1978	1979	1980	
Harclerode	Elmer	1921				
Harder	Ted	1949				
Hardesty		1957				
Hardy	Claude	1933	1934			
Hardy	James	1987	1988			
Hardy	Larry	1957				
Hargiss	Floyd	1909		1911		
Hargiss	Homer	1906	1907	1908	1909	
Hargiss	Leonard	1903	1904	1905		
Hargiss	Meade	1916				
Haring	Lee	1932	1933	1934	1935	
Harkness		1902				
Harlan	Dale	1931	1932			
Harlan	Mervin	1965	1970			
Harness	Vernon	1935	1936			
Harrington	James	1963	1964			
Harris	Bill	1914	1915	1916		
Harris	Frank	1924	1926	1930		
Harris	Jared	2002				
Harris	John-David	1999	2000	2001	2002	2003
Harrison	Beverly	1935	1936			
Harsh	Robert	1952	1953			
Hartwig	Fred	1913	1914	1915	1915	
Harvey	Bob	1954				
Harvey	Michael	2000	2001			
Harvey	Wilmer	1954				
Harwood	Solomon	1993				
Hatcher	Paul	1919	1920			
Havens	Brook	2001	2002	2003		
Havens	Tom	1978				
Havenstein	Sawyer	2014	2015			
Hawk	Collin	2012	2013	2014	2015	
Hawk	Robert	1955				
Hawkins	Steven	1980	1981	1982	1983	
Hawkinson	Kenneth	1963	1964			
Hayden	Chester	1949	1950			
Hayen	Bernard	1941				
Hayen	Charles	1939	1940			
Hayes	Everett	1940	1941	1942		
Hayes	James	1958	1959	1960		
Hayes	Jim	1954	1955			
Hayes	Richard	1935	1936			
Haynes	Matt	2001				
Haynes		1911	1912			
Haywood	Louis	1935	1936			
Healy		1972				
Heaney	Robert	1957	1958	1959		
Heats	Rowe	1934				
Hedges	Cale	2014	2015			
Hefty	Paul	1935				
Heidrick	Dylan	2014	2015			
Heigl	Doug	1969				
Heil	Mike	1973	1974	1975	1976	
Heim	Dan	1980				
Heimer	Travis	1994	1995			
Hellmer	George	1931				
Hellmer	Leo	1932				
Hemphill	James	2007	2008			
Henderson	Donald	1950	1951	1952		
Henderson	Edward	1936				
Henderson		1913				
Hendricks	Dennis	1940				
Hendricks		1909				
Hendrickson	Earl	1913				
Hendrickson	Garland	1973	1974			

Hendrin	Dennis	1966					Hoover		1926	1927	
Hendrix	Russell	1991					Hopkins	John	1929		
Hendrix	Sam	1912					Horn	Bob	1955	1956	
Hendron	Tyler	2015					Horn	Carl	1927	1928	
Hendry	Jason	1994	1995	1996	1998		Horn		1914		
Henicke	Johnny	2006	2007				Hornbaker	Andy	1975		
Henry	Brett	2002	2003				Hornbaker		1910		
Henry	Steve	1976	1977	1978	1979		Hosking	Ed	1953	1954	
Hensley	Frank	1967	1968				Hosler	Mark	1984		
Hepworth	George	1911	1912				Hosterman	Curt	1981	1982	
Herbic	Stan	1966					Houk	Russell	1997		
Herod		1917					Howard	Earl	1926	1927	
Herpich	Clarence	1962	1963	1964	1965		Howard	George	1932		
Herron	Joseph	1998	1999	2000	2001	2002	Howard		1905		
Hertig	Matt	1990	1991				Howell	James	1961	1962	1964
Hess	Kyle	2009					Howes	John	1960		
Hess	Orville	1930					Howze	Vincent	2009	2010	2012	2013
Hetlinger	Pete	1971					Hoyt		1940	1942	
Heyden	Merle	1921	1922				Huckabay	Brady	2013	2014	
Hickox	Duane	1938					Hudson	Richard	1937	1938	
Hicks	Frank	1959	1960	1960			Huebner		1926		
Hicks	Roy	1957					Hufford	Donald	1950		
Hidalgo	Thomas J.	1934	1935	1936			Hufford	John	1954		
Higginbotham	Sean	2008					Hull	Cleve	1932		
Hildyard	Arthur	1936					Hulpieu	John	1929		
Hill	Alfred	1912					Humbarger	David	1999	2000	2001	2002
Hill	Vincent	1954					Hunt	Aaron	2002		
Hill	Warren	1967	1968				Hunt	Ron	1972		
Hill	Wes	2000	2001	2002	2003		Hunt	Ryan	1995	1996	1997	1998
Hill		1922					Hunt	Walter	1914	1915	
Hilll	Will	2002	2003				Hunt		1920		
Hinson	Jerry	1970	1971	1972	1973		Hunt		1926		
Hirshler	Art	1912					Hunter	Harold	1926	1927	1928	1930
Hiskey	Marshall	1931	1932				Hunter	Ron	2002		
Hiskey	Verne	1930					Hurn	Kent	1961	1962	1963	1964
Hobson	James	1948	1949	1950			Hurst	Leonard	1911		
Hoch	Merton	1935					Huston	Paul	1957		
Hoffman	Eric	2002	2003	2004	2005		Hutchinson	Bill	1951	1952	1953
Hoffman	Peter	1977	1978	1979	1980		Hutchinson	Clair	1953	1954	1955	1956
Hogan	Darrel	1937					Hutchinson		1973	1974	
Hoglund	Don	1936	1937				Hynek	Larry	1970	1971	1972	1973
Hohmeier	William	2008	2009	2010	2011		Irwin	Scott	1958	1959	1960	1961
Holder	A.J.	1932	1933	1934	1935		Isaacs	LeRoy	1913		
Holland	Jason	1990					Ise	Walter	1903	1904	
Hollister	Edward	1938	1939				Isemede	Patrick	1977		
Holloway	Jay	1973	1974	1975	1976		Izzo	Roy	1973	1974	
Hollrah	Darin	2001					Jacka	Don	1941		
Holmes	Brett	1988	1989				Jackson	Demetri	2001	2002	2003	2004
Holmes	Stuart	1982	1983				Jackson		1905		
Holst	Donald	1950	1951	1952	1953		Jacobs	Bill	1967		
Holt	Kenny	1984					Jacques	Fred	1925	1926	
Holtfrerich	George	1921	1922	1923	1924		Jacquez	Mark	2000		
Holwick	Frank	1963					Jaggard	Guy	1907		
Honeycutt	Josh	2008	2009	2010	2011		James	Dennis	1972		
Honska	Otto	1906	1907	1908	1910	1911	James	Hadden	1912	1913	1914
Hoover	John	2005	2006				Jantz	Brad	1998	1999	
Hoover	Joseph	1964				1911	Javier	Gonzalo	1957	1958	1959	1960

Jenkins	Don	1967				King	W.T.	1906	1907		
Jennings	Dennis	1972	1973			King	Warren	1936			
Jennings	Doug	1980	1981			Kingan		1902			
Jennings	Roger	1986	1987	1988	1989	Kious	David	1975	1979		
Jilka	Adam	2002				Kipelio	David	1989	1990	1991	
Jilka	Ryan	2003	2004	2005		Kirbie	James	2011			
Jim	Jackson	1947				Kirkland	Sean	1995			
Johnson	Alan	1973	1974	1975		Kirkpatrick	Perry	1932	1933	1934	1935
Johnson	Corey	2012				Kisel	Jim	1969			
Johnson	Ken	1937				Kitterman	Shane	2001	2002		
Johnson	Leigh	1956				Kjekstad	Earl	1963	1964		
Johnson	Marven	1939				Klenda	Nick	2011	2012	2013	2014	2015
Johnson	Steve	1968				Kline	Harry	1937	1938		
Johnson	Thomas	1939	1940	1941	1942	Kline	Melvin	1937			
Johnson	Tod	1985	1986	1987	1988	Klotz	Robert	1949	1950	1951	1952
Johnson		1920				Knight	Derek	2009			
Johnston	Eldon	1939				Knight	Gale	1971	1972	1973	1974
Jones	Corey	2007				Knight	James	1933			
Jones	Dale	1948				Knoeppel	Paul	1941			
Jones	Harold Earl	1936				Knolle		1957			
						Knoor	Edwin	1925	1926		
Jones	Harold Elwood	1936				Knox	Burton	1941	1942	1943	
Jones	Lawrence	1956	1957			Knox	Carter	1938			
Jones	Leland	1947				Knox	Murray	1972	1973	1974	
Jones	Leland	1948				Knox	W.	1942			
Jones	Timothy	2009				Koelling	Matt	2007	2008	2009	2010
Jones	Tom	1966	1967	1968	1969	Kopfer	Larry	1967			
Joseph	Diedrick	1995				Koppenhaver	Chris	1993			
Josserand	Bruce	1912				Kotzman	Kyle	2008	2009		
Juhlin	Dean	1947				Kraft	Colin	2012	2013		
Juras	Richard	1962				Krehbiel	Lawrence	1936	1937	1938	
Kaberline	Ryan	1994	1995	1996		Krehbiel	Verne	1955			
Kadel		1949				Krey	Forrest	1931			
Kaiser		1918				Kruger	Leo	1934			
Kariuki	Antoni	2003				Kuck	Frank	1925	1926		
Katzer	Josh	1999	2000			Kuck	John	1925	1926		
Keach	David	2013				Kuestersteffan	Matt	1994			
Keller	C.	1969				Kukula	Howard	1929			
Keller		1931				Kuretich	William	1933	1934		
Kelley	Dylan	2012	2014			Kutnink	Marvin	1929	1931	1932	
Kellum	Forrest	1936				Kutnink	Paul	1920	1921	1922	1923
Kelly	Jack	1953	1955	1956		Kutschinski	Oscar	1927	1928	1929	1930
Kennedy	Aaron	2002				Lacer	Josh	2011			
Kennedy	Jared	2003	2004	2005		Lackey	Greg	1990			
Kennedy	Tom	1939	1940			Lackey	Harmon	1936			
Kent	Johnny	2000				LaCroix	Eugene	1936			
Kenyon		1902				Ladner	Herman	1914	1915		
Kepart	Kelly	1970				Laird	Lester	1937	1938	1939	
Kern	Sloane	2008	2009			Laird	Richard	1971	1972		
Kerr	Dereck	2001				Lamb	Donald	1947	1948		
Kerr		1918				Lamb	Ted	1949	1950		
Kersey	James	2005	2006			Lamb	Vernon	1947			
Kersey	Nathan	2013	2014			Lamkin	John	1956			
Kidd	Mike	1997	1998	1999		Lane	Howard	1922	1923	1924	1925
Killingsworth	Mark	1977				Lane	John	1946	1947		
Kimball	Ross	1999				Lange	Eric	1997			
King	Karl	1916				Langley	Phil	1957			

Lanning	Harlan	1933	1934			Lonard	Larry	1963	1964	1965	
Larkin	Jack	1947	1948	1949	1950	Lonberger	Kenton	2008	2009		
Larkins	Katrel	2006				Lonberger	Kyle	2009			
LaRoche	Thomas	2015				Long	Brad	2003			
LaRouche	Andrew	1992	1993	1994		Long	Lawrence	1956			
Larrabee	Mike	1978	1979			Long	Mike	1956			
Larson	Emil	1911	1912			Long	Wesley	1932			
Larson	Jean	1936				Lopez	Alberto	1991			
Larson	John	1909	1910	1911		Love	Glen	1971			
Laud	Orville	1939				Loveless		1920			
Lawrence	Davian	2011	2012	2013	2014	Lovely	Darryl	1994			
Lawrence	Gary	1968	1969	1970	1971	Lovett	Orval	1931			
Lawrence	Justin	2012				Loyd	Dustin	2006	2007	2008	2009
Lawrence		1936				Loyd		1902			
Laws	Mark	1973	1974	1975	1976	1977	Lucas		1903			
Lawton	Donald	1936				Lucas		1932			
Lee	Donald	1982	1983			Luedke	Randy	2012			
Lee	Ed	1988				Lunn	Steven	2004			
Lee	Henry	1932				Lusk	Howard	1948			
Lee	Ralph	1934				Lutschg		1928			
Lee	Travis	2005	2006	2007	2008	Lyles	Gary	1991	1992		
Lehning		1972				Lysen	Braden	2005	2006		
Leith	John	1927	1928			Mabry	Ray	1956			
Leitner	Carol	1954				MacFarland	Cliff	1902			
LeMaster	Bill	1996	1997	1998	1999	2000	Macha	Richard	1951			
Lengel	Ralph	1948				Mack	Gannon	2012	2013	2014	
Lenser		1925				Mack	Tyree	1933	1934	1935	1936
Lespagnard	George	1953	1954	1955	1956	Madden	Harry	1926			
Leuhring		1915				Madden	Vincent	1958			
LeVieux	Don	1951	1952	1953	1954	Maddux		1907			
Lewick	Hugh	1949	1950	1951	1952	Madeira	Brian	2014			
Lewis	Earl	1917	1918			Mahoney	Paul	1934	1937		
Lewis	Greg	1989				Majors	Mark	1989	1990	1991	1992
Lewis	James	1934	1935	1936	1937	Mallett		1904			
Lewis	Sylvester	1962				Mallory	Charles	1959	1960		
Liby	Robert	1938	1939	1940		Manhart	Jason	1995			
Liby	Virgil	1939				Manly	Harold	1920	1921	1924	
Lighter	Fred	1923	1924	1925	1926	Manly	R.	1920			
Lillian		1953				Mann	Kyle	2007	2008	2009	
Limon	Lester	1966				Manning	Jordan	2014			
Linder	Dwight	1973	1974			Maples	Keith	2010	2011		
Linder	Rex	1955				Mares	Adolph	1948			
Linder	Robert	1955				Markuly	Pando	1967	1968	1969	
Lindsay	Charles	1932				Marquardt	Harold	1934			
Lindsey	Stan	1984				Marquardt	Randy	1983			
Linsey	Alex	2012	2013	2014	2015	Marshall	Douglas	2007	2008	2009	2010
Lira	Tim	2004	2006			Martin	Andrew	1929			
Litchfield	Bill	1947				Martin	Brian	1989	1990	1991	
Littler	Richard	1949				Martin	Charles	1941	1942	1943	
Lloyd	Mark	1981				Martin	Codi	2015			
Locke	Al	1936	1938			Martin	Tim	1973	1974	1975	1976
Lockman	Cloudsley	1914	1915	1916	1917	Martin	Wade	2002			
Lockwood		1917				Massey	Dave	1928	1929	1930	1931
Logan	Tommy	1938				Masters	Brandon	1996	1997	1998	
Lohkamp	Anthony	1936	1937	1938	1939	Masters	Ira	1904			
Lojka	Glenn	1958	1959	1960		Masters	Tony	1973	1975		
Lonard	Bob	1961				Matheson	Dennis	1958	1959	1960	1961

Name	First	Y1	Y2	Y3	Y4
Mathews		1949			
Maton	Troy	1995			
Matthews	Chris	1979	1980		
Matthews		1973			
Mattox	Mike	1977	1978	1979	
Matz	Ken	1955			
Maudsley		1922			
Maxwell	Elmo	1931			
May	Jeremiah	2011			
Mayberry	Donald	1956			
Mayberry	Maynard	1949	1950	1951	
Maydew	Payson	2013	2014	2015	
Mayo	Melvin	1961	1962	1963	
Mays	Mark	1977			
McAdoo	Jeff	1975			
McAlister		1950			
McAllister	John	2001			
McAlpine	James	1937			
McArdle	Edward	1952	1954		
McCabe	Roland	1955			
McCafferty		1906	1907		
McCale	Tim	2011			
McCann	James	1963			
McClain	Vincille	1939			
McClanahan	Russell	1965	1966		
McCleary	Josh	1995	1996	1997	1998 1999
McClure	Andy	1931			
McCollum	Walter	1914			
McConley		1971			
McCoy	Elvin	1929	1930		
McCoy	Merle	1933			
McCoy		1922			
McCracken	Harwood	1934			
McCray	Kent	1978			
McDaniel	Paul	1967	1969		
McDonald		1909			
McDonnell	John	1964			
McElligot	Charles	1981			
McGahan	Lloyd	1919	1920	1921	1922
McGinnis	Bob	1939	1940		
McGinty	John	2001			
McGlinn	Marty	1966	1967		
McGovern	Adam	2008	2009	2010	
McGuire	Harry	1905			
McGuire	James	1927	1928		
McIntire	Duane	1957	1958	1959	1960
McKaig	Brad	1976	1977		
McKee		1925	1926		
McKeown	Casey	2000	2001	2002	
McKinness	Leslie	1942			
McKown	Earl	1922	1923	1924	1925
McMaster	Harold	1928			
McMullen	Eugene	1947	1948	1949	1950
McPhee	James	1976	1977	1978	
McPheron	Glenn	1917	1918		
Meairs	Clifford	1912	1913	1915	1916
Meairs	Robin	1920	1921	1922	
Meek	Leslie	1905			
Meeker	Ross	1973	1974	1975	
Meier	Don	1981	1982		
Mensah	Kirk	1994			
Merckling	Jason	1995			
Merriman	Carlos	1987	1988		
Merth	Robert	2014			
Methvin	Ted	1987	1988		
Mettler	Don	1942	1943		
Meyer	Benny	1956	1957	1958	
Meyer	Bernard	1918	1919		
Meyer	Eric	1999	2000	2001	
Meyer	Raymond	1939			
Meyer	Shane	1992			
Meyer		1911			
Meyes	Duane	1965			
Michels	Larry	1977	1978		
Mick	Richard	1992			
Middlekauff		1902			
Miller	Cody	2011	2012	2013	2014 2015
Miller	Edwood	1934			
Miller	Holly	1933			
Miller	Luke	2010			
Miller	Mike	1994	1995	1996	1997
Miller	Ross	1908	1909	1911	1912
Miller	Russell	1958	1959	1960	1961
Miller	Sidney	1906	1907	1908	1911
Millikin	Arthur	1973	1974	1975	1976
Mills	Joe	1956			
Minnis		1948			
Minton	Mike	1994			
Mitchell	Jermaine	1994	1995	1996	
Mitchell	Maynard	1948	1949		
Mitchell	Troy	1988	1989		
Mithcell	Steve	1961	1963	1964	1965
Mohr	Rodney	1970	1971	1972	
Molnar	Tamas	1996			
Montgomery	Stacy	1989	1990		
Monypenny	Bill	1915			
Moore	Arthur	1947	1948	1949	
Moore	Austen	2012			
Moore	Charles	1942	1947		
Moore	Clyde	1911	1912		
Moore	Justin	1993			
Moore	Lane	1986			
Moore	Martin	1981			
Moore	Melvin	1936			
Moore	Wayne	1941			
Moore		1908			
Moreland	Paul	1926			
Morgan	Forrest	1929	1930	1931	1932
Morgan		1911			
Morrell	Rich	1977			
Morrill	Bert	1930	1931	1932	1933 1933
Morris	Alvin	1939			
Morrison		1904			
Morrison		1910			

Mosier	Brian	2013	2014			Nolte	Jason	1998			
Mosier	Mike	1981	1982	1983		Noonan	Tom	1976	1977	1978	1979
Mosteller	Steve	1974	1975			Norman	Jay C.	1959	1960		
Mott	Gayle	1932				North	Eric	1978	1979		
Mullen	Earl	1938				Norwood	Cory	1995			
Munz	William	1964				Notheis	John	1951	1952	1953	
Murphy	Jack	1931	1932			Nufer	Clair	1920	1921		
Murphy		1913				Nulty	Michael	1969	1970	1971	
Murray	Harold	1957				Nunn	Gregory	1965			
Mustin	Pearl	1977				Oakes		1916			
Myer	Maurice	1921	1922	1923	1924	Oard	Kenneth	1961	1962	1963	1964
Myer	Wilbur	1924	1925	1926		O'Brien	Marshall	2004	2005	2006	2007
Myers	Earl	1954				O'Conner	Bob	1938			
Myers	Earl	2001				O'Conner	Larry	1970			
Myers	Elmer	1923				Oden	Robert	1957	1958	1959	1960
Myers	Roland	1940	1941			Oetker	Gary	1967			
Myers	Tony	1995				Ohlde	David	1959	1960		
Naanes	Eddie	1906	1907	1909		Olivier	Trenton	2003	2004	2005	2006	2007
Nanninga	John	1917	1918	1919	1920	Olson	George	1923			
Nanninga	Simon	1913	1916			O'Malley Jr.	Edward	1994			
Naughton	John	1934				Orajiato	Noble	2012	2013	2014	2015
Nee	Dennis	1969	1970	1971	1972	Orton	Russ	1981	1982	1984	
Neeley	Steve	1984				Oshel	Jonathon	1993	1994	1995	
Neff	Harold	1930				Osterhaus	Shane	1999			
Neiburgerhouse	Anvil	1935				Owen	Dougan	1936			
Neis	Charles	1919				Owen	Mark	1920	1921		
Nelson	Bryon	2011				Owen	Merritt	1929			
Nelson	Jon	1973	1974			Owens	Anthony	2006	2007		
Nelson	Stewart	1969				Owens		1910	1913		
Nelson	Warren	2008	2009	2010		Padden	Wilbur	1936			
Nelson		1917				Page	Grant	1931			
Nelson		1957				Palmer	Donnie	1993			
Neufeldt	David	1975	1976			Palmer		1926			
Neumann	Bill	1913	1914			Panovich	Dean	1986			
Neuschwanger	Elm er	1908	1909			Parkable	Bill	1948			
New	Mickey	1981				Parker	Chester	1938	1939		
Newbill		1902				Parker	Gayle	1976			
Newell	George	1962				Parker	Harry	1936			
Newkirk	Adam	1999	2000	2002	2003	Parker	Wilbern	1934			
Newland	Josh	2011	2012			Parks	Richard	1982	1983		
Nicholas	Ira	1929				Patterson	Darrell	1969	1970	1971	1921
Nichols	James	1913	1914	1916	1917	Patterson		1920			
Nichols	Robert	1941				Patton	Mike	1963			
Nichols	Steve	1970				Patton	Rick	1971	1972		
Nichols	Tony	1996				Paul	D.	1962			
Nichols		1921	1922			Paul	Everett	1930			
Nichols		1927				Paul	Weldon	1999			
Nicholson	Carol	1949	1951			Payne	Tim	1977	1978		
Nicks	Brad	1997	1998			Payne		1947			
Nietfield	Dan	1971				Peach		1920			
Nightengale	Brad	1980				Peals	Arthur	1970	1971	1972	1973
Nimitz	Gerald	1975	1976	1977	1978	Pearcy	Arlington	1925	1926		
Noches	Ramon	1939	1940			Pearson		1917			
Nofi	Joe	1965				Pecinovsky	Frank	1929	1930	1931	
Noll	Lloyd	1948	1949			Peck	Nathan	1999	2000		
Noll	Marion	1934				Pederson	Brian	1993			
Noll		1957				Peery	Sloane	1991			

Surname	First	Y1	Y2	Y3	Y4
Pefferman	Curtis	1964	1965		
Pennington	Glenn	1932	1934		
Pennybaker	Dale	1947	1948		
Pense	Mike	2000			
Peoples	Chris	2005			
Perkins	Dean	1977			
Perkins	Duane	1977			
Perkins	Howard	1939	1940		
Perkins	Russell	1980	1981		
Perkins		1916			
Perry	Harry	1932			
Pesek	Kory	2011			
Peters	Bob	1942			
Peters	Lee	1958			
Peterson	Chester	1939	1940	1941	1946
Peterson	Clarence	1962			
Peterson	Daniel	1911	1912		
Peterson	Gene	1939	1940		
Peterson	Henry	1912			
Peterson	Steve	1985	1986	1987	
Pettit	Jason	1995	1996		
Pfizenmaier	Kyle	2012	2013	2014	2015
Phillips	Vernon	1934			
Pickens		1908			
Pickett	Luke	1998	1999	2000	2001
Pierce	Bennie	1972	1973		
Pierce	Bill	1954			
Pierre	Desmond	1990	1991		
Pierson	Bruce	1979	1980		
Pierson	Wren	1912			
Pilkington	James	1958	1959		
Pingle	Eugene	1953			
Piper		1905			
Pitko	Mike	1963	1964		
Pitts	Carstell	1957			
Plank	Gary	1977	1978	1980	
Pletcher	Wesley	1953	1954		
Ploud	Briar	2010	2011	2012	2013	2014
Poff	Orsie	1931	1932	1933	1934
Ponder	David	1970			
Pontius	Arthur	1940			
Poole	George	1956	1957	1958	1959
Porter	Kirk	1983	1985		
Porter	Larry	1933			
Portofee	Marcus	2011	2012	2013	
Portwood	Bruce	1915	1916	1917	1919
Post	Gene	1954			
Post	Richard	1954			
Post	Ronnie	1955			
Postlewait	John	1937			
Potta	Ted	1969	1970		
Powell	Travis	1996	1997		
Powell		1930			
Powers		1908	1909		
Price	Jake	1995	1996		
Pringle	Roy	1922	1924		
Proctor	Ashton	2013	2014	2015	
Prophet	Kevin	1977	1978		
Prosser	Quentin	1939			
Provost	Edwin	1936	1937		
Purkeypile	Burl	1949	1952		
Purkeypile	Greg	1974	1975	1976	1977
Putman	Mason	2011			
Pyle	Alex	2008	2009	2010	
Pyle	Lucien	1920			
Quammen	Tom	1972			
Quasbarth	Alfred	1924	1925		
Quillen	Daniel	2008	2009	2010	
Radel	Jaylon	2015			
Raines	Raymond	1929	1931	1932	1933
Rains	Brandon	2001	2002	2003	2004
Ramirez	Augie	1989	1990	1992	
Ramirez	Jose	1989	1990		
Randall	Glenn	1927	1928		
Randle	Larry	2000	2001	2002	2003
Random	Dave	1976	1977	1978	
Rapp	Hubert	1936	1937		
Rauthlauf	David	1974	1975		
Ray	Doug	1977	1978	1979	
Ray		1940			
Raymond	Paul	1920	1921		
Raymond	Roland	1916	1917	1918	1919
Redd	Gayle	1963			
Redding	Wendall	1936			
RedMond	Darrius	2011			
Reed	Eugene	1951			
Reed	Harry	1951			
Reed	Lynn	1959	1960	1961	1962
Reed	Michael	1998	1999	2000	2001
Reed	Paul	1988			
Reed	Ralph	1935			
Reeves	J.	1969			
Regnier		1925			
Reichardt	Steve	1982	1983	1984	
Reilly	Jerry	1932			
Remal		1902			
Rempe	Michael	1992			
Resch	Bob	1937			
Ressler	Rex	1958	1959	1961	
Rewerts	Shannon	1999			
Reynolds	Robert	1987	1988	1999	
Rhea	John	1960			
Rhine	Orin	1907	1908	1909	
Rhinehardt	Steve	1973	1974		
Rhoads	Ken	1963			
Rhoads	Norman	1932	1933	1935	1956
Rice	Charles	1939			
Richard	Charles	1960	1961	1962	1963
Richards	Marvin	1917			
Richards	Ralph	1932			
Richardson	Shjuan	2010	2011	2012	2013
Richman	William	1911	1915	1916	
Richmond		1912			
Ridgeway	Art	1953			

Ridgeway	Paul	1927	1928	1929	1930		Ryman	Wayne	1925	1926	
Riedesel	James	1997	1998	1999			Saalfeld	Craig	2006	2007	2008	2009	2010
Riedesel	Joe	2000					Sack	Tom	1973		
Riggins	Bill	1937					Sadowski	Donald	1947	1948	1949
Riggs	Clarence	1939					Saidi	Samuel	2014	2015	
Riggs	Morgan	2011	2012	2013	2014	2015	Saint Clair	Chester	1960		
Riley	Brette	1936					Salley	Shawn	2001		
Riley	LeRoy	1914	1915				Sams	Arnold	1972	1973	1975
Rinehart	Steve	1973	1974				San Romani	Archie	1935	1936	1937
Rinnal		1902					Sanborn		1902		
Ristau	Geoff	1984					Sander	Wyatt	2015		
Robben	Jason	1997	1998				Sanger	Charles	1948		
Robbins	C. Roy	1964	1965	1966			SanMartin	Lucas	2009	2010	2011	2012	2013
Robbins		1964					Sarr	Alieu	1973		
Robe	Donald	1934					Sarracino		1936		
Roberts	DeWolff	1962	1963	1964	1965		Saville	Darrell	1955		
Roberts	Jim	1957					Sawyer	Eugene	1932	1933	
Roberts		1902					Scales	Dave	1940	1941	1947
Robertson	Bill	1922					Scales	William	1947		
Robinson	Charles	1914	1915				Schedevitz		1912		
Robinson	Ed	1952					Schenck	Jason	1986	1987	1988
Robinson	Mike	1962					Scheufler	Elias	1921	1922	1923
Robinson	Wallace	1942	1943	1947			Scheve	Aaron	1997	1998	
Robinson		1918					Schieffler	Dutch	1929		
Robison	Jim	1987	1988				Schierling	Valgene	1965	1966	1967	1986
Rodgers	Craig	1975	1976	1977	1978		Schlup	Steve	1977		
Rodina	Luke	2001	2002	2004	2006		Schmitendorf		1971		
Rodman	Raymond	1969					Schnakenberg	Trent	2001		
Rodriquez	Iggy	1999					Schnurr	Jim	1967	1968	
Roedel	Mikhail	2013	2014				Schoen	Spence	1994		
Roether	Dan	1951					Scholz	Chris	1998	1999	
Roger	Schutz	1971					Schrick	Ray	2000	2001	
Rogers	Omar	1965					Schroeder	Pat	1996	1997	1998	1999
Rogers	Pete	1967					Schuler	Josh	2008	2010	2011
Rogers	Peter	2014	2015				Schuman	Andrew	2010		
Rogers	Wayne	1965	1966				Schwartz	Kenneth	1947		
Rogers		1930					Scott	Ira	1911	1914	1915
Rohe		1909					Scott	Paul	1936		
Roland	Keith	1936	1937	1938	1939		Scott	Richard	1954	1955	
Rollings	James	1952					Scott	Tom	1974		
Romine	Aaron	1937	1938	1939	1940		Scott		1923		
Rosenberger	Zach	2011					Seachris	Corey	2003	2004	
Ross	Berry	2005	2006				Seawood	Charles	1961	1962	1963	1964
Rossillon	Joe	1956					Seiple	Lawrence	1931		
Rossillon	Norbert	1939					Sell	Steve	1967		
Roulhec	Kevin	2008	2009	2010	2011		Settle	Clayton	1909		
Rowley	Ed	1955					Sevier	Mark	1971	1973	1974	1975
Roy		1914					Sewell		1948		
Ruddick	Bernard	1942	1946				Seybold	John	1977	1978	1979	1980
Rupp	Robert	1952					Shadwick	Gerald	1950	1951	
Rusco	Jeremy	2005	2006				Shafer		1927		
Rush	Bill	1977	1978				Shaffer	Rob	1994	1995	1996
Ruskin	Bob	1937					Shaft	John	1956		
Russell		1916					Shanelec	Gail	1947	1948	1949	1950
Ruth	Roger	1948	1949	1950	1951		Shank	Harvey	1955	1956	1958
Ryan	David	1988					Shannon	Eustace	1934	1935	
Ryman	Harold	1924					Sharp	Charles	1932		

Surname	Given	Y1	Y2	Y3	Y4
Sharp	Mike	1971	1972		
Sharp	Walter	1927			
Sharpe	Lloyd	1916	1917	1918	
Shaw	Paul	1967			
Shaw	Willard	1939			
Shaw		1902			
Shea	Bill	1940			
Shearer	Lawrence	1932			
Shearer	Osborne	1932			
Shepard	Archie	1936	1937	1938	1939
Shepard	Kevin	1973	1974	1975	1976
Sherer	Darrell	1924			1977
Sherer	Merritt	1921	1922	1923	
Sheridan	Richard	1937	1938	1939	1940
Shewmak	Steve	1965	1966	1967	1968
Shirkey		1920			
Short	Walter	1941	1942		
Shuler		1916			
Shull	Charles	1935			
Shumate	Orilton	1951			
Shupe	Eldon	1913	1915	1916	
Sibbitt	Ronald	1953	1954		
Sidener	Doug	1981	1982		
Siehr	James	1951			
Sipe	Travis	2012	2013	2014	2015
Sipes	Bill	1937			
Sittenauer	Curt	1981			
Sjoblom	Darrel	1960			
Skaggs	Joseph	1909			
Skinner	Alex	2012	2013	2014	2015
Skinner	Haley	1940			
Skinner	William	1937	1938	1939	
Sloan	Ireland	1962	1963	1964	
Slocum	Derrick	1999			
Smalley	James	1939			
Smart		1905			
Smith	Allen	1940			
Smith	Beuford	1932			
Smith	Brad	1998	1999		
Smith	Charles	1937			
Smith	Chester	1940			
Smith	Colby	1991	1992	1993	
Smith	Don	1959	1960		
Smith	Donald	1934			
Smith	Eric	2000	2001	2002	
Smith	Harold	1941	1946		
Smith	Hilo	1968			
Smith	Ivan	1953			
Smith	Jerry	1959			
Smith	Jim	1941			
Smith	Jim	1956			
Smith	John	1941			
Smith	Jordan	2012	2013	2014	2015
Smith	Ken	1934	1935	1936	1937
Smith	Lee	1936			
Smith	Leland	1947			
Smith	Marrion	1998	1999	2000	
Smith	Robert	1948	1949	1952	
Smith	San	1916	1917		
Smith	Tromer	1932			
Smith	Will	2011			
Smith	Winston	1936	1937	1938	
Smith		1909			
Smith		1912	1913		
Smith		1964			
Smitheran	Brent	1997	1998	1999	2000
Smyth	Phillip	1947			
Snow		1932			
Snyder	Bill	1925	1926		
Snyder	Paul	2009			
Socolofsky	A.L.	1915	1916	1917	
Soden	Carl	1936			
Soggin	Wayne	1936			
Soice	Clyde	1924	1925		
South	Jimmy	1941			
Southieze	Charles	1971			
Sowell	Merle	1924			
Sower	Granten	1919	1920	1921	
Sparks	Fielder	1934			
Sparks	Ryan	2002	2004		
Specdt	Ernest	1927	1928		
Spicer	Jimmie	1934			
Spiker		1921			
Sprecker	J.D.	1953			
Squiers	Bill	1942			
Stacy	Gale	1947			
Stacy	Ryan	2009			
Stallbaumer	Doug	1987			
Stamper	Woodie	1992			
Stanbrough	Mark	1975	1976	1977	
Stander	Wayne	1957	1958		
Staples	Kenan	1998			
Stark	Erwin	1934			
Starks	Scott	1988	1989	1990	
Starnes	Pete	1931			
Stauffer	Greg	1968			
Stauffer	Robert	1939	1940	1941	1946
Stauffer	Robert	1950	1951		
Stauffer	Roy	1939			
Stearns	Chris	2005			
Stebbins	Ted	1932			
Steel	Robert J.	1912	1913	1914	
Steele	Richard	1966	1967	1968	1970
Steele		1908			
Steinbrink	Jonas	2003	2004		
Stenzel	LeRoy	1925	1926	1927	1928
Stenzel	Luke	2015			
Stenzel	Vernon	1929	1930	1932	
Stephens	Michael	2005	2006	2007	2008
Stern	Donald	1947	1948	1949	1950
Sterner	Steve	1971	1972		
Stevens	William	1957			
Stevens		1920			
Stevenson	Eric	1978			

Stevenson	H.H.	1912	1913	1914		Taylor	Bernard	1940	1941	1942	1943
Stevenson	Rick	1978				Taylor	Carlos	1951			
Steward	Manon	2011				Taylor	Josh	2003			
Stewart	Cleyon	1921	1922			Taylor	Merrill	1936			
Stewart	Clint	1971	1972			Taylor	Robert	1976	1977	1978	
Stewart	Levi	1923	1924			Taylor	Vernon	1908			
Stewart		1974				Taylor		1902	1903		
Stewart	Trevor	2006				Tedrow	Rex	1971	1972		
Stigge	Justin	1999	2000	2001	2002	2003					
Stillwell	Greg	1973	1974	1975		Teichgraeber	Woody	1935			
Stine	Jimmy	1954				Ternes	Brock	2006	2007	2008	
Stites	Lee	1914	1915	1916	1917	Terrell	Ray	1957	1958		
Stites	Russell	1917	1919			Thomas	Blaine	1969	1970		
Stokes	Maurice	1931				Thomas	Chris	1993	1994	1995	
Stokes	Robert	1947	1949			Thomas	Kenneth	1931			
Stone		1957				Thomas	Shawn	1992	1993	1994	
Stone		1971	1972			Thompson	Bobby	2015			
Storck	Leon	1961	1962			Thompson	Brian	1984			
Story		1940				Thompson	Claude	1922			
Stout		1920				Thompson	David	1975			
Stovall	Kenneth	1941	1942			Thompson	Dylan	2014			
Stroble		1948				Thompson	Fred	1909			
Stroda	Kyle	2002	2002	2003	2004	2005					
Strother	Cameron	2005				Thompson	Harold	1956	1957	1958	
Strube	Ben	1931				Thompson	Harry	1959	1960		
Strueby		1922				Thompson	Henry	1951	1954	1955	
Stuart	Alan	1973	1974			Thompson		1925	1926		
Stubblefield	Aaron	2006				Thornberg	Estal	1939			
Stucky	Myron	1979	1980			Thornton	Troy	1995	1996		
Stueve	Wes	1971	1972			Thrasher	Clyde	1942			
Stuke	Jason	1994	1995	1996	1997	1998					
Stump	Ron	1952				Thurston	John	2012	2013	2014	
Stutsman	Dean	1932				Thurston	Thad	1988	1989	1990	1991
Sughrue	Andrew	1922				Tibbs	Dukiya	2014	2015		
Sullivan	Colby	2002	2003	2004	2006	Tidwell	Billy	1951	1955	1956	1957
Sullivan	Paul	1967				Tiemann	Greg	1991	1992		
Sulzen	Richard	1975				Tiffany	Scott	1985	1985	1986	1988
Summers	Marcus	2006	2007	2008	2009	Tillemans	Steve	1999			
Summers	Ralph	1922	1923			Tilley	Robert	1966			
Summers	Ralph	1948	1949	1950	1951	Tolle	Howard	1923	1925	1926	1927
Sumner	Verne	1936	1937	1938		Tomlinson	Bryan	1916	1917	1918	
Supple	Dennis	1970				Topham	Greg	1979	1980		
Sure		1912				Topham	Jeff	1972	1976	1977	
Swaim	Francis	1936				Trager		1955			
Swaim	Jeremy	2011				Tranberger	Larry	1958			
Swaim	John	1964	1965	1966	1967	Travnichek	Vince	1984			
Swalley	Tyler	2010	2011	2012	2013	Traxter		1920			
Swanson	Lester	1932				Trencamp	Frank	1929			
Swift	Jamin	1997	1998			Tribble	Duane	1938			
Szymanski	Robert	1966	1967	1968	1969	Trites	Alan	1997	1998		
Talbert	G.	1969				Truaz		1921			
Talbott	Francis	1922	1923			Trusler		1912			
Tapler	John	1973	1974	1975		Trussler	Ivan	1915			
Tarro	Albert	1925				Tucker	Robert	1934			
Taskman		1915				Tufts	Guy	1940			
Tate	Merle	1923				Tuggle	Clem	1924	1925	1926	
Tauber	Richard	1935				Tuggle	Curran	1934			
						Turner	Broderick	2010			
						Turner		1902			
						Turner		1972			

Tyler	Richard	1973	1974	1975	1976		Warren		1905		
Tyron	Clyde	1938	1939				Washington	Eddie	1959	1960	1961	1962
Tyrrell	Steve	1990	1991				Wayman	Andrew	2009	2010	2011	2012
Unruh	Verlin	1954					Webb	Dennis	1973	1974	1975	
Upson	William	1923	1924	1925	1926		Webber	Charles	1915	1916	1917	
Utt	Les	1931					Webber	Dakota	2015			
Utter	Richard	1954	1955	1956	1957		Weber	Joe	1923	1924	1925	1926
Valliere	Donald	1947	1948	1949			Weber	William	1928	1929		
Van Campen	Harry	1911	1912	1913	1914		Webster		1929			
Van Campen		1917					Wecker	Brad	1989	1990	1991	1992
Van de Bruinhorst	Jack	1967	1968	1969	1970	1915	Wecker	Darryl	1961			
Van Ness	B.	1969					Wedd	Ralph	1941	1950		
Van Nice		1916					Wegler	Ben	1954			
Van Patten	Harry	1915	1916	1917			Weidenbach	Paul	1986	1987	1988	
Van Sickle	Ray	1971	1972	1973	1974		Weimer	Mark	1979			
Van Voorhis	Harvey	1919	1921				Weins	Luke	2003			
Van Weldon	Carl	1934					Wellman	Eric	2004	2005	2006	2007	2008
Vance		1931					Wells	Clayton	1987			
Vandergraft	Zacha	1914	1915				Wells	David	1992	1993	1994	1995
VanDonge	Ted	1988					Wells	Jim	1978			
VanVuren	Daniel	1995	1996	1997			Wells		1912			
Vassallo	Freddy	1940					Wernli	Jonathan	2013	2014		
Vaughn	Jim	1916	1917	1918	1919		Wesley	Laurence	1928			
Vaughn	Michael	2012	2013				West	A.J.	2014	2015		
Vaughn		1939					Weston	Carl	1924	1925	1926	1927
Velasquez	Ray	1955	1956	1958			Weston	Charles	1973	1974	1975	1976
Venniro	Travis	2013	2014				Weston	Ryan	2002	2003	2004	2006
Vierthaler	Dennis	1956					Whitcomb	James	1965	1966		
Vietti	Tim	1994	1995				Whitcraft		1923			
Vincent	Clay	1977	1978				White	Earl	1965			
Vininski	Richard	1962	1963	1964	1965		White	James	1970	1971	1972	
Vogelsberg	Andrew	2004	2006	2007			White	Lane	2014	2015		
Waddell	Dean	1949					White	Marlin	1940			
Waddell	Dwight	1947	1948	1949	1950		White	W.P.	1912			
Waddell	Keith	1947					Whitebird	Lawrence	1926			
Wagner	Marvin	1930					Whiteley	Kenneth	1962	1963		
Wahl		1931					Whiteley	Paul	1958	1959		
Waldorf	Bill	1907					Whitmore	Ellvern	1937			
Walker	James	1958	1959	1960			Whitney	Charles	2000			
Walker	LaRhon	2012	2013	2014	2015		Wichman	Anthony	1982	1983	1984	
Wall	Dwayne	2011	2012	2013			Widrig	James	1949	1950		
Wallace	Bob	1971					Wienandt	Michael	2001			
Wallace	Mike	1972	1973	1974	1975		Wiens	Luke	2000	2001	2002	2004
Wallace	Terry	1974	1975	1976	1977		Wiens	Richard	1940			
Waller	Luke	2001	2002	2003	2004		Wiggins	George	1952			
Walquist	Leone	1938					Wight	Roland	1941			
Walsh	Bill	1952					Wilcox	Donald	2011	2012	2013	2014	2015
Walston		1971					Wilcox	James	1937	1938	1939	1940
Walter		1955					Wilcox		1934			
Walters	Herman	1933					Wild	Rick	1975			
Wantland	Spurgeon	1930					Wiles	Steve	1967	1968		
Wapelhorst	Kent	1990	1991	1992	1993		Wiles		1916			
Wapelhorst	Kevin	1990	1991	1992	1993		Wiley	Albert	1935	1936		
Warner	Craig	1975					Wiliams	Michael	1998	1999	2000	
Warner	Pat	1967	1969				Willett	Frank	1929	1930		
Warren	William	1909					Williams	Clarence	1927	1929		
							Williams	Dan	2000	2001		

Last	First	Yr 1	Yr 2	Yr 3	Yr 4	Yr 5	Last	First	Yr 1	Yr 2	Yr 3	Yr 4	Yr 5
Williams	Darion	2012					Wolfson	Burton	1964	1965			
Williams	Elijah	1922	1923	1924	1925		Wood	Clarence	1934				
Williams	James	1971					Wood	William	1935	1939			
Williams	Kevin	1991					Woodbridge	Kermit	1927	1928	1929		
Williams	Lewis	1919	1920				Woodbridge	Phillip	1933				
Williams	Lois	1924	1925	1926	1927		Woodrell		1973				
Williams	Mike	1978					Woods	Derek	1994	1995			
Williams	Phil	1970					Woods		1920				
Williams	Ramel	1998	1999	2000	2001		Woodson	Dean	1966	1967	1968	1969	
Williams	Samuel	2009					Woodward	Royce	1951	1952			
Williams	Stanton	1983	1984				Works	James	1995				
Williams	William	1968	1969	1970			Worley	Jesse	1901				
Williams		1903					Wright	Frank	1906	1907	1908	1910	
Willis	Austin	2011	2012	2013	2014		Wright	William	1960				
Willis	Ken	1973					Wright		1918				
Willmott	Robert	1995	1996	1997	1998	1999	Writt	John	1938	1939	1940		
Wills		1927					Wyatt	Gary	1976				
Willson	Fred	1950	1951	1952	1953		Wyatt	Kirk	1987	1988			
Wilson	Anderson	1925	1926				Wygle	Bill	1947	1948	1949		
Wilson	Donald	1934					Wynn	Donald	1973	1974			
Wilson	John	1970	1971				Wynn	Ronald	1972	1973	1974		
Wilson	Kip	2001	2002				Wyrick	Randy	1975				
Wilson	Norman	1947					Yates	Albert	1935				
Wilson	Sam	1975	1977	1978	1979		Yergler	Roland	1947				
Wilson	Tom	1968	1969				Yoder	Evan	1977	1978	1979	1980	
Winkler	Wayne	1961					York		1929				
Winkler	Wendall	1964					Young	Charles	1937				
Winslow	Fred	1934					Young	Grant	1930	1931			
Winter	Todd	1995					Young	Wesley	1965				
Winters	Melvin	1946					Young		1914				
Wirta	Warner	1956	1958	1959			Youngstedt	Larry	1959	1960			
Wismeyer		1922					Yunger		1920				
Withee	Van	1940					Zane		1927				
Witt	Tyler	2001	2002	2003	2004		Zarker	Charles	1940				
Witten	Mark	1973	1975				Zickefoose	Jim	1966	1967	1970	1971	
Wixson	Robert	1947					Zimmerman	John	1936	1937	1938		
Woelk	Randolph	1940	1941	1942	1943	1946	Zimmerman	Paul	2012	2013	2014		
Woelk	Richard	1961	1962	1963	1964		Zungu	Bruce	1994				
Wolfe	Gary	1963					Zydor	Frank	1968				
Wolfe		1913											

Women's All-Time Track and Field Participants

The listing of names is as complete and accurate as could be obtained from the sources used. There is a possibility that some who participated in track and field are not in this list.

Last	First	Yr 1	Yr 2	Yr 3	Yr 4	Yr 5	Last	First	Yr 1	Yr 2	Yr 3	Yr 4	Yr 5
Allen	Amy	1999	2000	2001	2002		Banks	Dashika	2001				
Allison	Casey	2004					Barezinsky	Katie	2008				
Armstrong	Becky	1976	1977				Barnard	Lynda	1996	1997	1998	1999	
Axman	Karla	1983	1984				Barnes	Abby	1995	1996	1997		
Ayers	Amy	1991	1992	1993	1994		Barrier	Hannah	2001				
Bahr	Trish	1987	1988				Barton	Susan	1980				
Bailey	Mary	1992					Bates	Gloria	1985				
Baldwin	Bettina	1977	1978	1980			Baum	Tiffany	2008	2009	2010		
							Becker	Judy	1978	1979	1980	1981	

Surname	First				
Beckman	Tara	2003			
Bedenbender	Deneal	2000			
Bedenbender	Heather	2001	2002		
Bennett	Robin	1989	1990		
Berg	Katlyn	2006			
Biggs	Lori	1995	1996		
Bina	Brenda	1991	1992	1993	1994
Bissell	Catalina	2014	2015		
Blakeley	Cindy	1988			
Blevins	Elizabeth	2015			
Bloss	Emily	1998	1999		
Bohm	Gretchen	1987	1988	1989	1990
Bookout	Kylie	2008	2009	2010	
Borders	Melissa	2002			
Bradbury	Michelle	1992			
Brant	Morgan	2014	2015		
Brockmeier	Kara	2000	2001	2002	2003
Brough	Eileen	1978			
Brousseau	Jenny	1999			
Brown	Chary	1993			
Browning	Julie	1984			
Bruna	Courtney	2002	2003	2004	2005
Brune	Kristin	1998	1999	2000	2001	2002
Brunholtz	Kristen	2001	2001	2002	2003
Buckman	Kathie	1980			
Bulson	Pam	1977	1978	1979	1980
Burbee	Sarah	2005			
Burden	Melissa	1998	1999	2000	2001
Burden	Tiffany	1998	1999	2000	2001
Burns	Alicia	2002	2003	2004	2005
Buster	Shelby	2014	2015		
Butler	Shannon	2005	2006		
Cahoone	Diana	2006			
Camien	Marcy	1990			
Cannon	Melissa	1997	1998		
Carr	Erin	2008			
Carson-Heuer	Codie	2015			
Carver	Cathy	2000	2001		
Caryle	Robin	1979			
Cathcart	Angela	1993	1994	1995	1996
Chaltas	Connie	1976			
Childers	Robin	1999	2000	2001	
Chiroy	Abigail	2013			
Chmidling	Mary	1976			
Christensen	Renetta	1978			
Clanton	Chelsea	2008	2009		
Clark	Callie	2013	2014	2015	
Clem	Bridget	1996			
Clennon	Kim	1976			
Collins	Sarah	1999	2000	2001	2002	2003
Costello	Elizabeth	2015			
Cotman	Shayla	2014	2015		
Covington	Crystal	2002	2003	2004	2005
Croft	Jan	1978			
Cuadra	Lindsay	2013	2014	2015	
Cunningham	Brenda	1988			
Curtiss	Gillian	1996	1996	1997	1998	1999
Davenport	Justine	2009	2010	2011	2012
Davidson	Nancy	1978	1979		
Davis	Lysa	1996			
Davison	Kathryn	2008	2009	2010	2011
Dearing	LaDonna	1978	1979		
DeMint	Rachel	2008			
DeTiege	Celeste	1999	2000	2001	
Devine	Kathy	1976	1977	1978	
Diehl	Sarah	1996	1997	1998	1999
Diekmeier	Cori	2003			
Dill	Valerie	1976			
Dispensa	Kaitlyn	2014			
Dixon	Debbie	1978			
Doctor	Keiona	2015			
Dohrman	April	1999	2000		
Doubrava	Deandra	1995	1996	1997	1998	1999
Downey	Bryce	2001			
Dreiling	Mandy	2004			
Dumontelle	Jasa	2011			
Dunkin	Sara	2012	2013	2014	2015
Duran	Wendy	1998	1999	2000	2001
Dutton	Jonelle	1984	1985		
Edgerton	Cindy	1980	1981	1982	
Edwards	Laura	1993			
Egli	Rheanna	2014			
Elliot	Danielle	2005			
Euler	Kara	2006	2007		
Fairbanks	Alaina	2011	2012	2013	2014
Faught	Melinda	2015			
Fechter	Jayne	1986			
Feldkamp	Amy	2011	2012		
Ferguson	Sara	1999	2000	2001	
Finley	Skye	2004			
Fisher	Brooke	2015			
Fitzgerald	Maureen	1991	1992		
Flowers	Morgan	2014	2015		
Folk	Aubrey	2004	2006	2007	
Fowler	Olivia	1994	1995		
Frank	Kim	1977			
Frazier	Brook	2013	2014		
Frazier	Ingrid	1990	1991	1992	
Freeman	Sandra	1989			
Frehe	Morgan	2008	2009		
Frese	Amber	1999			
Frey	Dorothy	1978	1979	1980	
Frey	Tara	1996	1997		
Fuller	Taylor	2015			
Funke	Sara	1998			
Garhan	Susan	1982	1983	1984	
Garner	Chris	1981	1982		
Gerber	Jalayne	1997	1998	1999	
Gerstberger	Laura	1992	1993	1994	1995
Gilliland	Morgan	2014	2015		
Goad	Diane	1978			
Goetz	Melanie	2001	2002		

Last	First	Y1	Y2	Y3	Y4	Y5
Goetz	Rachel	2001	2002	2003	2004	
Goff	Kaylea	2009				
Gorges	Jill	1996				
Grabau	Kim	1978				
Gray	Nancy	1981	1982	1983	1984	
Graziano	Suzanne	1982				
Green	Ryan	2005	2006	2007	2008	
Grese	Amber	1998				
Griebel	Mary	1987	1988			
Gronewoller	Dawn	1997				
Grote	Stephanie	2005	2006	2007		
Gunn	Cecilia	1989	1990	1991	1992	
Haas	Cara	2005	2006			
Haight	Megan	2004	2005	2006		
Haines	Kim	1976				
Hamlin	Emilee	2001	2002	2003		
Hancock	Brook	1999				
Hansen	Carly	2011	2012	2013		
Hanson	Carolyn	1977	1978			
Hare	Kelly	1995	1996			
Harris	Catrina	2014	2015			
Haskett	Brenda	1984				
Hayes	Kaila	2010	2011	2012		
Hayes	Sophie	2015				
Hebb	Michelle	1990	1991	1992	1993	
Henault	Kayla	2014	2015			
Hennerberg	Vicki	1977	1978			
Henson	Tracy	1985				
Herrick	Patty	1980	1981	1982	1983	
Herring	Carley	2011				
Hickert	Danielle	2004	2005			
Hinshaw	LeaAnn	1976				
Hirt	Julie	1990	1991	1992		
Hoffman	Kay	1980	1981			
Holdeman	Tamra	1984	1985	1986		
Holloway	Tara	1998	1999			
Hopkins	Cherie	1995	1996	1997		
Howard	Monica	2014	2015			
Hudspeth	Tara	1998	1999	2000	2001	
Huggins	Amy	1990	1991	1992	1993	
Hughes-Stanton	Chastity	2009				
Humbarger	Alyssa	2001				
Hurla	Missy	1989				
Hurt	Courtney	2002	2003	2004	2005	2006
Jackson	Deja	2008	2009	2010	2011	2012
Jacobs	Jacquelyn	2009	2010	2011	2012	2013
Jagodzinske	Dana	1987				
Jennings	Renee	1984				
Jimenez	Sylvia	1977				
Johnson	Adrienne	1997	1998	1999		
Jones	Brandy	2004				
Jones	Kelly	1984				
Jordan	Emily	1998	1999			
Jordan	Valerie	2011	2012			
Kantack	Tricia	2001				
Kelley	Sharon	1990				
Kellie	Carrie	2013	2014	2015		
Kelly	Barb	1978				
Kelve	Kadri	2002	2003			
Kent	Brooke	2007	2008	2009	2010	
Kerwin	Mary	1991	1992	1993		
Kesner	Traci	1980	1981			
Keys	Lisa	1984	1985	1986		
King	Carmen	2012	2013	2014	2015	
Kirkaldie	Lacey	1999	2000	2001		
Kirkpatrick	Virginia	1980	1981			
Kivitter	Carla	1987	1988	1989		
Kliewer	Becky	1989				
Knackstedt	Barbara	1982	1983	1984	1985	
Koehn	Lex	1977				
Koerner	Chrissy	2004	2005	2006	2007	
Kolarik	Jean	1986	1987	1988		
Kronoshek	Suzie	1998				
Kunkel	Lindsey	2012	2013	2014		
Lamberson	Mandy	2005				
Lamberson	Megan	2004	2006			
Lane	Karen	1976	1977	1978		
Lansing	Kayla	2013	2014	2015		
Larimer	Shari	1983	1984	1985		
LaRouche	Amanda	1995				
Larson	Kristen	2003	2004	2006		
Lawellin	Jennifer	2003	2004			
Lee	Malacia	2015				
Lee	Robyn	2006				
Lehning	Andrea	1995				
Lemmons	Jennifer	2006				
Lemon	Laureen	1978				
Leverington	Heather	1998	1999	2000	2001	2002
Leverington	Megan	2000	2001	2002	2003	
Lewis	Elizabeth	2011				
Liddick	Kim	2002				
Lippert	Lindsay	2008				
Lohmeyer	Becky	1997	1998			
Lowe	Misty	2012	2013	2014	2015	
Loyd	Kristin	2002				
Lundgren	Brandi	2007	2008			
Lundin	Eleonor	1985				
Lunkwitz	Maria	1992	1993			
Lutes	Amy	1997	1998	1999		
Lynn	Jamie	1993				
Lytle	Tiffany	2001	2002	2003		
Maddux	Courtney	2011	2012			
Mains	Betsy	1984	1986			
Malotte	Elizabeth	2012	2013			
Marchant	Haley	2011	2012	2013		
Marisette	Marqueita	2010	2011	2012	2013	2014
Marsh	Keri	2001				
Marshall	Stacy	2002				
Martin	Amy	2012	2013			
Martin	Annette	1984				
Martin	Candy	1977				
Matschull	Sonya	1994	1995	1996		

May	Laura	1987	1988	1989		Potter	Amy	1986	1987		
McCammon	Kelly	1982	1983	1984	1985	1986					
McCarty	Amy	2002				Proehl	Laura	1992	1993		
McCoy	Sheredy	1999	2000			Purcell	Shari	1985			
McCumber	Lesa	2001				Raburn	Mackenzie	2008			
McIntyre	Dana	1993				Rand	Laura	1992	1994	1995	1996
McTaggart	Marla	1990	1991	1992		Ratzlaff	Cindy	1977	1978		
Medlin	Jessica	2012	2013			Ray	Jessica	1999			
Meeth	Alison	2015				Reeves	Amy	1985			
Melichar	Ashley	2003	2005	2006		Reynolds	Mackenzie	2007			
Mellen	Geri	1979				Richardson	Carina	2004	2005	2006	
Mikesich	Darcy	1981	1982	1983		Rinker	Martha	1977			
Miller	Darrah	2011	2012			Risner	Brenda	1990			
Milum	Jessica	2002	2003			Roberts	Patricia	1976			
Mona	Katelyn	2009	2010	2012		Robinson	Jennifer	2007	2008	2009	2010	2011
Morasch	Tina	1993				Robison	Lacey	1997			
Moreland	Cicely	1990	1991	1992		Rooman	Alicia	1998			
Morgan	Emily	2007	2008			Ross	Billi	1995	1996		
Mullen	Jennifer	1991	1992			Ross	Melanie	1976	1977	1978	
Munsell	Jami	1998				Rossbach	Jonel	2005	2006	2007	2008
Murphy	Aileen	1998				Rottinghaus	Nicole	2012	2013	2014	2015
Nemeth	Jennifer	2001				Runnebaum	Nikki	1997	1998	199	2000	2001
Nichols	Lynnsey	2007	2008	2009		Russell	Jodi	2011	2012		
Niehues	Brooke	2011	2012			Saunders	Nikki	2012			
Nielson	Lorye	1976				Schement	Sonya	2011	2012		
Nilsson	Katarina	1995				Schick		1977			
Noll	Annette	1986	1987			Schmitz	Brianna	2015			
Norris	Samantha	2009				Schneider	Erin	2001	2002		
Numberg	Lana	2004	2005			Schneider	Magali	1996	1997		
Nutt	Sarah	2000	2001	2002	2003	Schoenfeld	Emily	2014	2015		
Oakes	Natasha	2001	2002	2003	2004	Schroer	Laura	1978	1979		
Oberg	Jessica	1996	1997			Schroer	Theresa	1982			
Oberle	Chelsea	2014	2045			Searcy	Trudy	1987			
Oborny	Terra	1995	1996			Sedivy	Danielle	2004	2005	2006	2007
Oltjen	Sydney	2011				Shannon	Beth	1982	1983	1984	1985
Orth	Tiffany	2010	2011	2012	2013	Shepard	Iva	2015			
Orton	Michelle	1982	1982	1983	1984	Sherry	Jo	1991			
Owens	Bridgett	1981	1982			Short	Brenda	1977	1978	1979	1980
Page	Amy	1995	1996			Sill	Jaclyn	2005	2006	2007	2008	2009
Pankratz	McKenzie	2014				Simmons	Tobi	1999	2000	2001	2002
Pannbacker	Molly	2007	2008	2009	2010	Sledd	Sarah	2008			
Parhamhie		1977				Smith	Angela	1999			
Parrott	Ashley	2011	2012	2013	2014	Smith	Jennifer	1993	1994		
Pauly	Kayla	2002	2003			Smith	Kristi	2000	2001		
Payne	Michelle	1986	1987			Smith	Sandra	1997	1998		
Pedrick	Claire	2005				Snelling	Leann	1986			
Perez	Mercy	2015				Spencer	Ashley	2009			
Peters	Jan	1986				Spencer	Shonta	2008			
Phares	Cheryl	1980	1981	1982		Sponsel	Kristen	2011	2012		
Phillips	Connie	2005	2006	2007	2008	2009	Staats	Dominique	2013	2014	2015	
Pitman	Kari	1996	1997	1998	1999	Steimel	Mauri	2014			
Poague	Lindsay	2015				Stine	Kerry	1988	1991		
Polson	Heather	2015				Stine	Susan	1986	1987	1988	1989	1990
Posgai-Karjala	Annette	1994	1995	1996	1997	Stoll	Annette	1986			
						Stone	Erin	2002			
						Stone	Josie	2002	2003		
Post	Marcella	1990				Stover	Elizabeth	2010	2011	2012	2013	2014

Strader	Jennifer	1987	1988	1989		Woods	Terri	1979			
Strickland	Kati	2013	2014			Worley	Julie	1992	1993		
Stueve	Taylor	2013	2014	2015		Wuertz	Sarah	2000	2001	2002	2003
Swaney	Carol	1981				Yeargin	Latiyera	2015			
Sweaney	Erika	1989	1990			Yelliott	Kayci	2010	2011	2012	2013
Teichgraeber	Peggy	1984	1985	1987		Yingst	Janice	2001			
Tennal	Miklannet	2004				Young	Cassandra	1999			
Thompson	Brenda	1989				Young	Cheryl	1990			
Thompson	Shirley	1979	1980	1981		Young	Cindy	1979			
Tichenor	Sage	2015				Zeller	Amy	2003			
Tolin	Deanna	1989	1990	1991	1992						
Toricelli	Julie	1979									
Tucker	Diane	1997									
Turner	Nicole	2002									
Tyrell	Michelle	1988	1990	1991							
Utecht	Patti	1976									
Van Goethem	Vanessa	1997									
Van Gundy	Sharon	1977									
Van	Zavannah	2015									
Visser	Melissa	2005									
Wabaunsee	Ah-Sha-Ni	1993	1994	1995							
Wakefield-Hall	Ashley	2009	2010								
Walker	Desiree	1997	1998								
Wallace	Carolyn	2012	2013	2014	2015						
Walter	Sarah	1997	1998								
Ward	Carol	1978									
Waters	Hatsie	1977	1998								
Watkins	Ashley	2009	2010	2011							
Watson	Emily	2001	2002	2003							
Weaver	Renae	2008	2009	2010							
Webb	Bethany	2015									
Weide	Sherlyn	1991									
Weilert	Linzi	2006	2007	2008							
Weiss	Peyton	2012	2013	2014	2015						
Weller	Christy	2009									
Wells	Jaycee	2013									
Welte	Susan	2013	2014	2015							
Werner	Kim	1978									
Wetstein	Nikki	2011	2012	2013	2014						
Wewenes	Anne	1991									
Wheeler	Katie	1990	1991								
White	Jennifer	1999									
White	Rhonda	1988	1989								
Whitsitt	Leslie	1978									
Wiley	Donna	1982									
Williams	Becky	1999									
Willits	Sunny	1991									
Willse	Jaci	2010	2011								
Wilson	Casey	1999									
Wilson	Jackie	2002									
Wilson	Maggie	2012	2013	2014	2015						
Wilson	Sharolyn	1996									
Wolf	Jennifer	1994									
Wood	Jody	1999									
Wood	Lesha	1981	1982	1983	1984						

Resources

Athletic Department Track/Field and Cross Country Records and Releases. Emporia State University, Emporia, KS.

Bulletin (Emporia State University student newspaper). Emporia State University. Emporia, KS.

Crowther, S. & Ruhl, A. (1905). *Rowing and Track Athletics.* New York: MacMillan Co.

Emporia Gazette. Emporia, KS. Newspaper.

Ensminger, L.G. (1982). *A History of Men's Intercollegiate Athletics at Kansas State Teachers College, Emporia, 1942-1952, with implications of World War II.* Unpublished master's thesis, Kansas State Teachers College, Emporia, KS.

Markowitz (1962). *Football, for the Sport of it: A History of Football from 1893 to 1962 at the Kansas State Teachers College of Emporia.* Emporia, KS: Emporia State Press.

Official Records Book of the National Association of Intercollegiate Athletics. (1958-1983). (Published September yearly, beginning 1958). Kansas City, MO: NAIA.

Olympic Track and Field. (1979). Los Altos, CA: Track and Field News.

San Romani, Archie. (1960). (Speech delivered to the National Collegiate Track Coaches Association, title "New Horizons in High School Distance Running"). The Pan American Track and Field Journal, pp. 89-92.

State Normal Monthly. (1900, April). Vo. XII, No.7, p. 107. Emporia State University, Emporia, KS.

Student Index. (1902). Vol. 1, No. 17, p. 217. Emporia State University. Emporia, KS.

Sunflower. (1898-2015). (Annual Yearbook). Emporia State University. Emporia, KS.

Taylor, B. (1947). *History of Athletics at Kansas State Teachers College.* Emporia, KS. Unpublished master's thesis, Kansas State Teachers College, Emporia.

Watts, J. (1976). *A History of Women's Athletics at Emporia State, 1900-1976.* Unpublished manuscript, Emporia Kansas State College, Emporia.

Ziegler, Eearle M. (1979). *History of Physical Education and Sport.* Englewood Cliffs, NJ: Prentice-Hall Inc.

Photo Credits

Archives, WAW Library, Emporia State University
Pages 6, 7, 8, 9, 10 13 (McChesney), 30, 33, 37, 53, 54, 57, 60, 61 (Whiteley), 73, 76 (Boehringer)

ESU Media and Marketing, Emporia State University
Pages 11, 12,13 (1917 track squad), 14, 15, 16, 17, 18, 19, 20, 22, 23, 24, 25, 26, 27, 28, 29, 32, 38, 40, 44, 52, 55, 59, 61 (Welch), 62, 63, 66, 68, 71, 75, 76 (Delavan), 77, 78, 80, 83,2, 84, 86, 89, 91, 92, 94, 97, 98, 102, 103, 104, 107, 108, 109, 112, 113, 115, 116, 117, 118, 120, 125, 126, 127, 129, 130, 131, 132, 133, 140, 142, 144, 147, 148, 149, 150, 154, 155, 158, 159, 160, 161, 163, 164
Front Cover: San Romani, Honeycutt, Leverington

Archives University of Kansas
Page 77

Ron Slaymaker-ESU Athletics Museum
Page 64, 125

Mark Stanbrough
Pages 133, 134, 136, 138, 141

About the Author

Dr. Mark Stanbrough ran cross country and track and field for the Emporia State Hornets from 1974-1977 and was the head track and field and cross country coach at Emporia State from 1984-1992.

Dr. Stanbrough is a professor in the Department of Health, Physical Education and Recreation at Emporia State University in Kansas. He teaches graduate and undergraduate exercise physiology and sports psychology classes and is the director of Coaching Education. The Coaching Education program at Emporia State is currently one of only 10 universities in the United State to be accredited by the National Council for the Accreditation of Coaching Education. He was a co-founder of the online physical education graduate program, the first in United States to go completely online. He received his Ph.D. in exercise physiology from the University of Oregon, and undergraduate and master's degrees from Emporia State in physical education. He has served as department chair and has served on the National Association for Sport and Physical Education National Sport Steering Committee and is a past member of the board of directors for the National Council for the Accreditation of Coaching Education.

Mark has over 30 years of coaching experience at the collegiate, high school, middle school and club level. He has also coached at Emporia High School and Glasco High School in Kansas. He is a member of the Emporia State University Athletic Hall of Honor and the Health, Physical Education, Recreation Hall of Honor and has won numerous coach-of-the-year awards at the high school and collegiate levels.

After graduating from Silver Lake High School, Steve Hawkins competed in track and field/cross country at Emporia State University from 1979 to 1983. He served as a graduate assistant coach at ESU from 1983-1985. Steve is currently a Professor in the Exercise Science department at California Lutheran University in Thousand Oaks, California, and he also serves as chair of the department. He is a Fellow of the American College of Sports Medicine, and has served as President of the Southwest Regional Chapter of the ACSM. Steve has extensive teaching and research experience in the physiology of exercise, with particular emphasis on aging's influence, and he has published widely on master athletes, including chapters in two textbooks on aging and exercise. Steve has also taught at California State University, Los Angeles, and USC. Steve was inducted into the ESU Department of HPER Hall of Honor in 2009.

www.ingramcontent.com/pod-product-compliance
Lightning Source LLC
Chambersburg PA
CBHW080540170426
43195CB00016B/2621